THE HILT OF THE SWORD

The Career of Peyton C. March

The National Archives

P. C. March
Chief of Staff

Peyton C. March, Acting Chief of Staff, March 25, 1918.

THE HILT OF THE SWORD

THE CAREER OF PEYTON C. MARCH

EDWARD M. COFFMAN

The University of Wisconsin Press
Madison, Milwaukee, and London • 1966

Published by the University of Wisconsin Press
Madison, Milwaukee, and London

P.O. Box 1379, Madison, Wisconsin 53701

Printed in the United States of America
by North Central Publishing Company, St. Paul, Minnesota

Library of Congress Catalog Card Number 66-10493

To my father and the memory of my mother

". . . after all, Pershing's army
was the point of the sword
and the Home Organization
was the hilt."

Newton D. Baker to General Peyton C. March,
March 20, 1926

ACKNOWLEDGMENTS

SINCE I owe so much to the many people who contributed to this book, I regret that I am able to name only a few who helped me in its preparation. My father, Howard B. Coffman, initiated my interest in Peyton C. March and the First World War. At the University of Kentucky, Professors Thomas D. Clark, Clement Eaton, Holman Hamilton, Carl Cone, Gerhard Weinberg (now at the University of Michigan), and their colleagues in the History Department informed and advised.

Various persons aided my research effort. I am particularly indebted to Mr. Garry Ryan for his invaluable aid in attacking the long rows of record boxes in the National Archives. Professor Joseph Riggs of Memphis State University and Miss Jeanne Graham of Memphis, Tennessee, examined the Kenneth D. McKellar Papers, and Mrs. Robert Shaw of Lexington, Kentucky, interviewed Miss Mildred March for me. At the University of Wisconsin, Professor William A. Williams made available his notes on Russian-American relations in the period, and Professor E. David Cronon gave me leads into the diary of Josephus Daniels prior to its publication. Mr. Richard Resh served as my research assistant for a year.

Members of the staffs of the following institutions were generous with their time and frequently called my attention to additional material which improved this study: Manuscripts Division of the Library of Congress; Military Records Branch of the National Archives; Western Manuscripts Collection of the University of Missouri; Oral History Project of Columbia University; United States Military Academy Archives; Newberry Library of Chicago; the alumni offices of LaFayette College and West Point; the libraries of the University of Kentucky, Lafayette College, Yale University, Northwestern University, Memphis State University, and the State Historical Society of Wisconsin; and the public libraries of Easton, Pennsylvania, and Memphis, Tennessee.

Financial support which made this book possible came from the Kentucky Research Foundation, the Southern Fellowship Fund, the American Philosophical Society, the George C. Marshall Research Foundation, the National Security Studies Group, and the Research Committee of the Graduate School from funds supplied by the Wisconsin Alumni Research Foundation of the University of Wisconsin.

Since the personal correspondence in the March Papers is limited largely to the 1930's, I attempted to use the reminiscences of the General's contemporaries as a supplement. Although I was unable to talk with the surviving March children, I was fortunate in having the encouragement of Mrs. March and several interviews with her. I regret that she died on July 14, 1964, prior to the publication of this book. At the Army and Navy Club in Washington, D.C., Colonel George W. Hinman, Jr., was most helpful in arranging interviews and introducing me to General March's acquaintances. I am grateful to all of those who talked or corresponded with me. Their reminiscences gave me not only information but also, I hope, insight.

For the right to use and to quote from manuscript collections, I want to express my appreciation to Mrs. Peyton C. March (March Papers), Mr. F. Warren Pershing (Pershing Papers), Mr. Ralph Hayes (Baker Papers), Colonel Edward G. Bliss (Bliss Papers), Colonel George R. Goethals (Goethals Papers), Mrs. George Rockwell (Palmer Papers), Mrs. Kenneth N. Gilpin, Jr. (Mitchell Papers), and Mrs. Stuart Symington (Wadsworth Papers).

I want to express my deep appreciation to Mr. Emerson Beauchamp, who made possible much of my research in Washington. Among those who helped me at one stage or another of the book are some who deserve special mention: Mr. and Mrs. John P. Yoder, and Mr. Donald K. Graham of Washington, D.C.; Dr. Jacqueline Bull of Lexington, Kentucky; Mrs. Charlotte Davis of Atlanta, Georgia; Dr. Rexmond C. Cochrane of Baltimore, Maryland; and Dr. Carl E. Begley of Jacksonville, Florida. Professor Enoch Mitchell and Memphis State University provided a leave of absence at a crucial period. Professor I. B. Holley, Jr., of Duke University not only made available some of his notes on the John M. Palmer Papers but also read and criticized meticulously my manuscript. I am also indebted to Mr. Richard H. Kohn, who helped me with the index.

I am particularly appreciative of the aid given me by Dr. Forrest C. Pogue of the George C. Marshall Research Foundation. Dr. Pogue provided me with the opportunity to learn much about General Marshall as well as the benefit of many conversations over the field of recent American military history.

Finally, I want to acknowledge as the most helpful of all, my wife, Anne, who listened to the problems and who gave sound advice.

Madison, Wisconsin
December, 1964

EDWARD M. COFFMAN

CONTENTS

ILLUSTRATIONS

MAPS

THE HILT OF THE SWORD

The Career of Peyton C. March

PROLOGUE Born in the year Sherman marched through Georgia, Peyton Conway March lived to see the end of the Korean War. He entered an army led by Civil War veterans, yet saw his subordinates command in the Cold War. In the Spanish-American War, he led a pistol charge against a blockhouse. Two decades later, as the Chief of Staff of the army, he played a crucial role in that hinge of military change – World War I. He not only witnessed the modern age but helped lead the army into it. Tough, incisive, he curried no favors and suffered the consequences. Long after his retirement, Congress recognized his accomplishments. The public has yet to do so.

1 · THE BEGINNING OF A SOLDIER'S LIFE

In the fall of 1855, a tall, thin, young man joined the faculty of Lafayette College in Easton, Pennsylvania. Francis A. March, who would be thirty that October, impressed his students by his patient and gentle classroom manner. He enjoyed teaching and his sense of humor ornamented his erudition.[1]

A New Englander whose family had lived in Massachusetts since 1638, March did not plan on a career in education when he graduated with honors from Amherst at the age of nineteen. He wanted to be a lawyer and had begun practice in New York City when he suffered a lung hemorrhage. In search of a cure in a warmer climate, he journeyed to Cuba and to Key West. Then he secured a position as a teacher in a private academy in Fredericksburg, Virginia, where he stayed three years until he moved to Easton.[2]

Among his students at Fredericksburg was a tall girl, eleven years younger than he, Margaret Mildred Stone Conway. Mildred, as she was called, was a member of an old Virginia family, interrelated with many of the other distinguished families — Harrisons, Lees, Washingtons, and Madisons. One of her great-grandfathers, Thomas Stone, was a signer of the Declaration of Independence. More recently, her brother, Moncure, was laying the foundation for a career as a writer. In August, 1860, Francis returned to Fredericksburg and married his former pupil.[3]

As a teacher during the fifty-one years he served at Lafayette, March taught a wide variety of subjects — Greek, Latin, French, German, philosophy, law, political economy, botany, and philology in addition to acting as the librarian over a period of years. In the classroom, he was a pioneer in the introduction of the critical study of the English classics, particularly Shakespeare and Milton. Before and generally during this time teachers gave lessons only in the Greek and Latin classics.[4]

In the course of his career March earned an international reputation as a philologist. He wrote, compiled, and edited grammars, dictionaries, and various other works and led in the then developing scientific study of language. In recognition of his scholarship, Princeton, Amherst, Columbia, and, in 1896, Oxford and Cambridge bestowed honorary doctorate degrees on him.[5]

The College provided its distinguished Professor of the English Language and Comparative Philology with a large frame residence only a hundred yards from his classroom. The Marches needed a large home, since they had nine children – eight of whom lived to maturity. The second child and second son, Peyton Conway, was born here on December 27, 1864.[6]

In a letter which he wrote in August, 1870, to his five-year-old son, Peyton, the professor gave a hint of the warmth of the family life:

My dear son,

I am very glad to hear that you have helped mamma so much. Grandfather and grandmother, and Uncle Austin think Peyton would make a good farmer. They want you to come and ride the horses, and go to the pasture and drive home the cows. . . . If the boys were here we could go out, Frank and Peyton and TOM, and pick blackberries, big ones, ripe, sweet. I wish I could send a few to you. . . . Be careful of Tom and Aldy, and never cry much when you get hurt. Do as mamma says. What does the Bible say?

Yours truly,

F. A. MARCH[7]

As he grew older, Peyton thrived in literary surroundings. The books scattered all over his third-floor room reflected his studious interests. With his friend Ben Field, he played word games – competing to see who could come up with the most synonyms for a given word and who could remember and describe in detail the most characters in the novels of Dickens, Robert Louis Stevenson, and others.[8]

There was an athletic side to "Bob," as the family nicknamed Peyton. He loved to climb on rafters in the barn and sometimes on the school buildings. With three rivers nearby, he became a good swimmer. And he walked a lot. To keep fit, his father, whom the family called "Pater," in frockcoat and carrying his umbrella, would come down the hill and walk all over the town, across the Delaware River into Phillipsburg and even down to Andover Furnace on the New Jersey side. The barefooted

Bob and his brothers frequently accompanied the professor on these jaunts.[9]

After he finished his courses in the Easton public schools in 1880, Bob took the rigorous Lafayette entrance examinations. When he had demonstrated his proficiency in geography, arithmetic, plane geometry, English, Greek, and Latin, he became a freshman, three months before his sixteenth birthday.[10] Bob's class was a large one – numbering 102 out of a total student body of 293. While the large majority of the class were Pennsylvanians, seven other states, the District of Columbia, Brazil, and China were also represented.[11]

For the next four years, Bob excelled in all areas of campus life. He held various offices, including the class presidency; joined Delta Kappa Epsilon fraternity and numerous other organizations; and edited the joke column in the *Lafayette College Journal.*[12] Sports were his major extracurricular interest. As captain and pitcher of his class baseball team, he led it through two undefeated seasons. He also played second base on the varsity baseball team. Although a teammate said that he looked as "thin as a singed cat," he played on Lafayette's first football team as a halfback, specializing in kicking field goals. One of his fans was his father, who paced up and down the sidelines, following the game, when the football team played at home. During his student days, Bob also set the school record of 2:10 for the half-mile run.[13] When he reached his senior year, he was a tall (6′2″) and well-developed (160 pounds) young man.[14]

Bob did well in academic work and graduated with honors in his classics major. Lafayette was a good school which provided stiff competition. Of the 59 graduating seniors in the Class of 1884, more than half planned to continue their studies in law, medicine, and theology.[15] The two teachers who most impressed young March were his father and August A. Bloombergh. "A very extraordinary man," as his son described him later on, Professor March talked over problems with his son and led him in his intellectual development. Bloombergh, a former soldier of fortune, stimulated Bob's interest in history.[16]

In his senior year, Bob informed his classmates that his future occupation would be "Fightin' Injuns." Apparently he had nourished his military ambitions since childhood, when he had often been teased for playing soldier. Professor March may have encouraged this, since he did want one of his sons to go into the army.[17] During his junior year, Bob had gone to see the local Democratic congressman and had unsuccessfully sought an appointment to West Point. The next spring, Representative William Mutchler, whose several past candidates had had difficulty with the requirements of the Military Academy, crossed party lines and offered Professor March an appointment for one of his sons. March called in his eldest son, Frank, who was then teaching at Lafayette, and told him that the chance was his. Years later, Frank recalled: "I told my father I didn't want it, but that Bob did." His decision seemed to please the professor.[18] Because of this opportunity, Bob was not present on June 25, 1884, to receive his diploma with his class.[19] Miles away on a bluff high above the Hudson River, he was becoming acquainted with a harshly different environment.

"West Point was a place of exacting standards and acid tests." A serious cadet from Missouri, John J. Pershing, thus remembered the Military Academy in the 1880's. He added, "Work, order and discipline were requirements that tried the character and ability of every man." Another graduate of that era succinctly commented, "West Point was hard."[20]

For four years, cadets submitted to rigid control in a Spartan environment. From reveille at six to taps at ten, the cadets had to account for virtually every minute. During the school year (September to June), they lived in a four-story, gray stone barracks where two cadets shared each room. Twice daily an officer inspected all of the living quarters. In the summer months, they lived in the slightly relaxed regimen of a tent camp on the edge of the parade ground.[21]

On June 15, 1884, March and sixty-eight others entered the Academy and a week later began the training course which lasted the remainder of the summer. Heads back, chests out, stomachs in, hands at the sides, palms out with little fingers on the trousers' seams, they became what West Pointers call "beasts." Throughout the hot weeks Cadet March drilled and learned infantry and artillery tactics besides dancing and swimming the West Point way. But most of all it was "drill, drill, drill" with first classmen (seniors) and a large number of yearlings (sophomores) constantly ordering, berating, and generally harassing the "beasts."[22]

When the academic work began in September, March's class, inflated by new arrivals, numbered an even hundred. Out of this total, forty-four survived the four-year program in which mathematics and engineering were dominant. Since thirty-eight of his classmates had also attended college, March found competition rigorous. In the final academc standings, he ranked tenth in the class. The scholastic leader throughout the course was Henry Jervey, a South Carolinian whom March thought had "an unusually good mind." [23]

March was a good cadet. As a first classman, he was the ranking lieutenant, after wearing corporal's and sergeant's chevrons in previous years. Despite the strict regulations, he compiled a four-year total of just thirty-six demerits. Lower classmen had particularly sharp impressions of him, since he presided over the drill detail his last summer (1887) and was a member of the detail in 1885. Almost seven decades later, one of his charges described him: "Tall, slender, and erect with a countenance that seemed rather grim. . . . He was a strict disciplinarian but a fair one." He subjected them to severe room inspections and generally kept them in line, sometimes sarcastically, as one perspiring two-hundred-pound plebe (freshman) discovered: March looked him over and cracked, "Well, Mr. Dumbjohn, don't decompose out here." But Cadet Lieutenant March was all military; he did not indulge in hazing. Spencer Cosby, one of the 1887 plebes, later remembered that March seemed "the embodiment of what a West Point cadet should be." [24]

There was more to cadet life than drills and studies, but not much more. March had excelled in athletics at Lafayette but here he found no organized sports and had to be content with impromptu baseball games and kicking a football about with some friends. In the summer he could attend the dances and band concerts, go swimming or boating, and perhaps even play tennis. Although library books were available on a restricted basis, he made little use of that privilege, checking out only two novels during his entire stay.[25]

Visitors lent color to cadet life. Mark Twain with his corncob pipe and fund of stories provided a pleasant relief in the stern military atmosphere, as did Henry Irving and Ellen Terry when they presented *The Merchant of Venice* on a memorable night in March, 1888. More pomp surrounded the visits of the famed "Little Phil" Sheridan.[26]

The Civil War was very close to these young men. In August, 1885, March and his fellow cadets crossed the Hudson to salute the funeral train of U. S. Grant. Wesley Merritt, the strict Superintendent for whom March expressed a "profound admiration," was a constant reminder of the cavalry clashes in which he had worn a major general's stars. And

Merritt's successor, John G. Parke, who came in March's senior year, also carried a major general's rank from that war.[27]

Although the cadets in the 1880's made their debut in a military life dominated by the memories of the Civil War, they had their futures to consider. In the One Hundredth Night festivities of February 20, 1886, when the cadets celebrated the short time left before the end of the academic year, Cadet Marcus D. Cronin jocularly prophesied a comic-opera, German-American War in 1908. In that war, which Cronin misjudged in seriousness as well as in time, West Pointers of this era would play a notable part. In fact, of men in the seven Academy classes (1885 through 1891) during March's day, 138 would wear stars, including 23 from March's class alone. The West Point background was a common bond throughout the careers of these graduates; at the Academy they had had the opportunity of observing each other under the pressures of cadet life in a relatively small group, which at no time in March's four years ever numbered more than 344 men. Undoubtedly, this personal knowledge influenced future relationships.[28]

During March's first two years at West Point, he knew the tall, dignified former Missouri schoolteacher, John J. Pershing. "A fine figure of a man," serious, always meticulously uniformed, Pershing was not only the ranking cadet captain but also the president of the class of 1886. In the summer of 1885, March was a lance corporal in Pershing's Company A. They were not close, since rank and age separated them, but each had the chance to measure the other's merit.[29]

In his own class, which the last survivor remembered as a jolly one, March came to know several who would later gain distinction in the service: Jervey, the handsome Bill Judson, George W. Burr, J. W. "Dad" McAndrew, William H. Hart, Eli Helmick, Peter Harris, Bob Howze, and Bill Graves who started out with '88 but graduated in 1889. March's roommate was a Kentuckian, John S. Winn, who, like Pershing, was the First Captain and class president. Cadets respected March. W. W. Harts, who spent three years with him at West Point, said that he was "straightforward, positive, inclined to be serious rather than jovial." Another cadet wrote home in 1887 that March was "very bright and the most entertaining talker I have met here. . . ." His cadet contemporaries disagreed as to whether or not he was popular. One who was in his company in 1887–1888 thought that he was bitter in his first-class year because he did not make First Captain. No one else remembered this and, judging from his standing, he had little chance of achieving the rank.[30]

On June 11, 1888, amidst appropriate ceremony, March and his classmates received their diplomas. The young college graduate of four years before was now a ramrod-straight West Pointer with a shell of rigid military training overlaying the classical education he had acquired at Lafayette.[31]

Since there were more new West Point graduates than officers' berths in the small army of approximately 27,000, March became an additional second lieutenant until a vacancy occurred. On the last day of September, he reported as the junior officer to the Third Artillery Regiment at Washington Barracks in Washington, D.C. The six understrength batteries at this post functioned as the capital's ceremonial troops. In appearance the "Queen's Own" was "as smart as the Guards in London." As a result, March found a great deal of formality and a daily routine consisting largely of drill and evening parades. Occasionally, the men would fire their 1871-model Springfield rifles on the local range, but they rarely fired artillery pieces. They picked up practical artillery experience on their annual excursions to Fort Monroe, Virginia, when they underwent periods of training with the Civil War era smooth-bore cannon and the huge mortars.[32]

For six years Second Lieutenant March followed the routine of garrison life. He took instruction in signalling; went on recruiting duty; participated in the compulsory lyceum course; refreshed his knowledge of French; and even temporarily commanded the battery at times. Most of his superiors were Civil War veterans. When he joined the regiment, over half of the officers were in that category and the commander, Colonel Horatio G. Gates, had seen service in the Mexican War. One battery commander, "a portly relic . . . with a heart as big as a barrel," James Chester, had been a sergeant at Fort Sumter when the first shot was fired in 1861; and March's battery (K) commander, Captain Lewis Smith, was in his thirty-eighth year of service. Despite the disparity in age and experience, March earned the respect of these men, as one testified that he was "bright," showed "quick perception" and was "well informed in professional matters."[33]

Unlike his fellow second lieutenants, March was not particularly interested in the Capital's social whirl; yet he did take advantage of the opportunity to call on the White House on New Year's Day and, on one memorable occasion, he had an enjoyable time talking with Congressman Joe Cannon in his home. On the post in the Officers' Club, there were opportunities to play cards, use the billiard tables, or read newspapers and drink. Archibald Campbell, who joined the regiment in 1889, remembered, "There was a lot of drinking and playing cards"; but March did not participate much in either. He liked to shoot a pool game but he hated to lose. "He would pound his cue on the floor and stamp off," according to Campbell. Generally, he seemed distant to the other bachelors.[34]

He did not remain long in the bachelor ranks. Captain Smith's daughter, a tall and "very pretty" young widow, Mrs. Josephine Smith Cunningham, attracted his attention. Increasingly he visited the Smith home, where he listened as "Jo" played the piano and sang. On July 4, 1891, they married. They were to have thirteen years of life together, and six children.[35]

In the fall of 1894, came both his promotion to first lieutenant and a move. After a three-month visit to Easton, he and his family travelled to San Francisco where he joined the Fifth Artillery Regiment in the fort which guarded the Golden Gate. Again he immersed himself in the peacetime army routine. He did well and received his colonel's written praise: "Zealous, capable and efficient in the discharge of duty."[36]

Orders to attend the Artillery School gave March his first break from routine after nineteen months in California. At Fort Monroe he encountered a course covering a broad range of subjects – photography, engineering, chemistry, and electricity, besides artillery, mines, explosives and ballistics. For almost two years he and his twenty classmates worked hard mastering the theoretical and practical instruction. Clarence C. Williams, a younger West Pointer who took the course with him, observed, "Anything he had to do, he did well." But the competition was close in this industrious group of lieutenants: while March consistently ranked high, Ernest Hinds led the class. Because of the threat of war with Spain, they completed the course under duress. Finally, in the spring of 1898, the Artillery School graduated the class and suspended operations.[37]

In the ominous days of 1898, First Lieutenant March was completing ten years in the army. Intelligent, forceful yet reserved, he excelled in his chosen career, but garrison life in the artillery offered no opportunity for distinction. An Academy classmate, Robert Howze, already possessed a Medal of Honor, which he had won in a cavalry action against the Sioux. For an artilleryman, the peaceful round of drills, firing practice, paperwork, and school permitted no such adventure. Even with a war in sight, March doubted if he would be able to break from this pattern.[38]

2 · "THE MANY ACTS OF GOOD SOLDIERSHIP"

THE United States fought the Spanish-American War in the flush of Victorian romanticism. The sentimentality, the passionate glory-hunting, and the over-dramatization were elements more suitable to popular novels of the period than to the reality of fighting in tropical jungles. Far from the newsstands featuring the florid front pages, some men who met the reluctant enemy found glory, some disease, and a few, death.

In the Philippines March earned distinction. During the battle of Manila and in the ensuing brutal insurrection, he demonstrated again and again his courage and skill as a combat leader. Years later some of his critics, who did not know about his battle record, would frown at his lack of combat experience. The irony of their remarks must have been amusing to a veteran of so much fighting in the Luzon jungles.

War came in late April, 1898. On May 1, Dewey defeated the Spanish fleet in Manila Bay. At Fort Monroe Lieutenant March awaited orders which he feared would relegate him to a coast artillery post for the duration. A telephone call from the War Department ended the suspense. John Jacob Astor had presented a battery of light artillery to the government. Did the lieutenant want the command? "You may have twenty-four hours to decide." March replied, "I don't want twenty-four seconds . . . I accept the detail at once."

When his orders came he found that his new assignment was rather unusual. His unique organization at that point was "simply a check-book." It was up to him to recruit the men, buy the necessary uniforms and guns, no easy matter in the frantic spring of 1898, and to choose the destination of the unit. After a frustrating search he located an available battery of three-inch Hotchkiss mountain guns in Paris and purchased them by cable. The uniforms were less of a problem and he was able to buy from a New York importing firm British khaki tropical outfits to supplement the standard blues.[1]

He had no difficulty obtaining recruits. Over a hundred "good-looking, well-made, athletic young fellows" stood in a New York recruiting station line when he arrived. Before he started interviewing, March warned, "Any of you who think we are going to organize for parade may as well go away and save the time of the recruiting officer. . . . We want no one here who does not want to fight." He then announced that they would be enlisting in the regular army and that the unit was going to the Philippines.[2]

March wanted college men and got them – representatives of Harvard, Yale, Cornell, Pennsylvania, Princeton, and Lafayette. He reserved a few vacancies for men familiar with the needs and caprices of mules, since the guns would be drawn by these animals. Other slots he filled with veterans. The first sergeant, M. E. "Chappie" Holmes of the regulars, had soldiered with the British in India, as had Sergeant Dennis Cremins. Three others had served in the Canadian army, while Private J. W. Watterson bore a scar from a Sudanese spear and Private W. A. Fishbough reported service in the Matabeleland Border Police. Two others drew their pay as members of the New York police force throughout their tour in the Astor Battery. To officer the battery, March picked his Artillery School classmate, C. C. "Billy" Williams, and another West Pointer, Benjamin M. Koehler.[3]

On May 30, the recruits reported and began their training. For ten days they exercised, drilled, and studied the intricacies of the Hotchkiss gun at their temporary quarters in a new seven-story building owned by Astor at 552 Broadway. After this introductory work, March took his heterogeneous unit on an eighteen-mile hike to a campsite on some Astor land near Westchester. But the men only spent four days at what they called "Camp Blister" before leaving for San Francisco. They stayed not much longer at the port city.[4]

With an enthusiastic crowd cheering, bands playing, and steam whistles sounding, "Uncle Sam's swellest and least expensive military organization," as the *San Francisco Chronicle* labelled the battery, sailed on June 28. Their transport, the *Newport*, carried several other units and Wesley Merritt, who was en route to take command of the forces in the Philippines. Everyone, including the commanding general, was ignorant about the situation and the islands: one of Merritt's most confidential informational memoranda from the War Department consisted of material copied from the *Encyclopaedia Britannica.* On July 25, the *Newport* passed Corregidor and entered Manila Bay. Soon after their arrival the troops cheered as Admiral George Dewey came aboard to consult with General Merritt.[5]

The Admiral talked at length about Emilio Aguinaldo, the leader of the revolutionary movement. With the aid and encouragement of the Americans, this "thin, mild mannered man with a subdued voice"[6] returned to Luzon, gathered a force, and surrounded the Spanish in Manila. Since he assumed that the United States would follow the no-colonization policy it had announced for Cuba, Aguinaldo issued a proclamation of independence. Dewey and the two generals who had preceded Merritt had evaded the question of American intentions, but Merritt had instructions to assume absolute control.

While the high command wrestled with diplomatic matters, March attended to the mundane problems of landing and quartering his men. In the midst of a downpour the Astors manhandled their guns and equipment through a hundred yards of open surf to the beach. Once on shore they found scant comfort at their destination – a makeshift tent camp which offered little shelter from the daily rains. They remained at Camp Dewey for two weeks.[7]

During this period, while the American leaders negotiated with the Spanish, relations cooled with Aguinaldo. On a man-to-man basis, ill feeling, generated by mutual distrust, increased between the American soldiers and the insurgents. Although March often visited Aguinaldo's trenches on reconnaissance trips, he took more notice of a peculiarity of the natives' marksmanship than their attitude: they would conceal themselves, hold their weapons over their heads, and blaze away without aiming. Within a year he would have cause to remember this.[8]

At the time March probably was unaware that his commanders, as well as the Spanish, did not want the insurgents to use their guns. Since early May, Admiral Dewey had treated with Manila's commander – General Fermin Jaudenes – through neutral diplomats. After the arrival of the American expedition surrender was inevitable, but Jaudenes required a show of defense for honor's sake. Rules were sketched for

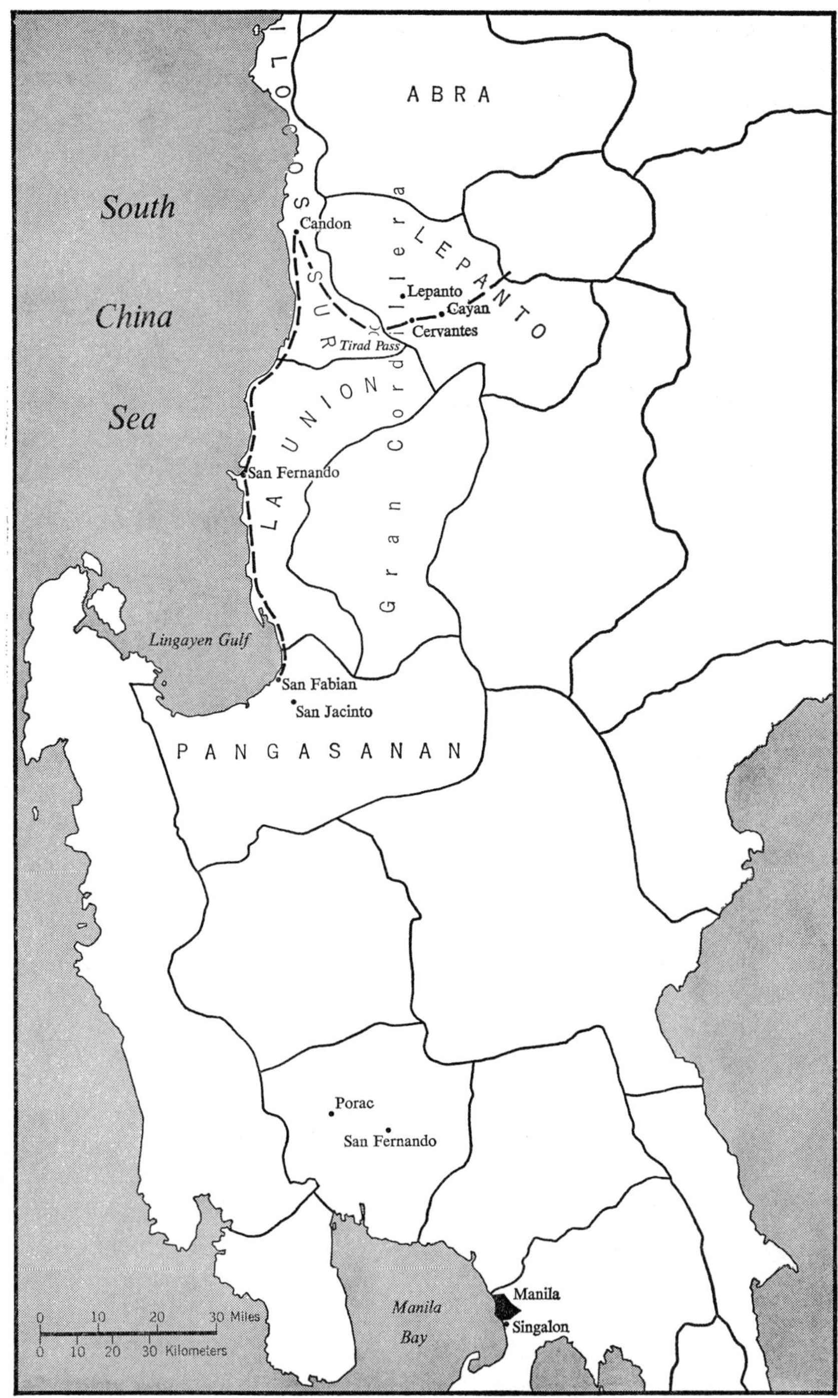

Northern Luzon, showing March's expedition, November–December, 1899. Map courtesy of the University of Wisconsin Cartographic Laboratory.

this action, but the Filipinos, whose intervention it was hoped could be avoided, were not brought into the negotiations.[9]

The "gloves were padded," as one correspondent commented, during the battle of Manila. Oscar Davis, who was on the scene, reported: "The tragedy lost its tragic character and became a comedy before the performance began, and the performance itself developed into pretty nearly a farce, with just enough of serious work in it to provoke regretful consideration." Both were the lot of the Astor Battery.[10]

For the advance Merritt placed two brigades on line. The one on the left, commanded by Francis V. Greene, occupied the trenches near the shoreline; the other, led by Arthur MacArthur, was inland, adjacent to the insurgents. The afternoon before the attack, March took his men, who were joyful about leaving their soggy camp, to a position on the right of the American line.[11]

The next morning, Saturday, August 13, reveille sounded at four o'clock. Rainy and windy, the dawn was not impressive. At 9:35 A.M. Dewey's warships opened fire. The huge projectiles sounded to March like express trains as they zoomed overhead. For the first time in their ten weeks of soldiering the Astors fired their weapons. Two Krupp guns promptly replied and continued the exchange. One unexploded shell struck the wheel of Sergeant Joe Beacham's gun and wounded three.[12]

Within two hours the Spanish deserted their trenches and the Americans began trailing them into Manila. MacArthur ordered March's battery to follow an infantry regiment in the advance. The troops moved forward cautiously until the head of the column ran into some opposition at the Singalon crossroads. The men halted and General MacArthur called for someone to lead a charge. March shouted, "I will lead it, sir." He drew his pistol and yelled, "Come on, men." A handful of Astors, firing their Colts and screaming like cowboys, joined some infantrymen and ran toward the Spanish position – a fortified house with sandbag emplacements across the road. The enemy concentrated their fire on the charging Americans. First Sergeant Holmes fell by March's side. Cremins was hit in the head and went down as if he had been tripped. Beacham reached for him, but March said, "He's dead – let him alone." With these two dead and three others wounded, March saw the futility of the attack. "Take cover," he ordered, and the men plunged into the undergrowth on the roadside where the leaves, clipped by the hail of bullets, rained down on them. Under this extremely heavy fire March worked his way back to MacArthur and reported the strong defense.

Then he noticed that the soldiers who had stayed behind with the two Hotchkiss guns had abandoned them. He promptly rallied the men and got the guns firing.[13] About 1:30 P.M. the "hellish fight" subsided and March volunteered to lead a scouting party. This time he found no Spanish in the position and continued on to Manila without further incident.[14] The war was over. While the Americans were not aware of it then, they learned later that President McKinley had ordered a suspension of military operations on August 12, but the message did not reach the Philippines in time.

After all the reports were in, it was apparent that the Singalon skirmish had been the most severe action of the day. Indeed, the Astor Battery's casualties of seven killed and wounded equalled the total losses of Greene's entire brigade, which had met virtually no opposition on its advance.[15]

In his report General MacArthur singled out the Astor Battery commander: "The brilliant manner in which Lieutenant March accepted and discharged the responsible and dangerous duties of the day . . . was an exceptional display of warlike skill and good judgment, indicating the existence of many of the best qualifications for high command in battle." He reinforced this citation with a recommendation for a Medal of Honor, but the reviewing board did not approve the award. Later March commented that he made the charge for the "moral effect." He admitted that he never expected to come out alive, adding, "It was only the abominable marksmanship of the Spaniards that saved our lives. . . ." Joe Beacham, who had been at his heels during the fight, supplied this afterthought: "I think he got overenthusiastic."[16]

For the next four months March and his men took part in the occupation of Manila. With the coming of fall, smallpox, dysentery, and typhoid began to take their toll, causing the deaths of two men in the battery. Relations continued to deteriorate with the Filipinos, yet, despite the occasional alarms, there was no actual fighting. Finally, in mid-December the homesick Astors began their return voyage on the transport *Senator*.[17]

Although March was leaving the Islands, he would soon return. After some seven weeks of travel the battery arrived in New York City, where it was mustered out of the service. Its commander completed his duties and then enjoyed a six-week respite with his family in Easton. Shortly after his arrival home he spoke to a group of Lafayette students who gathered in the rapidly falling snow in front of the professor's house.

He acknowledged their cheers and briefly told them of the part college men had played in the war. After the boys dispersed, a local reporter lingered to ask questions about the fighting which had just erupted in the Philippines.[18]

For at last the overstrained relations had deteriorated into war. In December, the terms of the final peace treaty, which ceded the entire archipelago to the United States, ended Aguinaldo's hopes for a peaceful transition to independence. On the night of February 4, 1899, an American sentry opened fire on two Filipinos who ignored his commands to halt and began the actual fighting. When the Easton reporter asked March for his comments, he replied, "I expected it and the outcome is settled in advance."[19]

Major General Arthur MacArthur, who was now a division commander, had written March in December, 1898, "If you wish to return to Manila and grow up with this country, I would be glad to have you as an aid." As March's leave neared its end, he forwarded this message to the War Department. By the end of May he was at the general's headquarters in San Fernando, a few miles north of Manila.[20] For over four months March stayed with MacArthur and gained experience as the division's adjutant general, judge advocate, and mustering officer. Despite the connotations of desk work associated with those duties, March took part in several engagements. In one of these, at Porac, he won a citation for his part in the pursuit of an enemy unit.[21]

At headquarters March had contacts with several interesting figures: the old Confederate general, Joe Wheeler; thirty-four-year-old Brigadier General Frederick Funston, who later captured Aguinaldo; and J. Franklin Bell, whose reputation would make him the army's Chief of Staff within ten years. The lieutenant's most valuable relationship, however, was with his commander. Arthur MacArthur encouraged him in his reading on Far Eastern problems. As March recalled, the general "had a standing order with Kelly, the bookseller of Hongkong, to send to him every book in stock published on Far Eastern matters, particularly those devoted to colonial administration of the various islands and parts of the Far East which were under control of the European Powers. I spent what spare time I had in reading these books as they came to the General, and trying to extend my knowledge of conditions existing in the Far East at that time." The general was much impressed with the artilleryman. Earlier he had written his son Douglas about March's heroism at Singalon. Again in August, 1899, he recorded his opinion of

March: "An exemplary officer in every respect, professionally capable, and physically strong."[22]

March's service on the general's staff ended with the formation of a new volunteer regiment. After Congress authorized 35,000 volunteers to combat the insurrection, the War Department cabled March on July 12, 1899, that he was to be a major in the Thirty-third Volunteer Infantry Regiment.[23] The Thirty-third was a picturesque and rugged outfit. Organized at Fort Sam Houston in San Antonio, Texas, nearly 60 per cent of its enlisted men were from Texas, Arkansas, and the Indian Territory. The senior officers were almost all regulars. At a time when the regular regiments were commanded by Civil War veterans, the volunteers were led by younger men. A captain in the Seventh Cavalry, Luther R. Hare, was the colonel; this "damn fine man" began his army career under Custer. The lieutenant colonel, John J. Brereton, also a regular captain, had been wounded in the Cuban campaign. Both of the other majors March knew at West Point: Marcus D. Cronin was the cadet who had prophesied the German war in the One Hundredth Night show in 1886; while John A. Logan, the son of the Union general of the same name, had spent a few months in both Cronin's and March's classes.[24]

The regiment trained briefly and then sailed for Luzon, where March joined it on October 29. After a few days on the defense line the unit received orders to reboard its transports. Rumors were rife: they were going home in disgrace because they had wasted so much ammunition on monkeys; they were going to Hong Kong for further training; or they were joining Wheaton's expedition. The last was correct. Brigadier General Loyd Wheaton was leading a force of 2500 men in an amphibious operation, which was part of a great pincer movement intended to trap Aguinaldo's army: while MacArthur continued to advance up the Manila-Lingayen Gulf plain, Major General Henry W. Lawton would move along the mountains to MacArthur's right; Wheaton's mission was to land at San Fabian, move inland to join Lawton and complete the envelopment.[25]

After a stormy voyage, the transports reached Lingayen Gulf and stood off shore while the supporting warships bombarded the enemy trenches. A member of March's second battalion described the scene: "In a few minutes the vessels were almost hidden, the spray was flying from the water near shore, trees were torn to pieces, houses were shattered, and dirt was thrown in every direction." March and his men came under the return fire in their plunging small boats as they approached the beach, but once ashore they found the trenches deserted. The major then left part of his battalion in San Fabian and took two companies about a mile from the town to establish an outpost near a long bamboo bridge.[26]

He knew that on the following day he would have to cross that bridge, since Wheaton had ordered a reconnaissance. The hard rain and constant howling of some dogs, together with the sounds of natives digging trenches on the other side of the estuary, made sleep difficult that night. The next morning March formed his men and led them across the 150-yard-long bridge as fast as he could. For almost six miles he pursued the enemy, who fled without much of a fight. Although the natives' marksmanship was generally poor, as March had noticed earlier, they took a toll of eight killed and three wounded in his command. Colonel Hare was impressed with the action and recommended March for a Medal of Honor for the bridge-crossing exploit.[27]

During the next week March took part in two other sorties. In one, the full regiment assaulted the *insurrectos* at San Jacinto, six miles east of San Fabian. On a very sultry day March had to lead his men through some three miles of the deep mud and water of rice paddies in a skirmish formation. His battalion was the first to reach the objective and suffered the consequences of casualties equal to the total of the other two battalions' losses. In this action March's "coolness" and "inspiring personal gallantry" won him another citation.[28]

While March was fighting in the jungles near San Fabian, the insurrection was disintegrating into a guerrilla war. By November 12, Aguinaldo had ordered an abandonment of open warfare, and then he had taken a small party into the mountains. During the following months March played a prominent role in the cat-and-mouse chase of the revolutionary leader. After the major returned to San Fabian from the battle of San Jacinto, he picked up orders to take four companies and move north along the China Sea coast to make contact with Brigadier General Samuel B. M. Young. Although one of Young's staff officers intercepted him and changed his orders, March drew criticism by stubbornly refusing to accept the new orders. The next day he met Young, who told him to move into the mountains and place his men between Aguinaldo's party and another large rebel band.[29]

On the third day of the hike through the wild mountainous terrain

March heard that the enemy was near and hurried his men to the foot of Tirad Pass. As they zigzagged single file on the narrow trail up the precipice, the Americans came under heavy fire. March ran up to the front of the column, sent word for the rest to come up, and pulled out his field glasses. He had difficulty locating the enemy position until he glimpsed an officer directing fire. The major pushed forward but, as several men fell, he realized that a frontal attack up the path was out of the question.

It was a formidable situation. On the left of the well-constructed stone barricade was a gorge several hundred feet deep; on the right was a steep peak which towered 1500 feet above the position. The Major decided that a flanking maneuver was the only choice. He sent a sergeant and ten sharpshooters across the gorge to a hill where they could fire on the trail behind the barricade and then he assigned a flanking move to Company H.

For two hours he paced up and down, anxiously glancing at his watch. The infantrymen huddled under ledges and drew fire by raising their hats on sticks. The insurgents jeered and occasionally sent rocks rolling down the slope. At times clouds enveloped the entire scene. Throughout the waiting, Lieutenant Frank D. Tompkins and his men of H Company were out of sight, climbing hand over hand. After the long wait, a crash of fire from his men on the peak demonstrated their success. Taking advantage of the enemy's distraction, March led the rest up the trail and took the barricade.

John T. McCutcheon and another news correspondent, who had accompanied the expedition and would later publicize this battle, identified General Gregorio del Pilar as one of the dead. This twenty-two year old leader of Aguinaldo's bodyguard had defended this Thermopylae with his sixty picked men until death. After this victory, the Americans knew that Aguinaldo was nearby.[30]

From Tirad Pass on December 2 to the end of the month March continued the chase. Three days after that battle he captured Aguinaldo's chief of staff, Venancio Concepción, and, on Christmas Day, Señora Aguinaldo, the president's wife, surrendered, but the supreme catch escaped. The dangerous game continued into 1900. Although March served as military governor of the mountain provinces—first in Illocos Sur and later in Abra—he still searched for Aguinaldo. On the most lengthy of his expeditions, a 110-mile hike over the most rugged country in Luzon, he fell into a swift-flowing stream and almost drowned. Private William E. Kilgore, who helped rescue him, later commented, "I often wondered if we convinced Aguinaldo and his men that we could hike without food, clothes, shoes, or rest." [31]

In January, 1901, March, by now a lieutenant colonel of volunteers, began the last phase of his Philippine tour. He went to Manila to take over the post of Commissary General of the Prisoners. For his remaining six months on Luzon he supervised not only the care of some 5000 insurgents in the various prisons but also the compilation of individual case records for each prisoner. The assignment in Manila also afforded him the opportunity to renew his acquaintance with General MacArthur. By July, Aguinaldo was in custody and the insurrection was virtually over. On the first of that month March reverted from his volunteer rank to his regular captaincy, which had come through during the spring. By the end of the month he was in San Francisco.[32]

At thirty-six, Captain Peyton C. March was a marked man in the army. His exploits with the Astor Battery and the volunteers had received wide publicity. More important, they had brought him the attention of senior officers as no garrison duty every could. After ten years of service in the "Old Army," bound by the restrictions of economy and of the past, he emerged from the ranks of good lieutenants to distinction.

Arthur MacArthur was particularly impressed with him. In 1901, the general wrote a letter recommending him for the post of commandant of cadets at West Point. While March did not get the position, MacArthur's explicit praise must have eased the disappointment. "March is a man of rare good judgment, decisive character, thoroughly informed in everything of professional nature. . . ." The general concluded: "The many acts of good soldiership that Colonel March has performed since the beginning of the Philippine War are too numerous to record, but it is a well known fact that no officer has rendered more efficient or brilliant field service than he in the Island of Luzon." [33]

As a troop leader March was decisive and direct. Beacham, the former Cornell football star, who succeeded Holmes as first sergeant of the Astor Battery, recalled: "He always did the right thing and the soldiers knew it. There was no hesitancy about it." Curt, even brusque, March was a hard disciplinarian who earned respect. At Bangued in Abra Province a half-drunk volunteer saw him in his quarters and yelled out an offer of a drink; 30 days in the guardhouse and $30 fine was the response. His many citations, which later brought him a Silver Star medal with four oak leaf clusters, recorded his courage.[34]

During the Philippine period March learned much, in addition to demonstrating his combat leadership ability. He saw the American volunteer soldier under severe conditions and later testified that he was "a first-class fighting man" who "learned quickly" and "was dependable." With this infantry service he transcended the narrowness of army branch loyalty which limited many of his peers. As a military administrator he bore the responsibility of governing two provinces and of maintaining the prisoners of war. Finally, he had the advantage of close contact and friendship with a ranking officer. By observing MacArthur as a division commander and as the military governor, he learned the complexity of such command positions without carrying the burden.[35]

When Captain March landed at San Francisco, he was on orders to return to garrison duty. But neither he nor the army would return to the stagnation of the garrison life he had left in 1896. The army was on the verge of a transformation and March and other young officers would be the instruments of this change.

3 · BETWEEN WARS

THE period between 1901 and 1917 was a time of steady advancement for March. As the army underwent fundamental reforms, he took advantage of the opportunities offered. During these years he balanced staff assignments with troop duty and continued to burnish his reputation.

Following a war there is usually a period of soul-searching in the military as the professionals attempt to learn from the problems of that war. Frequently the resulting changes in the system are rather superficial. But the widely aired scandals of planning, mobilization, and logistics during the Spanish-American War required more than desultory attention. Fortunately, an outstanding Secretary of War took office and made basic alterations in the army. Indeed, Elihu Root laid the foundations of a twentieth-century military establishment.

Root soon realized that many in the army only paid lip service to the principle, "That the real object of having an Army is to provide for war."[1] The events of the hectic days of 1898 clearly demonstrated that the labyrinth of administrative empire-building in the years since the Civil War had prepared the army to exist only in peacetime. With the aid of progressive military advisors, the Secretary penetrated to the heart of the problem.

The army was split into two parts: the line or combat units scattered in the posts throughout the country; and the staff bureaus in Washington. Lack of understanding and enmity characterized the relationship of the bifurcated service. Branch loyalty further complicated the situation, since the individual line or staff officer tended to think principally in terms of his specialty. This cleavage was symbolized at the top by the peculiar position of the Commanding General, who in fact had command over little more than his personal staff. Since the bureau chiefs spent the money and kept the records necessary to maintain the army, they worked in close association with Congress and dealt personally with the Secretary of War. The Commanding General lacked authority over the bureau heads; hence, in peacetime, he became isolated and virtually a bystander. On two occasions, these officers, angered by their impotence and the frequent dissension, had moved their headquarters out of Washington.[2]

Root realized that the army needed a co-ordinating agency other than the office of Secretary of War. In addition, the civilian executive in the War Department needed military advice on matters of broad policy to replace the particular special-interest pleadings of bureau chiefs. The obvious solution was a General Staff headed by a chief who would be the military advisor to the Secretary. To maintain this officer's military primacy, he would supervise not only the troops of the line but also the bureaus. For support in his mission, the Chief of Staff would depend on the General Staff to investigate and report "upon all questions affecting the efficiency of the Army and its state of preparation," and to plan for national defense.[3]

While the General Staff was a major part of his program, Root also advocated a new system of military education, culminating in the Army War College, which he hoped would furnish a large body of competently trained officers. Finally, he attempted to increase the effectiveness of the citizen-soldiery by standardizing and providing increased federal aid to the various state militias. By the time he left the War Department, Root had secured legislation which established the basis of a modern army.

When March debarked from the transport *Meade* in July, 1901, the General Staff was two years in the future. Meantime, the new captain would spend twenty months on troop duty. Before he joined his command, the Nineteenth Battery at Fort Riley, Kansas, he took a leave and became reacquainted with his family, including a daughter, now almost two years old, whom he had not seen.[4]

In the pleasant atmosphere of the old cavalry post March undertook the task of commanding a battery. There were drills and inspections in the mornings. During the afternoons he went over the paperwork and checked the drilling of recruits and the horse-training exercises. Occasionally he instructed in the school for young officers. For one three-week period in the fall of 1902, he and his battery participated in the first large field maneuver of a combined regular and militia force. March enjoyed the field work and frequently commented to one of his battery officers, "It's a great game, isn't it!" Beverly F. Browne, a brand-new second lieutenant, thought his captain "a wonderful battery commander" who expected his officers to do their jobs efficiently without his interference. Although March did not praise his subordinates, he did not berate them either unless they inexplicably failed.[5]

March's tour at Fort Riley came to an end in the spring of 1903, when he received orders to join the newly created General Staff in Washington. The initial General Staff Corps was the "flower of the service,"[6] selected by a board of generals who sifted the records in their search for the outstanding officers. A member of this board, S. B. M. Young, became a lieutenant general and the first Chief of Staff. While March had met Young at the Presidio before the Spanish War, the two did not become closely acquainted until they met again during the chase of Aguinaldo. Young recognized March's services on Luzon with commendations and even promised to take the younger officer with him to China when it looked as if the general would go there during the Boxer Rebellion. Among the forty-odd junior officers selected for the General Staff, many would wear stars in the next war: at one time, during the early days of the General Staff, March shared an office with Major George W. Goethals and Captain John J. Pershing.[7]

When the pioneering group started their tasks, they worked in three divisions. The First studied organization, training, administrative, and mobilization problems. The responsibility for military information or intelligence belonged to the Second Division. The Third prepared war plans and supervised the technical services – an assignment which caused this division to overlap some areas of the First Division's mission. Since none of the officers knew much about General Staff procedure, March remembered that they "turned to administrative work, which of course produced friction with everyone."[8]

To add to the inevitable difficulties of a new organization, the still recalcitrant bureau chiefs attempted to impede its development. Their power and animosity would continue into the First World War. Ironically, two of the most powerful bureau heads in that war, the Judge Advocate General, Enoch H. Crowder, and The Adjutant General, Henry P. McCain, had been members of the initial General Staff.[9] The men in authority changed, but the clash of special interests with the general supervisory role of the General Staff persisted.

For nine months March worked in Room 160 of the large State, War, and Navy Building, adjacent to the White House. As a member of the First Division's First Section, he wrestled with the questions of organization, distribution, armament, and training of regulars, volunteers, and militia in both mobilization and maneuver situations. These were trying times, since his wife was sick, but he would not permit his personal life to intrude on his official duties: on one occasion he remonstrated with his wife's step-mother for coming to see him at the office about his wife's illness.[10]

War half-way around the world pulled March away from his desk. For the past few years the ambition of Japan had clashed with Russian interests in Asia until, in early February, 1904, the two countries went to war. Before the month was out, March was on orders as an observer with the Japanese army. The day after he heard about his new assignment, as he was walking to work down Connecticut Avenue, he met the Russian military attaché. The Russian congratulated him, then commented, "The only question in my mind is whether you will be able to get out there in time. . . . It will be only a local affair." Later March would recall the appalling lack of knowledge of the strength of the Japanese army which this remark indicated.[11]

On March 5, March boarded the *Doric* at San Francisco. His companion on this voyage was the chief of his General Staff division, Colonel Crowder, who had asked for the mission in the hope of increasing his chances for promotion to brigadier general. A West Pointer, only five years older than March, this "vinegary" [12] Missourian was already far ahead of his contemporaries in rank because of his transfer to the Judge Advocate General's Department. He and March had known each other for several years. In 1898, they had crossed the Pacific together on the *Newport* and three years later they had renewed their acquaintance in Manila.[13]

When they arrived in Japan, the two Americans joined a group of European observers who had gathered in Tokyo to await permission to join the army in the field. While these officers and the various news correspondents took part in the busy social life and fretted for their release, the Japanese army had marched steadily north through Korea into Manchuria. On the last day of April, 1904, March and Crowder started on the two-week journey by rail, ship, and horseback to join the

Japanese First Army at Fenghuangcheng, thirty miles beyond the Yalu River in Manchuria.[14]

The Americans spent six weeks with Baron Tamesada Kuroki's army headquarters. They soon had to adjust to the polite Japanese restrictions on what they saw and on what they described in their reports. As Kuroki's chief of staff explained, "We are paying for this information with our blood." At Fenghuangcheng, March celebrated the twentieth anniversary of his entering West Point by dining with Frederick Palmer, the *Collier's* magazine correspondent. Although only thirty-one, Palmer was a veteran war correspondent. Since he and the other newsmen were better supplied than were the observers, they frequently entertained the military men with meals and sociable drinks. On these occasions Palmer became acquainted with March. The journalist was impressed with the tall, slender officer and recalled, "March had an extraordinary knowledge. He knew every subject and thought that he knew it better than anyone else. . . . He hated a waste of words and he was impatient with the lower class of minds." [15]

Most of the time March had to rely on the observers for companionship. They were a diverse group, representing several European nations. Among them were Lieutenant General Sir Ian Hamilton, who would command the Gallipoli expedition; two future corps commanders, who would oppose each other at Verdun; and an Italian major, who would command an army in the next great war. Although the two Americans got along well enough, March associated more with attachés his own age and rank. Besides, Crowder was ill much of the time with neuralgia, which caused him to spend some days in the hospital later in the fall. In particular, March became "very friendly" with the German captain Max Hoffmann, a burly General Staff officer. He gave the German lessons in English and checked his cable reports for proper language. Often they talked of common problems, for Hoffmann liked March's "intelligent military views and his straightforward and outspoken opinions." March found his friend well informed about the Russians, since he had served six months in that country. During World War I, Hoffmann was to put this knowledge to use and earn a distinguished reputation on the Eastern Front.[16]

In an irritated moment, Hoffmann, who was exasperated by the many restraints imposed by the Japanese, infuriated Kuroki's chief of staff by exclaiming, "You are yellow – you are not civilized . . . ,"[17] thus bringing into the open the racial feeling which lurked close to the sur-

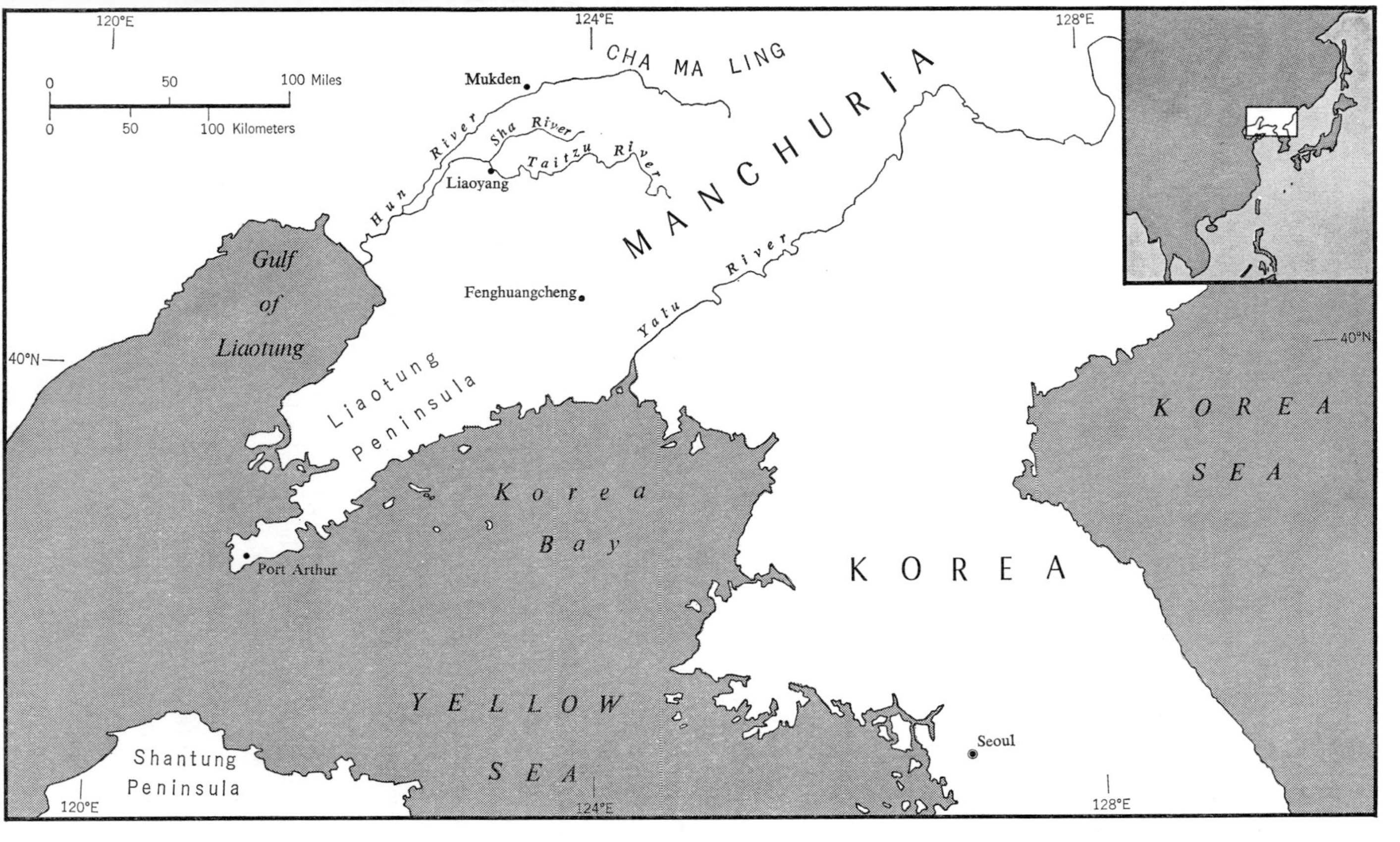

Theater of Russo-Japanese War, 1904. Map courtesy of the University of Wisconsin Cartographic Laboratory.

face throughout the war. The Japanese used race as an excuse for general restrictions, particularly for not allowing the foreigners to get closer to combat. Indeed, many of the privates thought the white men were Russians. Whenever they approached a recently captured village, Japanese officers had to ride ahead to warn the sentinels not to fire on the observer party. On one occasion March noticed a large number of soldiers with menacing demeanor gathered about the correspondents' tent. He asked the interpreter to translate their shouts. The old Japanese reluctantly admitted that they were yelling, "Down with the Americans."[18] March promptly complained, and the incident stuck in his memory. Supposedly the two nations were friends. In Japan, American diplomats were greeted with cheers and renditions of the "Star-Spangled Banner"; in the Manchurian war zone, however, troops aroused by success thought of the obvious rivalry.[19]

From the last week of June until November 20, March accompanied Baron Nishi's Second Division in the campaign which culminated in a great battle near the Sha River, some twenty miles from Mukden. The Japanese move took March and the others, first in very hot weather, then in the rainy season, through mountainous terrain which reminded Crowder of New Mexico. Throughout this period, when possible, March attempted to elude his Japanese guide to get closer to the fighting. He jotted down his observations in his notebook and occasionally used his camera to get a picture to supplement his comments.[20]

His particular mission as an observer was to report on field artillery. On August 30, when three Japanese armies converged on the Russian force at Liaoyang, he had a superb observation point on a promontory which gave him a panoramic view of the battle front. The entire Japanese line was spread out before him; beyond were the Russians. Above the scene, a captive Russian balloon floated, while in the distance he could see trains coming and going from the city. As he watched the artillery duel, March munched hardtack and muttered time and again, "This is great." Turning to Palmer, who was with him on the peak, he added, "To think I should ever see this!" – a great battle with modern weapons taking place before his eyes.[21]

At Liaoyang, the ten-day battle of the Sha, and various other fights, March saw a well-trained and disciplined army defeat its adversary in large-scale warfare. He filled his reports with a wide range of details, from the description of a battle to comments on the few sanitary precautions taken by the Japanese. In his specialty, artillery, he found that the Japanese guns were inferior to the Russian field-pieces, yet the Japanese overcame the deficiency with their superior training and superb morale. He considered the frequency of large night attacks, a tactic both sides used to counter the effect of modern magazine rifles and machine guns, "the most important development of the war." Also, the Japanese method of controlling units, their use of modern communications and of a general staff system modelled on the German version, made a lasting impression on him.[22]

After the battle of the Sha, March moved into comfortable winter quarters in the house of a British resident manager of a coal mine company. Although his reports took up time, the captain had some social life – celebrating the emperor's birthday with a champagne toast at Kuroki's headquarters, and attending dinners in honor of the birthdays of the kings of England and Italy. Earlier, during a lull in the campaign, he had read Alfred Thayer Mahan's *The Interest of America in Sea Power*, a collection of articles which summed up the concepts of the naval strategist. But in November he was more interested in news of the outcome of the Army and Navy football game and of Theodore Roosevelt's victory in the presidential election.[23]

On Sunday, November 20, he opened a cablegram announcing his wife's death two days before. She had been ill for some time but, nonetheless, she had borne him another son, Lewis, on May 10, 1904, shortly after his departure. That night he left for home. Four days before Christmas he arrived in Washington, where he found Jo's family in charge of things. "Everything in good order as could be expected," he wrote in his diary. His emotions he did not confide to paper. Until his older children reached maturity, a cousin and then his sister Mildred stayed with him most of the time and helped take care of them.[24]

On December 22, March went to the War Department. That afternoon he reported his experiences to the Chief of Staff and the Secretary of War. Across the street in the White House the President showed interest in his impressions of the Far Eastern war. Theodore Roosevelt, now in the midst of his efforts to bring about negotiations between the belligerents, had read all of March's dispatches, but he wanted to talk about the situation. The next day, March lunched with a "most cordial" President and his "very charming wife." Arriving at one, he stayed for three hours.[25]

In the course of the conversation March complained of the treatment of the attachés and, mentioning the "Down with the Americans" incident, he emphasized the attitude of the Japanese. Later, the President forced him into arguments on both points. Calling in Frederick Palmer, Roosevelt opened the question of the observers' position and listened to the artilleryman and the correspondent thrash it out. At a later dinner, he again raised the issue of Japan's attitude, using Senator Henry Cabot Lodge to counter March. By this time March was firmly convinced, as he told the Army War College students in a lecture, "if Japan wins this war, nothing less than predominance in the Pacific will satisfy her. The slightest study of the strategic weakness of our situation in the Philippines should show us that possibly the time may come when we shall have to play a hand ourselves. . . ."[26]

When he returned to his office in the War Department, March was disillusioned by what he saw. The American General Staff was a long way from being the effective agency that the Japanese General Staff was. Headed in these early years by Civil War veterans who had little understanding of modern concepts, the General Staff lacked a continuing policy, and still suffered from the enmity of the bureau chiefs and their friends on Capitol Hill. March advocated a reorganization based on his observations in Manchuria but his efforts failed.[27]

Soon he settled into the routine. As a member of committees on Bayonet and Sword, Intrenching Tools, and the Reorganization of the Artillery, he referred to his experience in dealing with these topics. In a joint study of physical training at the service academies, he met with naval officers. Since Captain Pershing had been ordered to join Kuroki's army before Mukden, March replaced him on the detail which helped make arrangements for the inaugural parade. But the artillery captain was restless. When he heard of a chance for promotion to major in the position of Assistant Chief of Records and Pensions office, he applied for the appointment, but he did not get it.[28]

His chance of quick advancement thwarted, March turned with increasing interest to his study of artillery organization. After the Spanish War a unified Artillery Corps had been created. Since this system of combining coast and field artillery was not working satisfactorily, a move was underway to split the corps into its natural branches. In his investigations March visited units at Forts Sill and Riley, and in 1906, he accompanied two batteries on the long march from Fort Myer, Virginia, to Chickamauga Park, Georgia, where he remained with them during a maneuver. When the General Staff board devised the reorganization plan, March worked out the field artillery organization. After the acceptance of the new program, he applied for assignment to that branch. When Beverly Browne asked for advice on choosing between service in the coast or field artillery, March replied that "he preferred the Branch of the Service that went to *meet the* enemy rather than the one that stayed at home and *waited for* the enemy." The new Chief of Staff, J. Franklin Bell, his acquaintance from Philippine days, endorsed his application: "I know of no officer in the Artillery whom I consider better qualified for service in the Field branch. . . ." [29]

Early in 1907, his promotion and transfer to the new branch came through. After spending the summer on leave, he joined the newly organized Sixth Field Artillery (Horse) Regiment at Fort Riley. The Sixth had unusual responsibilities in addition to its regular duties. As its commander, Colonel Montgomery M. Macomb, pointed out, "The War Department depends on that regiment to make all its experiments with materiel on the field; to pass on questions of administration; to examine field artillery officers for promotion. . . ." As a member of the Field Artillery Board, the Examining Board, and even the Board on Veterinary Instruments, March devoted much of his time to these activities; nevertheless, his principal task was to command the first battalion.[30]

Again he was in the element he liked best — command. Some of the officers, among them Beverly Browne, knew him, and others quickly learned his methods. One of his battery commanders, Ralph McT. Pennell, recalled, "He was a superior Battalion Commander in that he gave his Battery Commanders a free rein and . . . [held] them to a high standard for results." Pennell went on:

> His criticism of mistakes was terse, incisive, and clear. He could cut one down to size more completely and in fewer words than any other Commander I ever had, but not to cause resentment or hurt to one's self-respect. He did not humiliate a subordinate if it could be avoided. Once he was president of a Court Martial before which I appeared as a counsel for a soldier charged with some minor offense. During the trial I must have assumed some unsoldierly postures in my chair. After a while Major March arose from his seat at the head of the table and whispered in my ear. No one else heard him, but what he said was quite effective.[31]

Another lieutenant, James W. Riley, who served for a time as battalion adjutant, remembered that the officers were awed by him and the enlisted men were "just about scared to death of him." [32]

Practice marches and target practice took up much of the time.

When others complained of going into the field below strength and minus some equipment, March commented to his quartermaster, Browne, "You know this is really fortunate and may turn out to be a valuable experience — to learn what we can do with very short man-power — as it is certain to happen in war." [33]

For four months in 1908, the major had the opportunity to study field problems on a comprehensive basis. Throughout the country the army staged eight maneuvers with combined regular and National Guard units in an attempt to develop a more effective militia as well as to train the regulars. These exercises began with a camp of instruction and concluded with tactical problems in which combat conditions were simulated with actual opposing forces. At Fort Riley, guardsmen from Kansas, Missouri, Oklahoma, South Dakota, and Iowa joined the regulars for a week at a time. The problems also furnished the first opportunity to try out the new artillery organization in maneuver situations. March's mission was to prepare an instructional program, set up the problems, and write the rules governing the affair. In this preparation he called upon his Russo-Japanese War experience to emphasize night attacks and the increased effectiveness of modern weapons, particularly the machine gun. After he completed the preliminary work, he served as Chief Umpire. Once the maneuver began, he supervised the assistant umpires who accompanied the various units and reported on their observations. When the assistants completed their reports, they turned them over to March, who then went over these critiques with the unit commanders. Finally, he spent a month writing up the over-all report, which was published later that year. It was a "well-run maneuver," as one of the assistant umpires, Charles S. Blakely, later testified, and the general in charge, J. B. Kerr, commended March for his "masterly ability" in carrying out his assignment.[34]

All was not work at Riley. March liked games and frequently tested his talents. At the Officers' Club he would play billiards with Browne or the cavalryman Ben Lear. A veteran of Pershing's Moro expeditions, Lear thought that his billiard partner resembled his former commander in manner: both impressed him as harsh and abrupt, but quiet. At times March made a foursome at the bridge table with Browne, John E. McMahon, and William I. Westervelt. On the golf links he joined his next-door neighbor, Robert M. Danford, in a two-ball foursome with George H. Cameron and George W. Read. When Danford put him in a trap or in the rough, March, the younger officer recalled, enjoyed razzing him. Despite this, the major never encouraged familiarity. A tipsy captain found this out at the club when he addressed him as "Maje"; according to a witness, "He never finished the sentence and was entirely sober after about six words of admonition."[35]

March even played baseball on occasion. When Congress passed a bill increasing officers' pay, the Seventh Cavalry Regiment and the Sixth Artillery scheduled a contest to celebrate. While the lieutenants were making up a team, March walked in and announced that he was going to play. During the game he played with "remarkable agility," although he seemed to one young officer "to be about the age of Methusaleh." On one play he brought the spectators to their feet with a barehand catch of a line drive.[36] It was through baseball that he met an interesting lieutenant of engineers when he visited Fort Leavenworth as a member of an officers' team. Douglas MacArthur, who played first base on the Leavenworth team, introduced himself and "more or less attached" himself to his father's friend to look after his wants while he was visiting the post.[37]

In April, 1911, March left Riley. For almost four years he had enjoyed not only command but also, as a member of the Field Artillery Board, the responsibility of dealing with major artillery technical problems. During the next five-and-a-half years, except for a five-month respite at Riley in 1912, he was on detail to the Adjutant General's Department. First in a departmental headquarters at Omaha and later as a division adjutant general in Chicago and in Texas City, he supervised the flow of correspondence and the maintenance of records.[38] Finally, in October, 1913, March, by now a lieutenant colonel, went to Washington to take charge of recruiting in the Adjutant General's Office. On duty in the War Department he found several of his acquaintances, among them McMahon and young MacArthur, whom he saw frequently, on the General Staff, while Crowder, now a brigadier general, ran the Judge Advocate General's Department. The Chief of Staff at this time was Leonard Wood, a Harvard Medical School graduate and Rough Rider friend of Theodore Roosevelt. A competent administrator, Wood was "ruthless and ambitious," according to Assistant Secretary of War Henry Breckinridge, and determined to make the army a more effective organization.[39]

The year before March's arrival, Wood, with the strong support of the then Secretary of War, Henry L. Stimson, brought to a head the smoldering opposition of the bureau chiefs and forced the retirement of the strongest of the clan — The Adjutant General, Fred C. Ainsworth. An outstanding administrator with great influence in Congress, Ainsworth had used his power to thwart the General Staff. In an argument over the muster roll Ainsworth formally questioned the theory of General Staff control. Wood immediately took the offensive memorandum to Stimson. Aware of The Adjutant General's insubordination over a period of time, the Secretary acted decisively by ordering preparation of court-martial charges, whereupon Ainsworth retired. Stimson and Wood had won a victory for progressive thought but at the cost of injuring an influential man.[40]

March realized the significance of the Wood-Ainsworth fight. Although he was a member of the select group of six or seven in Ainsworth's successor's office, he remained a General Staff proponent. Nevertheless he earnestly attacked the problems of recruiting and of decreasing the paperwork. The threat of continued trouble with Mexico brought him the additional task of working up mustering-in plans for the militia units.[41]

For three years March served in the Adjutant General's Office. A General Staff officer of that period, George Van Horn Moseley, who had served under March as an assistant umpire in the Riley maneuvers, recalled, "His personality penetrated the office." When you thought of that bureau, Moseley added, "You thought of March in those days." The Adjutant General, Henry P. McCain, an Ainsworth disciple, believed him to be "an excellent officer, keen and alert with the courage of his convictions." In his dealings with the young Assistant Secretary of War, Breckinridge, who saw him frequently about recruiting matters, March was "very much the professional soldier — straight to the point, businesslike, stiff and formal," and "very intelligent." A clerk of twenty years' experience, Jesse H. Powell, found him "cold," a man of "few words," but one who made himself clearly understood. Powell knew that March "was not very approachable unless you had business with him — then he was right on the job." These characteristics made deep impressions on those who came into contact with him. Almost a half-century later an assistant to Secretary of Interior Franklin K. Lane recalled with a touch of anger March's brusqueness and his unco-operative reaction to a request.[42]

During the last year of March's tour in Washington, President Wilson made an appointment which would have ramifications in March's future. In the midst of the debate over preparedness, Wilson withdrew support from a plan proposed by his Secretary of War, Lindley M. Garrison, to create a large army reserve force. When Garrison resigned, the President named a Cleveland lawyer, Newton D. Baker, to the position. Soon after Baker took office, he made one of his most crucial decisions. A section of the comprehensive National Defense Act of June, 1916, apparently limited the General Staff to theoretical planning. The influence of the deposed Adjutant General, Ainsworth, was evident in this blow for the bureaus. Despite Judge Advocate General Crowder's endorsement of the bureau interpretation, Baker listened to his Chief of Staff, Hugh L. Scott, and other General Staff proponents, refused to accept the negative view, and maintained the General Staff position. He had ample reason later not to regret his decision.[43]

At the time, in 1916, the increased tension of Mexican relations took precedence over all other military affairs as the War Department dispatched an expedition into that country and mobilized the National Guard for border duty. Lieutenant Colonel March had the chore in this crisis of handling telegraphic correspondence between the War Department and the troops on the border. In addition to giving him the chance to follow the intricacies of maintaining a large emergency force in the field, this task also brought him into frequent contact with the new Secretary of War. This work came to an end, however, in the summer of 1916, when March put on the eagles of a colonel. On October 5, he took command of the Eighth Field Artillery Regiment.[44]

The Eighth was a new unit, created by a transfer of men from the Fifth and Sixth Regiments. Stationed at Fort Bliss, the unit occupied tents on the mesa on the outskirts of the post. The only buildings were mess shacks, which offered little protection in a Texas dust storm. The weapon which the six firing batteries had was a new, experimental gun – a 3.8″ howitzer, which, one officer recalled, "was not much of a gun."[45]

March moved into a storage tent and began establishing his command presence. Physically, he looked the part. Six feet, two inches in height, weighing 172 pounds, he walked with the erect West Point bearing. Moreover, he was decisive. "If you asked him a question," one of the lieutenants, Horace L. McBride, remarked, "he wouldn't say – I'll think about it or something to that effect – he would give you the answer immediately." His subordinates soon learned another trait, as McBride recalled: "He had steely eyes which would burn holes through you."[46]

The new colonel was frequently on horseback, visiting the various batteries and supervising their work. Since he thought war imminent, he did his best to prepare the regiment for combat. These were full days as the officers and men learned the traits of their new weapons, mastered the buzzer-type telephones, and gradually developed the knack of working together as a unit. In part, the limited amount of ammunition available for practice firing restricted the training. Throughout this period there were alerts caused by the Mexican situation, which meant placing the guns in position to fire on selected targets in Juarez, across the river. But the main concern was training, which was going on at such a pace that even the declaration of war in April, 1917, had little effect immediately. Seven weeks later the regiment left for Camp Robinson, Wisconsin, where it would continue its preparations for eventual overseas assignment. But March did not leave with his regiment. On May 30, he received a War Department telegram which directed him to report to Washington and to be prepared for prolonged duty abroad.[47]

Fifty-two years old, with twenty-nine years of commissioned service, March was ready for the professional opportunity the war offered. In a draft memoir which he wrote in 1928, he summed up his qualifications: "I had served in three arms of the line, the Field Artillery, Infantry and Coast Artillery; and had been part of the War Department Organization both as an Adjutant General and a General Staff officer. All this was rounded by observation in the field of the greatest war of modern times up to that period – the Russo-Japanese War. Few officers of my time had the good fortune to have any such varied experience."[48]

4 · A TIME OF PROMISE: JUNE, 1917 — FEBRUARY, 1918

WHEN March arrived in Washington early in June, 1917, there remained some eighteen months of war. For the first half of this period he commanded the American artillery in France. During the last eight months he was Chief of Staff in Washington, where his efforts were integrated with the actions of the War Department. In the early days of the war, March, because of his assignment, had little opportunity to know what went on in the War Department. Yet, while March dealt with artillery questions, Secretary Baker and his military advisers sought solutions to problems of large scope. Thus, when March became Chief of Staff, he would play a role for which others had set the scene.

In the spring of 1917, Secretary Baker, his Chief of Staff, and the Assistant Chief of Staff assumed increasing responsibilities. Although dissimilar in personality and background, the three worked well together. The civilian of the trio was a most unwarlike Secretary; indeed, he was rumored to be a pacifist. A physically small man, with hair as yet untouched by age, Baker looked at the world through his pince-nez with a serenity and kindliness that frequently misled casual observers. For beneath this calmness there worked a keen mind, analytical and logical, with a thorough grasp of facts.

Baker had come to the War Office in the midst of the Villa trouble in March, 1916. A West Virginian by birth, he had studied under Wilson at Johns Hopkins and then earned a reputation as a hard-working and courageous lawyer and reformer under the aegis of Cleveland's Tom Johnson. Wilson acknowledged his aid in the 1912 campaign by offering him the Interior Department. Baker refused, believing that he should carry out his program as mayor of Cleveland. Three years later, after the resignation of his War Secretary, Wilson again turned to the forty-four-year-old Cleveland lawyer. No longer restrained by local obligations, Baker accepted, to the good fortune of the army, the nation, and the President. As a cabinet member, Baker won the affection, admiration, and confidence of the President and the army. Throughout the war Wilson virtually left the military end of the great enterprise to his Secretary of War.[1]

To help him make the necessary decisions, Baker depended upon the advice of two old soldiers whom he genuinely liked and respected, Chief of Staff Hugh L. Scott and Assistant Chief of Staff Tasker H. Bliss, both of whom were eighteen years his senior. Major General Scott had gone from West Point to the Seventh Cavalry, where he replaced an officer killed in the Custer massacre. "He was the old frontier-type officer," Douglas MacArthur remembered — " a representative of the one-shot carbine, revolver, and saber army." Scott was fascinated by the Indians and became an authority on their customs, history, and sign language. Through the years he established a reputation as a pacifier and friend of primitive people — Plains Indians and the Moros in the Philippines. His friends ranged from Buffalo Bill Cody to Woodrow Wilson. Quiet, and somewhat deaf, Scott enjoyed nothing so much as reminiscing about the Indians. A wonderful old fellow, he was not at home behind a desk: the routine bored him and he was known to fall asleep in his chair during an important conference. He strongly supported the General Staff and conscription, but he was slow in making up his mind on the problems of the day.[2]

Major General Bliss, who somewhat resembled Scott in appearance, was his Academy classmate and a close friend. A student of Greek and history and a lover of the arts, the Assistant Chief, whom MacArthur considered brilliant, was known in the army as a teacher. He had taught at West Point and the Naval War College and was the first president of the Army War College. Skilled in languages, his broad intellectual curiosity caused him to explore many fields. Baker and Wilson delighted in his deliberate thinking, while Scott depended greatly upon him. Sitting at his desk and looking out the window, Bliss might have an absent expression in his eyes, but he was calculating all aspects of the problem at hand.[3]

Both of these officers were nearing retirement age when the war began. Scott gave up the office in September, 1917, to be succeeded by Bliss for a few months. An Indian fighter and a scholar, these men lacked one important characteristic necessary for their office in modern war. Their successor, March, recognized this and later wrote, ". . . neither of them had a certain ruthlessness which disregards accustomed methods and individual likings in striking out along new and untrodden paths."[4]

As war neared in March, 1917, work swamped the War Department General Staff. Only nineteen officers, an utterly inadequate number, were on duty to handle the tasks at hand. The fact that the bulk of these officers were at the War College, which was many blocks away from the Chief of Staff and the bureaus in the State, War, and Navy Building, further complicated staff procedure. Finally, the hostility of the bureaus continued to hamper the Staff's effectiveness.[5]

During the month before the war began, Bliss inquired for plans to raise, supply, and send to France an army of a half-million men. By the end of March, the War College Division reported that it would be two years and two months before the United States could provide anything but naval and economic aid to the Allies.[6] With the advent of war, business became more hectic. While Congress debated, the army had to act, regardless of the fact that the legislators had not yet appropriated necessary funds. Baker demonstrated his courage by calmly signing orders authorizing expenditures of yet unappropriated millions.[7] Crowder and the Judge Advocate General's Department helped solve another great problem of that period. Since Congress did not approve the conscription act until May 18, War Department officials did not know whether they were to depend on the draft or volunteers to supplement the regular army and National Guard. Crowder and his officers proceeded to establish the framework of the draft so that when Congress acted, the machinery was ready to function.[8]

The wheels of the war effort had begun to turn, but in what direction? What aid did the Allies want? By the end of April, France and England sent missions, led respectively by René Viviani and Arthur Balfour, accompanied by the captivating Marshal Joseph Joffre, former commander of the French army and the hero of the Marne, and General Tom Bridges, a wounded veteran, to inform the nation's leadership of Allied expectations. While all of the war-worn combatants talked of economic aid, Joffre bluntly asked for men to fill ranks decimated by trench warfare and to bolster the morale of the almost exhausted armies.[9]

The Americans could grant without much difficulty the request to send immediately a few regulars to show the flag for the sake of morale, but the all-pervading problem of shipping would hold back a large manpower contribution, even after the months necessary for mobilizing in this country a sizeable force. Bridges' and Joffre's junior officers suggested that this could be eased by merely recruiting the Americans into Allied ranks, thus avoiding the necessity for shipping the additional men and materiel required to establish an independent army. But Joffre, wisely recognizing national pride, encouraged the formation of an independent American Expeditionary Force.[10]

Selection of the leader for the American contingent was a major decision. During the evening hours when he could spare the time, Baker mulled over the records of all the generals on the active list. Although the Secretary had never met Major General John J. Pershing, he was impressed by the general's actions as commander of the Punitive Expedition, which had returned from Mexico only three months before. In early May, Baker made his decision, passed over several senior officers, including Leonard Wood, and called Pershing to Washington. When Pershing sailed on May 28, he knew that he had Baker's full support and that he would be allowed virtual independence in his administration of the American Expeditionary Forces.[11]

In the midst of the feverish activity in May, President Wilson ordered General Scott to accompany Elihu Root's mission to Russia. Pessimistic and protesting, the Chief of Staff left Washington on May 16, not to return until August, six weeks before his retirement.[12] Bliss carried on as Acting Chief of Staff, and dealt with the myriad details of mobilization. The War Department had to supervise the construction of camps, the ordering of supplies, and the promotions and assignments of officers. Despite the efforts of Bliss and his pencil, papers piled up on his desk.

Some officers passing through the War Department in the summer of 1917, thought that the Department was shambling to a possible collapse. Important papers were being delayed and, in some cases, lost. The various bureau chiefs, each determined to be supreme in his area, competed for available supplies. Politicians wrangled over camp sites for their communities. A lack of experienced officers and clerks added to the difficulty of the situation. As late as July 1, only sixty-four officers were on General Staff duty in the Department and, throughout the early weeks of the war, many of these officers clamored for and, in some cases received, overseas assignment, thus further depleting the staff of experienced men. Colonel Robert L. Bullard, after spending five days in Washington in June, noted in his diary, "if we really have a great war, our War Dept. will quickly break down." [13]

After Pershing arrived in France, the cable flow began across the Atlantic as Pershing and his staff carefully analyzed the situation and sent back recommendations and requests. Although both the War Department and Pershing's headquarters sought it, co-ordination seemed to elude them. Pershing and his chief of staff, James G. Harbord, were exasperated as their cables remained unanswered and were apparently lost, and as they noted the seemingly confused and unco-ordinated attempts to meet their requests. Officers who had recently been in Washington confirmed their worst fears about the War Department conditions.[14]

In Washington, as the end of summer approached, a major topic of speculation concerned the successor to the post of Chief of Staff after Scott's retirement on September 22. The two names mentioned in this connection were the obvious one of Bliss, who seemed to be running the office even after Scott's return, and that of Major General Joseph E. Kuhn, an engineer officer who had served as President of the War College. Since Bliss would reach the statutory retirement age in December, he appeared to be a less favorable choice than the younger man, but the gruff Acting Chief got the appointment. The next day, September 23, the famed builder of the Panama Canal, Major General George W. Goethals, wrote his son: "Confusion still reigns here. Scott is gone which is a relief, but I don't know that Bliss is any better for that job. Kuhn's chances seem to have gone a glimmering for some reason or other." [15]

A few days before Goethals expressed his displeasure, Secretary Baker had outlined his plan to President Wilson in conversation and later in writing: "You will remember that General Bliss also must retire in December of the present year, and that it is then proposed to bring a younger man, who has had an opportunity to observe the situations in France, for service in that capacity." [16]

The Secretary had his eye on such an officer – Peyton C. March. While March was in the Adjutant General's Office before the war, Scott had indicated March's ability to the then new Secretary. As Baker later commented: "From him I learned to understand and admire the completeness of Colonel March's grasp of the details of War Department business and the boldness and simplicity with which he reformed the intricate record system which had grown up in the course of years." By the time of Bliss' retirement in December, March would have been in France almost six months, long enough to become well acquainted with the needs and problems of the AEF.[17]

On September 10, in one of his frequent personal letters to the expeditionary force commander, Baker asked Pershing what he thought about March as Bliss' successor.[18] Two months later Pershing answered that he thought Major General John Biddle, an engineer officer and former Superintendent of West Point, might be a better choice; however, he could send March, whom he recognized as a strong leader, to serve as Biddle's assistant, where he would be readily available to take over if Biddle faltered. At the time Pershing wrote, Biddle had just returned from France and, despite his misgivings as to his qualifications for the task, he was already serving as Acting Chief of Staff, since Bliss was in Europe on a mission. Baker then decided to leave March in France at least for a few more months.[19]

During the last six months of 1917, March's career advanced in great bounds. When he reported to the War Department in June, he learned that the Secretary of War had nominated him along with seventeen other colonels for the rank of brigadier general and that his assignment was the command of the expeditionary division's artillery. He also found that the French would supply the guns and horses for his brigade — the famous 75-millimeter gun for two regiments and the 155-millimeter cannon for the third regiment.[20]

What March saw during his brief stay in Washington disheartened him. The War Department seemed to be floundering in paperwork. A huge backlog of correspondence filled up the Mail and Records Room of The Adjutant General's Office, and some of these papers were even lost in the process. A cable from Pershing concerning March's assignment had taken six days to pass through that office to the Chief of Staff. Bliss, who was the Acting Chief of Staff at the time of March's visit, spent hours on matters that March thought should have been handled in seconds. It was obvious to March that a transformation must take place, and he predicted that it would occur in the fall.[21]

On July 11, after an uneventful crossing of the Atlantic, March reported to the American headquarters in Paris. For the next month he would be a commander without troops. Although he and his small staff maintained a temporary office at 10 Rue St. Anne, he spent much of this period visiting British and French artillery units. On these tours he and a few selected officers would start at army headquarters and follow the artillery organization down the hierarchy. The French flexibility of organization particularly impressed his party. The French did not maintain a fixed number of units in army artillery but, at the discretion of the army artillery commander, distributed them to a particular corps headquarters as the situation required. As a result they had little heavy artillery in quiet sectors, while in active areas they massed their heavy weapons. The American observers also noted their use of camouflage and careful maintenance of materiel.[22]

After learning what he could from Allied experience, March then had to concentrate on preparation of his own troops for combat. Since his brigade would be the first artillery unit in the AEF, its training would serve as a pilot program for other brigades which would reach France later. Pershing's headquarters, in the middle of July, issued a general training directive which emphasized firing practice. Initially, French officers were to serve as instructors; upon completion of the first training cycle, however, Americans would replace them. As planned, the entire program should take eight weeks – the first six at a rear-area post, with the last ten days to two weeks in actual combat on a sector of the French front.[23]

Early in August, March moved his headquarters to the camp which the French had loaned as the artillery training center. Located near the Swiss border, the terrain about Valdahon was, according to a member of March's staff, Beverly Browne, "as fine and varied as Fort Riley or Fort Sill," with plenty of room for target practice. Here, on August 16, the First Artillery Brigade formally came into existence, although the three regiments (Fifth, Sixth, and Seventh) did not arrive until a few days later. Despite equipment shortages and a lack of experienced junior officers, the brigade promptly began its training. Throughout the cool September days up to six batteries at a time were on the firing range. At every opportunity March, a major general since mid-August, rode out to the range, where the *Chicago Tribune* reporter, Floyd Gibbons, saw him "in rubber boots standing hip deep in the mud of the gun pits. . . ." The men and their officers soon learned, as the Fifth regiment's commander, George Van Horn Moseley, already knew, that the brigade commander was "a driver with character."[24]

During September, three distinguished visitors came to Valdahon.

Georges Clemenceau, the man March thought the most interesting in France, stayed for several days. "The Tiger," a few weeks before he became premier, impressed March not only by his intelligence but also by his exceptional physical endurance. Although in his seventies, he refused either a horse or a car and walked out to spend every day on the range; even during inclement weather, the old man trudged along in high rubber boots. The General enjoyed the company of the famous politician. "Every night," March wrote, "we talked over a multitude of things, everything but war." Clemenceau reminisced about his experiences in the United States during the Civil War period. When March told him of his Lafayette background, the Frenchman knew not only about the college but also of Professor March's reputation. March recalled that, as a boy, he had been conscious of the debt America owed France for her aid in the Revolutionary War and that he hoped it could be repaid. This sentiment touched the old man.[25]

Soon after Clemenceau's departure, the commander of the French army arrived. Tall and robust, Philippe Pétain had done much to build up the morale in his army since the spring, but his doleful eyes reflected the cost of war. As he stepped out of his car, he heard the massed bands of the three regiments play the stirring "Marseillaise." Throughout the day March showed him the training in progress. During dinner March arranged to have a band play outside the mess hall. Finally, Pétain could stand it no longer; he asked if he could make a criticism. "Your bands don't play the 'Marseillaise' correctly. . . . They play it too slowly." March sent an aide to inform the bandleader. After the meal, as the two generals walked out on the porch surrounding the building, Pétain, still dissatisfied, said, "Let me show them." With March's assent, the French commander took the baton and drilled the musicians until they played the anthem at the proper tempo. Here was an officer who knew his profession, March thought, to "the minutest details."[26]

On Sunday, September 16, John J. Pershing came down for the afternoon. In a whirlwind tour, Pershing inspected some of the buildings, watched a French instructor teach a class, and, as March presented them, met the officers of the brigade. What he saw at Valdahon confirmed the AEF commander's opinion that his artillery chief was "energetic and alert." Harbord, Pershing's chief of staff, enjoyed the visit: ". . . it seemed like getting home again to hear an army band playing good old American dance music, to see the horses, the guidons, and good American soldiers once more." Harbord added in his diary that March "will go far in the war if he gets the chance."[27]

Before the brigade entered its final stage of training, March gave up its command to become the Chief of AEF Artillery, but in this position he continued his close supervision of the brigade's development. When the unit completed its training, March analyzed its experience. He saw no reason for changing the basic course and preserved the various orders and instructional material for succeeding units. He did suggest the possibility of giving the troops more preliminary instruction in the United States. In the front-line phase, he recommended that regiments rather than battalions go forward and that the commanders exercise actual command. Finally, he prescribed a definite ammunition ration for the target practice. As Chief of Artillery he had to supervise the training of other brigades. Since other artillery camps were now in operation, this meant that he had to travel a great deal in order to superintend the evolution of the recently arrived units into combat-ready condition and to prepare for the arrival of more troops.[28]

March ran into difficulty during this period with Pershing's staff over some of his views on training. Paul B. Malone, Chief of the AEF Training Section, pointed out that March's theories differed from G.H.Q. policy. March wanted the officers to stay with their units and considered the officers' school, which occupied the accommodations of the French Cavalry School at Saumur, a stop-gap solution. He also thought the Army Artillery School should be under his command as the Chief of Artillery. Malone objected that Saumur was part of the permanent system and that it should remain under a Commandant of Army Schools. He suggested that March be ordered to the headquarters at Chaumont for a conference. This was done, and G.H.Q. overruled the artillery commander. There were at least two other incidents in which Pershing's headquarters overruled March; however, these disputes apparently reflected little more than a strong commander's usual differences with a superior headquarters.[29]

In another area March's views were in more marked contradiction to G.H.Q. policy: he did not agree with the strict censorship rules. When reporters visited Valdahon, he let them observe the activities of the brigade and talked freely with them. One of the reporters asked if they could use the information which he was giving them and March replied: "You may say anything you like about my camp, good or bad. I believe that free and full reports in the American newspapers are a good thing for our army." His only exception was his request that they not refer to a new model of the French 155-millimeter gun. After the session ended, Major Frederick Palmer, the Chief Press Officer, whom March had known in Manchuria, told him that he was violating censorship regulations. March knew that Pershing's orders must be obeyed but this sort of censorship seemed needless. The Germans knew they were there. In fact, artillerymen had gained anti-aircraft practice firing on the occasional enemy planes which flew over the camp. As long as the Germans knew, he could see no reason for keeping the information from the American public.[30]

Although there were these occasions of differences between March and members of Pershing's staff, the two generals evidently remained on good, friendly terms through the artilleryman's stay in France. They had dined together shortly after March's arrival and then, in December, when March visited Chaumont, he stayed in Pershing's home for a few days. During the winter visit the two went over the various problems involved in developing the expedition's artillery.[31]

At the time the generals conferred, the AEF was in the midst of what Frederick Palmer called its "Valley Forge." It was a hard winter with unusually heavy snow. When the troops were not suffering from the snow and cold, they were wading in mud and slush. The shortage of heavy clothing and fuel made life all the more miserable for the soldiers. For weeks, the gloom of the brief, somber days was pervasive.[32]

The general situation abetted the weather in creating pessimism. The Russian withdrawal from the war and the Italian disaster at Caporetto overshadowed the American intervention. And the American contribution was slow in materializing – only 175,000 men, including four divisions, were in France at the end of the year. Major General Robert L. Bullard, who took command of the First Division in mid-December, confided forlorn thoughts to his diary, "So far as we are concerned, the war is practically lost," and later, "Alas, I think we came *too late*." The despondency became so widespread in late autumn that Pershing informed his officers that outward evidence of despair would result in removal from command.[33]

In the United States the mood was one of disappointment rather than despondency. A people accustomed to quick results began to fret at the spectacle of raw force being turned into an army. Sons wrote home about clothing and weapons shortages and the hardships of living in the cantonment cities, built from the ground in months. Congress sensed the nation's discontent and realized that something should be done. On the twelfth of December, the Senate Military Affairs Committee began its hearings on the progress of military preparations.[34] The testimony it heard seemed to corroborate the worst fears of the public. After several weeks of listening to the stories of failure, Chairman George E. Chamberlain, an Oregon Democrat, pronounced, "the military establishment of America has fallen down," and suggested that a War Cabinet of three men should be authorized to forward the war effort.[35]

Although he maintained an air of placidity which irritated the critics, Secretary Baker was aware that the War Department should be overhauled. Within a week after the hearings began, he announced the formation of a War Council to consist of himself, the Assistant Secretary, and five ranking officers. This advisory group, which would act through the Chief of Staff, was supposed to co-ordinate relations between the AEF and the War Department with particular regard to supplies. The Secretary also hoped that it would give the public a body which it could visualize as being in responsible charge. The officers, all old soldiers, named to the Council were: Bliss, the Chief of Staff; Crowder, the Judge Advocate General and Provost Marshal General; Erasmus M. Weaver, Chief of Coast Artillery; William Crozier, Chief of Ordnance; and Henry G. Sharpe, the Quartermaster General. The last two men had been strongly criticized during the investigation. This, together with the fact that three of the officers turned over their offices to younger Acting Chiefs, led to a natural assumption that Baker had created the Council in an effort to get the veterans out of the way honorably. On December 19, the Council met for the first time. During its several meetings in the next few months, the Council occupied itself primarily with a study of the supply problem.[36]

The Senate Committee was not satisfied with Baker's move. The anti-administration *Kansas City Star* demanded his resignation, while even some Democratic senators were said to have talked of getting him out of the War Department. In early January, Baker appeared before the Committee and batted back questions in what impressed even friendly observers as a flippant manner. Finally, on January 28, the Secretary stemmed the tide of criticism with a four-and-a-half-hour statement which he delivered before the Committee and an audience crowded into the large hearing room in the Senate Office Building. The high point came when he announced that the War Department expected to have a half million men in France soon, and another million and a half by the end of the year. This caught the imagination of his listeners and of the nation. David Lawrence, Woodrow Wilson's young journalist friend, described the speech to the President:

> He gave the best picture of the war and the responsibilities it involves that I have ever heard or read. He was forceful and had his back into the speech in such a way as to catch one's emotions. Everbody [*sic*] in the room was thrilled by his recitation of what we have accomplished in this war.[37]

Baker followed through with a reorganization of the General Staff. In General Order # 14 of February 9, 1918, he crystallized preliminary moves into a staff of five main divisions: Executive, War Plans, Purchase and Supply, Storage and Traffic, and Operations. This order charged the Chief of Staff, assisted by the War Council, with the planning and development of the army program. In an effort to ease the supply problem, Baker gave the power of supervision of supplies from the factory to France to the Director of Purchase and Supply Division, Brigadier General Palmer E. Pierce, and the Director of the Storage and Traffic Division, Major General George W. Goethals, with the latter doubling as Quartermaster General. A prominent businessman, Edward R. Stettinius, was appointed to assist them in their efforts. In order to make the General Staff more effective, Baker also provided office space in the State, War, and Navy Building for all of the divisions, with the exception of War Plans.[38]

In the key position of this reorganized staff Baker placed a man whom he knew to be "an energetic and effective administrator" – March. Even before the Secretary's dramatic appearance before the Senators, he had cabled Pershing, on January 26, asked for his Chief of Artillery, and emphasized his need: "I feel it urgently necessary to have him." On February 2, he made his decision public. The *New York Times* hailed the coming of the "foe of red tape," who had the reputation of courage, good judgment, and great executive ability. The *North American Review* rejoiced that at last "a real soldier in his prime" was taking over as Chief of Staff.[39]

Baker's actions in reorganizing the staff and in bringing March to the War Office indicate that he had read and had been impressed by General Scott's last annual report. In this September, 1917, testament to General Staff authority, the old Indian fighter clearly laid the theoretical foundation on which a strong successor could build a powerful organization.

There should be one and only one organ through which the Secretary of War commands the Army – the Chief of Staff . . . [who] should be the medium of recommendation to the Secretary and of execution for his orders. He should have ample authority for securing the coordination of all the activities of the military establishment.

The General Staff should be divided as now into two distinct bodies, one (a) to aid the Chief of Staff in his coordinating and supervisory capacity and be his organs of command, just as he is the Secretary's organ of command; the other (b) to make the studies required for the mobilization, organization, instruction, training, and movement of our armies [,] to gather military intelligence, and to investigate such special subjects as are referred to it.

Such a Chief of Staff and General Staff would give the army, Scott believed, "the best possible organization of the War Department, one which will furnish to all the extremities of the military establishment that rapid and vigorous impulse which can only come from perfectly concerted effort at the center."[40]

Baker qualified Scott's recommendations by granting broad authority to the expeditionary force commander and in setting up the War Council, but he brought to the position a strong man who was capable of acting with the power which Scott had envisaged.[41]

At the time of his return, March had served seven months in the AEF. During this period he had established the framework of the artillery program. He had put the training system into operation and had personally supervised the first brigade through the course. By February, 1918, over 45,000 men had undergone the training based on the Valdahon model. In addition, March had assisted in the general planning and had created the headquarters of the artillery command. Although he left before the American force appeared in strength at the front, he had set the standards and had given the impetus to the expedition's artillery. This would be to his advantage in Washington, where no officer could match his experience with the AEF.[42]

By the end of February, Baker was able to leave Washington for an inspection trip to France. At home, civilians were becoming soldiers in the recently built camps and the nation's vaunted industrial capacity was turning to military production. In France an expeditionary force was in existence and growing in number. As Republican Senator James W. Wadsworth commented, the United States was "rapidly turning the corner toward greater efficiency." The period of "promise, promise, and disappointment," in General Bullard's term, was coming to an end.[43]

5 · ACTING CHIEF OF STAFF: THE FIRST SIX WEEKS

IN HIS first six weeks as Acting Chief of Staff, March had to balance several complex tasks. He had to cope with such immediate problems as shipping, training, censorship, and relations with Russia. While he dealt with these matters, he had to shape the War Department to his mold; this meant additional reorganization and the introduction of new men into the various responsible positions. At the same time he had to learn to work with the civilian experts who played prominent roles on the home front. Then, too, he must establish and maintain an effective relationship with the AEF commander—not always an easy task.

For the remainder of his active service, General March was a part of the War Department. Its problems, and the army's problems, were his. Even though majors and lieutenant-colonels whom he never met judged issues and expressed written opinions on matters which perhaps never crossed his desk, March, in the end, was the responsible officer. It was up to him to provide the vigorous impulse and perfectly to concert the effort.

Although March did not want to leave France—the honor of being Chief of Staff seemed to him dubious compared to the distinction of commanding the artillery in combat—he had to respond to the Secretary of War's mandatory request. Before he left France, however, he spent several days in a careful examination of the American Expeditionary Force. His tour of inspection ranged from Pershing's G.H.Q. and the Services of Supply to the trenches. As a culmination of his study he had lengthy conferences with Pershing and Bliss, who was now devoting all of his time to the Supreme War Council on which he served as the American military representative. Pershing and March also met with General Ferdinand Foch and Premier Clemenceau. When March sailed for home he had a thorough knowledge of the military situation in France.[1]

On the first day of March, 1918, General March's ship docked in New York. Newspapermen, anxious for an interview, sought him out. The General pleased them with an interview which stressed that the people "must know the facts." He described conditions in France at some length, and made it clear that he thought news censorship was lamentable.[2] After the news conference he hurried to his home in Washington. Personally, it was a sad homecoming. His son and namesake, a twenty-one year old lieutenant, had just died on February 13, from injuries received in an air crash. Family grief was somewhat alleviated as he gave in marriage his youngest daughter, Vivian, to Captain Paul Frank on the day of his arrival.[3]

The next day, a Saturday, March went down to the massive gray stone building which housed the State, War, and Navy Departments. He found Secretary Baker gone to Europe and the Assistant Secretary, Benedict Crowell, acting in his stead. But the main reason for this informal call was to talk with General Biddle. In the five months that Bliss had held the title of Chief of Staff Biddle had acted in his place for three and a half months, but it was apparent that he had failed to take hold of his responsibilities. His actions or lack of action indicated that he considered himself a mere interim office-holder. In particular, he postponed too many decisions. He confided to his successor that he left the office at five and did not come back at night unless a special cable required his personal attention. Symptomatic of his mood was a conversation he had held a month earlier with Brigadier General William J. Snow, who had come into the War Department in the office of Chief of Field Artillery. When Snow asked him, ". . . who will define my duties, status, responsibility, prerogatives, and so forth? . . . who will put me in touch with field artillery conditions?" Biddle took his arm and answered, "Snow, the answer to both questions is, I don't know!" Indeed, Secretary Baker had recognized Biddle's limitations and had turned increasingly to General Crowder when dealing with important matters.[4]

The General Staff seemed to reflect its Acting Chief's attitude. Evidently it was a rarity for most officers to work on Sunday and at night.

When March showed up at the Department after dark, he found only one officer on duty, a major in the code room, while unopened mail sacks were piled up in the corridor: there was reason for the AEF complaints. With March there came a forceful cognizance of the requirements of 1918 warfare. Symbolically, the lights came on in the staff offices the night after his arrival and stayed on until the war was won. A few weeks later, March would be surprised to find one of his general officers absent at ten o'clock at night.[5]

After a reception on Monday noon, March 4, and the formal assumption of office by virtue of General Order # 22, the new Acting Chief went to work. On this first day he spent most of his time, aside from the reception and a brief news conference, with the War Council. Of the many problems facing him, he realized that the one which clearly surpassed all others was getting enough men and supplies across the Atlantic to aid the Allies effectively. The two prerequisites were additional shipping and more efficient co-ordination of the flow of troops and supplies to the ports. March's experience in France and his last-minute briefings by Pershing and Bliss impressed him with the Allies' dismal situation. France and England were looking to the United States for the balance of victory. Until sufficient help came they could do no more than hold the line. With Russia recently out of the war, the Germans could be expected to mass increasing numbers of troops on the Western Front in an effort to defeat the Allies before American troops could reach the lines in large numbers. Days were important. It was March's job to gain those days for the Allies by speeding up the troop convoys.[6]

The new Acting Chief of Staff immediately started pressing for increased shipments to augment the quarter of a million men then in France. Two days after he assumed office, he cabled Bliss to assure the Supreme War Council that the United States would ship a minimum of two divisions a month, beginning the first of April. This program stretched the current tonnage capacity to the maximum since it meant 92,000 men, including proportionate corps, army, and service troops. March also informed Pershing that he was making every effort to supply the needs of the army in France.[7]

The American government could push shipbuilding and seize neutral shipping but the greatest hope for enlarging the troop movement program rested in the hands of Great Britain. The English could help in a small way by allowing the AEF to debark more men at Liverpool and

Southampton, but American planners had their eyes on the great pool of British ships. In this respect Britain had a key bargaining point. The shrewd Prime Minister, David Lloyd George, later explained his country's position – the English were not particularly interested in loaning ships which were literally maintaining their lifeline of food and raw materials in order to bring American non-combatants to France.[8] On the other hand, the transport of riflemen and other soldiers who would actually be thrown into the trenches was another matter: Britain might willingly offer ships for such a program. Here were the boundaries of bargaining: the English had the ships and the Americans had the men. In return for carrying the American troops to France, England wanted to use them to fill up her depleted ranks. Of course, this would mean a temporary, and possibly permanent, setting aside of the American plan of establishing an independent fighting force because modern war requires a vast number of supporting troops, ranging from a company cook to a staff officer. The elimination of these men, necessary for an independent army, would enable the army to fill the ships to the limit with combat men.

In the spring of 1917, General Bridges of the British mission had broached this subject. And there was some American support. Herbert Hoover had suggested the amalgamation of his nation's available manpower into Allied armies in the event of war as early as February, 1917.[9] With the exception of Bliss, American military leadership, however, was convinced of the necessity of maintaining a separate and independent force. From the beginning of the war, the Allies had propositioned and pressured them to assent to various amalgamation schemes. But the United States had the desperately needed men as well as money; and it had square-jawed John J. Pershing, who banged his fist on the conference table, making it abundantly clear to the French and the English that he was in France to command a separate American army.

At the turn of the year, the Allies stepped up the pressure on the Americans. In an effort to avoid the confusion of dual control, the War Department in December gave its commander in the field full authority in this matter. By the end of January, Pershing had won his point with the English. They agreed to transport six full divisions, which would be trained with their army and then turned over to the AEF for service. Pershing's first letter to March, on February 24, 1918, announced that all was in readiness for these divisions.[10] If Pershing thought that this was the end of the affair, he was mistaken. By the time of March's return, Lloyd George had specifically requested of President Wilson that the United States send 120,000 infantry and machine-gun troops per month through July.[11] While the Allies wrangled over this proposal, the long dreaded German offensive smashed the Allied line. Fear now became reality and "hope stood still"[12] as the gray-clad infantrymen blasted gaps along the front.

Faced with the tragic possibilities of the German onslaught, the Supreme War Council's military representatives drew up a recommendation, to which Bliss agreed, that the United States must send only infantry and machine gun units to stem the attack. Baker, who was in Paris at the time, conferred with Bliss and Pershing, and reached the decision to advise Wilson to accept this proposition, with the clear proviso that it was a temporary measure. The AEF was to remain independent. That afternoon, March 28, Pershing went to see General Foch who had been given co-ordinating power over the Allied armies two days before. In one of the most dramatic moments in the war, the AEF commander, who had a keen sense of the dramatic, told Foch: ". . . all that we have are yours. . . ."[13]

In Washington, crowds anxiously scanned the war bulletins on the front of *The Evening Star* building. News of the German drive was coming through slowly. Even War Department officials were somewhat in the dark as to the actual events. Then came the call for troops. Wilson told Edward N. Hurley of the Shipping Board to go the limit in giving the army ships. March drove his staff to meet the situation's demands. Colonel Frank T. Hines and his Embarkation Service studied ship capacities. The Operations Division under Brigadier General Henry Jervey selected the units to go. March cabled Pershing: what arrangements have you made for supplies and transportation? Speed up the turn-around of cargo vessels, he urged. Since an increase in the expedition's strength meant greater logistical problems, the General Staff revised the supply schedules. The Acting Chief of Staff also had to deal with Lord Reading and Jules Jusserand, the British and French ambassadors, in addition to the civilian war boards and senatorial committees in working out the details of this program. Eight days after Pershing had offered America's all, March cabled details of the program. The British had agreed to carry 29,000 men per month in addition to a 91,000 minimum by other transports, some of which were also English. As March later said, this was "the sun breaking through the clouds."[14]

March's primary problem was transporting men to France, but it was only one of many phases of his work.[15] During his first month in office he also had to deal with the censorship policy against which he had spoken on his arrival. Prior to March, 1918, few American troops had been in action and casualties were consequently light. As more troops went on the line, the lists would naturally grow in size. The War Department announced on March 9, that, in deference to Pershing's desire for military security, it would not release the addresses of casualties. Whereupon the Committee on Public Information, the Creel Committee, refused to issue casualty lists since without addresses confusion might easily result. March gave a statement to correspondents that day explaining the reasons for the Department's action and concluded that it was the press' duty to support Pershing. Nevertheless, the suppression of casualty information caused widespread criticism. At the same time, journalists gave March the credit for permitting the publication of more detailed military information in the weekly review of operations.[16]

As news of the German offensive made banner headlines, correspondents noted that March and other War Office officials were having trouble finding out the facts themselves. The Acting Chief furnished the information when he got it, but the wait for Pershing communiques was long and when they came they were not very informative. March was forced at times to depend on Bliss for more complete details of the fighting. Although they believed that American units were engaged, the reporters had to turn to Allied newspapers for their information. Thus they found the first word of Pershing's offer to Foch in a Paris newspaper. Even the War Department learned of Foch's appointment as Allied generalissimo from the *New York Times.* In the midst of the excitement Baker cabled from France that all AEF information must come through Pershing's headquarters. March and Acting Secretary Crowell took the Secretary at his word and stopped issuing statements and even casualty lists until Baker answered their cabled query as to whether he had meant them to go so far. The *New York Times* criticized March for going beyond what it believed to be the spirit of Baker's order. After six days they heard from Baker and resumed publication of the lists. March had found that his desire to inform the people of their war was limited by the Secretary of War's support of Pershing.[17]

A fair promotion system is essential to maintain good morale, since for the soldier promotion is the ever-present goal. If he knows or even thinks promotions are being conferred haphazardly or unfairly, his incentive is diminished. As war quickens promotions and necessitates temporary ranks, peacetime systems are apt to prove inadequate. March and Pershing began debating promotion schemes and the advancement of specific individuals during March's first week in Washington.

In the summer of 1917, the War Department informed Pershing that promotions to general officer would be apportioned among the various arms and based on seniority and efficiency. Beyond that, the Secretary of War would give him full support in advancing and weeding out senior officers. After observing the Allied system Pershing became convinced that younger generals were necessary and that the rank should be attached to the position rather than to the individual. The AEF chief also recognized the fact that a careful balance of promotions should be maintained in the line and the staff.[18]

The first consideration, as far as March was concerned, was efficiency. Then, one must consider the morale of the officers serving in the United States. Another matter of particular interest to the former Chief of the AEF Artillery was that young artillery officers should command the artillery brigades rather than officers without experience with the guns. There also seemed to be a difference of opinion over a point which became increasingly sensitive. Pershing, accustomed to independence, evidently expected his recommendations in regard to AEF matters to be put into effect without question. March, as Chief of Staff and theoretically the nation's first soldier, viewed these recommendations as recommendations. Ultimately, this conflict of attitudes led to the question of the power of the Chief of Staff.[19]

Engaged in preparation of a list of promotions to one-star and two-star rank, March called upon Pershing on March 27 for recommendations. The AEF commander replied promptly with ten names for major generalcies and seventeen for brigadiers, the exact number requested. In addition, he suggested four men for one-star rank in staff corps. When Pershing received the final list, he was surprised to see that three of the ten major generals and well over half of the brigadiers were men whom he had not recommended, and at least one, William I. Westervelt, who had been March's adjutant, was serving under him at the time. Immediately, he fired off a cable, "For the Chief of Staff and Secretary of War," stating his disapproval and requesting that the Secretary of War be specifically informed of his views and that confirmation be held up until he sent an additional list of recommendations.

March answered this cable with a brusque assertion of the superiority of the Chief of Staff by bluntly informing Pershing that he commanded only a part of the army. Within that limited sphere, March considered his recommendations as "especially valuable," otherwise, he regarded his suggestions in the same manner as those of other commanders. March who was only a major general concluded this communication to the four-star Pershing: "There will be no change in the nominations already sent to the Senate." [20]

Although March had indicated in his cable that Baker, who had just returned from Europe, corroborated his attitude, Pershing wrote both the Secretary and March personal letters in an effort to reach an understanding. But Baker stood firm and March expressed surprise that Pershing should so adamantly question the War Department's judgment. In this regard, March must have realized that he touched a nerve.[21]

Closely allied to the promotion issue, although not a subject of controversy between March and Pershing, was the thorny problem of eliminating the unfit. On his fourth day in office March sent to the Acting Secretary a list of officers to be demoted because they had been found physically unfit. While these men retained their regular ranks, they lost their temporary ranks and command of combat divisions and brigades. Many of the senior officers of the army, including former Chief of Staff Hugh Scott, were in this category because of age or physical inability to carry out the arduous command duties. Pershing had looked over several of the division commanders when they visited France on observation tours and had sent March confidential memoranda specifically designating individuals whom he believed to be unfit. Naturally, the ambition of these men was to lead units in action. When the War Department relieved and, in some cases, demoted them, they were enraged. In the case of the ranking major general, Leonard Wood, there were political repercussions. It fell upon March to issue the orders and to accept at least partial blame from these men who had been his peers.[22]

In February, 1918, the astute war correspondent turned soldier, Frederick Palmer, wrote his friend and commander, John J. Pershing, "Our people think easily in Red Cross terms but with difficulty in shipping."[23] A trained observer, Major Palmer correctly diagnosed the American war spirit. The public was caught up in a crusade but it tended to answer the challenges unrealistically at times. It was a perfect atmosphere for witch hunting. "German" and "slacker" were opprobrious terms Americans used too freely. In Illinois a mob lynched a registered German alien and, in Alabama, the Ku Klux Klan rode again, searching out "slackers, drones, disloyalists and loafers."[24] Among the innocent victims of this perverted spirit were the military personnel who were not in combat units. Staff officers in the Washington area came under particular attack as politicians found them such convenient targets for criticism or for jokes about "deskhounds" or slackers in uniform. Obviously this reflected the civilians' ignorance of the organization of modern war, but rationalizations are difficult to sustain in the face of such feeling. Even the Acting Secretary of War added some fuel to the fire with an ill-chosen comment to a *New York Times* reporter: "There is very little about it [the War Department] today that is military. . . . The great military work of America, the work of the soldier, is being done in France."[25]

In March's first month a congressman suggested that the staff officers on duty in Washington be required to wear a white band on their sleeves. March acted quickly by calling for an investigation to see how many recently commissioned draft-age men were serving in the War Department. As far as a white-feather badge was concerned, he protested vigorously to the House Military Committee and to a reporter for publication. Against this background of public sentiment many staff officers eagerly sought overseas duty. For the professional there was the added incentive of his career, which might be ruined without the combat experience. Their chief never forgot this. Later he wrote about the officers who did not get to France because they were bound by duty in the War Department, "It is a tragedy in the lives of many of them, that most civilians do not remotely comprehend."[26]

While the AEF needed trained staff officers, the War Department also required them, therefore those in Washington at this time had little hope of leaving their posts. March attempted to bring an end to this dilemma by proposing a program which would also aid the war effort in a much larger sense. On March 15, he cabled his idea to Pershing. Co-operation and co-ordination between the War Department and its army in the field had been difficult. His own return was intended as a step toward improving co-operation. Why not put the plan of bringing back AEF veterans on a larger scale? In return for thirty officers qualified for General Staff duty, March would dispatch thirty of his staff officers then serving in the War Department. Eventually, as the plan progressed, there would be a complete turnover, and all General Staff officers on duty in the Department would be veterans and thus acquainted with AEF problems. This would be a continuing process even after that point was reached, as more recent veterans would rotate with the ones who had been in the Department for a period. March believed that this policy would give the War Department a better understanding of AEF problems and bring about a more co-operative spirit in addition to giving the Washington officers field service rather than having them, in his words, "punished for good work by being kept in Washington for the period of the war." [27]

This scheme aroused Pershing's suspicious chief of staff, Harbord, who warned the AEF commander that this was probably the result of March's "wild ambition." He added: "The best that could be said, if it is not hostile, is that it is selfish, inconsiderate, and ordered with no thought for your organization or intelligent comprehension of the task immediately before you." [28] In his reply to March, Pershing admitted the value of such an interchange but pleaded that he could not spare the trained officers. Nevertheless, he "earnestly" recommended that March carry out his side of the bargain. After another cable from March, who carefully explained that he did not mean to wreck the AEF and that any officers who could qualify for the black braid of the General Staff would be acceptable, Pershing gave in and the program began in May. Of the first group of thirty AEF officers, a War Department board regarded only three as fit for General Staff assignment. The AEF evidently did not desire co-operation as much as Pershing would lead one to believe. While the exchange continued in a half-hearted manner, Pershing's attitude virtually ended the hope of seeing France for the General Staff officers in Washington. Forty years later, two of these men would recall, with a touch of bitterness, the collapse of this plan.[29]

When March moved into the Chief of Staff's office, everyone expected him to make some changes. Of course, Baker had reorganized the staff in the middle of February but the Secretary had announced then that the incoming Acting Chief would have the opportunity to effect his own plans. With this in mind, Baker made it clear that the chiefs of the reorganized staff divisions would hold their offices temporarily until March approved the permanent appointments.[30] March knew the five men – William S. Graves, Daniel W. Ketcham, Henry Jervey, George W. Goethals, and Palmer E. Pierce – either personally or by reputation. Goethals, Graves, and Jervey were his friends. During the first few weeks all of these officers continued in their posts but the Acting Chief of Staff was observing them and measuring their actions.[31]

Reporters from the *Army and Navy Journal* and two other news organs anticipated that March might find the War Council a hindrance in developing the authority of his office. Bliss differed and advised March in his February conversations that this body had value. In his first letter to Bliss, March wrote that he had added Goethals and Stettinius to the Council in an attempt to fit it into his system but that "its future use and development will be taken up with the Secretary when he returns from abroad." There was no place for an Aulic Council in March's plans. Four months later, Secretary Baker abolished the War Council.[32]

In the office of the Secretary of the General Staff, one of particular importance, since its function was to pass on papers to be presented to the Chief of Staff and, in general, to handle his routine office matters, a ranking officer was one of the first to discover the March method. During one of the first presentations, this officer handed March a document with the comment: "I am not very familiar with this paper, General." March fixed his piercing gaze on the man and snapped: "Take it back and get familiar with it." Within three weeks there was a shake-up and a new Secretary of the General Staff, Colonel Percy P. Bishop.[33]

Although efficiency was becoming mandatory in the General Staff, it was still lacking in the supply program. The legislators had directed their attack of the past winter against this phase of the army's activity and Baker had included it in his February reorganization. Under March, change would become a continuing process. In April, he united the two supply divisions of the staff, Purchase and Supplies, and Storage and Traffic, into one division, Purchase, Storage, and Traffic. In this manner a single agency evolved to co-ordinate the army's supply as well as its transportation. He assigned the directorship of this large and somewhat unwieldy division to the chief of the old Storage and Traffic Division, Goethals. There were those who thought that the supply chief and March would not work well together, both being such dynamic men and generally similar in character, but an officer who worked closely with them during the war testified, "they got along very well."[34]

Goethals did not particularly relish the increased burden, since he was already doubling as Quartermaster General. March mollified him by giving the latter office to Lieutenant Colonel Robert E. Wood, a young West Pointer who had handled supplies under Goethals in the canal-building days.[35]

Neither Goethals nor March were impressed with Palmer Pierce, the chief of the old Purchase and Supplies Division. With the reorganization, the Acting Chief exiled this officer with a curt: "Pierce, I have cut your head off and ordered you out of the War Department."[36] The unfortunate Pierce lingered briefly as the army's representative on the War Industries Board, but the relentless March uprooted him and shipped him to France by the middle of May. He then called Hugh S. Johnson, Crowder's able young assistant from the Provost Marshal's office, and promoted him to replace Pierce.[37]

When March came to Washington he found the supply situation in a state of confusion, with the bureau chiefs still failing to co-ordinate their various programs. Goethals' job was to bring order out of this confusion. March commissioned him, "You are given complete charge of all matters of supply. . . . I hold you responsible for results, and I will take all the responsibility for anything you have to do to get them."[38]

The Ordnance Department, which supplied weapons, ammunition, and some accoutrements, also came under March's grand sweep. The efficiency-minded General decided that the incumbent Chief of Ordnance, Brigadier General C. B. Wheeler, was not the right man for the place. After talking this over with Stettinius, the civilian munitions czar, March cabled Pershing for the AEF Chief of Ordnance, Brigadier General Clarence C. Williams, who had been an Artillery School classmate and the executive officer of the Astor Battery. Pershing quickly acceded and sent this excellent administrator back to take over the Ordnance Department.[39]

During March and April, March overhauled other elements of the war machine. On his second day in office he approved the creation of a Tank Corps, based upon the recommendations of the AEF headquarters. Later in the month, he directed the War Plans Division to study the question of a separate Aviation Service. Under his guidance, the Cantonment Division expanded and changed its name to the Construction Division on March 13. A part of the Office of Chief of Staff, this division was in charge of all military building in the United States. In April he created the Coordination Section, with the special task of coordinating War Department activities and thus avoiding wasteful duplication. As one General Staff officer later commented, "He took the War Department like a dog takes a cat by the neck, and he shook it."[40]

Monday, March 4, 1918, marked a turning point in the American war effort, for on that day not only did a tough, decisive leader acquire the authority of Acting Chief of Staff but also a strong, clear visioned executive became chairman of the War Industries Board. Of all the civilian experts involved in the "nation at war," Bernard M. Baruch, the majestically tall, graying financier, was the most important. His letter of appointment from the President gave him almost unlimited power in carrying out his mission of "general eye of all supply departments in the field of industry."[41] March succinctly summed up the difference between Baruch and his predecessors: "He could do things instead of recommending them."[42]

When March returned to Washington, he found that much of his work would be dealing with civilian boards, particularly the War Industries Board and the Shipping Board. In order to carry out the army's shipping and supply programs, March and the civilian leaders necessarily held many conferences. Eventually, there would be a regular meeting every Wednesday morning in the room vacated by the War Council. At these meetings March would see the chairmen of the War Industries Board, Shipping Board (Edward N. Hurley), Shipping Control Committee (P. A. S. Franklin), War Trade Board (Vance McCormick), and the Chief of Naval Operations (Admiral William S. Benson). At times, Secretary Baker and other representatives also would attend this meeting. Here the war leaders shaped the nation's capacities into the war effort.[43]

In March, the civilian leaders found a soldier pushing relentlessly for results; there was no time for formality or diplomacy with this man. "He didn't invite you to sit down when you came in to see him," Bernard Baruch recalled. "He wanted all conversations to be short and to the point. He was all business." In this pioneering effort of civilian-military co-operation, March, once he understood the relationship, worked well with the civilian leaders, but there was never any place for formality or diplomacy.[44]

Soon after their meeting he tested Baruch, who held the essential priority power, and President Wilson's "Doctor Facts" solidly met the trial. The War Industries Board had allotted to the French a facility which made ammunition dump wagons. When March protested, Baruch threatened to take the dispute to the President:

> I told him [Baruch remembered] that he knew what the President's decision would be. The Army hadn't yet decided on exactly what they wanted. When they did, I would get the wagons for the Army; meanwhile, we would send these wagons to the French. This was the decision reached.[45]

After March knew just where Baruch stood, there were no more differences — with one notable exception.

Hurley of the Shipping Board marvelled at March's drive. He found that this General meant what he said when he exclaimed, "I am going to get the men to France if they have to swim." But the business executive also discovered that March was "prudent" and "far seeing" when he talked troop transportation.[46] Herbert Hoover, as head of the Food Administration, did not have so much contact with the army's top soldier as did Baruch and Hurley, but the future President had "the highest opinion of his abilities and the most pleasant relations with him. . . ." Troop shipments came first, and civilian relief second with this soldier, but Hoover believed that there could have been no better selection for the post of Chief of Staff.[47]

Within the War Department, March had to deal with various civilians brought in by the war's exigencies. The Commission on Training Camp Activities, an agency which sought to build up morale through systematic recreation, was not so impressive as the industrial and shipping boards; nevertheless, the Acting Chief came to recognize its value. Raymond B. Fosdick, the young Princeton graduate who headed the Commission, became fond of the "blunt, aggressive" General "after a stormy start." Fosdick knew a "sincere and honest" mind when he met one. March might protest singing lessons for soldiers, but when shown their value he would accede.[48]

In April, as part of the Department's reorganization, two new Assistant Secretaries of War entered the hierarchy. Actually, both were already performing their duties without the titles. Stettinius was one and the other was a Columbia University dean, Frederick P. Keppel. March wrangled with them over cables and stopped them from sending these messages without clearing through him. But Dr. Keppel, who had been a principal offender in that respect in March's view, comprehended the "extraordinary capacity for work, driving power and grasp of specific situation" of this General. Whether they liked him or not, his civilian co-workers, with the possible exception of Crowell, highly respected the Acting Chief of Staff.[49]

When March took over as the principal military adviser, he found himself in a familiar office. The big room, next to the Secretary's office, overlooking Seventeenth Street, had not changed since he had conferred in it with Chiefs of Staff in the past. The office was "Spartan in its simplicity," as March described it, and naturally military, with paintings and photographs of great commanders and former Chiefs of Staff. Its pre-war atmosphere had been altered by the war maps with the pins and threads symbolizing men in trenches three thousand miles away. Two or three straight chairs awaited visitors, but the aggressive General allowed little opportunity for sitting down and there was no loafing or chatting here. As he settled in the swivel chair behind the old-fashioned mahogany desk, March could see "nothing except things that would expedite the performance of military business." [50]

In the first six weeks this military business ranged from approving the use of his son's name for a new air station – March Field – and establishing a small arms school at Camp Perry, Ohio, to analyzing the possibility of using biological warfare. Although March concentrated on the war with Germany, his staff had to consider such matters during April as a threatened Indian uprising in Utah and Nevada and the perennial problem of trouble along the Mexican border.[51]

March might dismiss most of the questions presented to him with brief consideration but two problems demanded more thought: training and foreign affairs, in particular American involvement in Russia. While in France he had devoted most of his time to training. Pershing complained in early April about the lack of training of recent replacements, and Leonard Wood dropped by the War Department to add his comments on training. March wanted to construct a new replacement system. Heretofore, there had been no replacement depots. Ideally, the army trained and sent units overseas as organic wholes. As a rule, however, the War Department frequently had to call on these units for drafts to fill organizations which were closer to embarkation time. It was apparent that this approach not only damaged the morale of the troops but also defeated the purpose of training to a certain extent. March had observed these results in France and believed that it would be more efficient to establish camps which would be devoted to training men for specific arms or services. Thus if a call came for 5,000 riflemen, instead of drawing this number from existing units, the War Department could take them from an infantry replacement camp. These depots were still in the formative process as late as June.[52]

Foreign affairs came up on March's first day in office when his West Point classmate, Brigadier General William V. Judson, sent him a memorandum about intervention in turbulent Siberia. Judson, who had just returned in January from Russia, where he had been chief of the military mission, warned against allowing unilateral Japanese intervention. The Allies had worried about the Russian situation since the revolution in March, 1917. Now, because the Bolsheviks had taken this ally out of the war, the French and the British were anxious to divert the German Eastern Front forces. Talk ranged from the difficult and far-fetched suggestion of reopening the Eastern Front through Siberia to occupying the Trans-Siberian Railroad. The most interested ally in any such scheme would be Japan.[53]

In February the military advisory group of the Supreme War Council adopted Joint Note #16, which advised the Allied political leaders that Japanese occupation of the railroad from Vladivostok to Harbin was militarily valuable. The American representative, Bliss, not only gave in to Allied pressure on this point but even drafted the note. The United States government, however, withheld its approval at that time. The State Department was carefully fending off Allied pressure to become militarily involved in Russian affairs. March, meanwhile, kept himself informed through the cables from Bliss and the military attaché, Lieutenant Colonel James E. Ruggles, who by this time was in semi-exile with the ambassador at Vologda.[54]

March's observations of the victorious Japanese army in Manchuria had given him definite impressions of the Orientals. Where Siberia was concerned, he did not trust them. Frankly, he wanted the United States to be as little involved as possible in the morass of Russian internal affairs. Above all, he believed that American effort should be concentrated on the Western Front. When the War Plans Division recommended sending Judson at the head of another mission to Russia via Siberia and giving him the greatest latitude possible in the expenditure of funds and the broadest discretionary powers, the Acting Chief disapproved. Hands off, if possible, was his policy.[55]

As he started to work in the War Department, March told his old West Point friend, Bill Graves, that he did not relish his assignment, but since he had the job, he was going to run it his way.[56] On the basis of his experience and information, he had a definite plan of action when he reached Washington and found the war machine nearly complete. His plan was four-fold: reorganization of the General Staff; assignment of AEF veterans to the key positions of heads of the Quartermaster and Ordnance Departments; subordination of all other affairs to getting the men to France; and establishment of replacement camps.[57] Of these projects, the third represented the cutting edge of the total effort: the Allies' one great hope was American manpower. March knew this and realized that he must emphasize the speed-up of troop shipments. During his first month the flow of troops almost doubled the highest previous monthly crossings. In April, for the first time, over 100,000 soldiers made the oceanic voyage. From then until the first of November the figure never dropped below that number.[58]

At the end of his first six weeks in office March could look back on his accomplishments in all four aspects of his plan, but there was a debit side. His brusqueness, in particular, alienated people. His precipitate action in stopping publication of the casualty lists, although admittedly he was carrying out orders to the letter, had caused adverse criticism. And there was the friction, which was susceptible to expansion, between him and Pershing. March had not acted wisely in promoting without recommendation one of Pershing's subordinates. Although the strong evidence of his co-operation tended to offset this move, nevertheless it gave credence to suspicion which Harbord had engendered and was nourishing.

In April, the United States observed, without much pause for ceremony, the first anniversary of its entrance into the war. Through the months of trial and error the great democracy had made giant strides toward becoming a nation in arms. But the army, increased eight times in the past twelve months, as yet had not closed with the enemy in force as the small casualty lists testified. Before this could be done someone had to apply additional impetus from the top. The war effort, which was still "jelling"[59] at this time, had yet to be hardened into a blunt instrument of might.

Peyton C. March contributed to this metamorphosis. His grasp of modern war, his power of decision, his mania for efficiency – all led to the needed result of effective action. Soldiers on both sides of the Atlantic were aware of this new energy in the War Department. By driving hard and applying the whip, this tough soldier made the war machine move faster.[60]

6 · THE WAR DEPARTMENT BEGINS TO HIT ITS STRIDE

Every day March had to face problems which spanned the entire war effort. Although he made decisions in regard to these questions daily, in most cases, his solutions could only settle the immediate aspect of the issue; another phase of the same general problem might demand attention on the following day. Thus transportation, organization, promotions, press relations, and sensitive generals remained on the agenda with the pressure of time always present. In this period March began his working relationship with the Secretary of War. Within a few weeks Newton D. Baker measured his Acting Chief of Staff, deemed him successful, and gave him his reward.

Newton Baker arrived in New York on the morning of April 16, after a refreshing sea voyage. By that evening he was back at work with a vigor renewed by his inspection trip. As he shook hands with March, he was urged by Dean Keppel, "Mr. Secretary, you will have to remonstrate with General March. He is working too hard!" The quiet Baker smiled. Later when he and the Acting Chief were alone in his office, Baker started the conversation: "General, I suppose you received your orders to return to be Chief of Staff with rather mixed emotions." March answered frankly, "No, Mr. Secretary, it made me sick at my stomach." That subject closed, the two war leaders, joined by Provost Marshal General Crowder, began a long conference.[1]

When he surveyed the business handled during his absence, Baker found that the Acting Chief had taken some actions which he questioned. He was personally convinced that Wheeler was the right man to head the Ordnance Department. Also, in picking out details, he discovered that March had placed tobacco on the ration after the Secretary had earlier disapproved of such a move. Upon taking up both of these questions with the General, Baker came around to his advisor's point of view. Cogent explanations converted this anything but dogmatic man. Within a few days he knew the sureness of March's judgment and the rapidity with which the General studied details and formed opinions.[2]

He knew also the emphasis which its new occupant placed on the office of the Chief of Staff. Heretofore, the Secretary, upon the suggestion of General Scott, had occasionally summoned the Chief of Staff with a buzzer. One day, shortly after the Secretary's return, March heard a buzzing and answered the phone. It was dead. An officer, who was presenting some papers to him, said that it was Mr. Baker. March strode into the Secretary's office to find that he was wanted for something which he considered "wholly unimportant." After he expressed his indignation, the General returned to his desk and disconnected the offending instrument.[3]

There were some necessary adjustments, but Baker liked March and his accomplishments. On April 29, he wrote his friend, General Bliss: "You will be interested to know that General March is making a most favorable impression as Acting Chief of Staff. I find his judgment quick and sure, and he seems to have an ability to inform his judgment by a study of details which is rather rare in so quick a mind." A few days before, soon after his return, he had written, "I found that things in the War Department were progressing very satisfactorily." [4]

The Allied cry for "men, men, and still more men" [5] made a strong impression on Washington that spring. In response to this plea March participated in conferences with Allied representatives and the President even became involved in a rare excursion into the military field. Pershing used his grant of virtual autonomy from Baker and Wilson to play the dominant role in the shipping argument, but it was March who had to execute the decisions reached in the conferences.

The President cancelled a cabinet meeting on the afternoon of April 19th, in order to devote the time to conferring with Baker on troop shipments. Wilson, his right hand giving him pain from a burn received earlier in the day, went over and approved a proposed program which March had discussed with the British guaranteeing shipment of 120,000 infantrymen and machine gunners a month through July. A proviso added that if the situation allowed, the preferential shipping of combat units would cease before July 31, in order that the supplementary personnel, necessary for a separate American army, could be transported. Oddly enough, March did not cable details of this agreement to Pershing for one week.[6]

In the interim, Pershing met with Britain's recently appointed secretary of state for war, Lord Milner, in London and signed, on April 24, another agreement providing for the shipment in May of 126,000 troops, all elements of 6 divisions except artillery, with the remainder of these units to follow "immediately thereafter." Although these troops would train with the British, they would be used under American command. If the emergency continued, the agreement provided for an extension of this program.[7]

Upon his return to Chaumont, Pershing received news of the agreement Wilson had approved. Not only did the concession of a four-month program seem too generous to the AEF commander, but also the project appeared to endorse amalgamation of American men in British units. At least, Pershing thought that the Allies interpreted it to mean that President Wilson was favorable toward amalgamation. His chief of staff, Harbord, considered it a plain case of cutting the ground from under the AEF leader's feet and he blamed March.[8]

On the other side of the Atlantic, the Secretary of War and the British ambassador, Lord Reading, discussed the London agreement. Baker realized that this plan meant a more rapid build-up of complete divisions although the total number of men involved, considering the increased tonnage, would be about the same. Nevertheless, he told Reading that he would endorse the Milner-Pershing agreement since he believed that those two, being closer to the war, had a clearer understanding of the situation.[9]

The resultant confusion, plus the fact that the French had not been involved in either of the agreements, meant that much of the Supreme War Council meeting at Abbeville during the first two days of May would be devoted to the question. The Allies arrayed their leaders in an effort to pressure Pershing into agreeing to an infantry and machine gun personnel shipping schedule extending into June. Tension was high in the Allied officers' club where the conferees gathered as Lloyd George, Clemenceau, Foch, and Milner, stressing the emergency, pleaded that the war might be lost because of the Missourian's obduracy. The French premier also feared that the British were too ready to compromise. Pershing was "black as thunder the first day" and "very sulky," according to Sir William Wiseman, a close friend of Colonel E. M. House and one of the English representatives.[10] As Sir William listened to the American commander's arguments, he pencilled a note: "In other words not military reasons but purely political. . . . Is for the President to say not Pershing."[11] Finally on the afternoon of the second day, Pershing forced a compromise. He agreed to extend the London program into June on the promise of additional tonnage to carry auxiliary troops and a clear statement that the Allies agreed to the formation of an independent American army as soon as possible. "It was a big fight to get anything out of it," Pershing wrote March three days later.[12] Sir William expressed the general Allied reaction that it was "an unsatisfactory compromise."[13]

While Pershing and the Allied leaders debated the various plans, March and his staff drew up estimates and turned the figures on paper into khaki-clad men, equipped for battle, filing up gangplanks. A week after the beginning of the Abbeville conference, Baker, who was pleased with Pershing's stand on that occasion, announced that there were over a half-million Americans overseas.[14] But Abbeville was not the end of Allied agitation; the Germans would see to that. On May 27, the enemy spearheaded an attack toward Paris through the French lines in the Chemin des Dames sector. Amidst the dejection evoked by this offensive, the American army scored its first victory of the war as Hanson E. Ely's Twenty-eighth Infantry Regiment successfully staged an attack on the German positions at Cantigny and desperately held against counterattacks. Nonetheless, the German drive to the southeast pushed on toward the Marne.

As the Supreme War Council began its sixth session at Versailles on the first of June, American marines and infantrymen were fighting astride the Paris road west of Chateau Thierry. Once again Lloyd George, Clemenceau, Milner, and Foch pressed for more American combat troops. Depression permeated the atmosphere as the leaders debated anew the old question. Pershing stood his ground and reiterated that the logistical strain which increased combat troop shipments would induce would be too great unless proportionate numbers of auxiliary troops were dispatched.[15] "His straightforwardness" and "will to conquer" were apparent to Maxime Weygand, Foch's brilliant chief of staff, who agreed with Pershing and changed his general's mind by pointing out the practicality of holding some of the raw manpower in the United States a month longer.[16] Foch, Milner, and Pershing then signed an agreement recommending that, if Allied shipping could carry 250,000 Americans in each of the next two months, absolute priority should be given to 170,000 combat troops in June and to 140,000 combatants in July. Lloyd George, Clemenceau, and Premier Vittorio Orlando of Italy sent their own recommendation stating the seriousness of the situation and setting a goal of one hundred American divisions, at the rate of a 300,000-men-per-month increase, in France.[17]

Pershing came out of this conference convinced that the time had come for his country to take up "the brunt of the war."[18] This could be done most effectively, he believed, by an American army under its own flag. In Washington, March strongly endorsed the field commander's views and urged the rapid formation of complete divisions. The Secretary of War agreed and took their argument to the President.[19] Now that the AEF had demonstrated its excellence at Cantigny and on the Marne, the two generals had a more forceful case; however, time was of the essence. In the face of the German attack, Pershing secretly planned to move his headquarters from Chaumont to avoid being trapped by the enemy. In Paris, embassy officials were preparing to evacuate within the hour, and trucks were standing by to carry Bliss' office out of danger.[20] To the north, Harbord, now a brigade commander, and his marines hurt the enemy at Belleau Wood and Major General Joseph T. Dickman's Third Division displayed its *élan* on the Marne. The tide was turning but the issue was still in balance.

"Almost like a miracle,"[21] the Americans came in great numbers. Three men took turns in each bunk on six fast transports, as Pershing recommended and March approved overassignment of troop capacities. The President and Baker considered the shipment of soldiers in slow convoys too dangerous, however, and refused to permit it. At first, March disapproved of public departures, but later he gave his approval, and there were more, with troops on deck and bands playing. Even the submarine scare in early June did not stop the flow.[22]

As the army "over there" increased, the logistical problem became more complex. A breakdown in communication added to the difficulties in the War Department. For some unexplained reason, the supply people did not realize that the large troop shipment would continue. The leaders who attended the War Council meetings certainly knew, since discussions of shipping plans took up much of the agenda. Shortly after the war, criticism about this situation reached March who promptly labelled it "ludicrously false in its broad sense." He rebutted it by commenting, "The shipment of troops and the supply agencies were both under the same man, General Goethals . . . [the criticism] is like saying that General Goethals' right hand did not know what his left hand was doing."[23] Yet, the agencies in Europe evidently did not have official information to this effect until July. While the entire shipping-manpower-supply situation was fluid throughout this period, this does not excuse the lapse on the part of March and Goethals in failing to make the long-range requirements more explicit to their subordinate agencies.

"Roughly, we have estimated," Baker wrote Bliss, "that to maintain an army of a million men in France will require the continuous employment of 2,500,000 deadweight tons of shipping, and we have at present in service only about 1,300,000 tons. . . ."[24] And there were already over 700,000 men in the AEF. Could the French ports stand the strain of the deluge? Could the railroads? March and Baker posed these questions to the AEF commander. Pershing answered that, with the availability of Marseilles and the improvement of the railroad situation, he was confident of being able to handle the necessary tonnage. The development of supply sources in Europe would also help solve the problem.[25]

As soon as the various agreements expanded the convoys, another problem emerged. At the new rate the port calls would soon exhaust the supply of trained men. The War Department had to take drafts from organized divisions to fill up units at the port. March answered complaints by pointing out the need and added that he was developing a replacement system which he hoped would solve the difficulty by July. Replacement depots were getting a belated start due to the earlier opposition of Baker, Bliss, and Scott.[26] In May the selective service system mobilized its largest monthly quota to date and in June it held another registration. It was now "Work or Fight" for the young men of the nation. If the camps were inadequate to house the men, Pershing suggested billeting as he urged still larger draft calls.[27]

While he and March were pushing the nation into greater effort, they did not pause to be impressed by the records being broken. But the statistics were impressive as May troop shipments doubled the highest previous month (April) and June shot the record up another 30,000 to 278,664.[28] As the troops flowed into France, their training in many cases was not up to Pershing's standard. A division might include men in various stages of training, with some practically raw recruits. Various units also lacked open-warfare instruction. But March believed that the exigency demanded men. He had to fill ships and he hoped to work out other details as rapidly as possible, perhaps by July. Meantime, he was developing replacement centers and issuing instructions to stress open warfare. Besides, the Chief of Staff held that soldiers in this emergency did not require as much training as Pershing desired.[29]

Secretary Baker told Bliss before that wise old soldier left to assume his post with the Supreme War Council that he would not name a new Chief of Staff until he knew his man. Within two weeks after his return the Secretary realized that March was the man but there was a difficulty inherent in having the Acting Chief drop the "Acting" from his title. Bliss wore four stars only because he was the titular Chief of Staff, Congress having voted this rank, on a temporary basis, for the principal military adviser and the field commander in October, 1917.[30] When Bliss left the office he was supposed to revert to his permanent major generalcy, but Baker wanted Bliss to maintain his rank for the purpose of dealing with ranking Allied officers. The Secretary conferred with the Chairman of the Senate Military Affairs Committee on the possibility of his old friend retaining a brevet rank. When he found that the Senate Committee was unanimously in favor of this plan, Baker asked the President to nominate March as Chief of Staff with a proviso granting brevet rank to Bliss, whom Weygand, the French representative, called "steadfast" and "amiable."[31] On May 24, the Senate confirmed the recommendations with rank to date from May 20. March was then Chief of Staff in name as well as in fact.[32]

Generalissimo Foch paused in the midst of the tribulation of the enemy offensive to cable his congratulations. "I am happy to see you assume permanently the huge task of Chief of Staff of the U.S. Army which you were already performing in so brilliant a way."[33] Bliss prophesied, ". . . you will get out of it great honor, and that is the soldier's reward."[34] And there were other equally laudatory messages, but the one which, perhaps, pleased the new four-star officer the most came over a month later in a letter from Pershing:

I want to say that the affairs at your end of the line have moved much more smoothly and satisfactorily since you assumed the reins, and I have no doubt that your new organization will soon produce even more satisfactory results.[35]

The businesslike Chief of Staff did not alter his pace to reflect on his new status. With the expansion of the shipping program he had little time for such thoughts. He had appeared before the House Military Affairs Committee on May 2 and 6 to explain the necessity for an expanded army and its requirements.[36] On the last day of the month the House passed the Army Appropriations Bill without a dissenting vote. The Senate also approved and, on July 10, the President signed the bill which gave the army twelve billion dollars, according to the Washington *Evening Star*, "the largest sum ever voted by this country for the support of a military force."[37] This, together with the Overman Act, which granted broad powers to the President, clearly demonstrated the nation's determination to play a decisive part in the war.

"Now, All Together." "Over the Top." "Invest in Victory." "Buy Liberty Bonds." Thousands of "Dollar Fighters" paraded in front of President Wilson as government workers were let out to participate in "Liberty Day." "Four Minute Men" pounded home the doctrines of democracy's crusade. War was parades and slogans in April and May as Americans oversubscribed the Third Liberty Loan.[38] The nation's spirit aroused, its leaders molded this vigor into a war machine.

The General Staff was still evolving throughout these months of heavy strain. Although his Purchase, Storage, and Traffic Division had been in existence since mid-April, Goethals, who aimed at the goal of establishing his division as the army's sole purchasing agency, had to overcome bureau opposition, work out the details of his new organization, define its limits, and get good men. Robert E. Wood was back from France and now in charge of the Quartermaster Department. He was to see a lot of March during the following months, frequently consulting with him on supply projects. During this period he developed a high opinion of March, whom he thought resembled his immediate superior, Goethals, in character. Wood knew that the Chief of Staff "did not work out problems with people — he ordered." It was clear to him that March "was the War Department."[39] Another supply assistant, Hugh S. Johnson, got off on the wrong foot by provoking the Chief of Staff with a supply proposition which seemed impertinent to March. But

Goethals forged ahead and was succeeding, as Pershing's G-4 (chief of the supply section), Colonel George Van Horn Moseley realized. "We are in fine shape," he wrote his friend Wood in June, "except for some ordnance equipment." [40]

The Ordnance program was also undergoing alteration. The forceful Williams decentralized the organization yet closely co-ordinated its elements. Impressed by his service in France, the new Ordnance Chief changed from the old idea of dictating to the combat branches to the policy of acting upon suggestions from the using arms. He also brought industrial leaders into the bureau and gave them responsible posts. Both Wood and Williams found out that March, once he approved, would support their decisions "to the limit." [41]

Throughout the spring, March was solving personnel and organizational problems. He installed a newly promoted brigadier general, Lytle Brown, as Chief of the War Plans Division in May and appointed another new one-star officer, Frank W. Coe, to the office of Chief of Coast Artillery in June. During the spring, new organizations came into being which reflected the modern aspects of twentieth-century warfare. A Motor Transport Service became a part of the Quartermaster Corps on April 18, followed the next day by an Inventions Section in the General Staff. Two months later the War Department recognized the importance of poison gas with the creation, by General Order # 62, of a Chemical Warfare Service. Pershing, who had established a Gas Service in September, 1917, had advocated on several occasions a similar organization for the entire army.[42] Airpower, another new weapon, came into its own in late April when the Aviation Section separated from the Signal Corps. March continued expediting plans for the Air Service until in the hot, muggy days of the latter part of May an executive order augmented the authority of the Division of Military Aeronautics and created a Bureau of Aircraft Production.[43]

Under the pressure of war, business continued while the machinery was developing. In the spring of 1918, the Great War was becoming a World War for the United States as conditions in countries other than France drew the War Department's attention. From Italy came pleas for American troops to raise the spirits of people still somewhat stunned by the 1917 defeat. Wilson finally agreed to send a regiment of infantry to this part of the war front.[44] To the east, Russia remained a problem. Newton Baker wrote the President, in a vein his Chief of Staff would corroborate, "If I had my own way about Russia. . . . I would like to take everybody out of Russia except the Russians . . . and let the Russians settle down and settle their own affairs."[45] But March planned ahead in case the President decided to intervene. In May he told his assistant, William S. Graves, "If any one has to go to Russia, you're it."[46]

The Chief of Staff's office was within twenty blocks of the Capitol, thus, unlike the commander of the AEF, March was readily available for requests and buffets from the nation's politicians. Don't draft this man — commission that constituent — see if something can not be done here or there. Such things are normal, but war and its nation-wide embrace intensified the pressure congressmen and senators directed toward the top military man in Washington. In the midst of this atmosphere, March held to his belief that politics do not mix well with the development of military efficiency.

Colonel Bishop soon found out the new order when, as General Staff secretary, he asked March what he wanted to do about the letters asking favors for soldiers or officers. His answer was terse: "As long as I am in this job, I am not interested in a single . . . human being, as such. Answer them."[47] He included congressmen and senators in this policy. The appropriate division of the staff or bureau would answer requests or, if there were personal letters to March, his aide or assistant would handle them. The exception occurred if he were the only person who could reply and the letter deserved a reply. According to Colonel F. Q. C. Gardner, the officer who succeeded Colonel Bishop, even the President was effected by this no-politics policy. The first time that March received a request from the White House to commission certain individuals, he studied it, and then took it to Secretary Baker. After a conference, Baker put on his hat and went to see Wilson. There were no more requests of this nature from that source.[48]

When one congressman thought he had caught the Chief of Staff not following this policy, he hurried to the War Office and demanded why a wealthy meat-packer could get a direct commission for his son when one of the congressman's constituents had been denied one. March bristled: "If The Adjutant General has issued a commission in the way you say . . . we will have a new Adjutant General tomorrow morning." Prompt investigation proved that the young man had enlisted and passed a required examination.[49]

The "sharply military"[50] manner combined with the cold-blooded drive for efficiency and an apparent lack of tact did not gain March friends on Capitol Hill. Forty years later, two congressmen, Carl Hayden and Tom Connally, remembered that the General "did not welcome advice from civilians,"[51] and was "not a particularly popular officer."[52] After the war March crisply answered critics, "You can not run a war on tact."[53]

One concession that March intelligently made to Congress was the establishment of weekly conferences with members of the military committees of both houses. Impressed by the lack of accurate information the legislators seemed to have, the Chief of Staff realized that the army would profit from a policy of systematically giving the committee members the facts. With the aid of charts, maps, and later a written summary, March would explain the business of war to the people's representatives. After the abolishment of the War Council he used its meeting room for this purpose.[54]

In June he also instituted a weekly series of reviews for newspaper correspondents. At 11:30 on Saturday morning, beginning on June 15, the tall, immaculately uniformed Chief of Staff, followed by his assistants, marched into the conference room. Clearly and comprehensively, he elucidated for the reporters the war situation, using maps when necessary, occasionally punctuating his remarks with a slang expression. Over 800,000 men have gone to France and Allied hopes of stopping the German drive were rising, he told his audience on the first day. After his lecture, he permitted questions on certain subjects. "Sharp and precise," he impressed some of his listeners as a martinet; nevertheless, the reporters knew that March was easing army restrictions on news.[55]

Secretary Baker had agreed with March and upon his return made the statement that the army's system of providing information was "entirely unsatisfactory."[56] In May a daily communique from Pershing replaced the Weekly Press Bulletin which the War Plans Division distributed. Earlier in the month a presidential order had returned the disputed addresses to the growing casualty lists.[57] These measures followed up by March's weekly press conferences were definite advances in military public relations.

"Politics is adjourned," Woodrow Wilson keynoted in a speech before Congress in joint session. After perusing the President's message the

New York Times reader might turn to another headline on page 1 of the May 28 issue:

Order General Wood
To Home Duty On
Eve of Sailing

and question the President's statement. Leonard Wood and his friend Theodore Roosevelt were among the most bitter critics of the Democratic administration. To relieve Wood from command of the Eighty-ninth Division when it was on the verge of going to France seemed to indicate that the administration had not yet suspended politics. The irate general hurried to Washington and, on May 27, demanded a hearing.[58]

Aware of the explosive possibilities, March accorded the former Chief of Staff an interview. When the army's senior major general asked the foremost question – why? March bluntly told him that Pershing had specifically requested that he not send Wood to France and added that "the War Department is going to back him [Pershing]." [59] Going on to see Baker, Wood met with the same response. Finally, Wilson had to confirm the refusal personally.[60]

Wood limped as the result of an accident in Cuba. This disability had impressed Secretary Baker when he saw the general before the war, but Pershing objected to him because he knew that Wood would not be a tractable subordinate. In his first letter to March, Pershing had attached a "Personal and Confidential Memorandum" in which he elaborated on his main objection to Wood. In a vitriolic tone the AEF commander presented evidence of Wood's disloyalty to the President, the Secretary of War, and the War Department, and advised: "It seems high time that meddling, disloyal, political generals like this one be put where they can do no harm." Wood's habit of frank talks with the Allies and with his Republican friends frequently did result in conversations which less suspicious people than Pershing would consider disloyal.[61] March showed this memorandum to Baker and discussed the political implications of any move to relieve this officer. Within the army itself such action would draw criticism since Wood had a way of inspiring intense loyalty among younger officers and there was some anxiety about the reception of the news of the relief in the division. One report held that the troops were disheartened and that indignant officers had tears in their eyes as their general bade them farewell but Congressman Carl Hayden visited the unit and found the men generally indifferent. Wood, embittered, returned to Camp Funston, Kansas, and spent the rest of the war training troops and criticizing the administration and the War Department.[62]

The Wilson administration took a brave step politically when it supported Pershing in the Wood affair, but it was what the field commander expected, since he had received what he knew was "strong and sympathetic support" from Baker throughout his months in France.[63] Pershing realized also the strong backing he was getting from March who undergirded the foundation at home. "Things seem to be getting their stride there," the AEF commander wrote Hugh Scott in June, "and the staff seems to be working better." [64]

The distance separating March and Pershing did not lubricate the path of good relations. Had personal conferences been possible, they could possibly have solved or at least alleviated many mutually irritating problems. Correspondence failed to overcome this lack. Pershing wrote explanatory letters to the Chief of Staff from time to time in an effort to supplement the rather impersonal cables. As late as June 19, however, he had yet to hear from March, although the Chief of Staff had written him twice.[65]

Differences over promotions were annoying. There seemed to be an injustice in the Medical Corps advances, but March answered that the AEF commander had not accepted his suggestions to recommend officers of this branch.[66] Word of the disagreement over the April list of generals reached the pages of newspapers in June.[67] By this time, the two four-star generals had exchanged their views in courier letters which indicated that they both valued efficiency as the foremost reason for promotion. Their comments read much alike but March expressed his view in a peremptory tone while Pershing complained elsewhere to Baker that they should not promote inexperienced men over the heads of the experienced. Although he protested that he did not mean that promotions should be limited to AEF officers, he implied differently as he evidently intended "experience" to mean service in the AEF.[68]

Another list was in preparation in May as once again March asked Pershing for recommendations. The Chief of Staff warned, however, that the officers who made the new rank would have to return to the United States to take commands.[69] Weeks passed. By the middle of June the War Department had not sent the list on to the White House. Until he saw this new list the AEF commander would not know whether or not March and Baker had eliminated what he considered discrepancies in the promotion policy.

Supply was another irksome problem. The expeditionary force's General Headquarters — G.H.Q. — apparently made requests at times without considering the inherent difficulties or, on occasion, the impracticality that these requisitions presented to the Washington end of the line. A mistake in encoding or decoding cables might confuse the issue and make a difference of thousands of dollars. Constant changes bothered March to a great extent. Yet, when a seemingly impractical request came in, he checked with the AEF and explained the accompanying problems. First and last, he impressed the General Staff officers with their mission of supporting the AEF.[70]

March commented on one aspect of this question in a cable to Pershing in May. Officers in the AEF wore the broad leather waist belt with the strap over the right shoulder, the Sam Browne belt, although regulations did not permit this belt in the United States. The Secretary and the Chief of Staff asked Pershing to consider doing away with the belt as a part of the uniform because of the shortage of leather. When this suggestion came up in a staff meeting at G.H.Q., the officers unanimously disapproved. They believed that it added to *esprit* and also discipline because of its distinctiveness; moreover, it helped Allied troops to recognize American officers. In fact, this copying of the British uniform was one reason why some Americans resented it. Despite March's request, the AEF retained the belt. A small difference in uniform, the Sam Browne represented a larger difference between Pershing and March.[71]

Although war precluded most extra-curricular engagements, March did drop his duties occasionally to appear in public. He reviewed the high school cadets as they paraded on the Ellipse. Once Secretary Baker joined him for a ride on a five-ton artillery tractor in Rock Creek Valley near Connecticut Avenue.[72] More eventful, however, were his trips to the scenes of his youth.

In late May he journeyed to his birthplace to be honored. On the thirtieth, the townspeople of Easton presented a bejeweled sword to their former citizen. General March acknowledged this gift with a brief reiteration of what the War Department had been doing in the last few weeks, highlighting his remarks with the statement that more soldiers had gone to France during the month of May than were there when he left in February.[73]

The following day, Lafayette College, where his father had taught for over fifty years and his brother was now in his fourth decade as a teacher, awarded him, as "a thorough student, a gallant soldier, a keen intrepid commander," the doctorate of laws degree at a commencement in which twenty-eight of the seventy-one members of the graduating class were absent in the service. Later his fraternity, Delta Kappa Epsilon, gave him a jeweled wrist watch. To complete the honors, the alumni presented a horse to their fellow alumnus.[74]

Within two weeks he visited his other alma mater, the Military Academy. He arrived just in time to review the graduation parade on the Plain where he had marched in his last cadet review thirty years before. The sky was overcast but the ceremonies continued, culminating in a garden party at the Superintendent's home.

The next day, June 12, the cadet corps marched to the gymnasium to see the Class of 1919, 137 strong, received their diplomas a year early. They listened to three short speeches by the Superintendent, Colonel Samuel E. Tillman, General March, and Secretary Baker who awarded the diplomas and commissions. The Chief of Staff's few words drew editorial praise from the *New York Times*.[75]

The army needs trained leadership to defeat the enemy, March told the graduates. "Much will be expected of you and you cannot fail." But there would be glory for those young officers "face to face with the most glorious adventure – a modern crusade," in which the United States would be victorious. "We are going to put into this war the number of men necessary to win it, what ever that number may be." In closing, he exhorted the new officers: "I say to you, men of the graduating class, this is the greatest time in the history of the world to live in – go in and win." [76]

7 · "MEN, MEN, AND STILL MORE MEN"

THE shipping program reached its peak in the summer of 1918. During June, July, and August a daily average of almost 9,500 soldiers made the Atlantic crossing. In the midst of this gigantic accomplishment Pershing urged an even larger program. When March received this request, he had to study it in relation to the nation's resources. In the end he had to support a lesser project — one that was practicable. The difference was basic: Pershing planned in terms of the situation in France, while March had to act on the more comprehensive level of the entire war effort.

On Sunday, June 23, Chaumont was in a festive mood as the premier, Georges Clemenceau, paid his first visit to that town, where the American headquarters was located. A drive with General Pershing through the countryside and a brief visit to the American Eighty-third Division, quartered at nearby Montigny, followed the reception and the speeches. The Tiger of France, who, despite his large paunch and bushy white moustache, was much more vigorous mentally and physically than he looked at a casual glance, and the American commander, some twenty years his junior, talked of many things as their automobile passed through the rolling country. Returning to the chateau, they lunched with Generals Foch and Weygand, who had just arrived, before settling down to the real business of the day.[1]

Unlike some of the other inter-Allied conferences, the talk this afternoon was cordial. The French had come to ask the Americans for help in the form of divisions in a separate army. Before the end of the day, Foch would mention putting some regiments into French divisions, but Pershing stopped that abruptly. Their main reason for coming was to press home the plea for one hundred divisions which the generalissimo had made at Versailles three weeks before.[2] On that occasion the three prime ministers, Orlando, Lloyd George, and Clemenceau, had endorsed the program and had cabled their request to President Wilson. Now, the French leaders were trying to obtain Pershing's sanction to their petition. They found a ready listener. Since the Versailles conference, the hard-to-convince Missourian had reached the conclusion that the situation was indeed desperate. In recent personal letters he had confided to Baker and March that the Allies could not hold out "beyond another year." Since American troops in great numbers were the obvious answer to the dilemma, he had cabled, within the past week, a plan to build the AEF up to sixty-six divisions by May, 1919.[3]

As the conference progressed that afternoon, André Tardieu, French High Commissioner to the United States, suggested lowering the larger request, since he believed that it was beyond the nation's capacity, but the others were adamant. His separate command definitely understood, Pershing agreed to the proposal, and upped his previous appeal thirty-four divisions to the round number of one hundred divisions by July, 1919. Later, he would reminisce that at the time he thought an eighty-division program would have been an adequate goal; furthermore, the War Department "would do wonders if it would carry out even the sixty-six division plan." Nevertheless, he, together with Foch, signed the message to be sent to Washington. Clemenceau's trip had been successful.[4]

"To win the victory in 1918 . . . ," the phrase stood out in Confidential Cable # 1369 which contained the request, will require a draft of 300,000 men per month and a build-up of the AEF to sixty-four divisions in January and one hundred by July. Pershing added, "Am confident that . . . we shall be able to handle both troops and supplies" – with the help of Allied shipping and supply sources. The text showed that there was an error in transmission or coding – 1918 instead of 1919; yet the latter was awesome enough.[5] Frederick Palmer had mentioned in a New York speech five months before that Pershing was making preparations for one hundred divisions[6] and, of course, there was the Versailles request. But now Pershing had put his approval on record.

One hundred American divisions were equivalent to two hundred European divisions. The large, four-infantry-regiment, "square" division had been designed in order to make the most economic use of the limited quantity of trained command and staff personnel, and in the further hope that the larger unit would be able to sustain itself longer in combat. The huge division tended to confuse not only the interested layman following war news but also French leaders in the field. Numbering approximately 28,000, the division, when augmented by proportionate corps and army troops, would mean a total of 40,000 men for each unit of the hundred. When logistical support troops and replacements were added, the grand total of the AEF estimate came to five million men. Pershing anticipated that this force would be one-fourth greater than the combined Allied armies then on the Western Front.[7]

In his regular press review, held the day before the Chaumont meeting, March told the reporters that the War Department had sent 900,000 Americans overseas; in other words, "the United States is about five months ahead of its program." That month, the nation's ship production had set a new record, thus, with the help of the British, the army could easily hope to surpass the established goal of thirty divisions in France by December 31.[8] Already, March and Baker were looking forward to having one hundred divisions in Europe by 1920, if the war lasted that long. This latest request of Pershing's would mean compressing the two-year program into one. While the staff worked out the estimates of the large program, March and the Secretary of War realized the extreme difficulty involved in meeting this demand. "Getting the men is the simplest part of it. . . ." March wrote Bliss, as he recalled conferences with the various civilian boards.[9] Baker summed up their problem, "at present it looks as though I would need Aladdin's Lamp for the 100-Division program. . . ."[10]

March warned Pershing of the importance of not raising the Allies' expectations.[11] Baker sent a similarly worded cable to Bliss,[12] but there was not much need of this advice, since the idea had astounded Bliss anyway – and his estimate of the number of men involved was over a million and a half less than Pershing's. Bliss and the British representative, Major General C. J. Sackville-West, had come to the conclusion that Pershing and Foch must be contemplating a 1920 campaign. To confuse matters further, the U. S. military representative found, in talking with the French, that Clemenceau's estimate almost halved the difference between his (Bliss') and Pershing's.[13]

Combining Pershing's two requests and interpolating a third possibility, the General Staff figured on sixty-, eighty-, and one-hundred-division programs. The bulk of this work fell to the Operations Division, headed by one of the few men in the War Department whom March called by first name, his classmate, Henry Jervey. A frail, patient man, Jervey worked himself and his division hard. His associates recall his habitual gestures; crooking his right elbow and clasping it with his left hand, he would tweak his left ear with his right hand while contemplating such multi-faceted problems as planning increased troop shipments.[14] Concentrating on the all important tonnage aspect of the planning was the Purchase, Storage, and Traffic Division, and, in particular, the Embarkation Service led by the energetic, young Coast Artillery officer, Frank T. Hines, by now a brigadier general.

On July 12, Goethals forwarded his division's estimate to March. As he glanced over the report, the Chief of Staff saw that as far as shipping was concerned the sixty-division program, which entailed 2,500,000 men in France, could be accomplished. The eighty-division project, which Goethals estimated to be 3,355,000 men, would mean a cargo deficit of over 4,850,000 tons, while one hundred divisions (4,260,000 men) would raise the deficit to well over 15,000,000 tons.[15]

Men could be transported in the millions, but the "bridge of ships" could not support the requisite supplies. Already the increased troop shipments of the past four months, which had pushed the AEF past the million mark by the end of June, were straining available cargo tonnage. Despite the efforts of the supply people in France to pool supplies and to purchase, under the guidance of Charles G. Dawes, as much of their needs as possible in Europe, the long supply line across the Atlantic had to be maintained to the breaking point. The automatic supply was cut from fifty pounds per man per day to forty and, finally, to thirty pounds in hopes of putting into effect the eighty-division program.[16]

Another problem awaited War Department planners even if they could assume the solution of the tonnage question. Although Pershing confidently asserted that he could handle the largest program, Baker and his Chief of Staff were worried about the capacity of the French ports. It seemed to them that if all the berthing space in all of these ports were to be given over exclusively to the Americans, it would not fulfill requirements of the one-hundred-division scheme. In his report, Goethals emphasized this problem. He asserted that "considerable additional capacity must be provided in some way to meet even the minimum program," and pointed out that cargo would have to be discharged at 2.7 times the greatest previous daily average in order to carry out the one-hundred-division program.[17] This port situation alone seemed an "insurmountable obstacle to greater speed of transport," Baker later thought.[18] In order to evacuate supplies more rapidly from the ports, thus enabling them to handle more material, March and Baker considered a plan to send General Goethals to France to take charge of Pershing's supplies.[19]

At ten o'clock on Wednesday mornings, March and Baker, sometimes accompanied by other War Department representatives, would meet with the civilian leaders in the old War Council room. Baruch would be there with the facts about industry. John D. Ryan might attend and explain the air program. There would be three men, at times, to talk about shipping — Hurley, P. A. S. Franklin of the Shipping Control Committee, and the steel manufacturer Charles Schwab, who had taken over the Emergency Fleet Corporation. After a brief introductory outline of the war's developments by officers from the Statistics Branch, these leaders would compare their problems and progress for thirty minutes or so. During June and July, 1918, especially while ranging over the areas of supply, transportation, and ships, they measured the one-hundred-division program against the nation's capacity. Baruch knew that it would strain industry.[20] The shipping people would make estimates, but it seemed plainly impossible. March told them to take casualties into consideration in figuring cargo tonnage.[21] When questions were asked about how much space to allot each soldier on a transport, the Chief of Staff snapped: "We'll pack them in like sardines." There might not be transportation available to move troops from the ports to the lines. March's answer was, "What have they got feet for?" No wonder Baruch remembered him as a "driver." [22]

Shipyards were booming their way to another monthly record. On the Fourth of July, yards on the Gulf, Atlantic, Pacific, and Great Lakes strained for one hundred launchings and succeeded in launching ninety-five wooden and steel vessels.[23] President Wilson celebrated the national holiday by urging his people to victory in a speech at Mount Vernon: "The Past and the Present are in deadly grapple. . . . The settlement must be final." [24] The army now had about half of its over two million men in France, with a corps in action, and March announced on the sixth that, "we are now going after the second million." [25]

The credit side of tonnage was increasing, but the Germans were adding to the debit side. In July, mines and U-boats were sinking transports, and one cruiser. Fortunately, the transports were homeward bound, hence not filled with troops, but still men died and tonnage was lost. Earlier in June, Vice-Admiral Sir W. L. Grant of the British Navy went to the Chief of Staff's office and told him that Britain recommended discontinuing troop shipments from the American ports due to the U-boat threat. Grant's suggested solution to reduce the loss of tonnage, British in particular, was to build up Canadian ports and use them as ports of embarkation. Not wanting to divert American effort to construct port facilities, besides having to slow down or stop shipments in the interim, March turned down the suggestion and the transports continued.[26]

While the planning for the future was in progress, March was taking care of the present. He was planning to organize six new divisions and to draft 465,000 men in July. Things were going "at a very high speed," he wrote Pershing.[27] Over 300,000 men landed in France during July. A German prisoner of war, looking at the vast armada at Havre, exclaimed, "Mein Gott in Himmel!" and tears came into his eyes.[28]

There were many other aspects of the logistical problems than ships and men. As President Wilson pointed out later in July in a letter to Baker, which March saw and passed on to Goethals, "I am disturbed to find that the present industrial demands of the country for the supplying of war needs, either directly or indirectly, are in some instances far in excess of the productive capacity of the country. . . ."[29] Raw material shortages also made solution difficult. The woolen supply of the country would be stretched to the extreme in order to clothe the men necessary for one hundred divisions.[30] Artillery was a more important problem. Although the United States could hope eventually to produce the needed guns, for the time being the French must continue to furnish these weapons. Mobile artillery required horses which the French had largely supplied; however, they said that they would no longer be able to let the Americans have the required number of animals. Pershing promptly cabled for regular shipments of 8,000 horses per month. This meant converting desperately needed cargo ships into horse carriers. March suggested using motor transportation rather than horses to move the guns, but added that it was up to the field commander. Pershing replied that both animals and cargo were essential. Although he would try to substitute vehicles, he would still need horses since the War Department was behind in shipments of motor vehicles.[31]

Under the press of increased troop shipments, shortages, of which transportation was the most serious, were increasing. Irritating problems kept coming up. Units were arriving without their organic equipment. Some replacements lacked service records. Cabled debates over who had priority in the use of the newly developed Liberty engines took place. The constant changes in AEF requisitions were annoying to War Department planners.[32] And there was always the danger of a misplaced comma or a mistake in coding or decoding which would change the meaning of the message.

The shortages did demonstrate forcibly the lack of cargo tonnage available in proportion to the needs. The estimates of the shipping experts and the General Staff confirmed the shortages. It was obvious that there simply would not be enough tonnage in the coming twelve months to sustain the one-hundred-division program.[33]

On the day that American troops were joining the French in a counter offensive on the Marne, March submitted the General Staff's estimate to Baker, who informed the President, two days later on July 20, that he would brief him on the subject. The Chief of Staff recommended the eighty-division project which meant "in round numbers" 3,300,000 men overseas. To support these units in France, the army would maintain eighteen divisions (1,440,000 men) in the United States. As background for this brief two-page memo March could rely on staff studies which comprehensively explored the supply and manpower questions.[34]

The President gave his approval and the War Department started work on the project. March cabled the news to Bliss with the following ifs – Congress approves a change in age limits of the draft and appropriates the necessary money, France and Britain provide artillery and ammunition, and Britain's supply of troop and cargo ships necessary to overcome the tonnage deficiency continues. Of these questions, the problems of cargo tonnage combined with that of the capacity of the French ports still seemed the "greatest impediments."[35] Nevertheless, assuming that these obstacles would be cleared, America had set out "to do this great thing greatly."[36]

John J. Pershing did not then share the view that his country was doing all it could, although, as mentioned above, he later said that he did. His letters and cables continued to urge the one-hundred-division program. It seemed to him that the home-front leaders were simply not trying hard enough. Although supply shortages were mounting, as he continued to complain, he still pressed for the larger project. In regard to the tonnage difficulties, his advice was:

> If we start out with a continuous flow of men and material and supplies to the extreme limit of present American and Allied tonnage we shall be able to

force new tonnage into war service instead of debating the question beforehand with shipping people.[37]

Yet, on the same day, he cabled that "a very serious situation" was developing because equipment was not being shipped in proportion to the increased troop shipments.[38]

In contrast to Pershing's unwillingness to adjust his planning to the established program, the other four-star general in France took a more reasonable attitude toward the situation. Recognizing that even the eighty-division program would be difficult to accomplish, Bliss sent word that Foch was reconciled to this smaller project. Both generals knew that eighty divisions would give the Allies numerical superiority in the coming summer.[39] But Bliss must have misunderstood the Allied generalissimo, since Foch continued to urge the larger program. The military representative himself evidently wavered later. Fearing that the Allies would use the United States' failure to carry out the one-hundred-division plan as an excuse to continue the war, Bliss urged more effort to consummate the greater program. If the war went into 1920, he knew it would be at the expense of American casualties.[40] On August 25, he and Pershing conferred about the possibilities of the one-hundred-division plan. After their talk, Pershing went to Foch's headquarters at Bombon, where the recently promoted Marshal of France strongly advocated the larger program. There was no argument as the American commander helped Foch plan the latter's approach to Secretary Baker.[41]

Five days before Pershing met with Foch, a board under the direction of the Commanding General of the Services of Supply convened to study the requirements of the eighty-division program. These officers proceeded exhaustively to explore the ramifications of the project. Their idea of the eighty-division scheme did not coincide with that of the War Department: to these officers, eighty was merely the number of combat divisions; there would be an additional sixteen depot divisions, making a total of 4,585,000 men in France by July 1, 1919. Although this number differed by 1,225,000 from the War Department figure, AEF estimates would be based on it throughout the rest of the war.[42]

On August 7, the Chief of Staff went before the Senate Military Affairs Committee to explain the needs of the eighty-division program. This was the first of several appearances before the congressional committees in this connection. Outlining the War Department's plans, March clearly enunciated his strategical conception of the situation. The deadlock of the trenches could be broken only by massing enough men not only to penetrate the German defensive line but also to force its collapse.[43] The day after March's first appearance, the British did just that in a limited offensive in the Somme sector. General Ludendorff considered that the beginning of the end, but, at the time, the Allies did not realize the psychological effect of the day.[44]

The relentless Chief of Staff contended for more men: "we are going to win the war if it takes every man in the United States." [45] Specifically, he wanted the draft ages extended from the existing age limits of twenty-one to thirty to the much larger group of eighteen- to forty-five-year-olds. Talk of universal service was also in the air. March, the General Staff, many army officers, and some civilians favored it; however, Wilson vetoed bringing up such a proposal at this time.[46] After some debate, the new age limits were approved and September 12 was set as the registration date. Two days later, the Chief of Staff announced at his regular press conference that the army would need an additional appropriation of seven billion dollars to carry out its program. Good news accompanied this statement, as March described the victory of the First American Army at St. Mihiel. "America is going through with it," he told the press.[47]

Complicating the Chief of Staff's effort were the possible demands of the Siberian expedition, criticism of the strain on industry brought about by the new program, and the obvious fact that the War Department and Expeditionary Force plans did not mesh. When the AEF complained about supply shortages, March rebutted by pointing out that cargo vessels were detained too long in French ports. In early August, the British shocked the Americans by stating that they would probably have to withdraw some cargo tonnage from the "bridge of ships" because cotton and coal were needed in the home islands. Since the eighty-division program absolutely required British shipping, this would make it impossible. Exasperated, Woodrow Wilson commented: "This is serious, and — how characteristic after urging the 100 division programme! We must not insist that the decision be definite and final as to what they can do. Would that we were dealing with responsible fellows!" [48] Perhaps it was this news which made necessary a European trip Baker had been contemplating to confer on shipping and artillery problems.

Edward R. Stettinius had already gone overseas in order to represent the United States on the Inter-Allied Munitions Council. When he talked with Bliss and Pershing, he evidently became confused over the proposed program. The American leaders in France did not seem to understand that the eighty-division program had been approved by the President, but considered it as a proposal still to be debated. Bliss had been informed, but Pershing apparently had not been. When Baker arrived in September, he found the AEF planning on the ninety-six-division basis. Amazed, he cabled March to confirm what he thought was fact, that the official program was eighty, not ninety-six divisions.[49]

March was disgusted. Less than two weeks before, he had cabled a few details and forwarded by courier the complete particulars of the official program to Pershing.[50] On September 25, he bluntly informed the AEF commander that it was impracticable to carry out his program. The eighty-division project was official, and "you will give instructions that rate of shipments and requirements be worked out to correspond therewith." This was an order from March, as Chief of Staff, but he added, "Should it be possible to exceed it that will be done and you will be advised."[51] If March was mystified by Pershing's actions, the field commander was infuriated by the Chief of Staff's behavior. In the midst of the period of heaviest strain of the Meuse-Argonne offensive, he caustically informed March that while the lesser program might be "most convenient" for the United States it would not meet the requirements of the situation. He demanded that the AEF be allowed to plan its own program.[52]

Demanding ships did not mean that they would materialize, although on both sides of the Atlantic American leaders worked on the tonnage problem. Secretary Baker's talks with the British were successful.[53] It looked as if the War Department might carry out the eighty-division program; nevertheless, fourteen days before the war ended, General Goethals prophesied that the shipping situation would collapse — the Armistice saved the day.[54]

Perturbed by the confusion over the variance in programs, Baker asked Marshal Foch in early October how many American divisions he needed to win the war in 1919. The energetic Marshal promptly answered, "Forty." Taken aback, the Secretary repeated the question to the interpreter, but Foch had understood.[55] The war had changed since the hot summer days when battles hung in balance. The Allied armies now were breaking down the German defenses in the last great offensive.

As the anxieties of the summer faded, Pershing also came to believe that he had never really expected the United States to send one hundred divisions to France. He had urged it in such a desperate manner in hopes of getting a larger program than the War Department would have otherwise endorsed. Reading this portion of Pershing's memoirs, March must have smiled somewhat bitterly. The AEF commander's actions in 1918 certainly did not indicate that he was playing such a game.[56]

8 · THE RUSSIAN SITUATION: "EGGS LOADED WITH DYNAMITE"

While March and the General Staff wrestled with the complexities of the one-hundred-division program and stretched the national effort in the hope of getting as many men to France as possible, another problem came to a head. Should the United States support and contribute to intervention in Russia? If it did, March would have to consider the logistical complications of another expedition and divert men and material from shipment to France. Already the American government had rejected Allied requests in regard to Siberia alone several times but the Allied leaders persisted.

Russian matters had come to the Chief of Staff's attention during his first week in office. He was convinced then and later that there was no military advantage in intervention. He knew that the decisive theater was in France and that maximum effort there would hasten the war's conclusion. As military adviser to the President, March stated his views. As Chief of Staff he had to carry out the President's decision.

The proposal to intervene stayed alive because the Allies feared the effect of the transfer of German troops from Russia to France as well as the dangers of Bolshevism. Then, too, the Japanese had their imperial ambitions to nourish. Since February, 1918, Foch had strengthened the cause of intervention. When the Treaty of Brest-Litovsk took the former ally out of the war, the Allies became more panicky. Throughout the spring, naval forces stood off two Russian ports. Two American warships were part of these naval elements: the USS *Olympia*, famed as Dewey's flagship at Manila Bay, at Murmansk in the far north; and the USS *Brooklyn*, at Vladivostok. Beyond the watchful waiting of these two vessels and a small mission, the President refused to go.[1]

Still there were aspects of the problem which might make intervention purposeful. The German offensives in the spring forecast what would happen in the enemy received reinforcement in great strength from the east. Studying the matter from this angle, March remained adamantly opposed. In order to mount a force powerful enough to make its weight felt through Murmansk, the army would have to divert men, supplies, and tonnage from France at a time when all three were in desperate demand. To the Chief of Staff's logical mind, such an expedition simply was not feasible. In regard to Siberia, these same factors plus the great distances and the danger that the Japanese might twist the venture to their own advantage made such a move even more preposterous.[2]

The American stand against entangling troops in Russian matters was weakening as the President and the Secretary of State, Robert Lansing, began to think, despite the Chief of Staff's disapproval, that there were military advantages in landing a force in north Russia. When the Supreme War Council's military representatives recommended, at their Versailles meeting in June, the dispatch of a small Allied Force to Murmansk, they met with a receptive attitude. Such a force could secure the northern port from possible German capture, protect Allied war supplies stored there, and maintain an escape route for Czech forces supposedly en route. Secretary Baker and General March were unshakable. Their suspicions were aroused when they discovered that the small number of American troops envisioned by the military representatives was increased by the British, who expected to have command of the expedition. Even Pershing's approval did not change their position.[3]

The Secretary of War cabled Bliss to gain a clearer understanding of the situation.[4] The former Chief of Staff confirmed the fact that the Supreme War Council plan differed from the British proposal, one to two American battalions being called for in the first place while the British asked for three battalions with support troops. Bliss checked with Foch and found that the latter supported the less ambitious plan;[5] however, when the President approved the intervention on July 17, he accepted the British version, with the exception of the field artillery units. Three battalions of infantry (339th Infantry Regiment), a battalion of engineers, a field hospital, and an ambulance company were selected to form the American component.[6] "I then washed my hands of the whole matter," said the disapproving March. Pershing would have to draw upon his own forces for the men and supplies.[7]

On a dark, rainy day in early September, the Americans under Lieutenant Colonel George E. Stewart, commanding officer of the 339th, landed at Archangel. Two battalions were soon at the front fighting the Bolsheviks.[8] In Washington, there was a dispute over Stewart's instructions. The American Ambassador to Russia, David R. Francis, complained that Stewart refused to co-operate with him, but was working closely with the British commander. The Secretary of State criticized March because he refused to reveal to the State Department the American commander's orders. A few days later, the Chief of Staff cabled to Stewart instructions based on Wilson's Aide Memoire; in his difficult situation, however, Colonel Stewart probably found neither solace nor instructions applicable to his problems in the President's statement of the United States' general policy aims in Russia.[9]

During this month of September, the Allies exerted pressure to increase the American contribution. Bliss, who attempted to fend off the Allied request, passed the information on to March with the comment, "In any event I do not see how we can do anything more in Russia, even if we wanted to do so."[10] The Chief of Staff thought that the President would be interested in Bliss' analysis and forwarded the letter to the White House. After reading the message, Wilson observed, "I think you know already that the judgments expressed are my own also."[11] Following a meeting of March, Lansing, and Wilson on the twenty-fifth, a definite statement of the government's refusal to do more was issued.[12] For the men already in north Russia, holding a perimeter about Archangel was a hazardous business and one which would continue until months after the end of the war in France.

In the course of the discussions about Russia during the summer, Siberia also figured prominently. As it developed, the north Russian and Siberian expeditions proceeded concurrently.

While Lloyd George's suggestion of pouring two and a half million Japanese into Siberia to reconstitute the Eastern Front was out of the question,[13] the possibility of a limited intervention of combined American and Japanese forces was becoming more likely. Wilson was weakening under the weight of the Allied entreaties. Admitting that his Secretary of War and Chief of Staff were right from a military viewpoint in opposing Russian ventures, Wilson explained to Baker, "I have had to refuse to do so many things they urged upon me that I can not refuse this upon which they have so much set their hearts." His solution was to go along with their request, but, "to limit the American contribution as far as possible. . . ."[14] As late as the middle of June, Lansing and presidential confidant Colonel E. M. House were thinking of another possible solution which would avoid force. Why not send Herbert Hoover who had been so successful in aiding the Belgians to head a relief mission to Russia? While not discarded entirely (it would be mentioned in the Aide Memoire), this idea was not adopted.[15]

The President was thinking of stronger measures than advisory commissions. On June 19, he forwarded a memorandum, the composite of several opinions, advocating an intervention with 10,000 to 15,000 men for General March to analyze. When he read the document five days later, the Chief of Staff called a stenographer and dictated his reply. Recalling his observations of fourteen years before, he knew that the Russians hated the Japanese. A Japanese move in force into Siberia might easily throw Russia into the arms of Germany. Pershing, Bliss, and the deposed premier, Alexander Kerensky, corroborated this view. Besides, from a strictly military point of view, Siberian intervention, he believed was "neither practical nor practicable. . . ." Since it would not divert "a single German division," it would have no effect upon the war. There was no question in his mind: "All such schemes are absolutely futile."[16] Coincidentally, Bliss set down his views the same day in a letter to March. Since he had borne the brunt of much of the Allied pressure, Bliss had carefully studied the possibilities and had reached the conclusion that at best intervention would be based on a "guess."[17]

The Allies were certainly willing to wager American and Japanese troops on that basis. The Supreme War Council cabled Wilson in early July, recommending Siberian intervention as an aid to the Allied cause. Less than a week before, Foch had sent a similar request, but the French general was thinking of a small force – 12,000, of which the United States would furnish two regiments – while the Council was talking about 100,000 men.[18] On the same day, July 3, that Wilson received the Supreme War Council message, he was informed that a Czech force had taken Vladivostok.[19] The Czech Corps, which was recognized as a regular Allied force, had been moving toward that port for several months. Now, the sentimental appeal of helping these representatives of a minority nation entered strongly into Wilson's consideration. For two hot summer days, the President pondered the problem; then on the second day (July 5), he called a conference to meet at the White House the next day at two o'clock. Three cabinet members, the Secretaries of State, War, and Navy, and two military men, March and Admiral William Benson, were invited.[20]

By the time of this meeting Wilson already had in his hands a summary of March's plans for a move into Siberia, which Baker had given him on July 2. There were two understrength infantry regiments (Twenty-seventh and Thirty-first) in the Philippines; these units could be brought up to full strength and sent to Valdivostok in about a month after receiving orders. To supply the Czechs, there were 13,000 Russian rifles with over a million rounds of ammunition in the United States.[21]

On the day of the conference, the Chief of the Operations Branch of the Operations Division, Colonel E. D. Anderson, gave the Chief of Staff a more comprehensive memorandum on the expedition to supplement his own information. Anderson advised sending the two regiments at their present strength (together, the two units had 3103 officers and men, almost 600 fewer than the complement of one full-strength regiment) to Vladivostok. Since these were regular regiments, they would probably make a better showing than if they went in with a large proportion of recruits. Once they were in Siberia, March could fill the units with recruits from the United States. Equipment was available, and army transports operating in the Pacific could furnish transportation. The General Staff was demonstrating its purpose by already planning an expedition, on March's orders, before the decision to move was made.[22]

When they met in an upstairs room of the White House, the war leaders were aware that American marines had already joined the token Allied forces in Vladivostok. At this meeting the situation was discussed, particularly in regard to the Czechs and the recent Supreme War Council communication. Then Wilson proposed intervening with a force of 14,000, half American and half Japanese, in order "to guard the line of communications of the Czech-Slovaks proceeding toward Irkutsk. . . ." An attempt to re-establish the Eastern Front was out; and the American government would explain clearly that there would be no interference in Russian internal affairs nor impairment of Russia's political or territorial sovereignty.[23] Wilson presumably hoped that this would restrain Japanese ambitions. During this summer, incidentally, his advisor, Colonel House, told the Russian ambassador, "We feel that unless we send some troops over there, there will be no deterrent for Japan."[24]

The cabinet members approved the proposal; but when the President turned to March, he saw him shaking his head vigorously. "Why are you shaking your head, General?" He continued, answering his own question, "You are opposed to this because you do not think Japan will limit herself to 7000 men, and that this decision will further her schemes for territorial aggrandizement." March agreed: "Just that, and for other military reasons which I have already told you." Wilson commented, "Well, we will have to take that chance."[25] He had crossed the Rubicon. The Chief of Staff now must bring the expedition into being. Since the plan was already prepared, all March had to do was await the signal to put it into operation.

On July 17, the President issued, but not for publication, his Aide Memoire which described the government's intentions. To protect war stores and to aid the Czechs were the key reasons for Russian intervention.[26] That same day The Adjutant General telegraphed William S. Graves, who had recently become a major general and had received command of the Eighth Division at Camp Fremont, California, to select 5000 of his best trained men for service in Siberia. Quartermaster and ordnance supplies were being collected at the San Francisco supply depot, he was further informed. Instructed to observe the "utmost secrecy," the former Assistant to the Chief of Staff was also asked for recommendations.[27] Graves, recalling that March had told him in May that he would command such an expedition if one were sent, wired his suggestions and asked if he would be the commander.[28]

The Chief of Staff settled that matter when he went to Baker to tell him that all was in readiness. Three officers had previously applied for the command – Brigadier Generals (by this time Major Generals) E. F. Glenn and James Parker, as early as the summer of 1917, and, most recently, General Crowder, but March wanted Graves, whom he knew to be "loyal, level-headed, and firm." When he mentioned Graves' name, Secretary Baker approved: "Just the man."[29]

Since the Secretary had been interested in visiting Fort Leavenworth, where many conscientious objectors were imprisoned, he decided to go to Kansas and to visit the prison, using this as an opportunity to talk with Graves and personally to give him instructions. The division commander journeyed to Kansas City with orders to meet the Secretary at the Baltimore Hotel. Thinking that he would receive the Siberian command, Graves crossed half of the continent to the rendezvous. Unfortunately, his train being late, he was able to talk only a few minutes with the Secretary in the train station. Baker told him that he was to take command, handed him the Aide Memoire, and warned: "Watch your step; you will be walking on eggs loaded with dynamite." [30]

Graves read the policy document and pondered his assignment. He wondered why virtually nothing had been said about what was going on in Siberia at the time. The Secretary did furnish this much: the Japanese had already given the dynamite in the fragile eggshells a vigorous shake when they announced that they would not abide by the numerical limit suggested by Wilson.[31] On the morning of July 8, Viscount Ishii, the Japanese Ambassador, told Lansing that he was sure that his government would abide by the 7000 limit; however, sixteen days later his government evidently surprised him by insisting that at least a division (12,000 men) would go, and more if the situation demanded.[32] March's prophecy was materializing.

There was no turning back now, although the Chief of Staff was furious, believing that the Japanese would work the intervention for every advantage. At the same time the War Department assigned command of the expedition to Graves, it issued orders which established the force. The two regiments in the Philippine Islands were to proceed to Vladivostok; Graves was to form a staff, select 5000 men and sail with the first contingent; and the supply bureaus were to give priority to equipping the replacements. Supply matters were to be handled between San Francisco, rather than Washington, and Vladivostok, although the Philippine Department must manage initial supply.[33] The combined American contingents from the Philippines and the United States, totalling 296 officers and 9056 men, numbered well over the original limit.[34]

By August 16, the first elements of this force had arrived in Vladivostok. They consisted of 53 officers and 1537 men, led by Colonel Henry D. Styer, a West Pointer who had recently lost his star and was now commanding the Twenty-seventh Infantry. Four days later General K. Otani of the Japanese Army arrived, assumed command of the Allied force, and informed Styer that the present forces were "insufficient" to accomplish the mission of extricating the Czechs. By this time General Graves was en route on the transport *Thomas* with the first detachment of reinforcements from the United States.[35]

On his arrival in Vladivostok on September 2, Graves conferred with

Admiral Austin M. Knight, commanding the United States naval forces, and hurried off to see General Otani. In this first talk with the Japanese commander, Graves made it clear that no orders would be given for the American troops without his authority. After discussing the general problems, Graves cabled the War Department that the conditions in regard to the Czechs were "very satisfactory."[36] However, the American Ambassador to Japan, Roland S. Morris, who was in Siberia investigating the situation was hearing another side of the story. The Czechs, it seemed, were very much involved fighting the Bolsheviks in western Siberia. Morris recommended that American troops move to the vicinity of Omsk, some 2000 miles west of Vladivostok, to aid these men.[37] Graves, after he heard of this, cabled his own recommendation on September 11 that the bulk of his command be sent west of the Urals. If this plan was approved, he would need some more troops – a cavalry regiment and all of the field artillery and engineers in the Philippines. As an alternative, the expedition commander proposed distributing this command along the railroad.[38]

This struck a nerve. The fear of being drawn more and more into Russian affairs, with proportionate increases in the number of men, had impressed Baker in particular. At the same time Graves' recommendations were received, the Allies were appealing for more American troops to go to north Russia. On the afternoon of the twenty-fifth, March joined Wilson and Lansing in conferring about the various requests. They decided to make a definite announcement to the Allies that the United States would not send any more troops to Russia.[39] Two days later, March informed Graves that Omsk was out; under no circumstances was he to send any of his men west of Lake Baikal, but he could use his discretion in stationing men along the railroad.[40]

Graves' desire to enlarge his force and to project it into western Siberia almost cost him his post. When Baker returned from Europe and read, with March, the cables from Siberia, he recommended the general's removal to Wilson, but nothing came of this advice.[41] Actually, the expedition commander was operating under great disadvantages. The situation he walked into was difficult indeed, with the various Russian factions, the Czechs, the increasing Japanese force, and the agitation of the other Allies. To complicate matters, he had no background information on the situation other than that the Japanese would exceed the numerical limit and that they would probably try to play off the various Russian parties against each other in an attempt to prevent the establishment of a strong central authority. But he had no yardstick to evaluate the scanty information on Japanese numbers and presumed policy. March and his staff could be of little help in providing background information since they probably knew little more themselves. March had commented earlier on this lack of information in a letter to Bliss: "it is extremely difficult to see the light of day in a heaven so completely obscured as this is." [42] Looking back on his experiences, Graves concluded that at times "ignorance was not only bliss in such a situation, but was advisable." [43]

During the fall the American commander was fast becoming disillusioned with the Allies. After making an inspection trip along the railroad in October, he was certain that the Japanese had, rather than 12,000, some 60,000 men in their contingent. He was aware also that they were spending large amounts of money, bribing leaders of various Russian factions. Neither were the other Allies, represented by much smaller forces, intent on helping Russia, he then knew.[44] When the Armistice was signed, the situation was much as March had anticipated: the intervention had contributed nothing to the war effort, and the Japanese were perverting it to their own use.

9 · MARCH AND PERSHING: THE FRICTION OF WAR

PERSHING's burden of responsibility increased as the AEF grew. Until late spring of 1918, the major demands upon him were administrative and diplomatic; but as American troops went into battle, there was the additional mission of fighting his army. Aware of the danger of becoming involved in too many fields, Pershing had talked about this problem with March and Baker earlier in the year.[1] Countering his desire to devote himself more fully to the training and fighting of his army was a strong reluctance to relinquish any part of his independence. If he gave up his logistical or diplomatic responsibility, he would then have to co-operate with whoever assumed these tasks. Some of the diplomatic load had been taken over by Bliss who officially subordinated himself to the AEF commander; [2] however, at the crucial conferences dealing with troop shipment and amalgamation, Pershing represented the United States. He understood, correctly, that the President and the Secretary of War had meant him to be supreme in France. He viewed with suspicion any move which could possibly lessen his independence.

In the spring the logistical system of the AEF staggered under the tidal wave of troops and supplies pouring into France. Ports were not being evacuated fast enough as supplies piled up in a haphazard manner. Some of the blame could be placed on methods of shipping and lack of transportation facilities. On the other hand, the need for a forceful leader was also evident. There had been three officers charged with the Line of Communications, Service of the Rear, and finally the Services of Supply – Major General Richard M. Blatchford, Brigadier General Mason M. Patrick briefly, and Major General Francis J. Kernan. The commanding general since late November, Kernan was a seasoned officer with organizational ability. In fact, it was he who wrote Secretary Baker's instructions to Pershing in May, 1917. Despite his ability, Kernan lacked the more forceful qualities of leadership which would drive his organization to the necessary heights of success.[3] This was becoming apparent at both Chaumont and Washington.

In London, the principal concern in the matter was Pershing's presence at the conference table. After the difficult session at Abbeville, Lloyd George wrote Lord Reading:

> I do not believe that we shall ever get allied arrangements working satisfactorily until there is a civilian of first rank with real powers on this side. I have not the slightest doubt, for instance, that if Colonel House had been present at the Supreme War Council meetings things would have been settled to the satisfaction not only of the British and French Governments but of the American army as well.[4]

Sir William Wiseman corroborated his chief. Pershing seemed to him to be doing too much, acting "as an American leader rather than as a soldier."[5] Indeed, Wiseman had suggested to Woodrow Wilson in January that someone in France other than Pershing be given authority to deal with supply and tonnage questions.[6]

In late May, Wiseman and the British ambassador talked with House about this problem while Wiseman also confided his views, buttressed by his account of the Abbeville conference, to the President.[7] However, Lord Reading candidly advised House that it would be a mistake to do as Wiseman and the Prime Minister requested, "because it is so evident that what Lloyd George wants is someone to over-rule Pershing."[8] Nevertheless, House was convinced that the AEF commander had "too much on his shoulders." Prior to the British proposal, he had recognized this and, just as Baker and March had done, he had talked "frankly" to Pershing about it.[9]

On June 3, the "Colonel" wrote his friend, Woodrow Wilson, another letter about the situation in France. Drawing on his own observations and those of others, House was impressed by "the lack of coordination of our interests in France." He had come to the conclusion that the solution must begin at the top.

> What I have in mind to suggest to you is that Pershing be relieved from all responsibility except the training and fighting of our troops. All his require-

ments for equipping and maintaining these troops should be on other shoulders.

House reasoned that Edward R. Stettinius and Vance McCormick, the newspaper publisher, Democratic party leader, and Chairman of the War Trade Board, were the men who could best take the burden from the AEF chief. Stettinius, as Assistant Secretary of War, would be in charge of "all army work behind the lines" while McCormick would be the "Chairman of the American Board Overseas" and would co-ordinate the activities of all civilian agents in Europe.[10]

The President forwarded House's letter to his Secretary of War to be analyzed. Baker talked the matter over with March. The efficiency-minded Chief of Staff readily agreed to House's idea. While in France, March had not only talked to Pershing but also to Kernan about stripping AEF Headquarters of all staff except that part concerned specifically with military operations, thus making a clear dividing line between the combat forces and the logistical units.[11] On June 8, the Secretary wrote to the President, outlining three aspects of the problem of maintaining such a large American force in Europe. The obvious one was developing and fighting the army; this, of course, was Pershing's primary function. A second aspect was that of the logistical support of the army. Since this was essentially a military task employing thousands of soldiers, Baker believed that an army officer, rather than a civilian, should handle this task, but it must be a man with "sufficient breadth of view and swiftness of decision." The builder of the Panama Canal, who had done things other than build the canal and had done them well, seemed the logical choice: "General Goethals is the one man in the Army, so far as I know of its personnel," Baker informed Wilson, "who could be surely entrusted with the task." Baker theorized that Goethals would be in a co-ordinate capacity with Pershing, hence disassociated from his control. The final aspect was the diplomatic responsibility. Vance McCormick impressed the Secretary as the right man for this assignment.[12] House, Baker, and March all agreed that something should be done to relieve Pershing of the logistical and diplomatic problems, so that he could devote himself entirely to leading the army.

The tall, ruddy-faced, efficient Goethals had an international reputation because of his success in Panama. A West Pointer, he had been an instructor at the Academy when Pershing and March were cadets. Later he had worked in the same room with these officers when all three were serving on the first General Staff; however, he was closer to

March than to Pershing. They were friends of long standing. Leaving the service as a major general in 1916, he had started a practice as a consulting engineer before he was recalled to active duty in 1917.[13] When Baker broached the subject of House's letter to March, it was natural that the Chief of Staff should recommend his friend for the job. On the afternoon Baker reported his views to Wilson, March sent for his supply chief and told him the news.[14]

Goethals was excited at the prospect of going to France. Like most officers, he did not relish the idea of spending the war in Washington. Pershing had turned down his request in August, 1917, to take charge of engineering construction in the expeditionary force, and his previous hope to command the supply forces of the AEF had been dashed in December.[15] Now, it looked as if his chance had come. March was leaving for Schenectady, New York, to receive an honorary degree from Union College. From there he would go to West Point for the graduation ceremonies, hence it would be several days before he would know the President's decision. He would be back on Thursday, June 13, then he would discuss the matter again. Meanwhile, Goethals was to pick his replacement.[16]

There was still no verdict for the impatient Goethals when March returned. In anticipation of sailing, Goethals talked over plans with Stettinius, word of whose possible transfer to France had already leaked to the press. Not knowing whether he would get the command, Goethals debated the possibilities throughout the cool days of late June. March was still encouraging, so Goethals prepared to go—getting his inoculations, packing, and making reservations to sail in the same convoy with Stettinius. Whether or not he would be co-ordinate with Pershing, and he did not know for certain what his status would be, he wanted above all to get overseas.[17] A few days before he was to sail and exactly four weeks after March had mentioned the proposal to him (July 6), Goethals was once again called into the Chief of Staff's office. It was bad news. Baker had decided to consult Pershing. After he returned to his office, Goethals wrote in his Appointment Book: "As Pershing's objections are known this put an end to any thought of going over." [18]

Contrary to this belief, the issue remained in the balance. A few days later, Brigadier General William V. Judson, March's classmate who had been in Russia, walked in and informed Goethals that he was to be trained to take over Goethals' job. With the increase in supply problems and the expectation of the new eighty- or hundred-division program then being debated, someone had to take over the AEF supply. Until Pershing answered Baker's letter, March was assuming that Goethals would be the man. Even after the receipt of the cable announcing that James G. Harbord had relieved Kernan, and the logistical organization was being straightened out, March thought that the supply situation would bring about Goethal's assignment. Finally, by the middle of August, with news of the improved system and the adamant opposition of Pershing, the last hope was gone.[19]

Regardless of the War Department's intentions, Pershing was hostile to the Goethals suggestion. Evidently, he heard the first concrete word of the plan in a letter from March, written on July 5, which he received about two weeks later. In this letter, while not mentioning Goethals by name, March had written of the three aspects of the problem (about which Baker had written Wilson on June 8), and pointed to a solution: "It seems inevitable that a subdivision of your work must be made in the near future. . . ."[20] Baker's letter, written the day after March's, must not have reached Pershing until several days later. After discussing the pros and cons of the one-hundred-division program, Baker outlined the plan of sending Goethals. Following close behind this communication was another Baker letter, dated July 7, in which the Secretary emphasized that it was only a suggestion for Pershing to judge.[21]

On the morning of July 26, the AEF commander had a long talk with Stettinius, who could give him first-hand information of War Department thinking.[22] Convinced that he must act quickly, Pershing called Harbord, who had recently moved from brigade to division command and who was now wearing two stars. Arriving at Chaumont the night of the twenty-sixth, Harbord immediately saw his chief who explained the situation. To Pershing, Goethals' coming meant dual control which would invite disaster. Besides, he considered Goethals March's choice, and did not believe that he would be so co-operative as a man of Pershing's own choosing. Having thought of replacing Kernan for some time, he had decided upon Harbord since his reputation in the Second Division, his background as chief of staff of the AEF, and the Secretary of War's fondness for him in addition to his ability would give him a strong hold on the position. Pershing would also grant him more independence than Kernan had enjoyed. The two talked far into the night about the general situation in the War Department and the Expeditionary Force and of individuals. Finally, Harbord said that he need not defer a decision; he would take the job.[23]

The next day, Pershing cabled the Secretary that he was replacing Kernan with Harbord and, in regard to the Services of Supply, warned, "Any division of responsibility or co-ordinate control in any sense would be fatal." [24] Without waiting for a reply, the field commander formally appointed Harbord two days later (July 29), going the same day with him to Tours, headquarters of the Services of Supply (S.O.S.). After conferring with the various chiefs of services there, the party went on a whirlwind tour of the ports and supply installations. For a week, Pershing and Harbord inspected the logistical system. At the end of this trip, Pershing cabled Baker: "The work accomplished surpasses all calculations and is a monument to the ability of the men who during the past year have devoted their best energies to carrying out the great plans." [25] The AEF commander was perhaps spurred to such rhetorical heights by a cable Baker had sent through State Department channels on July 30. In this message the Secretary said he agreed with the unity of control idea, but the "personnel question" was still to be considered, despite Harbord's qualifications.[26]

Pershing's pleas, fortified by the results of his inspection, were convincing as far as the Secretary of War was concerned. His cables, followed by urgent letters, kept Goethals in a Washington now sweltering under the late summer heat.[27] By August 18, the hope of going to France was, for Goethals, "a closed chapter." March appointed the waiting Judson to the post of the supply chief's Executive Assistant; and Goethals, resigned to the decision, turned again to his work.[28]

In contrast to his opposition to Goethals and a drastic supply reorganization, Pershing raised no objections to Stettinius and to being relieved of the diplomatic burden. The idea of sending McCormick was discarded, Bliss' work being satisfactory; but Baker suggested, in his letter of the sixth, that the former Chief of Staff take over more of this function. Since Pershing's diplomatic ventures had been predominantly in the now settled arguments over troop shipment and amalgamation, he approved.[29] He had found Bliss to be most co-operative, although he had originally recommended Major General Hunter Liggett for the position of military representative.[30]

The S.O.S. had a more forceful leader. Stettinius was taking over the allocation of materials and of manufacturing programs. Diplomacy was turned over to Bliss. Now Pershing could devote more time to the duties of actual warfare. March was gratified with these results, but the AEF commander was not pleased with what he believed to be March's part in these changes.[31]

Concurrent with the discussions of the hundred-division program and of the Goethals proposal, the problem of promotions came up again. The list of generals which had been in preparation since May went to the Senate on June 28. Eight officers received the War Department's recommendation for major general's rank, while forty-three were up for their first star. On July 6, the Senate confirmed these promotions, which were generally approved, according to the press.[32] When the news reached Pershing, who was visiting Hunter Liggett's First Corps at the time, he was infuriated. He had been asked early in May to recommend officers to fill six two-star vacancies and thirty-three one-star openings. In the interim he had written a letter to the Secretary which suavely pleaded preference for AEF officers. But this was to no avail; the new list excluded several of his better officers whom he had recommended. Colonels Fox Conner, Paul B. Malone, Dennis E. Nolan, and LeRoy Eltinge, he believed, had demonstrated their effectiveness and were particularly deserving.[33]

Since he was near his former chief of staff's unit on the twelfth, Pershing joined Harbord, who was among those promoted in this list, for lunch. It was their first meeting in some weeks, and Pershing took advantage of the company of his intimate adviser to vent his feelings about the new promotions. Not only were some of his recommendations not taken, but once again AEF officers were promoted whom he had not endorsed, in some cases, officers junior to those recommended. Pershing and Harbord focused their attention on March. It seemed to them that the colonels who were left off the promotion list had differed with the Chief of Staff while he was Chief of the AEF Artillery.[34]

The day after his chat with Harbord, Pershing was remorseful. Perhaps he had gone too far in criticizing March.[35] He had just received a letter from the Chief of Staff which did explain the new list, at least in part. In particular, March accounted for the non-promotion of the recommended staff officers. While the staff section heads were listed on the table of organization as brigadier generals, the AEF commander did not recommend these officers for promotion as such, merely listing their names along with the other recommendations. This had puzzled

March and Baker, who feared that the policy of rotation from staff to line, which was now being practiced, might lead either to the demotion of these officers when they left the staff or to a number of superfluous generals. Pershing could see that neither of these eventualities would be satisfactory. Also, March showed his desire for co-operation, which pleased the field commander, by asking him to send another list specifically naming the officers he wanted promoted to head his staff sections.[36] Anxious to avoid starting gossip, Pershing wrote Harbord to forget their confidential talk: after reading March's letter and reconsidering the matter, he believed that the Chief of Staff had acted with "good intentions." [37]

Thinking the topic too serious to drop, Harbord answered Pershing in a frank letter, which warned of the dangers adverse criticism within the AEF of the promotion situation represented to his position as commander of the Expeditionary Force: "Either you are unappreciative of the fine work of men around you, or if not your recommendations do not carry weight at home." [38] This letter made sense to Pershing. "Good intentions" on March's part did not outweigh the facts and the threat to Pershing's status. With the Second Division commander's letter on his mind, he wrote the Secretary of War, pointing out the difficulties ensuing from the promotions, and suggesting a basis for future promotion procedure. He emphasized particularly the undesirability of promoting younger officers in the AEF whom he had not endorsed; to make the matter more galling, some of these men were promoted in preference to recommended seniors.[39] When he wrote March a few days later, he stated four principles which be believed should be followed:

1. That men from staff departments detailed for duty in the line should be required to take their promotions along with their fellows in the line and not also be given consideration by the heads of their staff departments as staff officers. . . .
2. That no officers of the American Expeditionary Forces should be promoted to the grade of general officer without official recommendation from here. . . .
3. That officers of the American Expeditionary Forces recommended for promotion to the grade of general officers should be given consideration in preference to any of their juniors serving in the States or with the American Expeditionary Forces. . . .
4. That vacancies occurring here in the grade of general officer should as far as possible be filled at once by officers serving with the A.E.F., upon the recommendation from here.[40]

Still worrying, Pershing wrote another letter to Baker, reiterating his plea for a re-examination of the advancements. To reinforce his request, he specifically named March as the culprit in the affair.[41]

Aware of the commotion the promotions were causing, but evidently not of Pershing's personal comments to Baker, March carefully went over the entire promotion problem in an August letter to the AEF commander. The solution, he believed, had been reached by establishing the policy of selection rather than seniority. As he wrote Pershing, "I suppose that the advocates of seniority rage but I am too busy even to hear them. The only thing that counts with me is results."[42] Neither he nor Pershing seemed to understand what the other meant by the terms selection and seniority. Both thought they were using the selection system, but Pershing considered seniority in his selective system to a greater extent than did March. The Chief of Staff continued his letter by discussing two other complicating factors: the necessity, proven by past experience, for giving the command of field artillery brigades to officers of that branch, and the custom of not returning some of the new AEF generals to fill vacancies in recently created units added to the difficulty of establishing a workable, satisfactory system. The new organizations were lacking general officers during the crucial formative period. March had made a move in the direction of solving the field artillery promotion issue by giving the Chief of Field Artillery the authority to recommend deserving officers.[43] The other matter would be up to the field commander.

If March hoped his letter would bring an end to the promotion debate, he was disappointed. The list of promotions published in late August, like its predecessors, provoked Pershing. While the AEF commander's recommendations for his staff section chiefs were confirmed, Colonel Paul B. Malone, a former section chief now commanding an infantry brigade, was omitted again and several other unrecommended officers were included. Malone, as chief of the training section (G-5) in the fall of 1917, had clashed with March over some aspect of the artillery training program. Now Pershing was convinced that, as he recorded in his diary, "The question of promotions involves some transactions on the part of the Chief of Staff at Washington which I am afraid would not look well in the light of an honest investigation."[44] To make matters worse, there was a shortage of brigadier generals to command brigades. Although March had told him to submit recommendations in anticipation of more frequent appointments, it would not mean much unless these recommendations were followed. He cabled a strong recommendation of Malone and asked that this be brought to Baker's attention.[45]

March promptly answered that the Secretary had seen all of Pershing's cables and had personally considered Malone's case, but that his work on the AEF staff did not rate advancement as far as the Chief of Staff was concerned. However, he would reconsider this case in light of the colonel's accomplishments as a brigade commander.[46] Malone received his long awaited star in the next list.[47]

When Baker visited France in September, Harbord expounded to him the complaints about promotions. The S.O.S. chief, with a jaw as square as Pershing's, minced no words in describing the situation and criticizing General March. The Secretary remembered that one AEF officer, Douglas MacArthur, had been promoted without Pershing's recommendation, but Harbord named others. This was displeasing to Baker, who promised that there would be no more of it.[48] Before the Secretary returned to the United States, the next list was issued. Pershing read it and noted, "some appointments have been made from AEF which were not recommended by me."[49] Also, about half of the new ranks were distributed to officers in the United States. In the few weeks until the Armistice, Pershing continued sending recommendations, but there were no more promotion lists. The day after the end of the war, March cabled that it had been decided not to promote any more general officers for the period of the emergency.[50] The war was over, and with it rapid promotion for regular officers. Remaining on the part of Pershing and some of his subordinates was a strong sense of irritation toward the Chief of Staff.

The promotion issue and the Goethals affair assumed a different, more important meaning, when considered in connection with the March-Pershing relationship. This impressed Baker during his hour-long chat with Harbord in September. The S.O.S. chief, who did not like March and who had been suspicious of the former Chief of Artillery ever since he had returned to the United States to become Chief of Staff, combined his personal attitude with the issues to form a strong criticism of March. The crux of the discussion was the unconfirmed report that the Chief of Staff wanted to succeed Pershing. Baker soothed

Harbord's fears by promising that he would tell March that the AEF commander's successor, if one were made necessary by death or disability, would be picked from officers in France.[51]

The Secretary knew that his Chief of Staff's ruthless drive for efficiency tended to hurt people's feelings. Pershing, accustomed to a large degree of independence had complained forcefully in letters about March's manner. In late July, the disgruntled commander had pointed out that the Chief of Staff was assuming a curt, commanding tone in his cables.[52] This tone gave the impression of a superior, and the Chief of Staff was not that, in the eyes of Pershing. The promotion method and the Goethals matter, which he had heard March wanted to order outright, accentuated his annoyance.

In the middle of August, Pershing's exasperation drove him to drastic measures. While in this mood, he wrote Baker, discussing the lack of co-operation between his headquarters and the General Staff in Washington. There was energy enough, but it seemed to him misdirected. A faulty General Staff organization might be the cause, he suggested, but teamwork was lacking. On the other hand, perhaps a change in leadership could lead to better relations. Pershing broached the subject:

> I have at times doubted whether you will get it [General Staff] going smoothly without taking someone who has actually gone through this organization here from beginning to end, as you know this is the only General Staff organization that our army has ever had. All this comes to my mind following the idea of an occasional change, of which you spoke when here as being your intention.[53]

The AEF chief, cautiously covering the mailed fist with the velvet glove, was pushing his prerogative to the extreme. Baker, who was well aware of March's accomplishments, did not act upon Pershing's advice. When the Chief of Staff learned of this letter after the war, he was infuriated. If he had known of it at the time, he declared that there would have been a "showdown." [54]

Pershing could certainly tell the difference in the operation of the War Department General Staff even if he disdainfully refused to recognize it as a General Staff organization. The aggressive March was pushing men and material overseas in quantities that would have been unbelievable earlier. But in the process of building up the General Staff in Washington, March was augmenting the role of the Chief of Staff, something that Bliss and Biddle had not done. Baker had granted

Pershing broad, independent powers as the expedition's commander. The other Chiefs of Staff had accepted their supporting roles, but March grasped the full meaning of the position of the Chief of Staff and the General Staff. Nevertheless, precedent in the American army was against him.[55]

The other Chiefs of Staff, dealing with a war situation for the first time, acknowledged Pershing's special powers. Bliss, for one, thought of his function as Chief of Staff as, "Except in name, the latter [Chief of Staff] was an Assistant Chief of Staff to the Chief of Staff of the AEF."[56] March would have none of that. Support Pershing, yes, but this did not necessarily mean emasculating the power of the office of Chief of Staff. Originally created to be the instrument through which the President and Secretary of War controlled the army, the position was supposed to carry with it supervisory power over the line as well as the staff. His service on the first General Staff, reinforced by his observation of the Japanese Army, convinced March that the Chief of Staff was the keystone of a modern army. As head of the military establishment, in addition to being Chief of the General Staff, the Chief of Staff, properly and of necessity, should make "many decisions about administrative and other matters which do not strictly pertain to real General Staff work."[57] To establish clearly this concept, March issued General Order # 80 in late August. The Chief of Staff "is the immediate adviser of the Secretary of War . . . and is charged by the Secretary of War with the planning, development, and execution of the Army program." The order provided the authority to balance with the responsibility by stating that this officer "takes rank and precedence over all officers of the Army. . . ."[58]

The February reorganization had not gone this far. While assigning the same mission to the Chief of Staff, it had qualified his position by adding that he was to be assisted by the War Council. Neither did the earlier order specify that rank and precedence should go to that officer. Similar rank would be held by the Chief of Staff and the field commander, according to a Senate act passed in October, 1917. Technically, since orders were issued throughout the army over the signature of the Chief of Staff, it could be argued that he was superior to the AEF commander; nevertheless, in practice, Pershing was supreme in France: President Wilson and Secretary Baker had taken advantage of Article # 761 of the Army Regulations, which authorized the Chief Executive to place part or all of the army under a single commander, "subordinate to his [the President's] general command," to give him that power.[59]

Coming into a situation set by nine months of operating under this system, March was hamstrung in effecting his concept. The duality of control with the Chief of Staff supreme in the United States, but charged with supporting a field commander dominant overseas, did not impress March as being the most effective way of fighting a war. The direct line of command from the President to the field commander, in effect, meant two military men of equal rank subject to the final authority of the civilian head of government. As March knew, the same Army Regulation under which this expedient arrangement was devised also stated, "The President's command is exercised through the Secretary of War and the Chief of Staff."[60] Logically, there should be one man advising the civilian executives at the apex of the military hierarchy. The proper sphere of a commander was to train and to lead his troops in battle. Within this area, March could understand the value of allowing Pershing broad discretion, and he certainly would not interfere with the actual strategy and tactics involved. But Pershing had virtually become the nation's top soldier during the months prior to March, 1918. Firmly entrenched in his jurisdiction, Pershing could argue that any attempt to limit his power, as in the Goethals case, would disrupt the entire AEF structure, developed under this arrangement. In turn, he also used the argument of dual control against the withdrawal of his logistical support from under his command.

"Pride of position,"[61] which is strong in military life, also undoubtedly played a part in Pershing's protests against what he viewed as encroachments on his authority. He believed that there should be no intermediary between himself and the civilian executives. Then, too, ambition for higher command could have occupied Pershing's thoughts. During the Meuse-Argonne campaign, he told Moseley, his G-4 (supply section chief), that when the United States had more troops at the front than any other ally, "then command should go to an American."[62] Naturally, pride was probably just as strong on March's part; however, Secretary Baker, having made the arrangement, supported Pershing in his belief. As far as Baker was concerned, March headed the army in the United States and had the mission of supplying men and material to Pershing who was supreme overseas. A controversy over whether or not the Chief of Staff was superior to the AEF commander was, in Baker's view, "purely technical" and "unimportant."[63] While he might assent to relieving Pershing of some of his burden, he would not carry out the project without the AEF commander's approval. Even then, his reason was to enhance Pershing's prestige as a combat commander. Somewhat naively, Baker, thinking of the Civil War, wanted to build up the image of Pershing as "our great fighting soldier" in the public view, as well as in his own.[64]

Adding to the complications of the relationship of Baker's two military chiefs was a rumor, particularly strong in France, that March wanted to succeed Pershing as commander of the Expeditionary Force. With this in mind, Pershing and his advisers considered the Goethals proposal as a part of the alleged plot. As early as April, the *New York Times* reported two rumors going the rounds in Washington: one was that March was dissatisfied and wanted field command, while the other suggested that Goethals might be going to France; however, the newspaper considered both groundless.[65] Leonard Wood heard, in late September, that there was friction between March and Pershing and that March hoped to relieve Pershing.[66] Returning visitors and officers from the AEF reported the extent the story had reached overseas. Major Frederick Palmer was certain that it was true.[67] Paul D. Cravath, a lawyer who had served on various missions in France, repeated it to Goethals. The supply chief, upon hearing the story and his supposed part in the scheme, squashed it: "So far as I am concerned it's without foundation," and concluded, "Well there's always a lot of gossip in the army with plenty of jealousy scattered loose."[68]

March later affirmed, "There never was any consideration given the question of a successor of General Pershing during my entire tour as Chief of Staff of the army, as far as I am aware. . . ."[69] At least two proposals were made on the part of the Allies but neither reached the War Department. In June, 1918, Jan Christian Smuts, the South African soldier-statesman made one, as he recommended himself to command the combat elements of the AEF while relegating the logistical command to Pershing, but Lloyd George stifled this proposition.[70] Clemenceau made the other in the midst of the nerve-wracking Argonne offensive, when the American attack was not moving as fast as he wanted. The Tiger of France also complained to Colonel House that "it was like going up against granite to get him [Pershing] to accept advice from Foch"; but Generalissimo Foch refused to support any move against the American commander.[71]

Stories have multiplied since World War I about the so-called feud between March and Pershing. During the war there were differences, some of which were not worked out, but the legend outstrips the facts. The cables and Pershing's letters reflect dissension, but the March-Pershing wartime correspondence, although revealing disagreements, maintains throughout a friendly tone. Here were two men, both strong personalities, installed in positions and involved in a situation which invited trouble. Add the tension, the continual crises, and the awesome responsibilities of war to the traditional conflict between the line and the staff and the lack of a General Staff tradition, and friction becomes a natural result.

10 · THE WAR DEPARTMENT STRIPS FOR ACTION

As the nation prepared for a greater war effort, March reorganized the General Staff and dealt summarily with vestiges of bureau power. He created organizations and abolished others within the War Department and he unified the separate elements of the army. Almost hidden by the large issues were the smaller problems which he had to solve as a part of his daily routine. Many decisions took their toll in injured feelings but the dominant factor for March was efficiency and he worked relentlessly toward that goal.

A frail, balding general, hobbling with the aid of crutches down the corridor toward the Secretary of War's office, was a familiar sight on the second floor of the State, War, and Navy Building in 1917. His appearance would seem to indicate that Enoch H. Crowder might better be on the retirement list than bearing the tremendous burden of administering the draft, but his sharp eyes revealed the force within this man. "Quick-tempered and highly sensitive," one of the most powerful men in the War Department, Crowder was a "brilliant lawyer" with broad experience in administration gained in the Philippines and in Washington, where he had been Judge Advocate General since 1911.[1]

As the army's chief legal officer, this "hard, prodigious worker"[2] wielded great influence, particularly in legislative matters, but he did not use his power constructively in the opinion of more progressive General Staff officers. In particular, Crowder "believed that the War Department should be run by the chiefs of the bureaus," hence he "was a foe of the General Staff." [3] A captain commented in 1915, that the Judge Advocate General was, "a positive obstruction to all constructive legislation." [4] The most glaring example of Crowder's attitude was his interpretation of the section referring to the General Staff in the National Defense Act of 1916. He seized upon this to re-establish the legal right of bureau control while relegating the Chief of Staff and the General Staff to a rather innocuous general planning role. Hugh L. Scott, who was the Chief of Staff at the time, took Crowder's opinion to Secretary Baker with the comment, "Mr. Secretary, I am handing you a case that will be the most important decision that you will ever have to make in that chair." [5] Baker, who had been in office less than five months, took the opinion, studied it and others as well as the Congressional hearing relevant to the founding of the General Staff. After carefully analyzing the various documents, he reached the conclusion that Crowder was wrong: the act did not emasculate the power of the Chief of Staff and the General Staff. In making this decision, Baker struck, in March's view, "the first blow toward the successful prosecution of the war." [6]

Early the next February, the day after the diplomatic break with Germany, President Wilson paid a surprise visit to the War Department. When he had gone, Baker called in Crowder and told him that Wilson had decided to use conscription to help raise the army in case war came. With the help of his assistants, Crowder prepared a plan which became, seven weeks after the beginning of the war, the draft law. The Secretary of War then turned over the administration of the selective service system to Crowder, with the title of Provost Marshal General. Operating, in a time of emergency, an unusual system, involving many civilians who manned the local boards, gave a large measure of autonomy to Crowder.[7]

By August, when conscription was well under way, Crowder was anxious to command one of the new divisions. A decision not to grant command positions on the basis of bureau service thwarted his desire.[8] Nursing his injured pride, the Provost Marshal General continued in Washington. With the departure of Bliss, he assumed increased power as an advisor to the Secretary of War. It was he with whom Baker talked about the proposed War Council, which Crowder envisioned as an instrument of bureau control.[9] Although the body was created and he was given a place on it, it never developed into the powerful organization of his plans. Despite his growing importance in Washington and his promotion to major general, the former Indian fighter still sought duty in France. Early in 1918, he poured out his feeling to his fellow Missourian and friend, Pershing, "For God [*sic*] sake do not let me get side tracked for this war. I will accept demotion down to Capt to get a chance."[10]

While his chances for overseas service were almost non-existent, there was a faint hope, in view of the rapid turn-over in the office of the Chief of Staff, that Crowder might achieve that position. At least Colonel Hugh S. Johnson, his loyal assistant, proposed his name in late January. Since March had already been recalled, Johnson suggested detailing March as Assistant Chief of Staff. His main point was that the Provost Marshal General was better known to the public and was "the greatest administrator, organizer and executive" available.[11] In this same period, Supreme Court Justice Louis Brandeis recommended that Crowder be named Acting Secretary of War during Baker's planned trip to France.[12] But Baker was not receptive to either of these proposals. Benedict Crowell, the Assistant Secretary who did act as Secretary in Baker's absence, later commented that the move to make Crowder Chief of Staff actually meant abolishing the position altogether.[13] Since Baker wanted March, Crowder had to be satisfied with his present work.

Frustrated and somewhat bitter, Crowder awaited with apprehension the arrival of March. They had served together previously on several occasions but Crowder had always held superior rank. During the early months of the war, March's rank caught up with Crowder's; now, as Acting Chief of Staff, he was superior to the Provost Marshal General. To have a one-time subordinate overtaking and passing a former senior, then serving with him, can lead to a difficult situation. In this case, trouble was even more apt to result because of the two men's strong characters and their opposing views of General Staff power.

On March's first morning in office, he met with the War Council and, presumably, saw Crowder. Later, at the regular Monday morning conference with the Secretaries and the bureau chiefs, he had occasion to meet the Provost Marshal General. The virtual autonomy of the selective service system probably irritated him; even though he was invited to inspect the bureau, he never did.[14] Non-interference with subordinates as long as he thought they were doing their job properly was one of his characteristics. Relations between the two officers were good at first. Crowder was pleased with March's "quick decisions" and told him so.[15]

With the plans for a larger army and the promulgation of the "Work or Fight" order, Crowder's name became an even more familiar one to newspaper readers in the spring. Then, in late June, while the Senate was debating the army appropriations bill, Senator Kenneth McKellar proposed rewarding the Provost Marshal General with promotion to lieutenant general. This suggestion was greeted enthusiastically, and an amendment providing for the increase in rank was added to the bill. Crowder, however, requested that the amendment be withdrawn, arguing that the local boards deserved the credit for the draft's success.[16]

Ten days after he turned down the promotion, he got an opportunity for overseas duty. March informed him that he was sending him on a special mission to Switzerland. Although the Provost Marshal General was still eager for foreign service, he believed that his work with the selective service was of more importance than going on this mission, and asked for a reconsideration. Not wanting to send him if he did not wish to go, the Chief of Staff replied that he would not be sent. "You were selected for this confidential detail," March explained, "because you have repeatedly expressed a desire to go abroad in any capacity."[17]

Then in late July, the new order of things in the War Department reached the Provost Marshal General. March wrote a strong memorandum to Crowder, directing him to stop sending out circulars on the subject of preliminary training for inductees and informing local officials of future quotas, because in so doing, his bureau was infringing on the jurisdiction of the General Staff. While the term "reprimand" was not used in the memorandum, the *Resumé of the Day's Work*, a mimeographed information pamphlet circulated within the General Staff, so described it.[18]

Crowder, his pride injured, hastened to answer the directive in a nine-and-a-half page, single-spaced typewritten rebuttal. Emphasizing the relationship with civilians and the previous bypassing of the Chief of Staff, the Provost Marshal General warned that if General Staff control were allowed, it would mean the virtual ruin of the selective service program. In reference to the two specific points of training and quota information, he pointed out that the first was minor and could be "disregarded" while the second actually was not an attempt to formulate military policy but merely an aid to the local authorities; besides, he wrote, March had been misinformed on the latter point.[19]

As he forwarded the lengthy communication to the Secretary, March stated his view on the case: it was a clear example of the bureau versus General Staff argument. Crowder represented a system which was anachronistic. In order to operate a modern war machine, General Staff supremacy must be maintained. There was no place for independent segments. The army was a whole, and its guidance should come from only one source.

> The fact is that all nations of the world are efficient in a military sense in proportion to their adoption of complete supervision of military activities by their General Staffs. And during this war this fundamental and imperative requirement has been revealed to such a degree that all the Allies have and will have no other system. Anything else means failure and disaster.[20]

March concluded this brief explanation of his action with a strong reaffirmation of his belief in General Staff control.

> If a Chief of Staff is a weak man, and the results obtained by his supervision are not satisfactory to the Secretary of War, the remedy is not to break down his authority and invest subordinates with that authority. The answer is to get a new Chief of Staff who can handle the job.[21]

While this struggle for power was going on within the War Department, all concerned were presenting a united front to the public. During the first days of August, March, Crowder, and Baker appeared before the Senate Military Affairs Committee, testifying in favor of an expansion of the draft limits. In order to send eighty divisions to France, they explained that the ages of availability must be extended from eighteen to forty-five.[22] Meantime, the two generals awaited the Secretary's decision on their arguments.

Baker mulled over his dilemma. As in the case of Pershing, he had created the problem himself by granting so much independence to a subordinate. Again, Bliss and Biddle had acquiesced, to the detriment of the General Staff theory. More firmly convinced of the value of General Staff control, March fought the infringements upon his jurisdiction. Yet what could the Secretary do? In both matters, he had maintained this bypassing of the Chief of Staff throughout the war. The personalities of the two opponents added to the difficulty of decision. Although he admired both men very much, he knew that March's ruthless manner injured much less sensitive souls than Crowder, whose pride, he realized, was easily hurt. After almost a month of contemplation, he made his decision shortly before he left for France.

The Secretary agreed that Crowder was correct in asserting that precedent was on his side. He and the Provost Marshal General had maintained a direct relationship. This arrangement he hoped to maintain in order that the selective service system should be considered largely a civilian matter, with a civilian official as the "court of last resort." In fact, Baker interpreted March as agreeing with the idea of civilian control. On the other hand, when the Provost Marshal General moved beyond the restrictions of administering the draft, he was to be considered a bureau chief and was thus "subject to the coordinating direction of the Chief of Staff." If the original orders to the Provost Marshal General had been more explicit, Baker believed that the present situation would not have arisen. Now, he was outlining the necessary jurisdictional limits. In regard to the "civilian part" of his duties, Crowder would be under the "direct guidance" of the Secretary, but in military matters, he would be subject to the "coordinating direction of the General Staff," hence the Chief of Staff. As to the specific question of training—the training circulars must be submitted to the General Staff for its concurrence. The policy problem should be worked out between the two generals.[23]

Baker had not slapped down his Provost Marshal General. On the contrary, he had corroborated him and even praised him. Nevertheless, he had set definite restrictions on Crowder's authority. March forwarded the paper with curt instructions to submit the material on pre-induction training for General Staff examination.[24] By this time, Crowder had entered another plea. The *Resumé* which referred to the original action as a reprimand had come to his attention. He wanted the Secretary to print in the *Resumé* a lengthy disapproval of March's move, including a statement that the Provost Marshal General did not have to recall for General Staff inspection training material already issued. When he received Baker's verdict, he sent the offending documents to the General Staff, but protested the drawing of a jurisdictional line between his office and that of the Chief of Staff. Since Baker was en route to Europe, Crowder reiterated his objection to the *Resumé* entry to the Chief of Staff and requested a Court of Inquiry to pass upon the justification of the reprimand. He pointed out that March had never taken up the dispute with him personally, but he ended the memorandum on the apologetic note that lack of regular officers in his bureau led to innocent violations of authority.[25]

Two months later, Baker, back from France some five weeks, wrote Crowder that he had not been reprimanded. To assuage his feelings, an item stating that the Chief of Staff's note was not a reprimand was put in the *Resumé* two days after the war's end.[26] Yet if Crowder thought he was triumphant in his encounter with March, he would have to admit it was a hollow victory. No longer was he within the inner circle of planners, as he complained to Pershing, "Circumstances have arisen . . . which deny me that knowledge of the home situation that would make it possible for me to write in any detail of what is going on here." In fact, he was worried over whether or not he would retain his old post of Judge Advocate General after the detail expired the coming February.[27] While he could not touch Crowder's power in quasi-civilian matters, March had succeeded in reaffirming General Staff supremacy in military affairs.

In the midst of the conflict between Crowder and March, another bureau chief was impressed with the Chief of Staff's methods. Henry P. McCain had been a first classman (senior) at the Academy while March was a fourth classman (freshman). Some thirty years later when March was serving in the Adjutant General's department, McCain had been The Adjutant General. In this office, McCain held to "the Ainsworth idea of The Adjutant General's Department's place in the army." [28] As in Crowder's case, when war came a one-time subordinate now ranked a former superior. Evidently, McCain and March got along well during the first few months, but, in at least one instance, The Adjutant General irritated his former subordinate.

The Chief of Staff was going over some routine papers with an officer from the Executive Assistant's office when Major General McCain came in unannounced through the hall door rather than through the Secretary of the General Staff's office. The Adjutant General interrupted, presented his problem, then walked over to the window and told a funny story. Joking, March thought, was out of place at a time like this. After The Adjutant General had gone, the Chief of Staff commented to the waiting colonel, "Some people don't realize a war is on — suppose I shall have to keep that door locked." [29]

McCain's regular tour as The Adjutant General was coming to an end in late August. During his tenure of four years, he had supervised the avalanche of wartime correspondence which passed through his department. As a mark of official approval, he expected a re-appointment. Abruptly, late on a Saturday afternoon, about ten days before his detail ended, he received orders from March to leave at once to take command of the Twelfth Division at Camp Devens, Massachusetts. Shocked and somewhat humiliated by the manner in which he was given his orders, McCain asked for a two-day respite, which was granted.[30]

In his press conference held the same day (August 17), March announced that The Adjutant General was "extremely anxious" for field command and that the division was "a reward for good service." [31] When he broke the news to McCain, he did not give him this reassurance. War Department rumor, as recounted by Crowder to Goethals, held that not only did McCain not want a division command but also that he had requested a demotion to colonel with the hope of staying in Adjutant General work since he felt better qualified in the area.[32] Upon leaving his office, he would be demoted to a regular colonelcy anyway, since the two-star rank was inherent in the post. By going to a division, he would still be a major general but on a temporary basis. This fact was not lost on him or on others, particularly since Sharpe and Crozier, other former bureau chiefs, had been recently given permanent major generalcies. And they were considered inefficient. Nursing his hurt pride, McCain assumed command of his division and, once in the unit, seemed to enjoy his work.[33]

To fill the vacancy, March called on a West Point classmate, Brigadier General Peter C. Harris, a records expert, who had worked out a more efficient system to replace the awkward muster roll. Not a long-time bureau officer, Harris, "a little bit of a man physically," [34] was an infantryman who had served a four-year tour on the General Staff before he was detailed to The Adjutant General's department in 1914.[35] Here was a man more to March's liking than one steeped in bureau background.

Later in August, the Chief of Staff sought to alleviate another bureau problem. Under existing law, the field of selection for bureau chiefs was limited to officers above the rank of major who had served at least four years in the particular corps or department. At this time, that meant that only one officer was eligible in one department while but three were legally available in another. March advocated extending the eligibility lists to include all officers who were permanently assigned to the particular bureau or who had served or was serving on detail in that staff corps or department. Despite the endorsement of Baker and Crowell, the necessary legislation did not receive congressional support.[36]

Where the General Staff was concerned, March did not have to worry about legislative sanction. Here he moved inexorably toward a more efficient instrument of war. Early in July, he wrote Bliss, "The reorganization of the War Department is about reaching a point where the machine is completely in hand." [37] The culmination of this rebuilding was a General Order, issued on August 26, which rescinded the reorganization order of the past February. This new order firmly delineated the positions of the Chief of Staff and the General Staff. March, after gaining Baker's approval, directed that the Chief of Staff, as the "immediate adviser of the Secretary of War on all matters relating to the Military Establishment," be given the responsibility for carrying out the army program, and the commensurate rank and authority. By this time, the War Council, which had been assigned the mission of assisting the Chief of Staff, had been abolished.

General Order # 80 went on to describe the functions of the four divisions of the General Staff. This order carried over two of the divisions from the February reorganization – War Plans and Operations. A third – Purchase, Storage, and Traffic – was a combination of the February divisions, Purchase and Supply, and Storage and Traffic.[38] The Executive Division was abolished and the Military Intelligence Division was created.

The Executive Assistant, although his division no longer existed, remained a key figure in the War Department. As the title implied, he was the principal assistant to the Chief of Staff and acted in that position when March was absent. General Graves held this office originally. After his promotion and departure from Washington in July, he was replaced by Major General Frank McIntyre, an Academy classmate of Pershing's, who had served on the first General Staff with March. Like Graves, McIntyre was personally close to March. Then, his background as Chief of the Bureau of Insular Affairs had given him a broad knowledge of governmental affairs. Tactful, dignified, charming, a fluent and convincing conversationalist, McIntyre evidently acted as a buffer for March. When asked a question requiring consideration, he would take off his glasses, twirl them around, look up at the lenses, then look at the inquirer, and give the answer and, as one of his principal subordinates, Colonel George W. Cocheu, commented, "the result ten years from now."[39]

The Operations Division, still under the directorship of Henry Jervey, March expected to be responsible for military matters other than supply. In order to achieve this mission, he assigned to it the additional functions of handling commissioned personnel and motor transportation. To carry out the first function, he established a Personnel Branch in September. This organization had the responsibility for the procurement, distribution, and promotion of officers. Since this meant that a centralized group would begin operation, March abolished the personnel branches of the various staff corps and departments. He promoted Percy P. Bishop, the Secretary of the General Staff, to brigadier general and placed him in charge of this branch. This was an advance in the field of effective utilization of officers, as well as in the area of centralized General Staff control.[40]

Motor transportation was also managed by a subordinate branch – the Motor Transport Corps. Pershing and Palmer Pierce had earlier suggested such an organization. In fact, a Motor Transport Service had been developed during the spring. March created this Corps eleven days before the publication of General Order # 80. The Chief of Staff picked Colonel Charles B. Drake, a former cavalry and quartermaster officer, to take charge of this unit, which controlled the design, procurement, storage, operation, and repair of the army's motor vehicles, in addition to the procurement, organization, and technical training of the personnel they required.[41]

The able Lytle Brown continued as the Chief of the War Plans Division. Other than losing to the Operations Division its Equipment Committee, War Plans did not change; it still maintained the primary function of planning, with the concurrent duty of supervising the army's training program. Two subordinate branches drafted proposed military legislation and collected records of historical interest, while an Inventions Section examined the large number of inventions which a war-alert public sent into the War Department.[42]

The third General Staff division – Purchase, Storage, and Traffic – controlled supplies. Goethals, now somewhat reconciled to staying in Washington, held the reins in this organization. Receiving the army program from the Operations Division, the P.S.&T., as it was abbreviated, dictated the requirements to the supply bureaus. The procurement, custody, and distribution of war material, with the exception of a few highly technical items, was its dominion. In a sense, the section of the General Order referring to this supply body clarified the General Staff's position as the controlling agent within the army.[43]

The division newly created in this reorganization, the Military Intelligence Division, had come a long way since the beginning of the war. At that time it was a section, consisting of two officers and two civilian clerks, in the War College Division. Before the Armistice, it would number 282 officers, 29 non-commissioned officers, and 948 civilians.[44] In addition to handling censorship, this unit had the responsibility of collecting, evaluating, and disseminating positive and negative intelligence. From the positive side, came the strategic estimate of the military situation; the Negative Branch had as its mission the task of preventing any influence, other than that of the enemy's armed forces, from impairing the efficiency of the army. One section of the M.I.D. was supposed to maintain a high standard of morale among the troops. In October this subordinate organization was expanded into a separate branch, the Morale Branch, under the Executive Assistant.[45]

Unlike the other Assistant Chiefs of Staff, the title given all division heads, the Director of the M.I.D., Marlborough Churchill, was not a West Pointer. A "tall, good-looking"[46] Harvard graduate with "a great deal of charm,"[47] he was an artilleryman. When the United States entered the war, he was a member of the military mission in France. Later, he served on March's staff at Valdahon. He came to the War Department as part of the General Staff exchange, being one of the three whom March acknowledged as proper General Staff officers.[48]

The correspondent of the unofficial service newspaper analyzed the new reorganization scheme, and commented: "Unquestionably under this new divisional arrangement there is a simplicity and directness of operation possible that seems to have been impossible under the divisional scheme now abandoned."[49] With these moves, the General capped the unified structure of the army, created earlier in the month. March's goal in the reorganization was "complete coordination."[50]

On the last day of July, at the mid-week press conference, a reporter asked the Chief of Staff about unification of the army. March replied:

> I intend to put on the collars of every man serving in the American Army the letters "U.S." which has heretofore been reserved for the Regular Army, taking off the letters, "N.G." and "N.A.," and making one Army of the United States.[51]

Up to this point, the wartime army had consisted of three components —Regular Army, National Guard, and National Army (primarily draftees). The fact that there were great numbers of wartime recruits in the first two components had already lessened the difference between them and the National Army.

Baker had discussed unification plans earlier in 1917, with both Scott and Bliss; but, at that time, the military advisers did not think it was wise to risk injuring the local pride of the National Guardsmen.[52] Throughout the war, even though the divisions formed were strictly labelled Regular Army, National Guard, and National Army, the trend was toward unification. The War Council recommended in January a legislative draft designating the army as the Army of the United States, particularly for the purpose of simplifying officer promotions.[53] As a matter of fact, the AEF was already operating on that principle in regard to promotions. Pershing customarily recommended officers from any one of the three components for promotion in the National Army.[54] By the middle of June, March ordered that all temporary appointments be based on this policy. The day before announcing the change in collar insignia, the Chief of Staff approved the AEF commander's request to do so.[55]

Rather than risk asking Congress to pass an enabling bill, March sent for Lieutenant Colonel Samuel T. Ansell, who was Acting Judge Advocate General while Crowder was involved in Provost Marshal General duties, and asked if it would be legal to unite the diverse elements by an order. With Ansell's favorable opinion, the Chief of Staff laid the prepared order before the Secretary of War. Baker, who was pleased with the decision, commented, "General March, there is no order which you have brought to me since you became Chief of Staff which it gives me more pleasure to sign than this." [56] On August 7, an unusually hot day even for Washington, March issued General Order # 73, which began, "This country has but one army. . . ." When pressed for the reason behind this step, the Chief of Staff emphasized the democratic aspect of leveling the different elements.[57]

On the day the First American Army jumped off into the assault near Montfaucon, commencing the Meuse-Argonne campaign, General March wrote Bliss about his reorganization, "The machine is moving now on definite lines at a very high rate of speed." [58] This was apparent to the former Chief of Staff, who answered, "That everything is work-

The United States Military Academy Archives

Cadet Lieutenant Peyton C. March, United States Military Academy, Class of 1888. Portrait from the Class Album.

U.S. Signal Corps photo. The National Archives

Astor Battery at "Camp Blister" in June, 1898. March (facing camera) and his executive officer, Clarence C. Williams, are standing at the right.

March Papers, Library of Congress

March accepting the surrender of General Venancio Concepción, Aguinaldo's chief of staff, at Cayan, Luzon, December, 1899.

March Papers, Library of Congress

Military attachés and their hosts with the First Japanese Army at Tokyoryo, Manchuria, September, 1904. On the photograph in the March Papers, the officers are identified as:

Seated, left to right: Lieutenant Colonel Hume (British), Lieutenant Colonel Corvisart (French), Colonel Crowder (American), Lieutenant General Hamilton (British), Lieutenant Colonel Gertsch (Swiss), Major Payeur (French), Captain Jardine (British).

Standing, left to right: Mr. Matsuo (Japanese interpreter), Captain Vincent (British), Captain Saigo (Japanese interpreter), Captain Dani (Austrian), Captain March (American), Major Caviglia (Italian), Captain Hoffmann (German), Major von Etzel (German), Captain Hegardt (Swedish), Lieutenant Colonel Satow and Mr. Nakamura (Japanese interpreters).

U.S. War Department General Staff photo. The National Archives

John J. Pershing and James G. Harbord with an unidentified civilian in front of the State, War, and Navy Building in May, 1917.

U.S. War Department General Staff photo. The National Archives

Secretary of War Newton D. Baker; the Superintendent of the Military Academy, Colonel Samuel E. Tillman; Assistant Secretary of War Frederick P. Keppel; and the Chief of Staff at West Point for the graduation exercises in June, 1918.

U.S. Signal Corps photo. The National Archives

Key personnel of the Purchase, Storage, and Traffic Division, December 7, 1918.
First row, left to right: Brigadier General Frank T. Hines, Gerard Swope, Major General George W. Goethals, Brigadier General H. M. Lord, and Brigadier General William H. Rose.
Second row, left to right: H. M. Adams, Colonel Edwin W. Fullam, Robert J. Thorne, Brigadier General Robert E. Wood, and Colonel F. B. Wells.

Wide World Photos

March and Secretary of War Newton D. Baker with General John J. Pershing at his reception in New York Harbor, September 8, 1919.

Beverly F. Browne

March, in his eighty-ninth year, with his friend Beverly F. Browne at Front Royal, Virginia, in the fall of 1953.

ing as smoothly as possible there is evident from the smoothness with which things work here."[59]

The cables on the ocean floor linked the army, separated by the Atlantic, and communicated the pulse of activity mentioned by Bliss. In the fall, some 14,000 words per day were streaming from the AEF with an answering 3,000 words from the War Department, at a daily cost of $2,800.[60]

One reason for the large cable expense was the steady growth of the casualty lists forwarded to Washington. March favored the publication of the names, in keeping with his desire to inform the people. It was their war, and they deserved to know the facts. In October, he approved the establishment of a centralized information bureau for the War Department.[61]

When it came to designating divisions and naming their commanders, the Chief of Staff drew criticism from the AEF G-2 (Intelligence) section. Brigadier General Dennis E. Nolan, the Chief Intelligence officer, feared that the German High Command, through reading American newspapers, would learn what divisions were operating in certain sectors before they determined this information in more laborious ways. Pershing was not pleased with March's freedom with facts, either, and had not been since the Chief of Staff was at Valdahon.[62]

While March opposed censorship generally, there was one area in which he did not encourage freedom of speech. An elderly medical officer discovered this when he published a critical editorial entitled "The Passing of the General Staff" in *The Military Surgeon*, a periodical published by Medical Corps officers. At the time March was feuding with Crowder over what he construed to be bureau versus General Staff control. He read this editorial, considered it an expression of disloyalty to the Chief of Staff, and promptly returned Colonel John Hoff, the author, to the retired list. The situation was too sensitive, in March's opinion, for such remarks on the part of a bureau officer. Within six weeks of the war's end, a War Department General Order appeared which expressly forbade criticism and the uttering or publishing of true or false information which might be detrimental to the government.[63]

The Chief of Staff also had to deal with the third dimension of war which the airplane represented. As far as March was concerned, the airplane was a supporting weapon to be used wisely but not as an end in itself. In keeping with his conception, he advocated air-ground training, air cover to protect harbors, and he urged reorganization of the air arm. In order to speed the manufacturing of aircraft, he organized the Spruce Production Battalions which helped bring out the necessary wood in the Northwest.[64]

During the summer of 1918, a British mission came to Washington to advocate the formation of a strategic bombing force. Major General William L. Kenly, Director of Military Aeronautics, endorsed their argument, as did the military representatives of the Supreme War Council later. March was somewhat wary of the proposal that one of their officers command the force. Later he would say that he did not agree with the principle; but at the time, he asked the Bureau of Aircraft Production to examine the possibilities of building 570 super-bombers (presumably Handley-Page) rather than the "in excess of 1500" Kenly had suggested. Neither the Chief of Staff nor the Secretary of War wanted to dissipate the productive effort; hence in his request, March added that the Bureau should take into consideration that the super-bomber production was not to interfere with the building of planes required for tactical and limited strategic use.[65] W. C. Potter, of the Bureau, replied on July 10 that if an immediate decision were made, it would be January, 1919, before the first super-bomber would come out of the factories. After that they could be produced at the rate of twenty a week. Finally, in the middle of October, after the Equipment Branch of the Operations Division had reviewed the various documents, March decided not to take action.[66]

One obstacle to effective airpower throughout the war was the ever-changing programs suggested by the AEF staff and the lack of concert between the army air technical agencies in the United States and France.[67] Adding to the problem was the dual organization – Division of Military Aeronautics and Bureau of Aircraft Production. Air enthusiasts even went so far as to suggest a separate Department of Air. While this was not carried out, Baker did co-ordinate air activity under an Assistant Secretary, John D. Ryan, who had formerly headed the Bureau of Aircraft Production.[68] By the middle of October, March could report to the Senate Military Affairs Committee that the production of airplanes was improving at a favorable rate.[69]

Airpower had come a long way since the early days of the war as the use of tactical air power in the fall campaigns demonstrated, but it was an even greater distance to the time of the strategic bomber fleets. The Infantry "with rifle and bayonet" still won wars, March firmly believed.[70]

Many diverse problems pass across the desk of the nation's key military adviser. In August, there was another flurry of incidents on the Mexican Border.[71] More germane to the war effort, March ordered the organization of six new divisions to help fill the eighty-division quota.[72] The next month, he dictated the move of the Infantry School of Arms from Fort Sill, Oklahoma, to Columbus, Georgia, where Fort Benning would become world famous as the Infantry Center.[73]

The large army program would require many junior grade officers. West Point could not be expected to meet this demand; nevertheless, by speeding up the course, several hundred additional lieutenants would join the graduates of the various officer training camps in filling the vacancies in the new divisions. March informed the Superintendent in July, 1918, that the regular four-year term would be shortened to three, following the example of the last two classes.[74] Within three months, he ordered that the two upper classes, totalling 511 cadets, be graduated on the first of November and that the course be cut to one year for the duration of the war.[75]

During October, the AEF was battering its way through the Argonne forest. At home a zealous nation went "Over the Top" in the Fourth Liberty Loan. General March was forced by his many duties to decline an invitation to attend the November graduation at the Military Academy. The war was moving at too fast a pace for him to leave the War Department even though his nephew, Francis A. March III, would be one of the graduates. As he wrote the Superintendent's daughter, ". . . things are booming here to a degree where I cannot see definitely a day ahead. . . ."[76]

11 · SUPPLIES, SHIPS, AND VICTORY

During the fall of 1918, the American war effort culminated in the Meuse-Argonne campaign. The demands of this battle generated a strong impulse across the Atlantic and the chain of supply underwent its greatest strain as the AEF called for men, guns, horses, trucks, and all the paraphernalia of war. In Washington, March, with the aid of Goethals and the new supply organization, attempted to overcome the obstacles and stretch the limits of tonnage and resources to maintain the lifeblood of the army in France.

In this last campaign much of the confusion and friction between Washington and Chaumont resulted from the fact that the American army had to make its major effort months in advance of the projected 1919 campaign. Although the army was not at its peak, it had to carry out its mission. In the end its effort was enough to give the impetus of victory over the Germans, but the trial left Pershing in a recriminatory mood toward March.

Success in battle stemmed not only from the attacking troops, but also from the guns with ample ammunition, aircraft covering the advance, and the supply dumps. Before the doughboys could begin their assault, they had to have supplies. Providing these necessities involved a network of organizations. Pershing would meet with his staff, which was "really part of him,"[1] and discuss the situation. Handling supply problems was the efficient West Pointer who had come overseas with one of March's artillery units, George Van Horn Moseley. From these staff conferences, the problems went to the Services of Supply, over which Harbord reigned at Tours. The next step was across the ocean to Washington where, as Bernard Baruch said, "Goethals was the Army supply."[2]

Throughout the fall of 1918, Goethals was in the process of reorganizing the supply structure, and, in so doing, firmly establishing the position of the General Staff. This particular project had its beginnings in a lengthy memorandum prepared by Hugh Johnson and given to March by Goethals in the middle of July.[3] For over a month, the Panama Canal builder waited impatiently for approval. Concurrently, Benedict Crowell, the Assistant Secretary of War, who did not get along very well with either Baker or March, was advancing a scheme to divorce purchasing from the General Staff and take it over himself. When Crowell heard of Goethals' plan, he decided to abandon his own idea in order to give the other's plan a chance.[4]

On the same day (August 26) that he issued General Order # 80, March approved the Goethals project, except that construction was to remain under the control of the Operations Division.[5] Immediately, Goethals began to effect his reforms. Henceforth, he would have executive rather than supervisory authority. Not only would the several bureaus have to turn over their purchasing systems to be consolidated, but their storage and finance facilities also came under the control of the Purchase, Storage, and Traffic Division. Transportation, in the form of the Embarkation and Inland Traffic Services, was already a part of this organization. One significant aspect of this consolidation was that the Quartermaster Corps was fused into this Great General Staff division, with the Acting Quartermaster General, Brigadier General Robert E. Wood, also becoming the Director of the Purchase and Storage Department.[6] Taking over all supply, with the exception of some technical items, was a tremendous task and one that was not complete by the war's end.

Goethals had some problems in the form of rearranging personnel. There was some objection within the organization to Hugh Johnson, but this was successfully solved by placing him as an assistant to the Director. Anyway, he was out of the division and in command of a brigade within two months after the reorganization began.

Administrative difficulties, Goethals hoped, would lessen after early October when he moved his office along with his division to the newly constructed Munitions Building in Potomac Park. He hated to leave his comfortable office in the State, War, and Navy Building, but, as he wrote his son, "the concentration of all units here will make administration easier and as the demands from the other side are constantly increasing I can handle the matters that come up better and more expeditiously." [7]

The fall offensives were pressing increased action throughout the complex supply network. In France the former combat division commander, Harbord, injected a new drive into the Services of Supply. Finding Kernan's organizational structure adequate, Pershing's ex-chief of staff contributed personal leadership in the form of constant inspections of the varied facilities. Where Kernan had rarely ventured beyond the vicinity of Tours, Harbord ranged all over the country to examine personally the men and installations. To begin with, the AEF commander had given his favorite subordinate increased independence, including the authority to communicate directly with the War Department on supply matters "not involving large questions of policy," thus saving the time taken up by channeling correspondence through Chaumont.[8]

As far as March was concerned, Harbord began his direct communication in an unpleasant manner. His first cable condemned the failure to ship Ford parts and ordered the Director of the Chemical Warfare Service to supply certain items. March promptly answered in a strongly worded cable which clearly placed Harbord as a subordinate who had authority neither to "condemn" nor to "give orders" to anyone in the War Department. The S.O.S. commander replied immediately that "condemn" was an error in coding while the apparent giving of orders resulted from the "condensed form" of the text; nevertheless, he added, "such requests will hereafter be in a more courteous form." [9] Harbord did not like March anyway, and now they had started off in this new relationship with a misunderstanding.

From the opening up of this channel of communication until the Armistice, the substance of the westward bound messages could be summed up largely in three words — give us more. With the increasing commitment of American troops to battle in the great fall offensives, the demand for men and supplies multiplied. Naturally anxious to achieve overwhelming superiority, Pershing emphasized the urgency of the situation in his request. The condition of both supply and personnel, he, as well as Harbord, considered desperate.[10]

Transportation, in particular, was a constant problem. Shipping was a primary necessity to get the men and material to France, but once they had arrived in the war theater, the army required horses, mules, motor vehicles, and railroad equipment in great numbers to move the troops and their supplies. Since the AEF anticipated that it could fill its animal quota by buying European horses and mules, Pershing had recommended discontinuing animal shipments in the spring of 1918.[11] But when the demands of the fighting began to strain the transportation system, Pershing asked for over 30,000 horses a month, beginning in October. March knew that this would mean a delay in cargo shipments of all sorts, since ships must be overhauled in order to carry animals. He warned the field commander that such a project was impossible unless tonnage devoted to other essentials was diverted to carrying animals. As it developed, he did not make the animal shipments at the requested rate.[12]

The situation in motor transportation was equally bad. In order to mount the St. Mihiel attack, Pershing had to take trucks away from the Services of Supply and to call on French aid to alleviate shortages in the fighting command. Throughout the summer and fall, he requested the shipment of additional vehicles. Unless increased shipments of vehicles were forthcoming, Pershing warned on October 2, his command would be faced "with a very serious crisis."[13] Put the trucks on the decks, Pershing cabled. March replied that this had been tried without success, but he would try it again.[14] Basically, the shortage could be traced to the lack of shipping. To complicate matters, the Expeditionary Forces' staff had been underestimating by some 40 per cent the amount of space the vehicles occupied on ships; hence, it never got as many trucks as it expected.[15]

Not all of the problems relating to transportation resulted from the shipping shortage. The Director General of Transportation, Brigadier General William W. Atterbury, formerly the General Manager of the Pennsylvania Railroad, was a rather difficult subordinate with a tendency to carry "a chip on his shoulder."[16] While Pershing commented on the "businesslike" way Atterbury ran his office, the Chief of Staff of the S.O.S., Johnson Hagood, thought that this department was the least efficient of the various organizations in the Services of Supply.[17] What vehicles were available were not adequately maintained. This also held true for animals, as Hagood compared the Remount Service's handling of its charges to the fiasco of 1898.[18] Sick horses were improperly tended, and contagious diseases spread. One of the causes for this inefficiency was the lack of trained personnel. In the haste to ship combat men, the War Department necessarily neglected S.O.S. requirements.

Confusing the issue even more was some ill feeling between the S.O.S. and General Headquarters. Harbord later blamed the railway car shortage on the G-4. Under the G-4 system, commanders who had control over trains near the front frequently held on to the rolling stock too long, thus bringing about a shortage in the rear areas. Friction also developed between these two headquarters over motor transportation.

In the closing weeks of the war, Moseley suggested a reorganization plan which would subordinate, to a greater extent, the Services of Supply to the Fourth Section of the AEF General Staff. The reaction of S.O.S. officers was to recommend the virtual abolition of the office of G-4. Harbord approved and forwarded this suggestion of his bureau chiefs to G.H.Q. and added this comment on Moseley's idea: "It is an actual reversal of the Commander-in-Chief's policy announced in August of throwing [a] greater amount of responsibility with commensurate authority to Services of Supply." Then, in a personal letter to Moseley, he warned, ". . . if the proposition to send General Goethals here is not entirely dead I look to see it revived, using this order as an argument." The war ended before Pershing made a decision on this organizational conflict.[19]

During the last six months of the war another shortage haunted both headquarters. The guns required ammunition in large amounts to support the men in the trenches. Early in the war the War Department decided to rely on the French to a great extent for these munitions. As the United States developed its war industry, it could be expected to start sending over shells, but shipments of a large amount of steel to be used by French munitions factories would continue even after the American manufacturers started adding to the output.

Pershing and Harbord would later point to the lack of ammunition in the summer of 1918 although they almost succeeded in building up a ninety-day reserve at the time.[20] After he arrived in Europe, Edward R. Stettinius joined in the plea for more.[21] Upon talking with Louis Loucheur, the French Minister of Munitions, Harbord thought that the monthly shipments of 75,000 tons of steel should also be increased by some 40,000.[22] Leland L. Summers, who represented the War Industries Board on the Inter-Allied Munitions Council, vetoed this suggestion, pointing out this demand added to the many others was far in excess of the nation's productive capacity. He and Stettinius knew that some of the Allied representatives considered the AEF estimates as being much more than actual needs.[23] Yet, what could March do when thus informed? His response was that the War Department planners realized this, but that it was up to Pershing to change the requirements.[24] After the war a study of the shells requisitioned and the number actually fired by the American army confirmed the belief of March and the others that the Expeditionary Force had grossly overestimated its requirements.[25]

On another matter the Chief of Staff did ask Pershing pointedly to reconsider his requests. When the field commander called for 194-millimeter guns, March answered that it would be a year before the factories, which would have to be constructed at a cost of millions of dollars, could produce any of these guns, and suggested that already available naval guns be used.[26]

"Unless supplies are furnished when and as cabled for our armies will cease to operate." A distraught Pershing, under the heavy strain of the Meuse-Argonne offensive, cabled this ultimatum on October 2. His army was lacking every type of supply, according to his estimate.[27] The chief of Pershing's supply section, George Van Horn Moseley, in a letter to Charles G. Dawes on October 3, gave a somewhat different interpretation: "We are getting along all right but Uncle Sam is not sending in the tonnage each month that we believe we have a right to expect, but we are licking the Boche. . . ."[28] Before the end of the month, Harbord reported figures showing the steady decline in pounds per man per day of supply shipments.[29] Combined with the news of the desperate fighting and hold-up of the advance, this supply problem seemed almost unbearable to Pershing.

In the War Department, March exerted pressure on Goethals but failed to inform Baruch of Pershing's cry of anguish. Goethals transmitted the urgency to his subordinates. In particular he looked into the cable problem by putting expediters to work and demanding that bureau chiefs adhere to the system of checking delays in replying to AEF cables. Although this system had begun in the summer, some of the section heads had not been complying with it.[30] In the civilian office of supply, Baruch was furious when he learned of Pershing's cable "only by chance." He called on March and had a "showdown," making it clear that the army must acknowledge the responsibility of the War Industries Board in supply matters.[31]

While March was remiss in not informing Baruch of the situation, neither he nor Baruch could do much in regard to the basic problem of the lack of sufficient tonnage to maintain such a large expedition properly. In the summer March had endorsed the eighty-division program with the realization that this shortage was a strong possibility and, for this reason, had refused to approve the hundred-division plan. Now, the results of the lack of cargo tonnage were becoming obvious, as March had feared, but he gambled on victory before the proportion of supplies and men became too unbalanced.

Yet, despite the urgent appeals, the AEF was generally well supplied and even built up reserve stocks in some classes of supply. "No man lacked ammunition or rations," General Moseley wrote in his diary on October 21.[32] "By comparison with our previous army, we made a magnificent showing. Our men were well equipped and, with few exceptions, always well fed," was the opinion of First Army commander, Hunter Liggett.[33] And Charles G. Dawes, the AEF's General Purchasing Agent, later commented: "It will be noted that the success of the shipping program in the United States was such that in the last five months preceding the armistice nearly twice as much tonnage was shipped from America to the American Expeditionary Forces as had been shipped the entire preceding year." [34]

In the summer, the casualty lists began growing rapidly until by the middle of October the daily list was taking up full newspaper pages in tombstone-like columns. The steady drain on his force caused Pershing much concern, which he persistently communicated to the War Department. In order to maintain his army, he wanted 300,000 or more men a month, the bulk in divisions and supporting units with replacements making up the rest of the quota.[35] In late August, he even asked for eight regiments of cavalry but March cabled that it would be impossible to comply with this request.[36] The demands of the heavy fighting in the fall forced Pershing to break up seven of his divisions to be used to sustain the fighting strength of other divisions. Within nine days of the Armistice, he called for 140,000 replacements, in addition to unit shipments, for the month of November. He demanded: "Can not this matter be given the consideration its importance deserves?" [37]

In spite of the efforts of the leaders in Washington, the troop shipments dwindled from the high point in July. The Shipping Board was not providing the necessary bottoms. To make matters worse, the AEF was still basing its estimates on the ninety-six-division program, thus the number of men arriving in France was considerably less than expected. March was aware that Pershing was operating on a different plan than the War Department, and informed him that he would not get his anticipated reinforcements.[38]

In October, the influenza epidemic brought about a large drop in the number of troops going to France. Men were dying on the transports although the troops were quarantined and then examined within twenty-four hours of embarkation. At the French ports the convoys were arriving with large numbers of infected men who had to be hospitalized. At home the War Department halted draft calls and curtailed training as army installations took on the appearance of large hospitals.[39]

With the specter of flu threatening every activity, the President came over to the State, War, and Navy Building to ask the Chief of Staff to suspend troop shipments. After pointing out that precautions were being taken, and that transports were carrying only 80 per cent of their capacity, March emphasized the necessity of keeping as many men as possible in transit to France. He pointed out what a boon it would be to German morale if they learned that troop shipments were stopped; and, he added, they would learn within forty-eight hours. He concluded. "These men [who die en route] have died for their country just as truly as any man killed in France. The shipment of troops should not be suspended for any cause." Wilson looked out the window, pondered, and nodded his approval.[40]

On the first day of October, newspapers headlined the capitulation of Bulgaria. Within five weeks, Turkey and Austria also surrendered, and Germany was asking for terms. As he considered the various problems of peacemaking, the President called March to the White House five times during that month. On one occasion, the Chief of Staff together with other advisers talked over the situation all night. Over two million Americans were in France and the Central Powers were falling to their knees, but Pershing did not want any limitations of shipments based on the possibility of an armistice.[41]

As the war neared its conclusion, Pershing again raised the question of his authority by advocating unconditional surrender terms when conferring with the Allied commanders and also by stating his views in a letter to the Supreme War Council. This latter "extraordinary communication" reached Colonel House while he was in a session with the prime ministers. He described the scene in his diary: ". . . after reading it I handed it first to Clemenceau who said: 'Theatrical.' I then handed it to George, who said, 'politics.' Everyone believes it is a political document and a clear announcement of his intention to become a candidate for the Presidency in 1920." [42] Three days later, House and the AEF commander had a "heart to heart" talk as they drove from Versailles to Paris. Pershing apologized for not consulting the President's representative and admitted his mistake. House then cabled this explanation to Wilson.[43] In Washington, Baker disapproved of Pershing's activity and prepared an admonitory letter which clearly informed the general that "the views of the United States upon any question of national policy could be expressed only by the President." But Wilson, who had received House's cable, advised his Secretary of War not to send the letter.[44]

With the end of the war in sight, the Chief of Staff issued orders on the first of November to cease shipping troops. This was not made public; not even Pershing was told. March gambled on the war's ending soon. This coupled with the fear that the German fleet might make a suicidal dash to sea in a fanatic gesture to destroy the transports, a possibility previously warned of by Sir Eric Geddes, First Lord of the Admiralty.[45]

On November 7, Washington went mad with excitement over the news of the war's end. Government workers walked out of their offices and mobbed the streets. Carousing went on into the night, even after the news was pronounced false. Four days later, the Armistice was really signed. After a few hours of quiet, crowds began to congregate, filling the streets as schools and government offices closed. Amidst much cheering and applause, Woodrow Wilson delivered a twenty-seven-minute speech outlining the Armistice terms to the combined houses of Congress. Later in the day, he and Mrs. Wilson reviewed a hastily organized parade.[46]

There was a large throng about the White House and the State, War, and Navy Building where the flags of the Allies were flying. The honking of horns increased the din of the merrymaking. Inside, the high command was slowing down the war machine. In Baker's office, Frank Polk of the State Department talked with Baker, Daniels, Crowell, Roosevelt, Hurley, and March about the effect of the Armistice. They wanted confirmation of the signing from Polk before they relaxed the war measures.[47] Draft calls and supply contracts were stopped. March cabled Pershing informing him of the procedure followed by the War

Department in regard to supply and troop shipments, the draft, and contracts.[48] A few days before, the Chief of Staff had announced that much of the army's work would continue even after the war's end.[49] But this day, he interrupted his schedule in the early afternoon to go to the Capitol and hear the President. In the well of the House, he joined the cabinet members and Supreme Court Justices in the chairs set up in front of the dais.[50]

During the exultant pandemonium, March signed his annual report and added it to the reports of the General Staff divisions which the new Secretary of the General Staff, Colonel F. Q. C. Gardner, had collected.[51] Finally, the Assistant Chief of Staff dictated a letter to the Smithsonian Institution, presenting the uniforms and flags which were displayed in the corridors of the State, War, and Navy Building.[52] The war was over.

12 · "THE RIGHT MAN IN THE RIGHT PLACE"

As Chief of Staff, Peyton C. March occupied the military pinnacle of the war structure in the United States. A strong man, he made his presence felt throughout the War Department. Within his jurisdiction, he assumed the responsibility, made the decisions, and guided the army to its goal. In the brief period of eight months, he pushed men and material overseas in enough quantity to enable Pershing and the AEF to turn the balance against the enemy.

During those eight months of trial and tension, March maintained a rugged schedule. At Fort Myer, where his daughter, Mrs. John Millikin, kept house for him, he got up at six in the morning; weather permitting, played tennis; showered; and went into Washington, arriving at the War Department by eight o'clock. From then until dinner, he was at his desk. Lunch was a glass of milk and a sandwich or an apple served to him in his office. He went home for dinner and allowed himself an hour before returning to his desk where he would work until midnight, Sundays included.[1]

Promptly at 11:30 each morning, March called in the Secretary of the General Staff. This officer and his assistants previously had culled a dozen or so papers out of as many as six hundred streaming into their office daily to present to the general. Colonel Bishop and later Colonel Gardner would briefly inform the Chief of Staff orally of the contents of each document. If there were some question of policy, this was brought out. March listened intently, saying "approved" or "disapproved" after each paper. If he thought he needed any more information, he would ask searching questions, but the entire presentation would usually be concluded within thirty minutes.[2] If a problem puzzled him or needed more consideration, he would take the paper, put it in his desk, and that night go over it and make his decision.[3] On the first page of the documents he personally examined, he wrote "M" and "OK" or some other comment in his large hand. The papers that required his signature might be cursorily signed "March C of S," or occasionally with his full signature and title.[4]

On occasion, he would call for his secretary at other times throughout the day. Then, pacing up and down in deep thought, sometimes with his hands clasped behind him, he would reel off rapidly and concisely instructions as to how he wanted several matters handled.[5]

Most material was presented to him orally; his remarkable memory enabled him to transact business in this manner. Once Colonel Gardner informed him of a problem arising from the allocation of Liberty engines. In the course of the presentation he gave the figures of the estimated production and of the recommended allotments to the different agencies. A month or so later, when a question of reallocating the Liberties arose, Gardner started to repeat the original figures only to be stopped immediately: March told him to go on and give the new estimates since he remembered the old figures.[6]

Not the type to encourage familiarity, March impressed his subordinates with his cold-blooded, ruthless drive for efficiency. Dedicated to his work, he "inspired in high degree, confidence, admiration and loyalty. He did not inspire affection." [7] He was "a very austere man," Richard C. Marshall, Chief of the Construction Division, thought, "but he left austerity at the door when you went in to see him." [8] Others would agree. They thought him impersonal and severe but fair, a man who allowed subordinates to express their honest opinions and to disagree with him. "I countered him once in a bitter difference of opinion as to an important policy and he wiped the ground up with me," General Bishop recalled. "But he told me I could see the Secretary of War which I did and the Secretary of War backed March." [9]

He assumed that subordinates knew their jobs. As long as they did their work well, he neither praised nor interfered, but supported them to the limit of his power. When General Snow, who had served with him in the Sixth Artillery before the war, reported soon after March became Acting Chief of Staff and proposed, "If I am to be Chief of Field Artillery, I am going to be what the name implies, and I am going to run the job, using your name freely, and not coming near you to bother you except in cases wherein I must have your signature to put something over," March tersely summed up all the instruction he would give: "Go to it, Billy!" [10]

When he organized the Personnel Branch, March merely gave brief instructions to Bishop. Beyond that it was Bishop's problem. March left him alone until a month or so later when he inspected his work. After his examination, he commented, "Everything you have done is all right; now what can I do for you?" Bishop replied, "General, this organization is all set up and working smoothly. I would like to go overseas." March startled him by bending over with rare laughter. He slapped his thigh and said, "You'll get your chance young man!" [11]

If a subordinate failed, he found himself standing at attention before the Chief of Staff's desk with March's sharp, piercing, blue eyes looking "right through" him, and the gray goatee bristling as his lips tightened until it seemed to point at the offender. March's criticism was incisive and clear. "You couldn't lie to him," Beverly Browne recalled.[12]

His tough, tactless method of handling matters was not limited to soldiers. Conversational amenities were not observed and "he would give the shortest, most final and dismissing replies." [13] The head of the Associated Press, Melville Stone, once stormed into Secretary Baker's office complaining about March's refusal to extend him a privilege.[14] Baker was pleased with his Chief of Staff's stand but wished he would be more tactful:

> I used to say to General March that he wasted a substantial part of my time, and he would ask how; and I would tell him that I had to go around with a cruse of oil and a bandage to fix up the wounds which he had made. These seemed unnecessary in the day's work, and if I would abandon the oil and bandages, I could probably devote more time to my own job, but he would go out and make more wounds.[15]

March "lived, breathed, and slept efficiency," according to the wartime Chief of Field Artillery.[16] The urgency in his stride, the speech clipped with firmness and decision, and the fearless approach impressed the War Department with a new drive. Although some of his contemporaries believed that the sharply military manner and tough methods disguised an introvert, few glimpsed this aspect of his character while he was Chief of Staff.[17]

The normal amenities seemed to him to be luxuries during a war. A Republican congressional leader, Julius Kahn, remarked to Leonard Wood in the fall of 1918 that the Chief of Staff was digging "a grave of personal unpopularity."[18] March's reply to such criticism was, "One is proud to be hated, if it is a consequence of doing one's work well."[19] And he continued to make enemies.

There was a lighter side. In September, he interrupted the business-like cable correspondence to send a terse announcement of the birth of his grandson: "For Major Millikin: Wife and son doing well. March."[20] In the way of amusements, he enjoyed an occasional cigar or a glass of Scotch and a hand of bridge,[21] but there was little time during these days for diversions. Dinner engagements, for example, were victims of the war, unless they were connected with business.[22] Nevertheless, he took part in those late after-hours sessions when Secretary Baker would fill his pipe, put his feet on his desk, and lean back to discuss the affairs of the day. In this "kitchen cabinet" sanctum, Baker's civilian aides discovered that the Chief of Staff had not only a wit but also an "engaging grin."[23]

Since his pitching days at Lafayette College, he had loved baseball, but it too fell before the war machine. The "Work or Fight" order was folding up the game as the players either had to secure war work or go into the service. Knowing of March's love for the game, several prominent baseball officials came to ask him to prevent a certain star from going overseas. As soon as the Chief of Staff realized what it was they sought, he abruptly snapped, "Gentlemen, my job is to get men to France, not to keep them in this country."[24] He did, however, take time off to watch the last game of the Washington season, which came to an early end on September 2, 1918. A crowd of 10,000, many in uniform, sang "Auld Lang Syne" as March threw out the "last ball of the season"; and then saw the Nationals beat Connie Mack's Philadelphia Athletics 8 to 3.[25]

"And by the words 'War Department' I mean the recommendations of the Chief of Staff, approved by the Secretary of War." March's statement in his memoirs explains the relationship between himself and Newton D. Baker.[26]

The small, gentle, seemingly frail Cleveland lawyer and the tall, formal, professional officer worked together very well and developed a mutual admiration. Baker, who carefully avoided giving offense, might deplore March's impatience with less intelligent people and his rough handling of everyone in general, but he respected the General's ruthlessly decisive use of power. Each afternoon at two o'clock, March presented the various policy questions to his superior. After listening to his Chief of Staff's explanation and recommendation, Baker, as a rule, would give his decision at that time. No longer did bureau chiefs approach the Secretary with special pleadings; March saw to that. At first, Baker objected but he soon realized the efficacy of this step.[27]

Baker profited from March's broad experience, which on occasion saved him from a naive gesture. One such instance also reflects the Chief of Staff's sense of humor. As the two leaders were inspecting a camp near Washington, Baker, who was particularly interested in the social and cultural welfare of the soldiers, examined a newsstand. After asking the attendant, "a hard-boiled regular private," a few questions and getting "prompt and snappy answers," the Secretary noticed that there was only one *Atlantic Monthly* in contrast to a dozen or so *Cosmopolitans* and several *Redbooks.* He wanted to know why this was the case. The soldier quickly replied, "Can't keep the *Atlantics* in stock, Sir. They are all sold out as fast as we can get them." March glanced at the camp commander, whose face was purple, but said nothing. Baker was pleased: "It really shows what a high average of intelligence we are getting through the draft." Then he added that he would write Ellery Sedgwick, the *Atlantic*'s editor, and tell him the good news. The next morning, March called the camp commander into Washington. When he presented himself, the Chief of Staff asked, "What did you do about your *Atlantic Monthly* man?" The officer answered: "I made him a Corporal, Sir." March, relieved, said, "I was going to suggest a Sergeancy. . . ." Later, when he went into Baker's office, the Secretary started commenting again on the incident, as he had just finished writing the letter to Sedgwick. Not wanting to carry the joke too far, March then told him that in fact the newstand had stocked 25 to 30 of the other magazines and only one *Atlantic*, which had remained unsold. The Secretary, who enjoyed a good joke, grinned, and later told the story on himself, but, as March commented, he "continued to be equally guileless the next time."[28]

Subjected to severe criticism, Baker, who was sensitive about his height, once told March, "These people wouldn't believe I was Secretary of War unless I was six feet tall and had guns strapped around my waist." The Chief of Staff was over six feet tall and looked the part of a war leader. The contrast between the two was tactlessly remarked upon by the wife of the commanding officer of Camp Humphreys when Baker and March were inspecting that post. She and Mrs. Baker were walking behind the two toward the speakers' stand when she observed,

"How small Mr. Baker looks compared to General March." Mrs. Baker was aghast, but the keen-witted Secretary saved the day: "Yes, Madame, General March is six feet two, and I am two feet six." [29]

Although he perhaps did not look the part, Baker earned the admiration of army officers for his work as Secretary of War. His warm personality and composure did not keep him from exercising control over the more outwardly stern subordinates. Having established a co-ordinate relationship between the Chief of Staff and the AEF commander, Baker tactfully maintained the balance despite the difficulties involved. When Pershing directed pointed criticism at March and his methods in personal letters, the Secretary, who knew his man, did not reply. He considered himself fortunate to be dealing with such a "zealous, devoted . . . loyal set of men," [30] and he realized from his legal experience "that facts, like jugs, sometimes have two handles, and that the handle you see depends upon the side of the jug from which you view it." [31]

In March, the Secretary of War found an officer upon whom he could rely to give straightforward advice and to wield the power of his office to its limit. That limit he imposed in regard to the operation of the Expeditionary Force, which he entrusted to Pershing. Better than any other observer, Baker could guage March's success. In this regard, he praised unstintingly March's contribution:

> The Chief of Staff was the head of the organization at home. His driving power, his high professional equipment, and his burning zeal imparted to our whole machine an impetus which never slackened on this side of the water . . . [as he] organized, expedited and stimulated our mobilization at home, and made effective that support and cooperation upon which, under modern war conditions, the success of the commander in the field depends.[32]

When he left the War Office, Baker expressed his regard personally to General March:

> You came into the office of the Chief of Staff at the most critical juncture of the war and brought with you untiring energy, prompt and authoritative decisions, and an intimate knowledge of the military act, on both personnel and supply sides. . . . [Your work] was not only tireless, intelligent, and successful, but . . . it was characterized at all times by a complete freedom from prejudice or favor, and by a courage which never shrank, no matter how unpopular or difficult the task.[33]

When March became Chief of Staff in the spring of 1918, the American contribution to the war effort was largely in the future, as the low number of casualties attested.[34] The foundations for victory were in place with Pershing and a token force in France, well over a million men in training in camps in the United States, and the nation's industry converting to war. The development to this point had been accompanied by no small amount of difficulty and criticism, and the continued evolution would also be arduous.

To the War Department General Staff, the arrival of Peyton C. March meant the end of the rapid turnover of Chiefs of Staff, with three officers holding that position in eleven months, and of the shaky beginnings based on peacetime methods. Ahead remained the primary requirement of getting enough men to France to break the German resistance and the requisite reorganization of the Staff. During the 8 months and 1 week March served as wartime Chief of Staff, over 135,000 more men (approximately 1,788,448) were transported to France than were in the entire army in April, 1918 (approximately 1,652,725).[35]

March did not construe support of the AEF as agreeing to all of its requests. Forced to operate within the restrictions of the co-ordinate structure created by Baker and the precedent of his predecessors, March was hampered in developing his own concept of General Staff control. He would back Pershing but with reservations. The field commander and his staff seemed at times to consider matters closed after making their demands. Of necessity, the Chief of Staff, who must get the men and material to the ports, could not always comply. The one-hundred-division program was a case in point. After a careful examination and analysis of the various factors, March decided to adopt a lesser goal. Nevertheless, as the civilian experts testified, March was most forceful in filling ships with men whom it was his responsibility to equip, train, and transport to the loading piers. Because of this he opposed the Russian intervention and, in the weekly conferences, fought for the needed tonnage.

March did not believe it part of his duty simply to approve Pershing's ideas and actions. In his opinion the Expeditionary Force would function more efficiently if there was a change in the logistical command. Whether or not Goethals would have performed better than Harbord as S.O.S. chief will remain unknown. Certainly, if Goethals had assumed authority over the S.O.S. in a co-ordinate status with Pershing, the influence of the Chief of Staff would have been greater in France.

On the promotion issue March did not act wisely. Although his idea of selection for efficiency is more logical than a selective system based largely on seniority, he should have taken more cognizance of the situation resulting from Pershing's independence and attempted to reach a compromise more agreeable to the AEF commander. Throughout the war, however, he did not appear to realize Pershing's influence in Washington. For instance, he evidently was unaware of the extent of the personal correspondence between Pershing and Baker.

March's supremacy was acknowledged in the United States. Here he created new branches – Air Service, Chemical Warfare Service, and Motor Transport Corps – and the various new divisions and sections within the General Staff. He abolished the distinction between the army's three components and liberalized the censorship policies. And with him, he brought other AEF veterans to take over key posts in the War Department.[36]

Based on none too stable foundations and a record of fumbling in the earlier days of the war, the General Staff by November, 1918, because of March, was a powerful organization. Its expansion in numbers alone indicates this development. At the beginning of the war, there were nineteen General Staff officers in Washington. By the Armistice, there were over a thousand. Of this number only four, who were all general officers and who included the Chief of Staff, had General Staff experience prior to the war.[37] Under March, the Staff functioned as the brain of the army as it expanded not only in numbers but also in power.

To secure the General Staff, March fought the remnant of bureau control in the form of Enoch H. Crowder and the War Council. By October, 1918, the Council was no longer in existence and the Provost Marshal General-Judge Advocate General was restricted in his power and influence. The General Staff was firmly established.

Four decades later, Bernard M. Baruch said of March as wartime Chief of Staff that he was "the right man in the right place." [38] But Newton D. Baker accorded him the highest praise which he could hope to receive when he wrote: "The war was won by days. Your energy and drive supplied the days necessary for our side to win." [39]

13 · COMPLICATIONS OF DEMOBILIZATION

During the war March had concentrated his efforts on building up, supplying, and transporting a military machine. Now that the war was over he and the General Staff had to work just as hard on reversing the great machine. In handling demobilization the Chief of Staff had to consider such problems as the return of the AEF, the discharge of the bulk of the army, integration of the AEF regulars in the deflated peacetime army, and the background noise of a flurry of criticism.

On the morning of November 11, 1918, shortly before the senators took their walk under the Capitol's dome to the House to hear the President deliver his address, they listened to two Western Republicans condemn war extravagance. William Borah of Idaho led the attack, supported by Utah's Reed Smoot, who expressed the nation's sentiment: "We have got to return to normal conditions." [1] In their offices across town, the War Department officials were trying to do just that.

Since the Armistice had come so suddenly "that it almost took our breath away," [2] as one General Staff officer commented, the army did not have a plan for demobilization. But it was clearly evident that the nation wanted its sons out of uniform and the burden of the expenses of war lifted as rapidly as possible. There were other considerations. The specter of hordes of unemployed veterans converging on large cities haunted March and the other planners.[3] Then, too, the requirements of industries whose working forces had been reduced by the wartime demand for men were constantly in the forefront of most thinking on the subject. Finally, the army must analyze its own needs. Military efficiency and readiness for possible contingencies were requisites in any decision. After all, it was only an armistice and too soon to make military forecasts, as Pershing warned in a cable on November 11.[4]

Prior to the abrupt cessation of hostilities, there had been some moves to determine the course of demobilzation. Two months earlier, during September, two senators proposed the creation of commissions to help handle post-war problems, but the President was not impressed by the need for haste.[5] When the Argonne campaign was in its early stages and victory seemed distant, the army showed signs of premonition. On October 8, 1918, Colonel E. S. Hartshorn of the General Staff suggested that the Staff study the question of demobilization. A few days later, March looked over the memo and issued orders to the War Plans Division to begin this investigation. For the next month, these officers collected opinions and weighed the evidence, but they were unable to keep up with the progress of the war – the Armistice came eleven days before they submitted their formal views.[6]

While the War Plans Division was working on the subject, March and Baker were considering various other suggestions, but the situation was complicated by Baker's status. Since the President had told Baker that he would be on the Peace Commission, the Secretary assumed that he would be occupied soon with his duties in Paris. Although Baker remained in Washington because his absence, combined with the resignation of Secretary of the Treasury McAdoo, might weaken the administration too much, it was March who dominated War Department thinking and made the decisions on manpower demobilization in this crucial period.[7] As for war material, Baker cancelled some contracts in the last week of the conflict and the Purchase, Storage, and Traffic Division handled the adjustment of contracts and disposal of surplus. In Europe, Stettinius and Dawes began the settlement of obligations.[8] In this area, March did not play the dominant role that he did in discharging the army.

Two choices were open to planners in returning the bulk of the army to civilian life. Should they gear the manpower demobilization to the economy or should they think in terms of speed and military efficiency? Either course would result in criticism by those who considered themselves slighted. Naturally most soldiers wanted to shed their uniforms as soon as possible. On the other hand, the release of over three and a half million men might have a serious effect on the economy. The British had made this their main consideration; hence their plan, devised in the summer of 1917, developed a system based on industrial needs. Before the end of the war, a civilian member of the Committee on Classification of Personnel, Robert C. Clothier, visited England, studied this plan, and, three days prior to the Armistice, submitted a report on the system of releasing men on the demand of the various industries.[9] On the War Industries Board, a former vice president of John Deere and Company, George Peek, who believed "demobilization is more of an industrial than a military question," was thinking along the same lines.[10] Simultaneously, Felix Frankfurter, head of the War Labor Policies Board, came up with a solution generally similar to Peek's. Their idea was to release farmers and professional men first, then workers who were urgently needed by such industries as transportation and mining, and finally those men whose employers specifically requested them. Neither seems to have considered the military ramifications of the problem.[11]

Peek's plan also introduced another factor for consideration – the agency of demobilization. He recommended that the Selective Service Local Boards manage the whole procedure.[12] In this he had the strong support of Crowder. The Provost Marshal General was proud of his empire of 4648 boards and it seemed obvious to him that those civilians who had brought so many into the service would be the logical ones to terminate the military life of the emergency army. Crowder's theory, detailed in a nine-page memo, neatly supplemented Peek's idea. Where the business executive had vaguely referred to a general plan of releasing the men through the draft boards and had emphasized the economic orientation of the program, Crowder pointed out the value of the boards in closing the soldiers' pecuniary accounts and maintaining manpower records. The general also thought his plan would solve the employment problem. It answered the question, who better could integrate the returned soldier into the economic life of the community than his friends and neighbors who had taken him from it? [13]

In the week following the Armistice, March analyzed the various plans. While he probably did not know about Peek's and Frankfurter's specific proposals, he was aware of Crowder's and he was familiar with the general idea of the industrially oriented system. He was also acquainted with the gist of the unfinished War Plans Division study which advocated bringing the AEF back in its existing organizations, mustering out the units at a few camps near the ports, loading the men on military trains, and giving them their discharge certificates as they left the train near their homes. As contact points with the ex-service-men, Lytle Brown's division wanted to maintain the local boards.[14] The Operations Division, which had supervised the mobilization and would perform the same function with demobilization, also contributed its thoughts on the subject. Its experts supported a scheme based on dispersing the army to thirty camps where post detachments would handle the terminal procedure.[15] March measured these plans on the basis of their accomplishing what he deemed the essential demands of demobilization – that it be done "in the promptest, fairest and most efficient manner."[16] After giving the several recommendations serious consideration, the Chief of Staff chose that of the Operations Division.[17]

On November 16, at his Saturday press conference, he made the "first authentic statement" on demobilization. Prior to this, Secretary Baker had made brief public comments which hinted that the army would release its men on the basis of economic considerations, but March made it clear that the army would demobilize by military units. He gave the reporters the order in which the units would leave the service, beginning with the organizations in the United States and culminating in the return and discharge of the combat divisions. To give concrete emphasis to his plan, he named specific units whch would demobilize within two weeks. The army would discharge as many as possible at camps near their homes. In these demobilization centers, the soldiers would undergo physical examinations, settle all financial accounts, and then leave with the privilege of wearing their uniforms for three months. Emergency officers could apply for regular commissions. Finally, he announced that millions of blank forms were already en route to the fourteen demobilization camps which he had designated the day before.[18]

March may have thought that the matter was settled, but opponents to unit demobilization did not. That night Peek and Crowder called on Bernard Baruch and went over their plan with the czar of wartime industry. Two days later, March and Assistant Secretary of War Benedict Crowell dined with Peek and Baruch. Again Peek pressed his plan. Crowell demurred with the excuse that it was not his responsibility. But the General took the memorandum, read it, and stated flatly that he had made the only practical decision and that demobilization would proceed along the announced lines.[19] In the first place, the task of analyzing the priority of individual soldiers would delay the discharge process; besides, it would destroy the integrity of the units. For example, administrative units needed for managing the demobilization might be riddled by the industrial plan. As for draft boards, he argued that the local civilian bodies were not adequate to the task. To implement release by the boards, he believed, would require attachment of military personnel to each board besides the need to provide facilities to house and feed the soldiers during the process.[20] Still unsatisfied, Peek and another member of the War Industries Board, Hugh Frayne, called on Baker on November 20. Despite earlier indications of his support for economic-based demobilization, Baker upheld March's stand.[21] Although he seemed to have failed, Peek's fight probably brought about a compromise which made the program more flexible. On November 26, the War Department authorized two qualifications to the system: the army would release hardship cases and soldiers who were "urgently needed" by industry. In anticipation of economic needs, the War Office ordered anthracite coal miners, railroad employees, and railway mail clerks released. Later, the army informed the Department of Labor that if demobilization proceeded too rapidly it could be slowed.[22] As a nod to Crowder's idea, Baker, in mid-December, asked the local boards to help the soldiers adjust to the economic life of the community.[23]

As early as January, 1919, March considered his decision justified by the British experience. Two months after the Armistice, he presented to reporters the comparative figures of British and American demobilization. The English, in applying their industrial system, had discharged men at half the rate of the American process. This sluggishness, combined with real and fancied injustices, provoked mass mutinies in the British Army at the turn of the new year. As a result, Winston Churchill, the recently appointed war minister, discarded the system and began releasing the men as rapidly as possible on the basis of length of service and age.[24]

As the "pyramid of [war] effort sagged down to a normal horizon," the War Department was not immune to the atmosphere of release from wartime tension.[25] "Everybody here felt like taking a rest," Crowder wrote an AEF friend.[26] While much remained to be done, March recognized this tendency by suspending the wartime meetings of the bureau heads and the Wednesday conferences, and by setting the policy of releasing all emergency personnel who could be spared.[27] This move had a special effect on the P.S.&T. Division where, as Hugh Johnson complained, "There was an immediate exodus of experts. . . ." He continued in a somewhat exaggerated and despondent vein: "The result was lethal. I sit apart and look on that great structure and almost weep." [28] Although most officers did leave as soon as they could, some citizen soldiers such as Lieutenant Colonel Herbert H. Lehman stayed on to adjust contracts.[29]

Congress wanted to make certain that the War Department officials did not relax. Throughout the entire demobilization period, the legislators forwarded constituent demands and goaded the army to release men more rapidly. As Democratic Senator Kenneth D. McKellar of Tennessee, rather needlessly, wrote March in December, "Apparently the sentiment in favor of demobilization is overwhelming, now that the war is over." [30] On the floor of the House, a Mississippi Representative, Percy E. Quin, sounded, amidst applause, a more earthy appeal: "In the name of heaven, let us get those soldiers . . . back home in civil pursuits. . . . Old Bossy and old Muley are calling for them. The bobwhites out in the corn field are calling for the boys back on the farm. . . ." The Mississippian hinted that the rate of demobilization would be a factor in the 1920 elections.[31] Other complaints ranged from not adopting the local board method to not having attractive discharge certificates.[32] March answered the more legitimate criticisms in two detailed letters to congressmen but the faultfinding continued.[33] On the constructive side, Congress did authorize a bonus of $60 and offer a special veteran privilege under the Homestead Act.[34] But the legislators did not enact a comprehensive reconstruction program and hampered the army's, as well as other government agencies', efforts by reducing appropriations.[35] Perhaps, with an eye on the polls of 1920, they were satisfied to leave the onus of demobilization on the War Department.

In the weeks following the war, while March saw his decisions implemented by the rapid discharge of troops then in the United States, he still had to consider the great problem of bringing back the two million soldiers in the AEF. On December 18, he wrote Pershing, "We have the machinery here now completely organized to take care of any number of men that may be sent back for demobilization. . . ." [36] Yet two other aspects of the question remained unsolved: how many of these men could be released and how much shipping could be garnered for the return voyage?

By the end of the first week of peace, Pershing thought he could answer the first question. Resumption of hostilities was not improbable, although there remained a faint possibility of revolution in the Central Powers. With the concurrence of Foch and Bliss, the AEF commander then recommended the retention of 30 divisions (an estimated 1,200,000 men) in Europe. He could begin shipment of rear-area troops, but he warned that the rail situation was so bad that he could not predict with accuracy the number of soldiers available each week for the voyage. He added that it would be a month or six weeks before the AEF could have a "reservoir of personnel" for embarkation.[37] At the end of the year, he recommended that ten divisions remain until the treaty was signed. In doing so, he overrode Foch's plea for twenty-two to twenty-five divisions. But by then Pershing did not want to concede even as many as ten divisions, as he indicated in a cabled request "that we take all our troops out of Europe at the earliest possible moment."[38]

In Washington, March noted this advice and authorized the early transportation of the rear-area troops.[39] Before the end of November, the Chief of Staff sent out the plan for handling the demobilization of the AEF. Regiments would go to the centers in the area from which the majority of the unit came. Prior to leaving France, those not from the area would transfer to casual detachments going to their locale.[40] He abandoned this initial procedure in three months as impractical and replaced it with a program of breaking up the division at debarkation points, collecting men from the same area, and sending them to the nearest centers for final processing.[41] One essential remained constant. Baker and March intended to bring the AEF home "as rapidly as transportation facilities are available. . . ."[42]

Since shipping was the limiting factor, as March informed one correspondent, the Chief of Staff began thinking about this before the war ended.[43] He called in Hines of the Embarkation Service, discussed the requirements, and laid plans for the conversion of cargo vessels into transports; as the AEF decreased in size, its supply demands would also, allowing reduction of the number of vessels required in this service. When Baker asked March about the problem, the General told him of the preparations. In December, work began on the first cargo ship. Eventually, the army converted 58 of these craft at a cost of $8,345,975. Despite this tremendous increase in troop-carrying capacity, March knew that the army needed still more. The navy contributed some space in its warships. Again, as in the spring of 1918, the War Department turned to foreign sources. As General Hines was going to Europe anyway to negotiate the Allied charges for the use of their wartime shipping, he supplemented the transport fleet by making commercial arrangements with various countries. Nevertheless, 84 per cent of the AEF returned in American ships.[44]

The returning tide moved more rapidly than the eastward flow. Beginning with 26,000 in November, the number transported grew until it reached a peak of almost 350,000 in June, 1919. Pershing announced the order of precedence in February and cabled in May that he had placed all but three divisions on shipping orders. By the end of August, these three had sailed and only 40,000 logistical troops and the occupying force in the Rhineland remained.[45]

The public wanted to greet its heroes by having them parade – a sentiment not shared by the soldiers who contemplated the resulting delay in their discharge. Although the General Staff was aware of this attitude, it acceded to the popular demand and authorized such ceremonies when possible. In the first six months of 1919, over 500 parades took place throughout the nation. The War Department wanted the soldiers cheered, but it refused the suggestion of a New York City official who advocated that civilians be required to give a military salute to all returned veterans.[46]

In the spring of 1919, army officials were more concerned over the men's employment opportunities than their ceremonial welcomes. As the stream of ex-soldiers poured out of demobilization centers, the job market was decreasing because of the cancellation of war contracts. Congress added to the difficulty of the situation by cutting the appropriations of the Labor Department's job placement agency, the U.S. Employment Service. In the War Office, Baker named Arthur Woods, a former New York City police commissioner, as a special assistant to supplement the Employment Service's efforts.[47] As March later commented, ". . . every possible effort was made by the War Department to obtain employment in civil life for ex-soldiers."[48] The army also offered those soldiers without job prospects the opportunity of remaining in the service if they wished.[49] Throughout the period, the two executive departments made progress in dealing with the problem. During his press conference on June 7, March reported that in the preceding four months only 30 per cent of the new civilians had applied for placement assistance. He noted that in the past five weeks the Employment Service had placed 66 per cent of the applicants.[50] Without broad economic planning and fettered by congressional penuriousness, the Labor and War Departments, aided by other agencies, achieved a final record of over 66 per cent placement of all registered applicants.[51]

In March, Baker and the Chief of Staff embarked on a coast-to-coast inspection tour of the demobilization centers. Ten days after the Armistice, they had visited Fort Dix to examine the beginning of the demobilization.[52] Since then well over a million soldiers had re-entered civilian life and thirty-two other camps had set up the necessary discharge arrangements.[53] Although each post was supposed to be going through the same procedure, some were taking much longer than others to discharge the men. For two and a half weeks, the two officials watched men go through the process, talked with local commanders, and analyzed the differences in the methods of handling the demobilization.[54] At their first stop at Camp Custer, Michigan, March found that Brigadier General Grote Hutcheson, the commanding officer, had reduced the terminal procedure to two days. After visiting the other camps, the Chief of Staff decided that Hutcheson's system was the most efficient and ordered all centers to follow his practice.[55]

The number of administrative personnel also concerned the high-ranking inspectors. March later told reporters: "At each camp I gave orders on the spot, when it was necessary, to cut the overhead personnel in half, and otherwise diminish the number of emergency men [those who had entered the service for the duration of the war emergency] who were retained."[56] In some cases, March authorized the hiring of civilians to handle the administrative duties.[57] Throughout their journey, daily telegrams informed the Secretary and the Chief of Staff of War Department activity and supplied them with the mounting statistics of demobilization.[58]

During the next month March alone made another brief inspection trip to several demobilization centers. The high point of this trip was at Camp Pike, Arkansas, when the Chief of Staff went through the discharge mill and did everything that the soldier had to do.[59] As a result of his own observations and the various reports, he was pleased with the system. On May 10, he told the press that the army had discharged over two million men and that the last of the first million of the AEF was on the way home. The six months of demobilization he considered "really a Twentieth Century performance."[60]

After the Armistice a barrage of criticism, much of it about the AEF, struck the War Department. There were horrible stories of misjudgment in combat and unnecessary casualties and less serious tales of antagonism toward the French and English, inefficient mail service, unpaid troops, and poor living conditions in the field and, particularly, at Brest, the great port of debarkation. A controversy also raged during the early months of 1919 over the maladministration of military justice, with Enoch Crowder bearing the brunt of the attack.[61] In part this was a natural post-war reaction. To a certain extent, anti-administration politics generated some of the criticism and, of course, internal army politics played a role, yet many of the allegations were true. Then, in addition, the fact that every major war had provided a general as a successful presidential candidate was a consideration of the time. Although as Chief of Staff March was exposed to glancing blows whenever the army came under attack, he was more directly concerned with the internal military complaints — the National Guard-Regular Army rivalry and the relationship of the War Department and the AEF.

The cause of much of the "griping" in the AEF as well as in the United States was the army caste system which provided special privileges for officers, on occasion at the direct expense of the enlisted men. Raymond B. Fosdick, Chairman of the Commission on Training Camp Activities, labelled this "the main root" of soldiers' dissatisfaction with the army.[62] Representative William Fields, Democrat from Kentucky, picked up the cause and threatened to stop the pay of any officers guilty of perpetuating caste practices.[63] And in February, Fields proposed an amendment to the Appropriation Bill which would make mandatory the elimination of caste within the service.[64]

Complaints against the caste system could easily turn into wholesale tirades against the army — specifically, the regular army. Accounts of discrimination against citizen-soldiers circulated on both sides of the Atlantic. The military way did not fit into the main stream of American democratic development, and, what is more, maintenance of a regular army in peacetime is expensive. The general post-war reaction inspired congressmen to attack the service. An Alabama Congressman, George Huddleston, put the regulars in their place: "Many of the officers are engaged in the business merely as a profession, which is a loafing job in time of peace, as it might be considered, not doing anything useful, except perhaps giving a little of their time to fitting themselves for a duty that may never come. . . ."[65] More knowledgeable representatives might well have winced at Huddleston's remarks, but there was more to come. Republican Representative Harold Knutson of

Minnesota phrased the issue in economic terms: "The time has arrived to democratize the American Army — better still, replace it with the National Guard, so far as possible. If we do that we will make an important step in retrenchment of our expenditures."[66] The National Guard Association, through its president Bennett Clark, went all out against the regulars: "It is the aim of all of us to build up the National Guard and smash the Regular Army."[67]

The symbol of caste in the AEF was the Sam Browne belt. This diagonal across-the-shoulder leather strap attached to a broad belt was cherished by the AEF officers as a distinguishing characteristic and hated accordingly by the enlisted men.[68] Since regulations forbade wearing these belts in the United States, the returning officers had to shed them before landing. On some transports, the troops staged mock funerals for the Sam Browne and sang, to the tune of "The Old Gray Mare," "The old Sam Browne belt is not what it used to be, not what it used to be, for it has been taken away."[69] While some officers joined in these festivities, others were anxious to retain the belt. Frank McIntyre, March's Executive Assistant, answered one such plea which a senator had forwarded: "Your friend will find, I think, that those officers and enlisted men who return from overseas will be envied for their opportunity and splendid accomplishments, but that there is no disposition to permit this envy to extend to their haberdashery."[70] Pershing, in a personal letter to Secretary Baker, made a strong appeal for the belt, but to no avail.[71] Later, he and his staff would flaunt their Sam Brownes and, when the AEF commander became Chief of Staff in 1921, one of his first orders directed that the belt be worn at all times outside of quarters.[72]

The Sam Browne symbolized the difference between the AEF and the army in the United States. Baker was conscious of the possibility of friction and talked about it with Harbord during his visit to France.[73] For many, a mystique enveloped the AEF. Desk officers in Paris were overseas veterans and heroes while men doing similar work in the United States were abused as "slackers" and "swivel-chair officers" on the floor of the Senate.[74] To a certain extent, the AEF people cultivated this distinction. After the Armistice, the great problem of integrating the two forces began. By September, 1919, the AEF would be a memory and the officers who planned and led it to victory would be attempting to find places in the peacetime establishment. At the same time, the emergency expansion in the War Department and the various combat and administrative units which did not cross the Atlantic would be greatly deflated. Since post-war military policy was in the throes of debate throughout 1919, army planners did not know exactly what the size of the army would be. Officers who commanded divisions in combat might well be disgruntled to find themselves commanding understrength regiments. The war was the high point in most of these professionals' careers. The sickening plunge from stars to eagles or leaves accentuated their post-war depression.

In this vein, on the day following the signing of the Treaty of Versailles, one of Pershing's ranking staff officers mused in the now peaceful atmosphere of G.H.Q.:

> This is one of the dreariest days of the war. I have knocked around the world so much that I am seldom ever lonely but yesterday was certainly a lonely day. The people of Chaumont celebrated the signing of the peace by lighting up the town with colored electric lights and by giving a grand ball. I did not turn out for this affair as it was much of a mob.[75]

For the AEF career officers, the uncertainties of peace were fearful to contemplate.

On the day of the Armistice, the War Department stopped appointments to commissioned rank and all promotions. Baker even refused a presidential request a few days later.[76] March thought it unnecessary to commission more officers at a time when he contemplated demobilizing the bulk of men in uniform. As for promotions, the logical course seemed to March to be complete demobilization, followed by placement of deserving officers in higher ranks in the reorganized peacetime army. He would reward the deserving emergency officers who were not remaining in the service by promotions in reserve rank or by decoration or both.[77]

Pershing immediately protested this decision. In a lengthy cable, he pointed out that various units were in the process of organization, which meant that many officers were occupying positions of responsibility beyond the rank held. He believed others deserving on the basis of their performances in the closing campaign. In short, to him and undoubtedly to those who were recommended for promotion the order was simply unjust.[78] March answered with his explanation for the order.[79] In January, the Secretary relented slightly and ordered him to authorize the AEF commander to make limited promotions up to and including the rank of colonel, not as a reward for past service but only to maintain the AEF "as a living organization." [80] Pershing attempted to mollify the recommended officers by writing those who would have received stars and by promoting as many as possible – 12,875 – under the new provision.[81] But this was not satisfactory, as former Assistant Secretary of War Henry Breckinridge, then serving as a staff officer noted: "After the Armistice, it was nearly amusing to see the emissaries of G.H.Q. rushing from one end of France to the other to promote everyone in sight. It was better than nothing but not good enough." [82] In this matter the War Department seemed at fault to many and Congress was quick to register this discontent.

March took the personal responsibility for handling the demotion of generals, but delegated the fate of lesser ranks to the Personnel Branch of the Operations Division.[83] Since demotion on a mass scale was inevitable, the Chief of Staff and the General Staff made many enemies among the AEF officers who believed that combat service was undervalued. As the transports returned, March would go over the list of generals on board, decide the disposition of these officers, and then allow them to maintain their emergency rank of demote them accordingly.[84] Most who lost their temporary commissions resented the junior officers who had not crossed the Atlantic but who now retained higher ranks. The fact that these officers were holding positions commensurate with their rank, while the AEF people had no units to command or to staff, did not ease the bitterness of the dispossessed. March gave some of them interviews but offered little consolation.[85]

In August, one of the recent AEF arrivals in Washington, Major General Charles D. Rhodes, recorded his disillusionment and suspicions in his diary:

> Everywhere, I find much discontent over the present unsettled conditions in army circles. Those who fought overseas are heartsick over the apparent envy and even malice which appears to confront us on the part of those who were unable to get to France. Although there may be some fixed policies affecting the demotion of returning officers, such policies are not apparent to the man-in-the-street, and to the casual observer appear to be based on favoritism. All of Pershing's generals, with but few exceptions, have been promptly demoted, while all good army jobs continue to be filled with "March adherents," with officers of the field artillery, "running strong." [86]

Two days later, Rhodes' turn came. He had survived an air crash in Europe and he would live through his demotion, but not without pain,

"Actually changed my double-stars today, to the old-time eagles, and the drop in rank is worse than my plane drop in France." [87]

March had important positions for some AEF officers, but this did not counter the general despair of those who lost stars. During the first six months after the war, he cabled requests for specific officers to head the schools, to serve on the General Staff, and to act as Judge Advocate General in Crowder's absence.[88] To the others, he could offer only the possibility of places in the projected large army which Congress was considering.

"In consideration of the problem of the future training of the United States Army at home," he wrote Pershing in March, "the selection of the general officer to supervise this work is of the greatest importance and the man whom I have in mind for the duty is [James W.] McAndrew." He requested Pershing's chief of staff, as he commented later, "because I wanted to have a man who had the last bit of knowledge we had acquired over there." [89] While Pershing displayed reluctance in releasing the general, he did, after some delay, allow McAndrew, who was also March's West Point classmate, to return to become commandant of the General Staff College. March also named AEF veterans Charles H. Muir and Douglas MacArthur to command respectively the Leavenworth school and the Military Academy.[90] On the War Department General Staff, he placed two AEF corps commanders – William G. Haan as War Plans Division Director and one of Pershing's close personal friends, William M. Wright, as Executive Assistant.[91] In addition to these appointments, several of the bureau chiefs were AEF veterans who took over the War Department counterparts of their jobs in France. The list of division and department commanders is another indication that March gave AEF leaders key positions: by January, 1920, well over half of these generals had won their distinction in France.[92]

In an effort to incorporate AEF experience into the General Staff, March reiterated his wartime appeal for trained staff officers to Pershing. Three weeks after the Armistice, he cabled for fifteen officers by name "or as many as can be spared immediately." [93] When Pershing chose not to spare nine of the group, March pressed the request: "trained General Staff officers who have experience in Washington and also in France are imperatively needed in making necessary studies bearing on future policies and legislation for reorganization. . . ." [94] In response to this urgent message, the AEF commander released three more and indicated that the others would soon follow.[95] Later, he rejected March's request for his aide, Colonel George C. Marshall, to serve in the War Plans Division.[96]

Even those fortunate ones who were offered good berths in the post-war establishment were not always pleased. Peacetime chores lacked the excitement and distinction of wartime action. Soon after he became an assistant to the Chief of Staff, Haan wrote a friend, "This job . . . is not altogether to my liking." [97] And George Van Horn Moseley was pleased when Pershing turned down March's request for him: "I . . . do not want to get mixed up in the War Department at the present time unless I know just what I am going into and the conditions under which I shall have to serve." [98]

Those less fortunate applied themselves to their routine tasks, dreamed about the AEF, pondered their present situation, and hoped that their old commander would be able to solve their problems when he returned. Evidently, they were thinking in terms of cliques; certainly Harbord, who had nourished suspicions of March since early 1918, thought the army divided. In June, he gave his "C-in-C" his opinion of the situation and reminded him of his responsibility to those who had served in France. "Everything indicates that the higher officers of the Regular Army are lining up in two general groups. a) Those who are in step with General March and whom he is using the great power of his position to place. . . . b) The group who look to you as Chief, who have served you with the best they had, and who, wearing your AEF brand, have no hope except through you." [99]

Earlier, when Harbord discussed the intra-army problems with Baker, the Secretary said in a questioning tone: "I do not exactly know what to do with General Pershing. There does not seem to be anything in the United States for a General." Harbord seized upon this opening to bring up his solution to the post-war difficulties: make Pershing Chief of Staff and let March retain his four stars as commander of the Army of Occupation. Baker was startled; but, after a pause, he commented, "General, I think that is a very good suggestion. It seems to me to have merit. I will think it over. I had not thought of that solution before." The S.O.S. Chief passed this along to Pershing with this observation of the Secretary: "Personally, I think he is a fine straight little man." [100] Events in June may have altered this opinion. At that time, Herbert Bayard Swope published a story in the *New York World* which asserted that President Wilson had "tentatively approved" a plan giving Pershing the office of Chief of Staff and March command of the Rhineland contingent, but Baker denied the story.[101] Later, on the day the Treaty was signed, June 28, Wilson actually made such a proposal to his War Secretary and added that they would discuss it upon his return.[102] Baker evidently disapproved, as nothing came of the suggestion, but rumors about such a change continued to circulate.[103]

The bitter reaction of the AEF officers to their situation was natural but, in a sense, unrealistic. The basic cause of most of their complaints was the reduction of the army from some 3,700,000 men to approximately 750,000 in one year. If the President had named Pershing Chief of Staff and given those wearing his "brand" complete control of the military organization, the fundamental state of the service would not have changed. Undoubtedly, many individuals would have been pleased, but then those experienced officers who would have to be replaced, in turn, would have had legitimate complaints. It was a dilemma which Baker and March attempted to solve by maintaining the existing organizations, by turning some key jobs over to AEF officers, and by hoping, all the while, that their plan for a large army would relieve the discontent of those former ranking Expeditionary Force officers scattered throughout the country in the deflated army.

Although this was an intra-organizational controversy, repercussions reached Congress, particularly about the frozen promotions and the demotions. Senator John B. Kendrick, Democrat of Wyoming, wanted to force promotions of all those recommended prior to the Armistice, and the Senate approved a resolution which ordered an investigation of the promotion situation.[104] Meantime, anti-administration politicians made use of the plight of the unpromoted citizen-soldiers and regulars as a convenient weapon against the War Department.

For civilians the struggle within the army, if known, had little meaning, while complaints from relatives in the AEF were of greater importance. In January, Fosdick, who had been in Europe for several weeks, reported on the post-war AEF: "The situation over here is, I believe, little short of desperate, and the worst part of it is that the regular Army men who are running it do not seem to realize it. . . . The feeling of bitterness among the troops is growing."[105] He then described the lengthy drill sessions and the living conditions of the Second Army in particular. "They live in the mud, they sleep in the mud and they eat in the mud."[106]

Despite Fosdick's belief, Pershing and his regulars were aware of the morale problem. As diversions for troops awaiting shipment, Pershing encouraged horse shows, marksmanship contests, boxing, baseball – athletics generally. In addition to this entertainment, the G.H.Q. established a broad educational program which embraced illiterates as well as college graduates.[107] As his contribution to morale, Pershing began inspecting the various divisions. During these ceremonies, he would talk with officers and men in the ranks, particularly those wearing wound chevrons, and conclude with a brief speech to the assembled command about its accomplishments.[108]

Pershing could rely on the accolades of victory, the three thousand miles of the Atlantic, and the sturdy defense of Baker and March to shield him from virtually all criticism. After all, as one congressman said, investigating this hero would be like "investigating the Duke of Wellington after the Battle of Waterloo. . . ."[109] Nevertheless, as his friend Frederick Palmer wrote to Harbord in March, "There has been a certain amount of gossipy criticism of Pershing prompted by foreign propaganda partly, and more largely, by gentlemen with their own lightning rods out who hear that he might be a candidate for president."[110] This last seemed to be demonstrated by the charge that the Thirty-fifth Division (Kansas and Missouri National Guard) had lost 7,000 men in the Argonne because of the lack of artillery and aviation support. The Governor of Kansas, Henry J. Allen, who made this charge, was a close political ally of Leonard Wood, whom he was to place in nomination at the Republican convention in 1920. Although Allen did not specify Pershing but rather held the "highly organized inefficiency of the whole system" responsible, one might ask who organized and controlled the "system" in the AEF.[111]

Pershing was aware of the dangers of post-war reaction to his position. His friends in France and in the United States informed and advised him about the possible threats. Harbord warned that every war has its "sacrificial goat" and that the "C-in-C" would be a prominent candidate from this war.[112] The S.O.S. chief also recounted the various points of criticism and analyzed the causes. "The Republicans are to a certain extent interested in discrediting the whole conduct of the war under the present administration. . . . When the Republican attack upon the administration gets to be a little binding, an effort will be made to 'pass the buck' to you."[113] His West Point roommate, Billy Wright, wrote in June, "The Nat Gd is responsible for much if not all of the anti-A.E.F. sentiment in the country."[114] Frederick Palmer enumerated the complaints and pointed out that "Washington seethes, and the big figure on the other side of the Atlantic was bound to be the victim of jealousy." He added this caution: "don't let any damfool talk the Presidency."[115] Harbord, always the good staff officer, advised his chief to prepare a defense: "It seems to me that it is a very grave duty for you to have a thorough study made to determine (1) all the facts along possible lines of attack, and (2) those most favorable to your own side."[116] Palmer further recommended: "Prestige, silence, wisdom, destiny."[117]

On September 8, the conquering hero arrived in New York on the *Leviathan.* Surrounded by his entourage of staff officers, his crack parade regiment, and the records of his Expeditionary Force, the tall Missourian came home to a great welcome. Baker and March arrived by train early that morning and hurried to join the welcoming party. At a brief ceremony on a Hoboken pier, the Secretary presented to the AEF commander his General of the Armies commission which President Wilson had signed just before leaving for his ill-fated western tour.[118]

"Gen. John J. Pershing, U.S.A., the victorious leader of the greatest army every assembled under the flag of the United States in the greatest war in all history," as the *Army and Navy Journal* described him, spent a busy period in New York City – greeting 50,000 children, each waving an American flag, in Central Park, attending formal dinners, and leading the First Division and his composite regiment down Fifth Avenue.[119] Although March had to return to Washington after seeing Pershing arrive, he came back to review the parade.[120] For the first time in history, according to the *New York Times,* a full division with combat equipment paraded. It took three hours for the 25,000 men to pass the reviewing stand in front of the Metropolitan Museum. Pershing looked magnificent on horseback as he rode slowly through the streets lined with flags and bunting and paved with the roses and laurel which the crowd cast in his path.[121]

Two days later, he arrived in Washington at Union Station, where Baker and March again extended greetings.[122] And on September 17, the "C-in-C" led the First and "Pershing's Own" along the Pennsylvania Avenue route taken by the Civil War armies in their Grand Review fifty-four years before. Once more, March and other dignitaries watched proceedings from the reviewing stand.[123]

In the nineteen months since he had left France to become Acting Chief of Staff, March's position had changed considerably. He had earned not only the four stars and title of Chief of Staff but also the confidence of the Secretary of War. He and Pershing had maintained close contact through cables and a less frequent but more personal correspondence by letter. During the anxious days of 1918, friction had developed between them when three thousand miles and different problems prevented them from completely understanding each other's situation. The urgency of affairs lessened with the Armistice but the differences remained with this distinction – now the focus was shifted to the United States as the troops were withdrawn from Europe. The AEF was no more. Even the token "show" regiment which Pershing led in parades would soon disperse and the victorious commander would have no troops to command. The foremost position in the army was occupied by the man who watched from the stands as the hero was pelted with flowers, but the foremost soldier in rank and reputation was the stately figure leading the parade. Here was a paradox. As long as Pershing remained in Europe, the problem was not so apparent. Once he returned and stood between Baker and March to wave at the throngs, a decision seemed imperative.[124]

Relations appeared to be affable, although newspapers had rumored that this was not true. Nevertheless, Baker awarded the Distinguished Service Medal to March on Pershing's recommendation, and the citation Pershing cabled alluded not only to March's work as commander of the AEF artillery but also to his "service of inestimable value" as Chief of Staff.[125] Their correspondence continued after the war but the personal letters ceased with a friendly exchange in the spring of 1919.[126] While Harbord, whose suspicions had not lessened in the past year, warned Pershing of the danger of March's position, a civilian friend, Martin Egan, pointed out that there were no signs of maliciousness from that source.[127] As criticism mounted against the army, the War Department took the brunt of it, but neither March nor Baker attempted to shift this burden to Pershing. Yet, the organizational structure of the two generals' relationship encouraged friction. The physical presence of both men in Washington would increase it.

For March, greeting Pershing was one of the many events which filled his calendar in addition to his regular schedule at the War Department. During the year he had gone on inspection trips, attended Theodore Roosevelt's funeral, visited West Point at graduation time, and, in the meantime, continued to hold weekly press conferences.[128] In a lighter vein, he had thrown out the first ball of the baseball season and watched Walter Johnson shut out the Philadelphia Athletics.[129]

Many issues took up his time. In June, there was a flare-up on the Mexican border and some American troops briefly crossed the boundary.[130] Throughout 1919 labor disturbances and race riots brought calls for federal troops. Although both Baker and March were reluctant to use regulars in these situations, regulars nonetheless appeared on the scene in several instances — on one occasion in the city of Washington itself to stop a race riot.[131] Despite the varying degrees of seriousness of these problems, the two principal issues of the time for March were demobilization of the wartime army and reorganization of the peacetime army.

By the time of Pershing's return, the discharge process was virtually complete. March viewed the results with pride. The army had released some 3,280,000 officers and men in the 10 months since the Armistice. In comparison with the mustering-out following the Civil War, the figures were impressive, as the War Department had more than tripled the 1865–1866 number.[132] This was not accomplished without criticism. March's plan of demobilization drew fire then and later, but the question remains, what would have been a successful alternative? Certainly the principal one suggested had deficiencies, as the British soon found. The industrial plan required, in order to be practical, the classification of soldiers to determine priorities. This would have kept the men in uniform much longer than they, the public, and Congress desired. The lack of a comprehensive economic reconstruction program also would have hampered the effectiveness of such a plan. Finally, the military establishment had needs which civilian planners did not consider.

Throughout this period, March evidently took little part in the liquidation of war surplus. He was more interested in the manpower question with which, because of his pre-war experience in The Adjutant General's Office, he was better prepared to deal. The civilian experts and trained logistical officers handled the surplus problem.

Although demobilization was almost over by September, 1919, the problem of reorganization and military policy was entering into the apogee of discussion. The ramifications of this issue were far-reaching. Promotions and demotions and the integration of the returning regulars of the AEF into the peacetime organization were part of this, as were the reaction of a war-weary Congress, the political animosities of some and the ambitions of others both military and civilian. To many, the solution of the multi-faceted problems of the post-war establishment was Pershing. The Chief of Staff, to them, was an obstacle or even a dangerous opponent.

14 · PLANS FOR A POST-WAR MILITARY POLICY

After the Armistice, consideration of long-term military policy became mandatory and Peyton March did not shirk his responsibility to advise his civilian superiors on this subject. He took a tentative plan from the General Staff, molded his version, and ignored those who criticized his methods. With the support of the Secretary of War and the approval of the President, he adamantly defended his policy. Since there were other proposals from within the army, from the National Guard, and from Congress, and the military future of the nation was at stake, controversy was inevitable. Although March did compromise slightly on the point of universal training, he refused to take a flexible position on any other aspect of his proposals. This rigid posture caused bitter opposition to him and to his ideas.

As the various factions shaped their plans and drew the battlelines for debate, March, as Chief of Staff, had to concentrate on other problems as well. Within the General Staff, he made major personnel changes. Then, in an effort to communicate War Department views directly to ranking generals, he ordered a conference of department and division commanders, but the fact that he did not attend, other than to make brief introductory remarks, limited the effectiveness of the meeting. Finally, he created additional opposition by his attempt to reform the West Point system.

In 1916, there had been a large-scale debate over military policy. Although the passage of the National Defense Act in June of that year had calmed the controversy, the experiences of the war had reopened the subject. And many of the same leaders on Capitol Hill were present in 1919 to defend or to propose their pet projects from the earlier period. On both occasions, the size and function of the regular army, the power of the General Staff, and the place of the National Guard and universal military training — the civilian, in other words — in the military system were topics of argument. Inseparable from the issue of the citizen in arms were the practical questions of the degree and methods of professional control, the exact type of military training, and the organization of the military establishment. For some, the conflict centered on a regular army organized to expand readily according to wartime demands versus a professional army acting primarily as a training cadre for citizens who would compose the bulk of an emergency force. But in 1919, other factors added to the complexity of the problem: the disposition of the wartime organizations, particularly those resulting from the new weapons — the airplane and gas; and the lobbying of bureau chiefs restive under the General Staff control increased by the war. Finally, the public reaction against the military and the overwhelming urge for government economy were to make it almost impossible to reach any sound solution.[1]

While the actual conduct of the war dominated most thinking on military matters through 1918, even during that hectic time both Congress and the War Department gave some attention to post-war policy. In April, 1918, three members of the Senate Military Affairs committee, Oregon Democrat George E. Chamberlain, and Republicans James W. Wadsworth of New York and Harry S. New of Indiana, talked of providing for post-war universal military training.[2] During their June conventions, the Rotarians and the American Medical Association endorsed a universal training policy.[3] Later, in July, March ordered the War Plans Division to work out such a program.[4] On August 29, Lytle Brown forwarded to the Chief of Staff his division's plan, which proposed a nine-months training program. General Brown concluded the plan with the comment, "The United States will occupy a particularly favorable position for the initiation of universal military training at the end of the present war." [5] With the major campaigns of the fall still before the army, the end seemed distant so March apparently pigeonholed this project.

In the middle of October, March and Jervey, the Operations chief, talked about a permanent military establishment and agreed that the army should consist of 20 combat divisions, supplemented by 4 depot divisions, organized into 5 corps; at reduced strength, the total number of troops would be 400,000 or 500,000. Jervey asked Brown to initiate a study on this basis.[6] On Armistice Day, a committee of four officers in the War Plans Branch of the War Plans Division received this order:

> The War Plans Branch is directed to submit plans for the organization of the Regular Army as it is to be after the War.
>
> It has been suggested by the Chief of Staff and Director of Operations that 1 Field Army reduced in strength to 500,000, be taken as a basis on which to proceed.
>
> Work to be expedited.[7]

With this guide, the committee proceeded to collect the views of the chiefs of all the bureaus and staff agencies on what their role would be in creating and maintaining a field army of this size. While the War Plans group made its investigation, the Coordination Section prepared a proposal to retain with a few alterations the existing War Department organization. The Executive Assistant forwarded this paper to Brown to include in the planning body's study.[8]

Before the committee could complete its analysis, March asked for an outline of its plan. Already he had discussed the project with the Secretary and had secured not only his, but also the President's approval of the 500,000-man army. Since Baker was impatient over the length of time the War Plans Division was taking in its work, March pressed the Director to turn in the results. Brown pulled together the material on hand and sent him a general sketch.[9] On the last day of the year, he gave the Chief of Staff a more thorough version, but one still "incomplete" and "fragmentary" according to his subordinates.[10] March was giving much thought to the problem of military policy. In the middle of December, he commented, "My work here has increased, if anything, with the reversing of the machine and mustering out of men combined with the preparation of a complete reorganization for the Regular Army which we intend to present to Congress very shortly." [11]

March deemed "prompt action . . . imperative." [12] For, as Goethals noted, "Everything is confusion and it will not settle down until the reorganization of the Army is definitely fixed." [13] When the Chief of Staff received Brown's first draft, he gave it to Jervey and McIntyre for comment. Their criticisms were similar in that they did not agree to the proliferation of the administrative staff nor to the territorial organization of the field army based, in part, on the possibility of universal training. Both believed that the executive branch through the War Department, rather than Congress, should specify organization and that promotion by selection was in order.[14]

March read over Brown's plan, decided that he could not use it, and outlined his own views to McIntyre and Jervey. With their aid, he devised his own design for the post-war army. In the outer office, Colonel Thomas M. Spaulding of the Operations Division shaped the notes of their conclusions into a legislative bill. It seemed to him that March virtually "dictated" the bill. He recalled, "When it was finished, McIntyre said to me: 'Well, it's not such a bad bill.' "[15] William G. Haan, who later served as War Plans Division chief, thought that there was "a lack of tact . . . in preparation."[16]

During the preparation of the bill, March kept Baker informed of the progress. When Spaulding finished his draft, March edited it and sent copies to the Secretary, the Assistant Secretaries, and the General Staff division chiefs. Baker then called a conference in his office to discuss the measure. Assistant Secretary Crowell, Jervey, McIntyre, Brown, and Goethals joined March after hours to meet with the Secretary. Significantly, as a demonstration of their waning power, none of the bureau chiefs were present.[17]

In "this free and complete discussion which lasted until midnight," March took up the bill by sections and answered all objections and comments.[18] The Chief of Staff dominated the meeting and "at the end, it was decided to submit the bill to Congress as it stood. . . ."[19] March later wrote, ". . . there was substantial agreement among the civilians as well as the military men present at the conference. . . . We all wanted to do what was best for the country, and none of us was influenced by any other motive."[20]

On January 16, 1919, the chairman of the House Military Committee, Representative S. Hubert Dent, Jr., of Alabama, introduced the War Department bill with the comment that it was by request. Throughout that day, he and his Committee colleagues heard the Secretary of War and the Chief of Staff explain their bill. "The general idea of the bill," March testified "was to put into legal form what the present organization of the army is. . . . [It] embodies the experience of the war. . . ."[21] The bill thus contained provisions for a strong General Staff and the various recently created branches, with the exception of the Chemical Warfare Service. It also provided for an army of 509,909 men without specifying the organization beyond the number of men in each branch. Finally, the bill included a plan for promotion by selection.[22]

The congressmen were disgruntled. None of them wanted a large peacetime army. And the bill did not mention universal military training or the National Guard. Baker attempted to allay their criticisms by explaining that the large army would be temporary: "in making the estimate we had in mind the possibilities of some part of the American army being required for a more or less limited period to see that the terms of the peace agreed upon were carried out." He believed that the subject of universal training should also depend on the results of the peace conference. The National Guard, he added, would remain as formed under the 1916 National Defense Act. But his explanations did not satisfy the Committee.[23]

Dent warned that it would be "impossible" to pass such a measure in the remaining six weeks of the session. Rather than trying to obtain legislation on permanent military policy, the chairman suggested that the War Department merely request funds for maintaining necessary troops during the transition period.[24] Another Committee member, John C. McKenzie, was more frank: "I do not believe that any bill providing for an army of 500,000 men in time of peace will ever get through the House of Representatives." [25] The hearings ended on that note.

Naturally, congressional leaders expected AEF experience to play a part in post-war planning. The War Plans Division committee also desired to consult the overseas contingent before reaching a final solution; however, March wanted immediate action and did not allow time for such consultation. In his testimony, he made one reference to the AEF participation when he mentioned that he had asked Pershing to return some General Staff officers to aid in forming policy. If the Chief of Staff was reluctant to seek AEF views, the "C-in-C" was equally averse to supplying them; but March did not tell the congressman that Pershing initially had refused to honor his request in its entirety—sending only six of the fifteen officers requested.[26]

In keeping with its independence, so carefully maintained throughout the war, G.H.Q. developed concurrently its own military policy. The genesis of the plan was in the office of the G-5 training section. By December 6, 1918, the chief of this section, Harold B. Fiske, was able to circulate a comprehensive memorandum to the other staff agencies in Chaumont. This lengthy paper advocated a standing army of 252,400 officers and men, universal military training with a seven-month training period, abolition of several bureaus, a powerful General Staff of permanently detailed officers (similar to the German system), abolition of the militia, and absorption of the Marine Corps into the regular army. After securing the comments of his colleagues, Fiske made minor revisions and prepared the plan for Pershing's signature.[27]

The wary "C-in-C" was not ready to endorse any such proposal. The time was hardly propitious for him to approve a plan which would arouse opposition from bureau chiefs, friends of the Marine Corps and militia, and those against universal training. By this time, the House had already refused to consider the less extreme March bill and newspapers were broadcasting criticism of the army's wartime effort. His astute friend, Frederick Palmer, the journalist, would later warn: "I hope that you will not be drawn in to any statement official or otherwise about our future military policy. Its [*sic*] certain that it will not be worked out for many months to come." [28] On Pershing's staff, Fox Conner and George Van Horn Moseley expressed similar views at the time.[29] After considering the memorandum, Pershing told his staff on February 7, 1919: "There are a good many things in this that have already become the subject of controversy, and for us now to spring the thing here as our scheme, would involve us over here in a good deal of discussion which would be entirely out of place at this time, so simply withdraw all the memoranda on the subject and have them placed on file, and drop the matter for the present." [30]

Since liaison between the War Department and G.H.Q. was faulty, March learned of the G-5 plan through two rather indirect sources. A fellow artilleryman, A. J. Bowley, enclosed a copy with a personal letter in late December. Then one of the returning staff officers brought in the December 6 draft when he reported.[31] Although the Chief of Staff sent Pershing a copy of the War Department bill, he waited until March 7, 1919, to do so, but he did brief the AEF commander on the opposition in Congress and the bureaus at that time.[32]

Although the AEF plan did not reach the public except by rumor, Senator Harry S. New, whom a Senate colleague called "practical" and "philosophical," offered an approach to military policy which differed from the March program.[33] On the last day of January, 1919, after condemning the War Department bill on the basis "that it smacks too much of that very militarism which is righteously abhorrent to our national ideals. . . . ," New proposed a bill (S. 5485) to establish a universal training period without pay for a period not to exceed one year. He added that this should be the nucleus of the military establishment. Then, on the Senate floor, another senator shifted the subject to international obligations, which Henry Cabot Lodge turned into a discussion of the Versailles conference.[34]

Despite the abrupt change in debate, the Senate did not forget New's bill. The Military Affairs Committee picked it up and sent it to the General Staff with instructions to study and to make recommendations on a universal training system. In the War Plans Division, this mission fell to three AEF veterans who had joined the staff at the Chief of Staff's cabled request. The head of this group was, in March's opinion, a "very able officer," well known throughout the army as a student of organization and policy.[35] John McAuley Palmer, "a little fellow of the school-professor type," had already developed two plans of national military policy, the last one based on universal training, during his pre-war service on the General Staff.[36] An infantry officer, he had gone to France with Pershing as his chief of operations. In this capacity, he directed the initial planning not only for operations but also for training. Forced to leave the staff by bad health, Palmer, after an interlude in Italy, returned to the AEF to command a brigade in the Argonne campaign. During this battle, the "quiet and studious" colonel greatly impressed one of his regimental commanders by his deliberate action as he took over the brigade.[37] In the closing days of the war, Pershing recognized his achievements by recommending him for a brigadier generalcy but the War Department's ban on promotions prevented him from wearing a star.[38] After the Armistice, Palmer was one of those whom Fiske asked to comment on his G-5 plan. He was pleased generally with the project and advised Fiske, "I think it presents an absolutely sound scheme of organization."[39]

When he learned that he was returning to Washington to work on reorganization planning, Palmer went to Pershing for instructions. He later reminisced, "When I reported to the General he declined to give me any instructions. He said that he had had not time to study the matter in detail and that he did not wish to commit himself in any way."[40] While at Chaumont, he stopped in the G-4 office to chat with Moseley, who had served with him on one of the pre-war General Staff committees. Palmer told his friend his destination and they discussed "questions of army organization." Afterwards, Moseley confided in his diary, "Unfortunately, he has little experience here practically, with the problems confronting us, and he still speaks from a very theoretical standpoint." [41]

On his arrival in early February, Palmer found that March had taken the matter away from the War Plans Division and had already presented his policy to Congress. Although he was disappointed, since the War Department bill seemed to him to be "completely at variance with the traditional military police of the United States," there was nothing for him to do but to turn to routine tasks. But when the New bill came in for analysis, Palmer saw an opportunity to reopen the question of policy.[42]

Since the other two officers assigned to study the bill agreed with him, they began a study which culminated in the "Outline of a Plan for National Military Organization based on Universal Military Training." Its fundamental principle, Palmer wrote Jervey, "is an organized reserve army" perpetuated by universal training. In recognition of the fact that citizen armies were necessary to fight wars, he wanted to establish and train an organized citizen force during peace. At the core of their plan, he and his collaborators placed a universal obligation consisting of a period of no more than eleven months of continuous training in the nineteenth year followed by four years in the organized reserve, which included the National Guard. Palmer thought that the plan would work with a standing army of 165,000. While he did not detail organization beyond advocating a territorial scheme of sixteen corps areas, each broken up into three divisional areas, he proposed that the regular army consist of an expeditionary force ready for immediate action, the foreign garrisons, and troops necessary to operate the training and reserve system.[43]

During March, 1919, he circulated this program throughout the War Department and obtained the general endorsement of virtually all of the bureau and General Staff sections. When the "Outline" completed its rounds, Lytle Brown read it with the concurring memos and forwarded them to the Chief of Staff with these remarks: "I recommend that it be approved as the ultimate solution . . . with the consideration always in view of passing from the plan already adopted to meet the conditions of today, to this plan as settled policy." [44]

March did not accept Palmer's plan. In his mind there was a difference between universal training and compulsory service. Training of a minimal amount, calculated not to disturb the body politic was all right, but compulsory service – a long training period combined with extended service in an organized reserve – he considered neither "American" nor "desirable." His disagreement with Palmer rested on a fundamental difference of opinion on policy. March believed that the most effective security was a standing army prepared to expand to roughly double its strength in an emergency. In case of war, conscription would supplement this existing force. On the other hand, the Chief of the War Plans Branch subscribed to a "citizen army" concept ("compulsory military service" in March's nomenclature) which de-emphasized the regular army.[45]

The expandable army idea went back to a plan advocated by Secretary of War John C. Calhoun in the 1820's and emphasized in Major General Emory Upton's *Military Policy of the United States* later in the century. Palmer would trace his citizen army ideas to George Washington and maintained that it was more in keeping with the American military experience and traditions. He well remembered the warning his grandfather, the Civil War political general John M. Palmer, had given him years before – "not to become a narrow regular army partisan."[46]

Palmer failed to make his point. While he "did not have an opportunity to speak with the Chief of Staff," he did see McIntyre and explained the case to him.[47] In the interview he based his argument on the facts that Congress would not approve the War Department bill and that the returning veterans favored universal military training. Only a month before a canvass of draftees at Camp Devens showed an overwhelming majority for such a military policy. McIntyre heard him out but when he called him in a few days later he informed Palmer that the matter was settled. As the disapproval order stated, he was merely "to faithfully develop the plans already approved by the Chief of Staff" with the assumption "that there will be no compulsory service during peace. . . ."[48]

Despite the apparent finality of his order, March did make a modification in the War Department bill. After convincing Baker that they should make a gesture toward universal training, he added a provision for three-months training in the citizen's nineteenth year.[49] This angered Palmer, since the notification which he received included the statement "that the ultimate object is to place in the field promptly a field army of about 1,250,000 men, with the necessary provision of replacements." Clearly, March's move was to support the expandable army concept and amounted, in Palmer's view, "to a complete abandonment" of the citizen army idea.[50] For the Chairman of the War Plans Branch, it was the crucial decision, as he later wrote Senator Wadsworth: "What a pity it is that General March did not approve our report on the New Bill and send it to you in April, 1919, instead of persisting in his big standing army plan. With that early start, I think you would have succeeded in getting universal training through Congress." [51]

There was another approach to the citizen army idea. At March's request, Major General John F. O'Ryan formulated his ideas into a plan which Palmer noted "was very much like" his own universal training scheme.[52] A dapper New York lawyer and the only Guardsman to command a combat division throughout the war, O'Ryan believed that the amateurs and the professionals should present a united front in military policy. His solution was to merge civilian and regular components into one federal army composed in bulk of citizen soldiers with obligatory three-months training and supplementary service. Although, in his opinion, the regular army was "obsolete," he would retain 100,000 to 120,000 professionals, but the regulars would share policy making with the citizen soldiery. Such a plan, he thought, would gain the approval not only of the civilians but also "a great number" of regular officers.[53]

While Palmer and the newly appointed Director of the War Plans Division, William G. Haan, approved O'Ryan's plan, March and some other General Staff officers did not. An indication of the War Department's attitude is in a memorandum prepared for the Chief of Staff in his office. This paper, in its comparison of the O'Ryan proposal with official War Department policy, concluded that the former was less efficient and economical and, moreover, that the change from a volunteer civilian body to a "compulsory service . . . purely Federal National Guard" would be "un-American" and "might be a menace to our institutions." [54]

Nor did all National Guard leaders accept O'Ryan's solution. The National Guard Association, harshly critical of the regulars, worked up its own plan which eventually reached Congress as the Frelinghuysen bill. Instead of a merger with the regulars into a citizen army, this faction of the Guard wanted increased separation. They advocated a relationship of their favorite organization with the army analogous to that of the Marine Corps and the navy. In particular, they wanted to take National Guard affairs away from the War Department regulars and to lodge them in a separate bureau headed by a Guard officer advised by a council of representatives from each state's contingent.[55]

March's approach to the problem pleased neither faction of the Guard. He, together with Baker and many congressmen, believed that the National Guard should operate under the provisions of the National Defense Act of 1916, hence he did not refer to it in his bill. Since the position of the National Guard was one of the crucial items in the pre-war policy debate and the Guard had won a favorable compromise measure, it would seem that the Guardsmen should applaud this stand. But the War Department's requirement that Guard units must number at least one hundred men nullified the possibility of such goodwill. Since the Guard was weakened after demobilization, this restriction would hamper its revival by eliminating the many traditionally small, understrength but enthusiastic units. It also increased the Guard's hostility toward the War Department and the suspicion that March was not interested in this civilian component as a possible defense force but only as a domestic state police agency. Although the Chief of Staff attempted to allay this fear by publicly endorsing "a strong National Guard" and by explaining, when he appeared before a congressional committee, that in case of war the Guard would again become part of an army such as he had created in the summer of 1918, he was not successful in quelling the criticism.[56]

As the various advocates proposed their views and took up their positions on military policy, March still carried on the multiple duties of Chief of Staff. While he made occasional trips, including a visit to Philadelphia to see Lafayette play the University of Pennsylvania in football, and a two-week voyage to Panama with Baker, March spent most of the time at his desk.[57]

There were changes in the General Staff in addition to a reduction in its strength. March paid homage to AEF experience with two key appointments in the staff. In May, 1919, he ordered William G. "Bunker" Haan to replace Lytle Brown as Director of the War Plans Division.[58] At the end of the year, the dependable McIntyre turned over his position as Executive Assistant to William M. "Billy" Wright. An AEF corps commander who had been close to Pershing since they roomed together at West Point, Wright, although lacking the polish and tact of his predecessor, was a delightful person who charmed acquaintances with his wit.[59]

The Purchase, Storage, and Traffic Division, the continuing focus of controversy, also had a new chief. In March, 1919, after several months of preparation, an ordnance general and Academy classmate of the Chief of Staff, George W. Burr, relieved Goethals, who returned to civilian life.[60] Throughout 1919, as in 1918, there were instances of friction between the supply organization and the Operations Division. Although March attempted to settle the issue by defining each agency's role, he failed to eliminate this problem.[61] Much more difficult were the division's relations with the bureaus. The new Quartermaster General, who also held the office of Director of Purchase and Storage, Harry L. Rogers, wanted the division to stop the administrative work which he argued properly belonged to the bureaus. Formerly Quartermaster General of the AEF and a man with a strong congressional connection, Rogers seemed to represent the standard bureau attitude. Burr answered such criticism by maintaining that he was attempting to return the organization to its General Staff functions of co-ordination and supervision, but the bureau chiefs were not mollified, as their testimony before the congressional committees indicated.[62]

March and Baker had to spend most of their time considering service-wide problems. To profit from wartime lessons, March appointed an artillery board soon after the Armistice.[63] The next year, a similar board studied infantry and cavalry experience.[64] More immediate was the challenge of maintaining an adequate force despite the drain of demobilization and the lack of a permanent policy. By virtue of a special act, pressed through Congress in September, 1919, enough emergency officers remained on duty, but the enlisted strength dwindled, despite recruiting efforts, to 217,000 by the end of 1919. With some regiments reduced to less than 200 men, training was virtually impossible. Then, morale, as one lieutenant colonel who had worn a star during the war pointed out, was "certainly at a low ebb." Not only the demotions but also the War Department reorganization plan, the depleted conditions of commands, pay, and finally uniforms bothered this officer and many others, as evidenced by the congressional hearings.[65]

In an effort to promote understanding of the War Department policies and to gain a solidarity of effort throughout the army, March, at

Haan's suggestion, called a conference of department and division commanders.[66] For a week in January, 1920, these officers, predominantly former AEF commanders, listened to General Staff and bureau chiefs explain their views on the administration of the army. Since the atmosphere was informal, the visitors freely discussed their problems and made policy suggestions. They were pleased with March's recent order which decentralized War Department control by turning over some of its functions to them. But they did not seem so enthusiastic about the vocational education program which Secretary Baker and Haan emphasized. Demotions, poor morale, housing difficulties and uniforms (prohibition of AEF shoulder patches and the Sam Browne belt) provoked comment and criticism. At the end of the conference, the generals agreed that the meeting was useful and recommended that it become a permanent annual affair.[67] But Harbord, who now commanded the skeletonized Second Division, did not believe that it was as valuable as it might have been. As he wrote Charles G. Dawes, "The conference of Department and Division Commanders was profitable and at times interesting, but it lost fifty percent of its value by the failure of the Secretary of War and Chief of Staff to be present." Both spoke briefly on the first day, but neither attended the give-and-take sessions throughout the week. Thus they did not hear the interchanges about morale and they missed, as Harbord pointed out, "the effect of actual contact, the glance of an eye, a glimpse of the undercurrents, an estimate of the earnestness with which men feel." [68] Within the week of the conference's conclusion, March further injured the opportunity for rapport by turning down the unanimous request for shoulder patches and the Sam Browne when a favorable decision might have improved not only relations with the field commanders but also morale generally.[69]

One of the officers present at the conference represented a reform considered crucial by March and Baker, Douglas MacArthur, whose career, in March's words, "has been brilliant from the day he graduated at the head of his class at West Point," was in his seventh month as Superintendent of his alma mater.[70] MacArthur had found the Academy in a straitened condition when he arrived in June, 1919. Understrength in cadets, still suffering from the effects of graduating two classes (one after only sixteen months training) in one day, the object of civilian criticism, and controlled by the conservative Academic Board, West Point needed renovating.[71]

The Chief of Staff, who believed that "no system of education and training . . . can stand still and be successful," seized the opportunity to make some basic changes in the school.[72] Although he accepted the goals of the Academy, he drew upon his own educational background and the experience of eminent educators to propose a broadening of the curricula in a cultural vein while telescoping the course from four to three years. Within a week of the Armistice, the War Department queried the permanent faculty on this matter. The Academic Board's lengthy reply, endorsed by the seventy-year-old Superintendent, recommended no change.[73] Despite the concurrence in this conservative view by the *Army and Navy Journal*, a strong congressional element, John J. Pershing, and the War Plans Division, March, with the warm support of the Secretary of War, continued in his drive for reform.[74] In May, 1919, he informed the Superintendent that the course would be changed to three years and he announced publicly that he had found the man to make the transition.[75]

Recuperating from a leg wound, the heavily decorated former commander of the Forty-second "Rainbow" Division was awaiting reassignment in Washington. When MacArthur reported to the Chief of Staff, March said, "Douglas, things are in great confusion at West Point. . . . Mr. Baker and I have talked this over and we want you to go up there and revitalize and revamp the Academy. It has been parochial in the past. I want to broaden it and graduate more cadets into the army." The handsome brigadier general, still in this thirties, demurred, "I am not an educator. I am a field soldier. Besides there are so many of my old professors there. I can't do it." March knew his man: "Yes . . . you can do it." [76]

And, despite the opposition of the conservative professors, MacArthur did it. With the help of his Commandant, Robert M. Danford, whom March remembered from Fort Riley days, the young general set about refitting the Academy for its place in the twentieth century. By studying civilian universities and ordering his faculty to visit these colleges, MacArthur alleviated the isolation of the school. He also cracked down on hazing and lessened restrictions while increasing cadet responsibilities. The alteration of the course length was not successful. Although MacArthur instituted the three-year system, Congress, in passing the appropriation bill in March, 1920, ordered a return to the four-year course; but the other reforms remained and March was satisfied that MacArthur was "an exceptional Superintendent." [77]

Throughout this period, although the Chief of Staff naturally had to devote most of his time to other matters, and the Military Academy reforms were of particular importance to him, the question of future military policy remained dominant. March and others could make their proposals on that subject and fight for them but the final decision was the prerogative of Congress.

15 · CONGRESS FORGES A MILITARY POLICY

As Congress contemplated the ramifications of military policy, it had to consider the pleas of the various interest groups within the army, the National Guard, and the governing factor of an economy drive. And the legislators had to study the issues involved in the midst of a post-war reaction, marked by extensive criticism of the military. A freshman Republican representative from Kentucky, the first World War veteran to be elected to the House, King Swope, later summed up the prevalent attitude: "Everybody had a bellyful of the damn Army." [1] Regardless of President Wilson's activities at the Versailles peace conference, Congress could not forget that the nation had just fought the war to end all wars.

March's plan – the Baker-March bill – with its basic features of a strong General Staff, a standing army of over 500,000 men, and the three-month universal training program was shocking to the public's elected representatives. In an outburst on the House floor, a member of the Military Affairs Committee, Percy E. Quin, expressed the dominant mood: "They propose that outrage in time of peace. My goodness think of it." [2] His peers did and indicated their views by their cuts in the army appropriation bill and by their harsh personal criticism of the Chief of Staff.

While the men on the Hill also pounded Baker, Secretary of the Navy Josphus Daniels, and the War and Navy Departments generally, they gave especial attention to March. In January, 1919, one of the Democratic members of the House Military Affairs Committee even warned

Baker, "Your Chief of Staff is causing most of the adverse comment I hear." [3] The memories of his wartime rebuffs were too fresh for the politicians to forget. Indeed, almost two decades later, a former congressman, the then Secretary of State Cordell Hull, remarked, when he met March at a White House function, "I remember very well how you used to turn me down during the war when I came to your office for something." [4] March operated on the theory, "You cannot run a war on tact." [5] But the war was over and Congress would no longer tolerate what it construed to be arbitrary action.

One cause of congressional complaint was that March did not answer personally the letters addressed to him. Since the bulk of this correspondence was routine, his staff channeled it to the proper War Department officials for reply unless he was the only person who could settle the matter. Although it might be logical and efficient, this system irritated the members of both Houses. When Jervey answered a request for demobilization information, Senator Kenneth D. McKellar complained to the Secretary of War and then refused to accept March's explanation. He told the Chief of Staff, "We furnish you with such stenographic and clerical force as you desire. When we call on you for an expression of an opinion, it seems to me that it is as little as can be done that we get a prompt answer to it." [6] Before March received McKellar's reprimand, he had informed his staff that they should prepare replies to congressional mail addressed to him for his signature. Thus in one 5-day period he signed 237 routine responses to queries about discharge dates of individual soldiers.[7] But his change of policy was not soon enough to halt criticism.

"The lid was off. . . ." as March later noted.[8] Among his critics, Democratic Representative James A. Gallivan of Boston was particularly amusing, judging from the laughter and applause he caused in attacking the mail policy on the House floor on January 14, 1919. A few days later, he was more serious when he read into the *Congressional Record* a vitriolic letter which charged March with "blunderingly mismanaging affairs." [9]

In the Senate early in February, Joseph S. Frelinghuysen remained serious throughout his lengthy speech on the conduct of the war and demobilization. As he detailed his criticism, this enthusiastic member of the Military Affairs Committee did not spare the Chief of Staff. "From day to day," Frelinghuysen told his fellow senators, "he took to himself greater authority, unitl he was almost supreme, almost a law unto himself." The New Jersey Republican then concluded that March should be held responsible for military delinquencies.[10]

During these early months of 1919, stories about congressional hostility toward March and the legislators' desire to "clip his wings" circulated beyond the halls and offices of the Capitol in the newspapers. One included accounts of his treatment of Crowder and McCain and advised him to be "a diplomat as well as a soldier." As it is now, this Boston *Evening Transcript* article stated, some Congressmen say that March "aspires to be the Ludendorff of the American Army." While a reporter in the Washington *Post* did not equate the Chief of Staff with the hated German military leader, he unjustly accused him of withholding the Pershing reorganization plan (Fiske G-5 plan) from Congress. This correspondent, George R. Brown, had some idea of the contents of the G-5 plan, but he obviously did not know that Pershing had neither endorsed it nor submitted it formally to the War Department. But on the basis of his limited information, Brown concluded, "A situation has developed which is calculated to make the chief of staff rather than the Secretary of War the storm center of the coming inquiry." [11]

Seventeen blocks from the Capitol, in the State, War, and Navy Building, reverberations reached the office of the Chief of Staff. March wrote his Intelligence chief, Marlborough Churchill, then in France, "Conditions in America with reference to the Army are very bad." He thought he recognized the cause: "There is a concerted political drive on in Congress by the Republicans, and no attempt at defense by the Democrats, which embraces every phase of military activity both in the A.E.F. and the War Department, and," he added wearily, "apparently this will continue until the President takes a hand in the game himself, if he will." [12]

Partisan politics permeated the debates and heightened the legislative reaction against wartime executive-military dominance of affairs. During this period, the White House and the Navy Department were coming under fire along with the War Department. The time was not auspicious in Congress for a clear-headed appraisal of military problems. As an interested observer in France, Moseley, wrote General John F. O'Ryan in the spring, "The atmosphere will not be sufficiently clear for many months to enable Congress to seriously consider a military policy." [13]

Although the time was not propitious, Congress had to consider one area of military policy. The Baker-March reorganization bill, as Crowder wrote Pershing in reference to the January hearing, "was kicked out of the House Military Committee room," but consideration of the appropriations for the coming fiscal year could not be evaded so easily.[14] In February, 1919, Dent presented to the House the War Department's estimates based on the 500,000-man army for the next year. During the ensuing debate, he made it clear that this was a temporary one-year measure and that the Military Affairs Committee unanimously opposed a permanent standing army of that size. For five days the congressmen discussed the various aspects of the problem, ranging from rumors of paying trench rent to the French to questions about demobilization, troops in Russia, military justice, the caste system, and the use of typewriters.[15] While the sense of the House would not support one representative's suggestion to replace the army with the National Guard, there was enough hostility to cause the House's most knowledgeable member on military matters, Vermont Republican Frank L. Greene, to comment, "I am afraid, that we may . . . permit the pendulum to swing too far the other way, and that we will be as extreme against the army as we have been liberal for it." [16] Nevertheless, the lower house passed the bill on February 18, and sent it to the Senate. After making some amendments but retaining the 500,000-man army basis, the Military Committee reported it to their colleagues. Despite the appeals of the two party leaders, Chamberlain and Wadsworth, the Senate neither debated nor voted on this legislation in the closing days of the session.[17]

In May, 1919, the Sixty-sixth Congress began its first session with Republicans chairing the committees. Since neither of the Democrats, S. Hubert Dent and George E. Chamberlain, who had headed the House and Senate military committees had been particularly co-operative with the War Department, the change was for the better. The new incumbents, as March wrote later, had done "fine constructive work" during the war; however, both were opposed to the large standing army which the War Department advocated.[18] In the House, Julius Kahn, an immigrant in his tenth term as a representative of a San Francisco district, had earned the army's gratitude by leading the fight for conscription in 1917 when the Democratic chairman, Dent, had come out against it. Kahn, "a clear thinker," and a "delightful" fellow in his late fifties, was dedicated to universal military training.[19] The Senate Military Committee had as its chairman James W. Wadsworth, Jr., a member of the distinguished New York family. An athletic man who would be forty-two in August, Wadsworth was the "strength of the committee" although still in his first term. "Brilliant," "thorough," and "trusted," this senator was not without military experience: [20] in the Spanish War, he served as an enlisted man in Puerto Rico; later, he saw a brief period of combat as a civilian aide in the Philippine Insurrection; more recently, he had held a lieutenant's commission in a National Guard cavalry troop.[21]

During the last month of the expiring fiscal year, Kahn introduced a new appropriations bill in which he and the committee had specified the army's average strength as 400,000. Taking into consideration the large number of troops still in the service awaiting demobilization – a number which Kahn estimated to be 700,000 or 800,000 – this meant, he believed, that at the end of the fiscal year the army would consist of just over 200,000 men.[22] On the floor, various congressmen discussed the disposition of surplus material, overseas commitments, and details such as the maintenance of one insane Puerto Rican soldier.[23] The fact that the army was buying and improving some real estate – at Camp Benning, Georgia, among other places – caused comment at a time when legislators were anxious to cut expenses. According to Representative Greene, this practice was responsible in part for the congressional hostility toward the army's appropriation requests.[24]

March also came in for some blows. Fiorello La Guardia of New York objected to the figure 400,000, and, in reference to March's advocacy of the even larger 500,000-man army, he exhorted the legislators, "He has no consideration for the desires of Congress. He has all the despotic will and autocratic characteristics of Ludendorf[f] and the military genious of the Crown Prince." The Air Service veteran added, "When I was a soldier I soldiered . . . when I legislate I want to legislate, and I do not want Peyton C. March to tell me what I have to legislate." [25] He reinforced his statement with a motion to cut the army to 300,000. With La Guardia's amendment, the bill passed the House.[26]

The Senate was more amenable to the army's request. Despite questions about surplus and the redoubtable William E. Borah's probes about the impact of the Versailles Treaty on military obligations and disarmament, the senators approved a bill for 400,000 men and approximately $167 million more than the House deemed necessary.[27] These discrepancies meant a conference. After two meetings, the conferees agreed on a compromise favorable to the House, since they sliced $100 million off the Senate appropriation. The result – $775,241,543.50 – was some $410 million less than the estimate which the army submitted in January. Rather than providing for 500,000 men, Congress voted to support an average force of 325,000. By the end of September, 1919, when demobilization would be virtually complete, the army should reach 225,000 and remain at that strength for the rest of the fiscal year.[28]

On the day the president pro tem and the speaker signed the bills – the first day of the new fiscal year – Senator William H. King sadly remarked to his colleagues, "We have exhibited in this bill a hysterical tendency toward economy. . . ." [29] As a member of the Naval Affairs Committee, the Utah Democrat had seen the navy appropriation bill pared in a similar fashion.[30]

March knew of the congressional opposition to him and to the policy he represented. Even before the June appropriation cuts, he could read about the hostility in either the press or the *Congressional Record.* In addition to these sources of information, a General Staff officer who was attached temporarily to the House Military Committee furnished him with a private view of the congressmen. In April and May, 1919, Lieutenant Colonel Thomas W. Hammond accompanied several members of the Committee on a tour of the AEF. After this six-weeks association, Hammond submitted a report to the Chief of Staff. Although the colonel warned that the congressmen's views on military policy were "quite far apart" from those of the War Department, he thought that closer co-operation on the part of the War Department would remedy the situation. For, as he wrote, "I believe the members of the Committee are very desirous of bringing about a better feeling and understanding." But he warned, "Now that the war is over they feel that it is up to the War Department to show definitely and conclusively just why measures recommended should be passed." [31]

Despite this, the Chief of Staff was optimistic about the chances of the large army proposal. He assumed that he had clarified the reasons for the War Department request in his appearances before the various congressional committees. Besides, he believed that the program had strong support in the Senate. After all, Senator King had introduced a resolution for a 500,000-man army before he and Baker had presented their bill.[32] And it was more encouraging that the military committees of both houses had endorsed the large army on a one-year basis and that the lower house had passed the measure in the last weeks of the 65th Congress.[33]

Although the signs of congressional disapproval increased, which would indicate his misjudgment of the attitude of Capitol Hill, March continued to reorganize the army on his own terms. When a reporter asked if his actions would require additional legislation, he replied that at present the 500,000 men were authorized under the existing war-time laws. "When Congress gets through with passing a final plan for the army that will be conformed to." But, in the meantime, since the army was "a going concern," he considered definite decisions necessary.[34]

It was a time of tension and uncertainty. While Wilson and the Allied leaders were hammering out the treaty, the question of post-war overseas commitments remained unsettled. Within the army, the problems of demobilization, integration of the AEF into the army at home, and, generally, the return to an effective peacetime basis were crucial matters. In this period, March did not regard the organization and the 175,000-man strength provided by the 1916 act as adequate. Even the flamboyant Brigadier General Billy Mitchell, although primarily interested in Air Service needs, agreed and testified that the pre-war army had been only "a sort of national constabulary and not an organization for war."[35] Yet, by proceeding to reorganize the army with apparent lack of regard for congressional sensitivity, March was not aiding the army's chances for advantageous legislation.

Congress was not reticent in its reaction against March. Its action on the administration bills to grant March a permanent full generalcy for his wartime service was illustrative not only of its animosity but also of its naïveté in regard to the conduct of modern war. After the Armistice, as the victorious nations proceeded to award their leaders, Baker asked Congress to give permanent commissions to the five officers holding emergency ranks of general and lieutenant general. Although the Democratic chairmen of the military committees introduced the bills, they did so without enthusiasm and the measures disappeared.[36]

During the next session, Woodrow Wilson, in a special message to Congress on July 18, 1919, recommended that March and Pershing and Admirals William S. Benson and William S. Sims be given permanent four-star rank. The President specified that the AEF commander should have precedence in rank over March.[37] "When the message was read in the House," Preston Brown, who had commanded a combat division in France, wrote Harbord, "the mention of General Pershing's name brought forth great cheering and applause, a really remarkable demonstration. The entire House rose during the cheering. On the contrary when General March's name was mentioned, everybody sat down, and there were a great many shouts of derision and hoots of 'No, No, sit down, sit down.'" For Harbord's benefit, Brown analyzed the event: "The whole gist of this is that the break between Congress and the Chief of Staff has become public. . . . you could not get a bill through Congress increasing the armed forces by one corporal under present conditions."[38]

The Senate was not so demonstrative, and Brown exaggerated when he said all of the congressmen sat down at the mention of March's name, but the outburst was "surprising," as the *New York Times* commented, and, "if not unprecedented, at least it has no recent precedent."[39] Other journals joined the *Times* in condemning the House for its emotional display. The *New York Sun*, after recounting the event, remarked, "The majority, Democrats as well as Republicans, do not like Gen. March or his methods. They resent what they describe as his autocratic, dictatorial methods in dealing with Congress and in his general dealings with his subordinates."[40]

Behind closed doors, members of the House Military Committee argued the resolution. When it came to a vote, the 15 present split – 8 for and 7 against honoring March. Of the 6 absentees, half supported the resolution. But several of the Democrats who voted "yea" weakened the majority stand by stating that they thought a lieutenant generalcy was more suitable for the Chief of Staff although they would go along with the President's request.[41] The opposition was more adamant. In August, La Guardia and five others, including one Democrat, publicly registered their protest against awarding such high rank to anyone who did not earn it "on the field of battle."[42] In this statement, they showed their lack of understanding of the management of war. Baker attempted to explain the value of March's service and made the point in a letter to Senator Wadsworth that the efforts of Pershing and the Chief of Staff were "complementary" – "together they wrought the result . . . of victory unsullied and beyond dispute." Then he joined Kahn in putting pressure on the legislators to bring the resolution to the floor for a vote, but they failed.[43] Congress was only interested in rewarding Pershing.

Although some Republicans had stood up for the Chief of Staff, one cabinet member considered the congressional opposition a party move.

On October 6, 1919, in a conversation with a member of the Senate Naval Affairs Committee, the Secretary of the Navy broached the subject of Benson's and Sims' promotions, which had suffered the fate of March's. Michigan's Republican Senator Truman Newberry told Daniels that if Congress rewarded the two admirals it would have to promote March, and this was not on the Republican program. Daniels pencilled in his diary, "Playing small politics." [44]

Prior to Pershing's triumphant return, both houses voted to give him their thanks as well as the high rank. As Missouri Representative Champ Clark said on the floor, "we honor ourselves in honoring him," to which his colleagues responded with loud applause. Another Democrat was more enthusiastic: "I would like to see the people of this country and this House put aside our partisanship . . . and make him the unanimous choice of the conventions that assemble next year and elect him President of the United States. [Applause.]" [45]

"Pershing a candidate for the Presidency? Why, bless your soul, he has been a candidate ever since the war began." Thomas D. Schall, a Minnesota Republican, struck "a discordant note" a few days later. The blind Congressman said that when people asked him if he did not think Pershing's planning won the war, he answered, "Hell, no; it was the unparalleled courage and tremendous resourcefulness of the American officers and men at the front that won the war, despite the deplorable blunders, inefficiency, and lack of service of the general headquarters." [46] "To talk about Pershing's humanity is to talk hypocrisy." In this regard, he held the AEF commander responsible for the problems such as mail and army prison conditions in France. He also pointed out that the general, whom he called a "snob," had recently refused to testify before a congressional subcommittee. Throughout his excoriation, he emphasized that Pershing used his censorship power over the press to build up his public image. The former Progressive concluded, "He is deserving as a cold-blooded manipulator, a scheming politician, and for that I am willing to give him the palm." But the nation heartily disagreed with Schall and only three other congressmen joined him in voting against promoting Pershing.[47]

On September 18, 1919, twelve days after Schall's blistering attack, the General of the Armies stood in the same chamber with the senators as well as the representatives in the audience. The President pro tempore of the Senate and the Speaker of the House made a few remarks, with the latter summing up the occasion, "Human nature loves to personify its ideals. It loves a hero and hero worship." Then Champ Clark presented his fellow Missourian "as 'Exhibit A,' showing forth to the world what sort of men Missouri grows when in her most prodigal of moods. . . ." In a brief speech, which the audience interrupted twenty-six times with applause, the "manly and attractive" Pershing accepted his honors "as a recognition of the achievements of our splendid Army." [48]

While Pershing's reception was a gesture to past accomplishments, it was also an interruption in the discussions about future military policy. For the military committees, at last, were dealing with this crucial problem. On August 7, 1919, the Senate committee opened hearings, followed four weeks later by the House, on the pending legislation. Throughout the fall, approximately a hundred witnesses paraded their knowledge, ignorance, prejudice, and ambition before the committees. March inaugurated both hearings and spent two days before the Senators and eight days before the Representatives. After him there came a heterogeneous array of civilians and soldiers – including Secretary Baker, Assistant Secretary of the Navy Franklin D. Roosevelt, former Secretary of War Henry L. Stimson, Pershing, Lieutenant General Robert L. Bullard, Major General Leonard Wood, various combat corps and division commanders, bureau chiefs, General Staff officers, two enlisted men, a woman, and an Episcopal bishop who held a brevet brigadier general's rank from Civil War days. In the course of the proceedings, the witnesses, many of whom appeared before both committees, discussed all manner of military subjects from nurses' rank to the use of Indians but the essential points discussed were the type of military policy (including the size of the army and universal training), General Staff power, and the new branches – particularly the Air Service.[49]

In early August, Baker sent the War Department's reorganization bill to Congress. With the exception of the addition of a three-month universal training program, it was the same bill which he and March had offered in January. In his forwarding letter, the Secretary refused to give his official approval of the measure because Pershing had yet to be consulted; thus he presented the proposal "only as the basis of hearings." [50] During their investigation the senators would also consider two other bills – a universal training proposition and a bill for an independent Department of Aeronautics. When it began its deliberations a month later, the House Committee studied its version of these three bills plus a fourth on the same general subject.

On the first day of the hearing in the upper house, California Republican Senator Hiram Johnson posed a fundamental question: "Now, then, General, what is the necessity . . . for a permanent army of 576,000 officers and men? . . . I can not quite fathom why at this particular time, when we are facing an era of universal peace, we should have an army many times larger than we have ever had in our history before."[51] Both March and Baker had previously explained the need for such a force in the various hearings on appropriations and, in January, at the brief House reorganization hearings. March, quick in response and very military in his manner as a witness, maintained that the half million men were necessary for adequate defense. In the course of his House testimony, he explained that the bulk of this number would go into a field army which would be readily expandable to full strength of over a million in time of emergency. Baker was more tentative in his testimony: "I can see no reason why a smaller number would not do as well." But he later told the Representatives, "if the league of nations is not formed, 500,000 is a child's play army, compared with what the United States will have to have unless some arrangement is made by which international disputes will be amicably adjusted. . . ."[52] In this view, he was following the lead of the President who was making a similar appeal in his ill-fated speaking tour. At his last stop before his collapse, Wilson frankly told a Pueblo, Colorado, audience that the choice was to support the league or to "maintain great standing armies and an irresistible navy."[53]

Although March did not phrase the issue in those terms, his War Plans Director, Haan, wrote a friend, ". . . it is to be remembered that the Chief of Staff is not quite independent in his position. He has two superiors, both of whom have something to do with the policy that is to be expressed in bills that go to Congress." The Chief of Staff, however, did not allude to this relationship and defended the measure on its military effectiveness, denying its dependence "upon the league of nations or anything else. . . ."[54]

When the question of obtaining the necessary large numbers of volunteers arose, Baker and March pointed to the new educational program which the army was undertaking. Baker was greatly impressed with the success of similar projects in the post-war AEF and advocated dividing the enlisted men's time equally between military and non-military vocational or educational training.[55] The General Staff was more pragmatic, as one memorandum noted: "It is the plan of the War Department to encourage enlistments in the proposed army by affording educational and vocational training." [56] To support the plan, the army sent out recruiting posters advertising the army as a "National University." [57]

Despite March's adamant stand for the large army, the many officers who appeared before the committees did not support him. Although Senator Wadsworth would remark later that they were afraid to oppose March, the testimony shows that virtually all of them took issue with the Chief of Staff on this point.[58]

The most convincing of these officers was Palmer. Earlier in the summer, he had heard Wadsworth, in an address at the Willard Hotel, appeal to potential witnesses to be frank in their testimony.[59] The colonel was impressed and later told his friend, Thomas M. Spaulding, "I am going to kick over the traces." [60] Meantime, as the hearings continued, a large number of young officers advised Wadsworth to call Palmer to the stand: "He can tell you some things. He can make suggestions of a constructive nature." After consulting with his colleagues, Wadsworth decided to ask him to testify.[61]

On October 9, the committee room was filled with junior officers as Palmer came in carrying "a stack of papers a foot high." The senators glanced at the papers and groaned, "He'll talk to us and we'll go to sleep." This was not the case, as Wadsworth later recalled, "In half an hour he had us fascinated. In an hour, he had torn Peyton C. March's bill into scraps – figuratively speaking – and thrown it in the wastebasket." [62]

The intellectual colonel dismissed the March plan: "In my opinion, the War Department bill proposes incomplete preparedness at excessive cost, and under forms that are not in harmony with the genius of American institutions." [63] Others had said that during the course of the hearings. Over three weeks before Palmer's appearance, Tompkins McIlvaine, Chairman of the Military Training Camps Association of the United States, the group which prepared the Chamberlain universal training bill, had called the larger army, "uneconomic, undemocratic, un-American." [64] But Palmer had, in his plan of the previous spring, a constructive program to offer and he made an excellent presentation of his citizen army idea.

The senators were deeply impressed, as Wadsworth said: "He was so clear and logical, so American in his point of view. . . . We knew that at last we were getting what we were after." When Palmer appeared on the second day, the Chairman recalled, "it was like going to school. He was not domineering, he wasn't offensive, but he was philosophical." [65] The colonel marshalled knowledge based not only on his experience both in the staff and the line but also on his reading in history and strongly buttressed his arguments. To Wadsworth and the other committee members, he seemed to be the answer to their problem. They had been dissatisfied with March's proposal from the beginning. "We knew instinctively that the American people would never stand for that sort of thing," Wadsworth commented. "We didn't know the answer, but we instinctively knew this wouldn't do." Then Palmer came in with the solution. After hearing his testimony, the Committee conferred and "in about two minutes by unanimous vote" directed Wadsworth to request assignment of the colonel as its military adviser to aid in drafting legislation. Despite March's opposition, Baker acceded to the request.[66]

Although Palmer had "demolished" the War Department bill,[67] the lawmakers still had to hear from John J. Pershing. During the six weeks since his triumphant processions, the General of the Armies had escaped reporters and crowds of admirers and enjoyed the hospitality of Cameron Forbes in Naushon, Massachusetts, and of the Fox Conners at their estate in the Adirondacks.[68] In the last part of October the nation's hero returned to Washington and spent two days interviewing a stream of General Staff officers and bureau chiefs.[69] He also telegraphed three of his AEF commanders, Hunter Liggett, John L. Hines, and Charles P. Summerall, and requested their views on army reorganization.[70] In addition to these sources of information, his aide, Colonel George C. Marshall, brought to his attention the galley proofs of the testimony of various witnesses before the committees.[71] As Pershing told March, "I thought I would get the views of everybody and then decide what mine should be." [72]

On the day before Pershing was to appear at the hearing, March came to his office in the southwest corner of the second floor of the Old Land Office Building, now the location of the G.H.Q., to give his opinion of the various provisions of the reorganization bill. The Chief of Staff "was all wound up and had a lot of ideas he wanted to talk about." As Pershing leaned back in his chair and listened, March bent forward, with his elbow on Pershing's desk and emphasized his views by pointing his finger at the General of the Armies. He spoke so rapidly that the stenographer had difficulty getting the flow of words on paper.[73]

While the two generals ranged over most of the topics of the debate – an independent air branch, the elimination of the Chemical Warfare Service, and the attitude of the bureau chiefs – they focused their discussion on three subjects: the power of the Purchase, Storage, and Traffic Division; universal military training; and officer promotion by selection. In answer to Pershing's first question, March led off:

> The division that I organized, the P. S. & T. is misunderstood by many and misrepresented by others. If you are going to have co-ordination of supply, it doesn't make any difference what you call it, you have to have some purchasing branch in order that the different branches of the Government will not be competing with one another. . . . The fight between the independent bureau system and the one control was much in evidence. These corps that received appropriations did not want to give them up. . . . they knew that patronage goes with money.

Since March was drawing criticism from both advocates and opponents of compulsory training, he explained his reasons for the short period of training which the advocates criticized. "But we have a better chance if we ask for three months than if we ask for nine months. What we want is the principle accepted." He added that public opinion was turning against the idea. The one argument of the interview came up over promotion. March pressed hard for promotion by selection rather than seniority above the rank of lieutenant. Pershing countered, "The Army itself, with few exceptions, is decidedly against this." The Chief of Staff indicated that the Secretary of War was "a warm advocate" and continued to explain his plan. But Pershing was not entirely convinced and concluded the topic with the assertion, "Well, Congress will not give you promotion by selection." [74]

This was not Pershing's introduction to March's ideas on military policy. Almost eight months before, on March 7, the Chief of Staff had sent him a copy of the March-Baker bill and commented on the situation in Washington. At the time, it seemed to March that while the House would probably oppose the large army which the War Department requested, the Senate appeared favorable to it. The bureau chiefs with their congressional supporters were fighting against a strong General Staff, but March believed that the experience of the war had confirmed the value of General Staff control. He concluded, "I only regret that so many miles separate us at the present time and prevent our having personal consultations on this and many other military matters." [75]

On October 31, 1919, the day following his talk with March, Pershing made his appearance on the Hill, where the senators joined the House Committee in the caucus room of the House Office Building to hear his views on military policy. Throughout the three days of his testimony, the legislators displayed a deference toward the general – the only witness to appear before a combined session. In turn, the hero was a pliable witness who made his points, but who, if pressed, would shift to a compromise position. Also, as Haan commented, "he is talking on conservative lines and is taking into consideration the expense that goes with it." [76] Well prepared by the inverview and by consultations with his staff, Pershing seemed to think of himself as the spokesman for the entire army, which he pointedly dissassociated from the War Department: "My experiences in War Department affairs as such has been very limited. I am only viewing it from the side of the Army, from the point of view of the Army as to its efficiency of operation in the field." [77]

As he read his initial statement, the General of the Armies established his opposition to the March plan: "In discussing preparedness it is to be remembered that our traditions are opposed to the maintenance of a large standing army. Our wars have practically all been fought by citizen soldiery." [78] His proposed policy would include a professional army of 275,000 to 300,000 officers and men, supplemented by a federalized National Guard and a universal training program in which, after six-months training, the citizens would serve in organized reserve units.[79] His estimate of the size of the regular army was in agreement with the figure given by Palmer, and, although he did not so describe them, his views were an endorsement of Palmer's plan. When he was done, a *Stars and Stripes* headline succinctly expressed the effect of his testimony:

Pershing Gives
Finishing Blow
To Baker's Bill.[80]

Pershing also struck a blow in the attack which developed in the course of the hearings on the War Department General Staff. Congress' hostility toward this organization was demonstrated by its readiness to criticize it for all of the army's problems. Senator Chamberlain gave an extreme example of this attitude in a fifty-seven page polemic which he published in early September, 1919. The crux of his indictment was in a comment he made on the Baker-March bill: "militarism run mad." [81] Despite his knowledge of the situation as explained by March, Pershing would not approve the wartime actions of the General Staff – particularly the controversial supply (P.S.&T.) division. With little tolerance for the demands of an emergency, Pershing flatly stated that the General Staff should not operate in the supply field.[82] Throughout the discussion, however, he carefully maintained the distinction between his AEF general staff and its counterpart in Washington, with the implication that his staff was more successful.[83] In his three days of testimony, he made no effort to counter the prevalent hostility toward March's organization.

Naturally, the bureau chiefs were critical of the wartime arrangement which clipped their power and they had strong influence in Congress. As they testified before the committees, the bureaucrats constantly emphasized the evils of General Staff control, as represented by the P.S.&T. Division, and advocated a return to the pre-war system.[84] Even March's former Astor Battery executive officer, C. C. Williams, whom he had brought from France to be Chief of Ordnance, joined in the criticism.[85] The bureau point of view was expressed best by an exchange between William L. Sibert, whom March believed to be the leader of the opposition to a combined supply service, and Wadsworth. When the Senator asked pointblank: "Do you want to go back to the conditions in 1916?" The Director of the Chemical Warfare Service replied: "I would rather have it that way." [86]

The feud was bitter, for the bureaucrats were fighting for their official positions and privileges. March made it clear that he intended to abolish the old system which had demonstrated its inefficiency in the last two wars. To supplement the wartime encroachments of the General Staff, he provided in his bill that bureau chiefs, with the exception of the Surgeon General, would be generals of the line. In the past, Congress had passed on the appointments of bureau heads to their posts with ranks peculiar to their positions. This practice emphasized the close relationship of these officers to the lawmakers. If this prerogative were eliminated, bureau heads would be in a position similar to any line commander. Although the Chief of Staff might consider the move a logical evolution toward efficiency, both bureau chiefs and their congressional supporters viewed it as heinous.[87]

While not yet so influential with Congress as the bureau chiefs, another element in the army showed its strength in these hearings. Inspired by dreams of the future, the advocates of an independent air force made their ideas prominent in 1919. Billy Mitchell, since spring an assistant to the Director of Military Aeronautics, had stated during the Senate appropriations hearings in June that an independent department was a necessary requisite for a good air force. At that time, he introduced the appealing theme, "there is an air feeling all over the world now – it is a sort of an impelling force in itself." [88] In the fall, Benjamin D. Foulois, who had flown with Orville Wright in the army's first plane, emphasized the argument that only trained flyers should control this technical arm.[89] Both appeared during the hearings and frankly stated their views.

Nearly all of the senior officers were opposed to this proposal, which was advanced in bills introduced by Harry S. New in the Senate and by the California Republican Charles F. Curry in the House. March, Pershing, and the others granted the Air Service a position equal to the established arms – infantry, cavalry, and artillery – but no more. In this respect, they had the support of the Secretaries of War and Navy and the bulk of the navy's ranking officers, who were having their own problems with air officers. No one would deny that the air arm had made great advances during the war, but concurrent with these advances, there developed inter-arm friction between the air and the older branches.

The airmen seemed different, as Foulois and Mitchell contended, and their discipline appeared lax to the non-flyers. "The early trouble with planes," March complained, "was accompanied by continuous trouble with the personnel." [90] Following the war, the Chief of Staff appointed an artillery officer who had distinguished himself as the commander of the famed Forty-second "Rainbow" Division to head the air branch. A West Point classmate of Pershing's, Charles T. Menoher, although considered somewhat easy going, was supposed to stiffen this discipline. Without flying experience and opposed to air independence, he was soon criticized by such air enthusiasts as Fiorello La Guardia, a veteran of air combat missions, who ridiculed the Director on the House floor with the assertion that he "did not know a flying machine from a freight car." [91]

Despite the powerful opposition, Mitchell, late in July, 1919, wrote Henry H. "Hap" Arnold, "I think things look better every day for the Air Service." [92] He may have been rejoicing over the gain of an important convert — the Assistant Secretary of War. In May, Baker had dispatched Benedict Crowell with a group of officers and industrialists to Europe to study air developments. Although Crowell's instructions forbade him from exploring the subject of an independent organization, the Assistant Secretary came back convinced that this was the logical solution and recommended it in his report. When he read the document, Baker was furious over Crowell's disobedience and considered forcing his resignation. After thinking it over, however, he decided to publish the report with a cover letter which stated that he believed it went too far in its advocacy of a "single centralized air service." [93]

As a part of the army, March and Baker said that they would support strongly the Air Service, but neither could condone the creation of another department. During the hearings, Menoher pointed out to the senators one aspect of the problem — that if interservice rivalry between the army and the navy was bad, a third force would compound the friction.[94] Franklin D. Roosevelt, Assistant Secretary of Navy, agreed: "Two is company and three is a crowd." [95] Privately, the Director of Military Aeronautics advanced the argument that the aircraft had not yet reached the stage where it could be considered a separate arm. March, Menoher, and the other opponents of an independent air force acknowledged its great value as a supporting weapon but they believed that this value would depreciate if the arm were taken away from the control of the senior services.[96]

The airmen were not satisfied with the offer of equality with the other arms. What they wanted was equality with the army and the navy. Foulois explained their position to the congressmen in December:

> There has been most influential testimony . . . by the opponents of a consolidated Air Service as to the importance of aviation, yet right on top of these statements they say they will not sacrifice the interests of the other branches of the service for aviation. Due to this latter statement, I contend they will not effectively develop aviation under military control, although they all say it ought to be done.[97]

Later, he remarked, "March was saying publicly that the Air Service was important but the War Department castrated it." [98]

These flyers realized that Congress was in an economy mood. After all, in the past spring the House had sliced the War Department's appropriation recommendation of $83 million for air development to $15 million.[99] They reasoned that if the War Department remained in control it would not punish the older branches for the sake of the new organization. Menoher's statement that "the General Staff has not cut down our appropriation by one cent or disapproved it in any way" did not allay this fear.[100] They were more concerned with his other remark: "The Infantry I consider as the backbone of the Army always, it is the one determining factor. . . ."[101] And March was in complete agreement with the Director.[102] Pershing concurred, but his testimony was so phrased that Mitchell and others thought they had his support. But ten weeks after his appearance before the committees, the General of the Armies, at Menoher's request, made very clear his opposition to an independent air force.[103]

As the proceedings continued, it was obvious that there was opposition to March not only on the major points but also on various other details of his proposal, such as abolition of the Chemical Warfare Service and promotion by selection. He believed chemical warfare inhumane in its danger to non-combatants and emphasized, with Baker's support, the justness of his promotion plan. But Chamberlain indicated the congressional antagonism toward this arrangement for the chemical branch and the Senate subcommittee unanimously agreed on another promotion scheme weeks before the hearings ended. With March's ideas scrapped, the congressional committees started preparing their own proposals with the help of their military advisers.[104]

In the spring of 1920, Congress debated the reorganization bills presented by the respective military committees. During March, the House discussed and passed the bill which Kahn's committee, assisted by Colonels Hammond and Spaulding, prepared.[105] The next month, the Senate passed Wadsworth's bill on which the subcommittee, aided by Palmer and his "right-hand man" John W. Gulick, had labored day and night for weeks.[106] Neither March nor Pershing played much of a part in this phase of the reorganization. Pershing was content that Palmer would represent views similar to his.[107] Meantime, the General of the Armies, on orders to inspect army posts, toured the nation and acted more like a presidential candidate than an inspector. The Chief of Staff waited for the developments over which he had no control. When he attempted to relieve Palmer on the basis of the staff-detail limitation (the "Manchu Law," which required relief from detail after four years), he was stymied by the strong Senate opposition.[108]

Initially, Wadsworth's group considered a provision giving Pershing the office of the Chief of Staff as long as he was on the active list. But when Baker protested, they dropped the measure.[109] While March was far from popular on the Hill, at least some congressmen were beginning to defend him. In January, 1920, Gallivan soundly abused him, as he had the year before; however, in contrast to the lack of pro-March comment on the first occasion, three legislators rebutted and criticized the Massachusetts congressman.[110] A few weeks later, Senator McKellar even gave March credit for contributing to the victory in 1918. But Congress did not act on the proposal to make him a permanent lieutenant general.[111] At this time, establishing general military policy was more important and more desirable on the Hill.

Throughout the spring, March, Baker, and army officers generally followed the congressional deliberations on the reorganization bills. The bureaus were particularly active in propagandizing their demands. When possible, officers flocked to the Capitol to represent their special interests and to crowd the galleries during the debates. At one point, Congressman King Swope commented on the lobbying, "It has been difficult to tell whether the army headquarters is down in the Army and Navy Building or here in the corridors of the House of Representatives." [112] Civilians arguing the merits of universal training and National Guard policies added to the pressures on the legislators.

Early in the year, the House measured the political factors involved in universal training and concluded that it was not wise to advocate such a program. Southern Democrats led in this opposition on the basis of their fear of training Negroes. Despite the personal request of the President, they continued their resistance.[113] Other groups joined them in making any such proposal impolitic. Before the military committee brought the bill to the floor, it dropped universal training. Kahn was heartbroken. As he drove home on the night of the decision, he muttered, more to himself than to his companion, "those spineless cowards — those jellyfish!" [114]

Although the Senate committee, under the tutelage of Palmer, carried the universal training program into the debate, the Republican senators feared that the Democrats would ignore Wilson's wishes and make the matter an issue in the coming election. Even Palmer's most enthusiastic supporter, Wadsworth, realized the implications. Later he wrote, "the prominent Senatorial leaders of both political parties kept insisting that, 1920 being a Presidential election year, it would be political folly to permit such an issue to enter the campaign." [115] Thus, Senator Frelinghuysen, a leading Republican on the committee, offered to eliminate universal training from the measure and quickly won Senate endorsement. There remained, in Wadsworth's words, "the framework of a sound military structure, but we failed to fill it with men!" [116] This amendment emasculated Palmer's citizen army program. Only a skeleton organization and a provision for training volunteers survived.[117]

With universal training out of the way, the bills passed both houses. Fragments of opposition did bring up other points, such as a smaller army. This annoyed Wadsworth, who wrote Baker, "I know some worthy citizens, who, if they had the chance, would reduce the Army to 1,216 men, provided that the officers should be elected by the enlisted men, and forbid the general to wear a certain cut of breeches because such a garment apes the British." [118] Others were not satisfied with the bills for various reasons. Pershing's father-in-law, Senator Francis E. Warren, a Civil War veteran, voted for it but wistfully asked for an increase in cavalry.[119] In the House, eighty-four year old Isaac R. Sherwood, who earned a brevet brigadier generalcy in the Civil War, opposed the General Staff with the remark that there was none during that War.[120] Tennessee's Senator McKellar also opposed the increased General Staff and, generally, the bill which he called "a hopeless mess," "unAmerican," and "iniquitous." [121] But a sizeable majority in each House disagreed with this opinion.[122]

Since there were two bills with fundamental differences, a conference was necessary to settle those differences. Even before the House passed its bill, Kahn predicted this in a letter to Pershing: "Confidentially, the bill in the final analysis will have to be rewritten by the conferees." [123] For five weeks, Wadsworth and a contingent of four senators met with Kahn and four other congressmen to mold the final bill in meetings which Palmer and the other military advisers attended. As far as the regular army was concerned, the discrepancies were minor and quickly settled. The remnant of Palmer's citizen-army plan and the place of the National Guard were the major points of dispute.[124]

The House bill had nothing comparable to Palmer's plan and had continued the National Defense Act of 1916 provisions in regard to the

National Guard. Although March and Baker had advocated this status for the Guard, neither had suggested the one principal change in this civilian component. The House measure provided for a Guardsman rather than a professional in the crucial office of Chief of the Militia Bureau. In its bill, the Senate followed General O'Ryan's plan for federalization of the Guard by organizing it under the army clause rather than the militia clause of the Constitution. Evidently, the majority of Guardsmen were against this. Members of the House certainly thought so as demonstrated by their refusal to compromise on this issue and by their victory over the senators on this point.[125]

The bill which came out of the conference was largely the House bill, written as a series of amendments to the 1916 Defense Act. The task of writing the bill seemed impossible to Palmer, but Spaulding was equal to it.[126] All that survived of Palmer's plan was a trace of his citizen-army organization, without even the provision for training of volunteers, and a section which provided for equal civilian and military representation on a General Staff committee to consider civilian component matters. This, the Colonel consoled himself, was the "keystone" of the legislation.[127]

When the final bill reached the White House, the President considered vetoing it and asked Baker to draft the veto message.[128] The Secretary had told him that several of the provisions were contrary to the War Department recommendations. But, faced with the continued effect of a lack of permanent policy as well as the possibilities of a political fight over the federalization of the National Guard, Baker advised him, "I have debated with myself a long time about the bill; it is far less excellent than it was as reported by the Senate Committee, and in its present form shows that there are, unhappily, many things which this war has taught us but which we have not learned." Baker concluded, however, "All things considered, I feel that the public interest justifies your signing the bill, although I feel that frankness requires me to say that it is not as effective [a] reorganization measure as the country ought to have."[129] On June 4, 1920, Wilson signed the measure.[130]

The Act which evolved out of the months of discussion was comprehensive. In addition to providing for civilian components and for more flexibility of organization generally, it continued such wartime creations as the Chemical Warfare Service, the Finance Service, and the Air Service, with the last still a part of the army. Congress, however, did not follow the advice of March and authorize a Transportation Corps. The legislators tried to solve in this measure the onerous supply problem by turning over much of the authority to the Assistant Secretary of War, who would function virtually as a munitions minister under the Secretary. This probably appealed to the bureau chiefs since it allowed them to bypass the Chief of Staff in their dealings with civilian superiors. These officers, no doubt, also appreciated the fact that Congress did not carry out March's recommendation to appoint them from the generals of the line.

Congress attempted to answer the pleas for reform in three other sections of this lengthy Act. It tried to solve the perennial promotion issue by the establishment of a single promotion list. Then, the Act created the positions of chiefs of infantry and cavalry in order that those branches would have the same representation as the other branches in the War Department. The third reform was of more general interest. As a result of investigations developing out of the criticism of wartime military justice, Congress revised the Articles of War. The new Articles extended the rights of enlisted men and provided generally for better administration and more flexibility in matters of military justice.[131]

Although General Staff officers were annoyed by various sections of the law and its omissions, they found the provisions dealing with their corps generally agreeable. As George Burr, the Director of P.S.&T., commented, "The continuance of proper General Staff supervision and control is assured."[132] For these officers, the fact that Congress did not follow tradition and detail the army's organization was another favorable point. Finally, as Colonel J. C. Gilmore, Jr., Chief of the War Plans Branch, wrote Haan, "The advantages that will accrue from the bill greatly outweigh the disadvantages. It is the opinion of the War Plans Branch that the bill as a whole provides a military policy and flexibility of organization far superior to anything we have had in the past, [and] that this policy and organization can be satisfactorily developed under authorities granted. . . ."[133]

This policy was neither March's nor Palmer's. Both had lost out to the post-war, anti-military reaction, the drive for economy in government, and the general desire for a return to "normalcy." Although elements of sound policy survived in the bill, Congress gave an ominous portent in the appropriation bill which it also passed in the closing hours of the session. Despite the reorganization bill's authorization of a force of some 298,000 officers and men, Congress appropriated funds for less than 200,000 for the coming year.[134]

The Chief of Staff was not available for comment when the reorganization bill became law. On May 30, 1920, he had sailed for Europe to inspect the Army of Occupation.[135] Since the previous fall, the matter had been out of his hands anyway. His mission now was to execute the congressional directive which, he admitted in his annual report, "has afforded a definite basis for proceeding with the reorganization of the Army." [136]

16 · THE TRIALS OF PEACE

FOREIGN commitments added another dimension to the work of the Chief of Staff. The war was over, but even after the bulk of the AEF returned, American troops remained in the Rhineland and other detachments carried on various assignments in Europe and Asia Minor. And the enigma of Americans fighting an undesired war in north Russia and waiting for decisions in Siberia haunted March. By the time the General sailed for Europe, most of the miscellaneous missions and the troops in Russia were back home, but the Americans still maintained their watch on the Rhine. When March returned to the United States, he had before him his last year in office. During this period, the prevalent atmosphere of isolationism and economy dominated all military developments and set the pattern for the succeeding years.

As the *Northern Pacific* got under way in New York harbor, March chatted on the bridge with his two aides, his son-in-law, John Millikin, and his former subordinate of Fort Riley and Valdahon days, Beverly Browne. "We are going to have a wonderful trip." After this remark, he pondered the future: "If the Army Bill doesn't pass, we can just go over to the Philippines." He paused and then added in a holiday mood, "You can't beat it." Browne responded that you could. Prohibition had descended upon the country six months before, but he had some Scotch on board.[1]

On the afternoon of June 7, 1920, the party debarked at Antwerp. Since the commander of the occupation army could not be there, a staff officer, Brehon B. Somervell, greeted them. They spent the eighth in Brussels. While there, the Chief of Staff favorably impressed Newton

Baker's friend, Ambassador Brand Whitlock, who wrote the Secretary, "I greatly enjoyed talking with General March and was so pleased to see what great loyalty he bears you." During the visit, Whitlock presented him to King Albert and the handsome king entertained with a luncheon in the palace.[2]

The next day, March arrived in Coblenz, headquarters of the American Forces in Germany. He and Henry T. Allen, the commander of the A.F. in G., talked over the interesting news of the day. Pershing had submitted his resignation on the eve of the Republican convention. Although he denied that his decision had any political significance, he was well aware of the political possibilities. After speculating on the General of the Armies' surprising move, the two then discussed the future of the service under the reorganization law. Since the bill had passed, March commented that he would not go to the Philippines but must return to supervise the reorganization work.[3]

March was anxious to begin the inspection of the command. From a peak strength of 262,000 officers and men in February, 1919, the force had dwindled to 16,000. With these troops, Allen carried out his mission of holding the Coblenz bridgehead and guarding the Rhine from Bacharach to Remagen (approximately ninety kilometers of riverline). Together with similar Allied bridgeheads, the Americans' foothold served as points of departure into Germany if the situation warranted a deeper penetration. Prior to the signing of the Versailles Treaty, Allied leaders considered such a step probable. Indeed, in May and June of 1919, the Americans moved troops into position and prepared to resume hostilities. But despite the fact that the German political situation was still unsettled in 1920, the possibility of war had become remote.[4]

In the personable "Hal" Allen, March found an officer well equipped for the particular demands of his position. Allen wore the diplomat's uniform of morning clothes with as much ease and grace as the stiff-collared khakis. After his graduation from the Military Academy, this Kentuckian interspersed tours in the cavalry with attaché duty in St. Petersburg and Berlin. A fluent linguist, he had equal accomplishments in combat – serving with distinction in Cuba, as Chief of the Philippine Constabulary, and as a division commander in the AEF. In the summer of 1919, Pershing picked him for the post at Coblenz. Under Allen, the A.F. in G. became, as Lieutenant General Bullard wrote, "the most highly polished and burnished soldiers that the government of the United States ever had." [5] Service on the Rhine was an enviable assignment but Allen's standards were demanding.

Although March had maintained a correspondence with Allen and had given him support as well as broad discretion in his task, the Chief of Staff wanted to see personally the troops on the Rhine. On the afternoon of June 10, he saw the entire command in formation on the great field by the bend in the Rhine near Andernach. For three hours, he rode through the ranks questioning the men and checking the equipment.[6] This inspection set the pattern for the ten days March spent in Germany. To Allen's surprise, the Chief of Staff followed closely the "stiff program of inspections," [7] but the A.F. in G. commander wrote a friend, "It is always a pleasure to be inspected by soldiers possessing military qualifications and a proper sense of proportion." [8] Living quarters, hospitals, kitchens, stables, ranges, disciplinary barracks — all came under the General's scrutiny. He also managed to pay brief visits to the British, French, and Belgian bridgeheads in the brief period. As his tour came to a close, he enjoyed a dinner provided by the officers of his old regiment, the Sixth Field Artillery, which now included his nephew, Lieutenant Francis A. March III, on its rolls. There were other entertainments, dinners, and sports contests, but the demands of March's schedule did not permit much relaxation. On June 12, he conferred at length with Allen and the attaché from Berlin, Colonel Edward Davis, who had served with the Chief of Staff in the Thirty-third Volunteer Infantry in the Philippines. Based on their information on the German internal situation, March cabled Washington to support Germany's request to maintain temporarily an army of 200,000.[9]

Before he left the Rhineland, March wrote up his critique for Allen. He confirmed his comments on the good appearance of the command and its quarters but called attention to the need for marksmanship training and for emphasizing educational and vocational activities. But the Chief of Staff was consistent in his sparing use of commendation, as he wrote Allen, "My idea is that to get any value from an inspection of the kind I made of the American Forces in Germany, indiscriminate praise is of no worth. . . ." [10] After March returned to the United States, the Secretary of War comforted Allen with a letter which said that the Chief of Staff was "enthusiastic" about the troops in Germany.[11]

From the Rhine, March moved into France where he spent a day examining the battlefields of the Argonne and Chateau Thierry before going into Paris. As his guide, Browne, who had won a brigadier's star in the AEF, showed him the Crown Prince of Bavaria's underground bunker-palace near the Aire River and a sector of the Champagne front where shell fire had churned the landscape into the appearance of a large sand dune. Then they paid their respects at the Romagne cemetery. Once in Paris, March renewed his acquaintance with the various French leaders who competed with each other in entertaining him. Pétain began with a dinner which was followed by luncheons and receptions given by Foch, Buat, and others. At these gatherings, the soldiers compared notes on the war now twenty months in the past.[12]

By this time, virtually all of the once great American contingent was out of France except for a Graves Registration detachment. The AEF's Services of Supply, redesignated the American Forces in France, had remained under Brigadier General William D. Connor until December 31, 1919, to handle the remaining logistical problems and to close up the ports and depots.[13] Earlier the same month, General Bliss and the last remaining officers and men participating in the Peace Commission had left Paris.[14] While most of the other military missions scattered throughout Europe and Asia Minor had also completed their work, at least two remained in Poland and Armenia, but the General did not have the time to search out these small relief expeditions.[15]

March wound up his European visit with "a very short stay in London." Another round of functions during which he met Prime Minister David Lloyd George and other dignitaries took up most of his time, but he did manage to attend a tennis match. Unfortunately, his boat sailed before a scheduled luncheon of the Army Council so he missed meeting Winston Churchill.[16]

On June 28, he boarded the *Northern Pacific* at Bristol for the return voyage.[17] Two days later, while at sea, he took off two stars. The various attempts to secure a permanent full general's commission having failed, he reverted to his regular rank along with the other officers still holding temporary commissions. For the remaining year in office, he would be ranked not only by Pershing but also by four other major generals. Perhaps the sting of this reduction was eased in part by a gracious letter from the Secretary who praised him for his wartime efforts and by the award of the Distinguished Service Cross on July 10, two days after he arrived in Washington. On the basis of Arthur MacArthur's recommendation of a Medal of Honor for the Singalon charge, Baker pinned on him the nation's second highest decoration for heroism.[18] In addition to this ceremony, March held a press conference. The troops were in "splendid shape" and had "very high" morale, he told the reporters. And co-operation between the French and the A.F. in G. "could not be closer." [19] His trip had been successful.

By the time March sailed to Europe, the most provocative foreign entanglement was over. From the beginning, he had opposed sending troops to Russia, and, as he noted later, "events moved rapidly and uniformly in the direction of the complete failure of these expeditions to accomplish anything that their sponsors had claimed for them." [20] Although he remained informed of the situation of the Archangel contingent, he had virtually no control over its destiny. Graves and the larger Siberian force were under his supervision but the diplomatic factors prevented him and Baker from carrying out their desire to evacuate them immediately. With the Armistice, the morale of the troops in these "fantastic sideshows" naturally suffered.[21] Particularly in north Russia, it was difficult to explain to the troops why they were staying.

Although March advocated withdrawal and pressed his views on the Acting Secretary of State, Frank Polk, as early as December 14, 1918, the expedition was frozen in place until the icebound north Russian harbors thawed.[22] On June 3, 1919, however, the first element left Archangel. By the end of July all of the troops were gone except the headquarters, which sailed on August 23.[23] The British followed within five weeks leaving the White Russians to hold out for another five months until the Bolsheviks closed out this "ugly little" chapter of the war.[24]

At the time of the Armistice, the situation of the American troops in Siberia was not so serious as that of their comrades on the Archangel perimeter. Yet, potentially their position was more dangerous, since the additional factor of Japanese ambitions complicated this phase of the intervention. Eventually, the Japanese admitted that they had sent 72,400 men to this section of Russia. Although they soon withdrew some 14,000 of these soldiers, they continued to maintain a strength which dwarfed the 9,000-man American contingent in the area.[25]

Throughout this period, Japan attempted to serve its imperial ambition by maintaining a power vacuum in the internal affairs of far eastern Russia. In order to do this, the Japanese supported the notorious Cossack leaders – Ivan Kalmikov and Gregorii Semenov – who pillaged the countryside and made stability impossible. The goal of the Asian power, it seemed to some American observers, was to establish dominion over the Siberian maritime provinces.[26]

March and Baker were very much aware of this threat. From the beginning, March had warned of Japanese aims and the Secretary echoed his fears. Twice in November, 1918, Baker advised the President to withdraw the American force. In his second letter, he wrote, "I dread to think how we should all feel if we are rudely awakened some day to a realization that Japan has gone in under our wing and . . . completely mastered the country. . . . my own judgment is that we ought simply to order our forces home by the first boat. . . ."[27] In a conference with the Acting Secretary of State in mid-December, March reiterated this advice to withdraw.[28]

Contradictory advice came from the other side of the State, War, and Navy Building during 1919. The Russian experts in the State Department advocated a change of policy in order to combat Bolshevism.[29] The available instrument for such a policy was the government which a former czarist admiral, Alexander V. Kolchak, had established at Omsk. The French and British supported Kolchak and wanted American aid in the fight against the Bolsheviks. But many Americans were asking the same question that William Borah posed in the Senate in September, 1919: "What are we doing in Russia?"[30] Facts, rumors, and prejudices contributed to the confusion. After months of agonizing over the issue, Wilson wrote Baker, "I am a good deal perplexed in judgment about it."[31]

The President's perplexity made the task of the American commander in Siberia very difficult. William S. Graves, according to his staff officers, possessed a "world of common sense" and "could be as hard as nails if he thought he was right."[32] He needed these attributes to withstand the pressure of the Allied representatives, the Japanese, and events. Despite the opposition of the State Department and the apparent antagonism of General Churchill of the Military Intelligence Division, Graves refused to budge from the letter of his instructions not to interfere in internal affairs.[33] As the foundation of his position, Graves relied on his friend and former classmate, the Chief of Staff. In May, 1919, March wrote him, "Your attitude toward the Allied representatives in Siberia and toward the Russians has been wholly correct and will not be altered unless the President himself alters the purpose of the Expedition itself."[34] The general was also comforted when March bluntly encouraged him: "Keep a stiff upper lip, I am going to stand by you until —— freezes over."[35]

During the fall of 1919, the Kolchak government disintegrated, as Graves had predicted it would, and American relations with the Japanese deteriorated. In early October the situation reached such a dangerous point that Newton Baker asked the Secretary of Navy if the navy could defeat the Japanese sea forces and informed the prostrate Wilson, through the President's physician, about the crisis.[36]

By this time, it was apparent that if the Americans remained in Siberia they would soon be fighting the Bolsheviks. On the last day of November, Secretary of State Robert Lansing wrote in his diary: "We will gain nothing and help nobody by keeping forces there. As it is, I think it will be difficult to withdraw without loss of life."[37] Four weeks later, March cabled Graves to expect within a few days orders to withdraw. The Chief of Staff cautioned the general to keep this information secret.[38] Graves carried out his instructions; however, because of the lack of co-ordination between the State and War Departments, he informed the Japanese commander of the evacuation prior to the formal diplomatic notification.[39] This failure of the executive departments to coordinate on such a crucial point reflected not only the basic difference of opinion on the Siberian intervention but also, as the diplomat Dewitt C. Poole indicated, "a lack of really good relations between Newton D. Baker and Robert Lansing."[40]

The exodus took place in the first months of 1920. On January 17, the first contingent – 1754 strong – sailed, followed by the remainder at intervals, until the last departed on April 1. On that day, the American commander inspected a Japanese honor guard, boarded the *Great Northern*, and mused over his experiences as the Japanese band played "Hard Times Come Again No More."[41]

Two days before he sailed, Graves drove about Vladivostok with his intelligence officer, Robert L. Eichelberger. They noticed that the Japanese were digging trenches and placing sandbags against their barracks' walls. This seemed to corroborate the information they had that the Japanese were planning to seize the city as soon as the Americans left. On April 4, 1920, the Japanese did attack and take over control of Vladivostok. Eichelberger, who remained for a few extra days, watched them lead the long lines of captured Russians through the streets.[42] The Japanese stayed on until October, 1922.[43]

March believed that the events in Russia had proved him correct in his opposition to involvement. The intervention had no effect on the war against Germany. Nor did it mollify the Allies as Wilson had hoped. And, from the beginning, the American presence generated friction with the Japanese, who followed the ambitious course the Chief of Staff had predicted. The confusion and conflict over purpose between the State and War Departments combined with the underlying indecision of the President increased the difficulties of the operation. To send such a small force into the chaos of Siberia, March concluded, "was a military crime." [44]

By the time of March's return from his European inspection trip, reorganization planning was in progress. The affable Wright, who acted as Chief of Staff in March's absence, informed him of the initial steps a week after the Act passed. Before the effect of the bill reached the rank and file, boards must prepare plans and carry out basic functions which the Act required. The War Department promptly appointed these boards, which then began work on their tasks.[45]

The officer corps demanded particular attention. Three boards dealt with the various problems of selection – general classification of fitness, General Staff eligibility, and promotion to the rank of brigadier general. A lower ranking board started the chore of creating the single promotion list. Of the twenty-three officers serving on these boards, Pershing, his three army commanders and fifteen others wore AEF service chevrons. The single list board, however, depended largely on the knowledge of a non-AEF veteran – Thomas M. Spaulding – who had studied this problem ever since his cadet days. These officers labored throughout the summer to meet the requirements of the new legislation.[46]

Within the War Plans Division, Haan named two committees to provide the basic outlines of reorganization policies for the regular army and the civilian components. The ten officers on the regular reorganization Special Committee included six called in from duties outside the War Department. Again, the AEF was strongly represented by Fox Conner, Pershing's Chief of Operations, and George C. Marshall, Pershing's aide, and others. This committee completed its task by the time of March's return – July 8.[47] The other committee, Palmer's "brain child," was the group authorized by Section 5 of the Act. The purpose of this committee was to give citizen soldiers an equal voice in the preparation of plans and policies which concerned the citizen army. Because of this, the law required as many National Guard and reserve officers on the committee as there were regular officers. Despite the difficulties of obtaining civilians of proper background who could afford to leave their jobs for several months, the committee began its work by the first of September.[48]

"What the army needs more now," March wrote the Chief of the Operations Branch, "is to go ahead with the reorganization prescribed by law; and with the training of the new officers and men."[49] On August 31, 1920, he approved the basic principle of organization recommended by the special committee.[50] During the following months, he noted and approved the tables of organization with which the Section 5 committee and the War Plans organization committee were supplementing this policy. Some of these planners were still working on this laborious assignment as late as the summer of 1921.[51]

The Army of the United States, under this plan, would consist of nine corps areas, each with a regular division, two National Guard divisions, and the nuclei of three Organized Reserve divisions. To a certain extent, the expandable army idea prevailed since the regular units were skeletonized for peacetime operations. Before the Special Committee made its recommendations, Senator Wadsworth wrote Palmer, now serving at Governor's Island, "I am afraid that General March and those close to him are still clinging to their dream of a great big regular army which they hope to start with highly skeletonized units and fill up later on."[52] Wadsworth had heard of a plan which a board was developing and had mistakenly assumed that the planning was being done under March's influence. Actually, the specific plan which he mentioned in his letter was that of the AEF Superior Board on Organization and Tactics which would receive Pershing's endorsement in July. This board recommended the formation of twenty-one understrength divisions.[53]

The organization policy which March actually accepted perhaps mollified Wadsworth, but other solutions met with criticism from the officer corps. The single list proved to be no panacea and resulted in many protests at Senate hearings and in further analysis by the War Department. Finally, a board which met after March left office decided that although problems continued, the single list remained "highly important to the efficiency of the Army."[54] Harbord noted another cause of distress among officers. "The whole Army is very much stirred up apparently by recent publication of the initial list for the General Staff, from which a good many people, who thought they would be on it, were omitted." [55] There would have been even more disgruntled officers if Baker had not forced Pershing's board to expand the list.[56] Selection for this elite group, placement on the promotion scale, and the classification process were certain to cause dissatisfaction among many. When these results were combined with the problems of the high cost of living and lack of adequate living quarters, morale suffered greatly.

Most of all, the army's morale was a casualty of the nation's desire for "normalcy." Through their representatives on Capitol Hill, the people simply refused to support attempts to maintain an adequate military posture. Looking back to the war years from the reference point of political prejudice, a powerful Republican congressman told his colleagues, "We are going to try to put an end to some of the waste and extravagance which has characterized the conduct of the Military Establishment in recent years." [57] In the Senate, Borah warned after Harding's inauguration, "The Secretary of Treasury states that the only way in which relief [in government expenses] can be had which the President says must be granted is through the reduction of the Army and the Navy." [58] And the men on the Hill were anxious to carry out what they construed to be their mandate. Even the navy and the National Guard, both of which many politicians used as excuses for cutting army expenses, came in for appropriation reductions.[59] Pershing's aide, George C. Marshall, later summed up the period: "the cuts, and cuts and cuts came." [60]

Baker and March tried to bolster the army by recruiting up to the 280,000 authorized by the June 4, 1920 Act, but, since the appropriations provided for only 175,000, this was hopeless. Although they were getting the men, their defiance of Congress created great bitterness. Finally, the two Houses united on a resolution which stopped the army recruiting.[61] Within a week, Wilson's endorsement of the actions of his military advisers and a veto of the resolution reached the Capitol. Immediately, both Houses passed the resolution with overwhelming majorities over his opposition.[62] Again in the appropriations for the coming year, Congress ignored military advice and urged a further reduction in strength. March unsuccessfully argued that while he appreciated the financial problems and the need for economy, "A careful consideration of the Regular Army's place and functions in the national defense scheme indicates clearly and unmistakably that any reduction below 200,000 enlisted men . . . will diminish very largely the national protection provided for the United States by its military defense system." [63]

In the debates on appropriations in the spring of 1921, talk of reduction to 100,000 men began to circulate and 150,000 increasingly seemed a reasonable figure. Senator Borah supported his pleas for reduced strength by his participation in a general arms-limitations movement. Anyway, he considered the army necessary only for police purposes.[64] Senator Gilbert M. Hitchcock, a Nebraska Democrat, contributed the comment that all the soldiers were doing was "occupying quarters and having a few drills." [65] Another senator quoted the low appropriations of the 1870's, 1880's, and 1890's as a standard, while a congressman suggested that 50,000 would be proper size for the army.[66]

When Wilson, in his last days in office, pocket vetoed their first attempt, the politicians pressed for even smaller appropriations in their second bill.[67] The more knowledgeable among them protested. Wadsworth pointed out that, relative to the population, the army was smaller than that of any European power, including defeated Germany.[68] In the House, Frank Greene said that the army was no longer standing but "sitting down," and later added that Congress should not "bamboozle" the public on this matter.[69] Yet these few scattered protests were ineffective in the face of the prevalent mood toward the military. In June, 1921, Harbord wrote Pershing, "There is hardly a committee meeting in either house of Congress on matters touching the Army that there is not hostility expressed toward the service and particularly toward the General Staff. Much of it due to ignorance in which the members charge to the General Staff every military policy or act which thwarts their wishes." [70]

"March was not too diplomatic with Congress," commented a veteran news correspondent.[71] Instead, in the words of a member of Baker's office staff, he had "studiously and impartially irritated Congressional leaders of both parties by refusing to consider any request which seemed to him to have narrow *political* implications." [72] In itself this might be laudable; however, at the same time, the congressmen suffered, according to Harbord, "from discourtesy and curtness at the War Department in matters where they were within their rights." [73] In this situation of mutual lack of understanding and sympathy, March and the War Department naturally were more vulnerable than Congress. Despite the advice of the congressional liaison officer, T. W. Hammond, the Chief of Staff apparently did little to ameliorate the prevalent congressional attitude.[74] "He made practically no appointments with members of Congress in general," the Secretary of the General Staff wrote later, but routed such callers to his Executive Assistant.[75] Although McIntyre and Wright could usually satisfy the legislators, this did not eradicate resentment toward March.

Although the congressional economy moves and hostility imposed difficulties and limitations, March and the General Staff continued on their tasks. They revised the organization plans to accommodate the strength reductions and, as support for the regulars waned, they encouraged the development of the civilian components. The War Plans Division, in particular its Section 5 Committee, studied National Guard problems and planned for the establishment of Citizens' Military Training Camps for volunteers.[76]

As it carried out its assignments, the General Staff itself changed. During August, March brought in Pershing's intelligence officer, Dennis E. Nolan, to replace Churchill as Director of the Military Intelligence Division.[77] Earlier in the summer of 1920, he relieved Burr from the P.S.&T. Division and assigned him as Assistant Chief of Ordnance.[78] He created a board to study ways of reducing paperwork and "in general, the bettering and simplifying of the system."[79] At times, March acted as Secretary of War in Baker's absence.[80]

Within the General Staff, the controversial supply agency underwent the most thorough reorganization. Since the Defense Act directed a fundamental change, the General Staff had to adjust accordingly. The Assistant Secretary of War was now the quasi-director of munitions, with the bureau chiefs reporting directly to him, rather than through the Chief of Staff, on matters of procurement. Crowell, who had argued for even greater powers during the reorganization hearings, did not benefit from the revision. He had not been on good terms with Baker and March for some time and his advocacy of an independent air department had served to increase this personal friction. But, aside from this, the normally congenial Secretary found relations with his Assistant "often difficult" and March frankly disliked the man. On June 23, Crowell resigned to be replaced at the end of July by a Richmond, Virginia, businessman, William R. Williams.[81]

Under the new system, the P.S.&T. Division not only changed its name to the Supply Division but also moved back to the State, War, and Navy Building from the Munitions Building offices.[82] In November, Lieutenant Colonel John L. DeWitt, who had been the Supply officer (G-4) of the First Army, complained that it should devote more time to planning and suggested a reorganization on that basis. A month later, the Secretary of War authorized a modified version of this plan.[83] Since Burr had transferred to Ordnance, March named Wright to head the division concurrent with his duties as Executive Assistant.[84] As the new organization went into effect, one of the senior colonels warned all members of the division to be "constantly on the alert to insure economy in all practicable cases and whenever possible."[85]

During March's last months in the War Department, the Air Service again came into prominence. Despite their failure to get congressional approval of an independent department, the air advocates were not disheartened. In January, 1920, Billy Mitchell wrote "Hap" Arnold, "We are in the midst of our appropriation hearings for this year, and will have a hard time holding our own, but still we will come off much better than any other department of the Army." Then, he returned to his favorite topic: "I think prospects are very bright for a United Service for next session."[86]

On February 1, 1921, the flying general proposed the battleship bombing test and asked for March's approval. After talking it over with Baker, the Chief of Staff forwarded Mitchell's plan, with the admonition "Rush" on the buckslip, to the Joint Army and Navy Board for consideration.[87] Once it was approved, March went along with the requests for more money to finance the operation.[88]

By the time Mitchell completed his successful tests, March was no longer Chief of Staff; hence he had no official comment. Mitchell had sunk the *Ostfriesland* and won immortality, but he never dissuaded March from the belief that the aircraft was essentially a supporting weapon on land and sea.[89]

Inauguration Day, Friday, March 4, 1921, was dry and sunny, a perfect day for the solemn ceremony of changing administrations. As the crowd began to gather in the streets, March joined the other dignitaries to witness the events on Capitol Hill. Minutes before the Republicans assumed executive power, he waited in the President's room, just off the Senate Chamber, for Woodrow Wilson to perform his last official duty. Supported by a servant, the crippled man hobbled in, sat down, and proceeded to sign the proffered bills. After greeting Harding and others, Wilson looked about the group crowded in the small room, saw

March and spoke to him. For the only time in his life, the General admitted tears. He never saw the President again.[90]

March also bade farewell to Secretary Baker. When the now ex-Secretary left Washington, the General led a large group of officers to Union Station to see him off.[91] Before Baker departed he wrote a letter emphasizing the value of March's services and concluded: "I give myself the pleasure of adding as a personal word, my deep appreciation of your loyalty to the policies of the President and of the War Department. . . ."[92] These two men brought together by the pressures of war not only had worked well together but also had become friends.

The new Secretary, who promptly refused March's resignation, was John W. Weeks — a bald, portly former Massachusetts senator with a walrus moustache. The Chief of Staff confided to his son-in-law that Weeks was "an able man" and would "make a good Secretary of War."[93] Baker echoed this sentiment and referred to his successor as "a man of large experience, courage . . . [with] a good deal of knowledge of the War Department and military policy."[94] A graduate of the Naval Academy, Weeks had resigned from the service to enter business. In 1905, he began his political career in Congress, serving first in the House and then for one term in the Senate. Although Weeks was generally quiet on the floor, he was "exceedingly useful and influential" in committee sessions, according to his colleague James W. Wadsworth.[95] This would be to the War Department's advantage, Baker wrote Hugh Scott, "The Congressional attitude toward the Army at present is bad and it is particularly for that reason that it seems to be fortunate to have the Secretary of War a man of weight and influence among the legislators."[96] There was no indication of partisanship in the change of War Department administrations. Both Weeks and Baker saw to that as they discussed the problems and attended the many dinners and lunches during the period. Finally, the Republican showed his respect for the Democrat by joining March in the farewell assembly at Union Station.[97]

Although March remained Chief of Staff, rumors of a successor flew throughout military circles. Curiously, in this speculation, the name of the nation's ranking soldier was not often mentioned.[98] Pershing's position as General of the Armies presented a problem. What does a nation do with a victorious commander when the war is over? In the past, the United States had been able to solve this readily by making the hero Commanding General of the Army; but Elihu Root had eliminated this office when he created the General Staff in 1903. Besides, the notoriously difficult relationship between the Commanding General, theoretically in charge of the line, and the bureaucrats, who more or less actually controlled the army during peace, had been one of the major reasons for Root's reform measures.

Since the war, Pershing had found occupation initially in retaining command of the AEF until the bulk of this force left France. When he came home, he kept a large remnant of his staff to work with the records and to handle the remaining details. Then Baker dispatched him on the lengthy inspection tour which also afforded him the opportunity to accept the accolades of the general public. But there was still no definite task for him. On the eve of the Republican convention in June, 1920, he admitted as much: "It now appears that my duties are not likely to be of a character that will require more than a portion of my time." On this occasion, he applied for retirement, with more than a casual interest in his own presidential possibilities.[99] But Harding won the nomination and the hero, who had figured little in the political maneuvering, decided to stay in the army.

During the reorganization debate, some of the legislators talked of making Pershing the permanent Chief of Staff in a manner reminiscent of the old Commanding General plan, but Baker protested. Despite his careful guarding of Pershing's independence during the war, the Secretary was loyal to March and he also saw in the congressional desire to give special prerogatives to Pershing the specter of the Commanding General system.[100] When the bill passed, Congress merely assigned the General of the Armies to the war council where he joined the Chief of Staff, the Secretary of War, and the latter's Assistant in deliberating on military policy.[101]

In the months following the enactment of the reorganization bill, Pershing chaired one of the boards and regularly presented his recommendations for general officer promotions and assignments;[102] but, in his office in the old Land Office Building, he was isolated from the center of power in the War Department. To a certain extent, this was to his advantage: no one could blame him for the many difficulties which beset the army in this period. March, Baker, and the War Department received the criticism. Out of power, Pershing possessed the advantage of potentiality.

As long as March remained Chief of Staff with Baker's support, Pershing's employment was a dilemma. The situation might be less difficult with Weeks in office. A diplomatic assignment as ambassador to France or England was a possibility, but a more plausible solution, with a degree of sentiment, was to allow him to retain the trappings of Chaumont – a G.H.Q. Although the staff and name had continued until September, 1920, it was primarily a records office.[103] The revived G.H.Q. would function as the headquarters of the army as organized under the reorganization act. In case of war, the Secretary would not have to create and man such an office under the pressure of the emergency. During the awful days of 1917, when Pershing had to choose a staff for his expedition, he naturally disrupted the War Department General Staff and other military activities. Thus the plan would not only make a place for him but also provide for a future crisis. Among those who favored such a proposition were Tasker Bliss and the AEF's brilliant operations officer, Fox Conner.[104] The General of the Armies also saw the possibilities of the idea.[105]

In April, 1921, Weeks announced that Pershing would form a G.H.Q. and described the functions of this headquarters. Although the Secretary affirmed that it would in no way interfere with the Chief of Staff and the War Department General Staff, the *Army and Navy Journal* commented that it obviously would, since the powers Weeks assigned to the Commanding General, G.H.Q., were specifically granted to the Chief of Staff under the reorganization act. The military journal concluded, "Unless some very sharply defined plan is arranged for General Pershing and his War Department G.H.Q. . . . complete disruption of the present system appears inevitable, at the top at least."[106] Even before Weeks made his public announcement, opposition emerged from a source close to Pershing. When the "C-in-C" explained the scheme to Harbord, the loyal subordinate telegraphed a protest to his old chief and elaborated in a letter.

The Chief of Staff is charged under the law with certain of the things you suggest that a G.H.Q. should undertake. No matter how much confidence he might have in you he could not divest himself of his responsibilities. If it was attempted without law and on orders only it would breed trouble at once. If the law were changed it would so minimize the position of Chief of Staff that the right sort of man would not wish to accept the position, for it is easy to see that it would mean that you and the G.H.Q. would run the Army except as to purely administrative and supply functions in the War Department. It is wrong in principle to change an organic law to fit an individual case. You have less than four years to serve and they do not intend, probably, to give you a successor as General. To disrupt the whole law as it affects the duties of the Chief of Staff would be wrong, and would make instant and continuing trouble in my opinion.[107]

After another month, Weeks changed his mind somewhat: Pershing would get his G.H.Q. and be, in fact, the Commanding General, but he would also have the title of Chief of Staff. In an effort to avoid legislative action and to answer the criticisms Weeks outlined a new approach. Pershing would have a separate office in the State, War, and Navy Building and be responsible for the organization and training of the army. At the time he gave the General of the Armies these titles, the Secretary named Harbord as the Executive Assistant. In this position Harbord not only would physically occupy the present office of the Chief of Staff but also would supervise the administration of the War Department. In case of war he would become Chief of Staff in name as well since the Commanding General would take the G.H.Q. into the field. This part of the plan, of course, was an attempt to avoid the friction which had emerged between the War Department and the AEF during the war. Under this system, presumably, the Commanding General/Chief of Staff would have established such a relationship with his subordinate Executive Assistant in peace that no question of authority would arise in war.[108]

This seemed to be a return in great part to the old Commanding General system. There would be a Chief of Staff in name who also held the title of Commanding General and actually performed the duties of the latter office. A General Staff would continue to exist, but many of its major tasks would be handled by the G.H.Q. Most of the other wartime missions not turned over to the G.H.Q. were already out of General Staff domain because of the reorganization act. Under this law, the bureau chiefs reported directly to the Assistant Secretary of War, not through the Chief of Staff, on procurement matters. The great powers which the General Staff exercised during the war would virtually be gone. The stage appeared set for a return to the pre-Root era, with the difference that the Commanding General might be more powerful and a General Staff would be available for planning.

For six weeks after the Secretary's announcement of Pershing's appointment, March remained in office. He did not comment publicly on the Weeks-Pershing policy, but he must have regretted the weakening of the General Staff system which he and Baker created during the war. During June, a final irritation was that the General Staff, reduced from a wartime high of over 1000 to 93 officers, was operating with even fewer officers because of the lack of transportation funds to bring newly assigned officers to Washington.[109] On June 30, March signed his last letters, paid a farewell call to President Harding, and walked out of the War Department.[110] Without ceremony, Pershing and Harbord moved in the next day. Harbord took over March's office and directed that all papers previously prepared for the Chief of Staff's signature be routed to his desk.[111]

When Pershing and Harbord entered the War Department, the army was in difficulty. Despite the protests of President Harding and Secretary Weeks, Congress had ordered that it be reduced to 150,000 by October, 1921.[112] Generally, as Wright told Pershing, "the Army is like a yellow dog running down the street with a tin can tied on it, and everybody on the sidewalk throwing rocks."[113] Although Weeks and Pershing might have better personal relations with the Republican Congress than their predecessors, they could not halt the reaction. The war was over and the army had reverted to its peacetime place as an unwanted national instrument of force to be used only in emergencies which everyone hoped would never occur.

Once in power, the new regime began to make its presence known. Within a week, a War Department circular ordered all officers to wear the Sam Browne belt – the talisman of the AEF officer. In another symbolic move, Pershing brought John M. Palmer back into the War Department to study and advise on policy matters. Although the G.H.Q. idea lingered, there seemed less reason for maintaining a separate organization now that the AEF leaders were in control.[114]

When March gave up his office, he also left the army. At the time Weeks announced that Pershing would become Chief of Staff, the Secretary said that March would stay on duty in Washington.[115] Since this did not appeal to the General, he applied for retirement, although he could have continued on active duty until 1928. Weeks accepted this decision with regret and wrote him, "Not only during my short term in this Department but during my service in the Senate I have had an opportunity to observe your conduct of the important position you have held and I appreciate fully the very important results you have been able to accomplish."[116] There were other notes of praise. A *New York Times* article, in February, had commented, "It is undeniable that in a surprisingly short time he brought order out of confusion and achieved a success which probably will cause discriminating critics to rank him as an organizer and executive without a superior in our military history."[117] Despite this achievement, as a *Times* editorial pointed out in June, the United States had failed to honor him as the Allies have rewarded their chiefs of staff. Evidently, "he will be Major Gen. March to the end."[118] The *Army and Navy Journal* added to the applause: "To his soldierly qualities, untiring industry and unsparing zeal, history when written, in the proper perspective, will undoubtedly give full due."[119]

Praise and criticism now were matters of history. For March's days of power were over.

17 · YEARS OF RETIREMENT

During his retirement March traveled, read, and maintained a lively interest in current events. When he published his memoirs, there was a flare-up of controversy and, in World War II, his candid comments on the military situation drew national attention. Throughout most of this period, however, he could walk on the street or ride the bus in Washington with few people realizing who the tall, distinguished-looking gentleman was. Nevertheless, some knew of him and his work and, in 1953, Congress recognized his achievements with its Thanks by Joint Resolution.

On his last day in office, March, accompanied by Secretary Weeks, called on the President. The General had already explained his immediate plans to Weeks and, as he sat in the President's office, he repeated them to Harding. As March recalled the conversation later, "my plan was to go to Europe and travel through the Central Powers . . . to find out for myself conditions actually existing there; and then return to the United States through Russia and learn, if I could without too much official shepherding, something about the then practically unknown Soviet Government and how its plans were working." [1]

Harding heard him out and then cautioned him to be careful in his travels through the former enemy countries. As for the Russian trip, the President told him, "I wish you wouldn't do that, General. We simply can't protect you there under present conditions." Since he considered the executive request mandatory, March regretted having mentioned this part of his plan. Weeks was more enthusiastic about the European tour and encouraged the General to report his observations.[2]

That night March went to New York, where he stayed for a few days before boarding a transport. Once in Europe, he made a brief visit to Coblenz and then traveled on to Berlin.[3] There his old comrade of the Thirty-third Volunteers, Colonel Edward Davis, the military attaché, welcomed him as a house guest.

After the years of tension, March began to unwind. The Davis family thought him a "very agreeable" guest, "genial, in fact, jolly." He enjoyed the two little girls not yet in their teens, and was the producer and financial backer of a play the children staged for the family. Yet, even in relaxation, he was restless. "The General liked to keep on the move. No matter how busy he had been during the day, he always liked to play a few games of cards before retiring." Colonel Davis recalled those pleasant days, "I took him all over Germany by automobile and he proved himself a tireless traveler." [4]

While March was in Berlin, his friend of Russo-Japanese War days, Max Hoffmann, learned that he was in the city and came in from his country place to see him. For March it was not only a delightful but also an informative reunion. In his halting English, which improved as they talked, Hoffmann told the American General "everything" about the Eastern Front where he had played a leading role during the war.[5] "Off and on, for days," March remembered, "[Hoffmann] talked his soul out to me." [6]

The high point of March's stay in Germany was what he termed "an extremely interesting and valuable conversation" with his former adversary, Field Marshal Paul von Hindenburg. Through Davis, Hindenburg and Ludendorff had asked March for an interview during his inspection tour in 1920, but at that time complications prevented the meeting. In late July, 1921, however, March and Davis boarded a special car and went to Hanover to see the aged war lord at his home. Since the Field Marshal had sent word that he would be in full uniform, March donned his field uniform for the occasion.[7]

The two soldiers enjoyed the interview. March was impressed by the "massive figure of a man. . . . direct and straightforward" with "a surprisingly kindly eye." [8] Davis thought that the Field Marshal was "in his usual good humor and genial form" and reported that he answered "General March's queries without reservation or any sign of rancor or regret." [9] In addition to discussing the recent war, they talked at length about the American Civil War and the "rehabilitation of the distressed nations of Europe." March was pleased to learn that Hindenburg had not underestimated the American fighting ability and was somewhat surprised not only that the Field Marshal knew a great deal about the Civil War but also that as an instructor years before in the General Staff College he had introduced a study of the campaigns into the course work. On the more immediate subject, March asked as he was leaving, "Do you ever go up to Berlin?" The old Field Marshal answered, "I never go to Berlin, and I never will go to Berlin." Later, the General commented on the famous soldier's political career: "The march of events was too strong for him." [10]

From Hanover, March journeyed to Essen, where he visited the Krupp works. He had promised Weeks and Harding that he would examine the great munitions factory and find out if it really had converted to peacetime efforts. After spending two days going over the plant, he reported to Weeks: ". . . it is impossible for any war material to be constructed sub rosa. . . . I saw what I wanted to and was not led around to see things which they thought I should see." [11] On his return to Berlin, the Krupp manager, Otto Wiedfeldt, who had missed seeing him in Essen, asked to talk with him. When March and Hoffmann met the industrialist, Wiedfeldt proposed that Germany and the United States join in rehabilitating Russia. Since his nation had not recognized the Soviet regime, the General said, it would be useless to pursue this idea. March recalled, "Wiedfeldt rose at once, bowed from the hips and marched out, deeply offended." When he heard afterwards that Wiedfeldt was going to Washington as ambassador to the United States, March went over his notes and described the interview to Weeks.[12]

While in Berlin, March also talked with the Chancellor and various members of his cabinet. Upon his initial arrival in the capital, he found an invitation to a tea at the old Bismarck Palace. At the appointed time, he joined the German leaders around a small table on the grounds of the executive mansion. Chancellor Julius Wirth and the others, in "great frankness," discussed with him the German situation. March was particularly impressed by "the brilliant Rathenau," whom he called "one of the ablest men . . . I met abroad in any country." In his letter to Weeks about this experience, he concluded, "It seems to me to be of the utmost importance that a strong American Ambassador should be appointed at the earliest practicable date so that America can be represented here by somebody who can speak with authority. . . ." [13] In the fall, March heard that Harding was considering him for this position, but the General thought that the task required an economist.[14]

After his stay in Germany, March moved on to Austria. In Vienna, the government gave a dinner for him and opened its highest offices to him. He met and talked with Chancellor Johann Schober as well as with the less powerful president, and supplemented these conversations by traveling by automobile through that country and neighboring Hungary.[15]

Italy was next on his agenda. Here he not only wanted to see the recent battlefields but also to renew his acquaintance with Enrico Caviglia, whom he had known as a military observer in Manchuria. More entertainment awaited him, and he was the "object of most cordial attentions" in Rome.[16]

Originally he planned to spend five months abroad, but he found the continent so interesting that his stay lengthened to five years. During this period he visited most of the European nations as well as Turkey, Egypt, and Morocco. By the time of his return, he had met virtually all of the leading statesmen and had had long talks with Mustapha Kemal, Primo de Rivera, and Benito Mussolini. While Weeks remained Secretary, March reported on his observations in informative letters which the Secretary passed on to the President and the State Department.[17]

In 1922, March incurred the wrath of Henry T. Allen, still commander of the A.F. in G., by advocating to Weeks that the occupation force be withdrawn. The former Chief of Staff advised Weeks that the nation would have to choose between reinforcing the contingent or bringing it home. The former alternative he considered "unthinkable." When Allen obtained a copy of this letter, he attempted unsuccessfully to argue the matter with March. But the tide of American public opinion was against the occupation commander. Within a few months, in January, 1923, the last American troops ended their watch on the Rhine.[18]

During the several weeks March stayed in Coblenz, Harbord visited the city and promptly wrote Pershing about the former Chief of Staff. He had heard rumors that March was writing a book about the war and that, while in Paris, he "was very much with Marshal Pétain." Harbord was particularly shocked because of March's attire at the Fourth of July reception on the terrace of the Coblenzerhof – the General appeared in evening dress with the one decoration of a Grand Commander of the British order of St. Michael and St. George.[19]

March did not spend all of his time studying the political situation or renewing acquaintance with old soldiers. He later said, "I wanted to see the Acropolis, the Parthenon, the great galleries of Europe . . . the Passion Play at Oberammergau, to hear a production at La Scala in Milan. And I saw and heard them all." He also visited the great universities of Oxford and Cambridge which had honored his father.[20]

The last three years of his stay also served as a honeymoon. While in Rome, he met the young and vivacious Cora McEntee at the American Embassy. On August 25, 1923, in a quiet ceremony in London, they were married. Although they traveled extensively throughout the continent, "loafing through Spain far from the tourist track," in northern Africa, and Turkey, they spent much of the time in a villa at Nice.[21]

Finally in December, 1926, the Marches returned to the United States. When a *New York Times* reporter asked him about his impressions of Europe, March told him that the Europeans hated the Americans. Later, he added that this was probably because of the war debts issue and jealousy of American prosperity. He also noted that while the dictators – Mussolini, Kemal, and Rivera – were making drastic improvements in Italy, Turkey, and Spain, they represented a disquieting trend. "The prevalence of the dictator idea . . . in the Governments of Europe," he commented to the newsman, "and the open contempt for any republican form of government expressed by the dictator, is a very discouraging feature of the whole situation."[22]

After visiting his brother in upstate New York and ranging as far west as Denver, March rented a house in Bayside, Long Island.[23] As in Nice, his home had a tennis court, which he put to great use. When an acquaintance remarked that tennis was a strenuous exercise for a man of his age, March replied, "If it is, do you know any better way for a retired general to die?"[24] The residence had other advantages, as the General wrote Baker: "We are about a mile from Fort Totten, and can hear the bugles and band, and the sound of the sunset gun, daily. We look out over Long Island Sound from our bedroom windows, and find the place more and more charming."[25]

Amidst these sounds, which must have brought memories of his many years on military posts, the General began to think seriously of writing his memoirs. Baker and others had urged him, even while he was Chief of Staff, to tell his version of events of the war.[26] During the intervening years, Baker had continued to press him on this point. In 1926, he wrote, "You should write the Home Front story. The fine officers whom we kept on this side against their will, will never have justice done them unless you do it. And after all Pershing's army was the point of the sword and the Home Organization was the hilt." [27] A year later, the former Secretary asked if he might not write a preface to the proposed book.[28] Finally, in October, 1927, March announced that he would write such a book. He informed the press, "I'm going to tell the truth." [29]

Writing seemed to pall on him. In the year following his announcement, he did work up an article, which the *New York Times* published, on the great shipping problems and he started a draft of the memoirs.[30] But, after pencilling eighteen pages on his career prior to March, 1918, he dropped the work.[31] At this time, he did give some thought to a tentative title – "The Hilt of the Sword." [32] Two years later, he published another newspaper article which, with emphasis on Pershing's vitriolic opposition, told why Leonard Wood did not go to France.[33] This aroused Pershing, who attempted to stop its publication, and irritated Baker, who wanted his generals above all to avoid controversial bickering.[34]

Before March was to begin serious work on his memoirs, two other basic accounts appeared which helped goad him to the laborious task. After ten years of preparation, in early 1931, Pershing brought out his two-volume story of the war. Later that year, Frederick Palmer, who had known both March and Pershing in Manchuria and France, produced a two-volume study of the wartime home organization. As the principal source for *Newton D. Baker: America at War*, the experienced war correspondent used the Secretary's papers.[35] March refused to furnish information for Palmer and seemed to resent the fact that he was writing such a book.[36] When he received the copy which Baker presented him, he wrote the Secretary that he had looked up the references to himself "in company with Mrs. March, and we simply screamed at what he had to say. Nothing like seeing ourselves as others see us." [37]

Pershing's story, of course, had a much greater impact on both Baker and March. Although the AEF commander wrote a generally colorless account which, for the most part, avoided intra-army controversies, Pershing did refer to War Department failures. When Baker read the serialized sections in the newspaper, he wrote March, "He saw his own problem but seems wholly to have failed to grasp ours." [38] The former Chief of Staff was more blunt: "Of course, the Pershing stuff is the veriest blah, and very distressing to those who know the facts. He has no imagination, as you say, and does not visualize our problems at all." [39]

A few days before, in February, 1931, March had visited Washington to deliver a lecture at the Army War College. While he was there, as he wrote Baker, he

> found officers at the War Department & War College . . . completely disgusted with the Pershing attacks on the Department and the mis-statements he has made about what was done at home in his support; without which he never could have moved a foot. Secretary [Patrick J.] Hurley told me that he had gone to Pershing personally, & remonstrated with him about the character of his attacks on the War Department. Hurley begged me to write the real story & placed his Department at my disposal for that purpose. Gen. [Douglas] MacArthur offered me a room, stenographers & any officers I wanted to hunt up papers, & data I needed, if I would come to Washington & write the War Department story. And of course I have got to do it, now.[40]

That fall March and his wife made the move to Washington.[41] With the co-operation of the War Department, the general began serious work on his book in Room 157 of the State, War, and Navy Building.[42] Soon after the move, he wrote Baker, "I find that the work has been very much expedited by the fact that I remember within near limits exactly the documents I want which minimizes the lost motion of having to hunt for everything." [43] The fact that he had signed a contract for the book's publication probably encouraged his efforts; after being approached by several publishers, he had accepted a sizeable advance from Doubleday, Doran and Company.[44]

In addition to examining the records, March also relied upon his memory and his correspondence in writing his book. From Goethals' son, he borrowed the supply chief's valuable wartime diary. He questioned MacArthur about his experience with replacements in 1918. Then, he had read Pershing's and other accounts.[45]

As the publication date neared, Russell Doubleday asked the General to consider delaying the sale of the book because the Depression was having such a bad effect on the literary market. March refused: he wanted to go on record while Pershing and the other war leaders were alive. On this point, he was adamant. "I undertook this work as a public duty and in the interest of historical accuracy," he wrote the publisher in September, 1932.[46]

During June he read the galley proofs of his book.[47] In August, a few newspapers began running part of the book in serial form. During this hot summer month, he and Mrs. March vacationed in Michigan.[48] On their return to Washington they visited the Bakers in Cleveland.[49] In September *The Nation at War* reached the bookstands.[50]

The General wrote his story of the war in a crisp, concise style. He used a topical rather than a chronological approach and was brutally frank in his comments on men and issues. In particular, he criticized, in a polemical fashion, the General of the Armies.

The *New York Times* reviewer joined others in commenting on the controversial aspect of the memoir.

> Finally, one cannot escape the impression that General March suffers from internal injuries because of a nation's forgetfulness or unawareness that as Chief of Staff he was General Pershing's superior officer. . . . It is somewhat ironic that General March's recital of his many constructive achievements as Chief of Staff are compelled to compete with his animadversions upon General Pershing for the reader's interest. . . . General March is heedless of the impression which he personally may make upon his leaders.

The reviewer conceded, "It is apparent that he is not courting popularity but that his chief concern is to place himself upon record." [51]

The most interesting review was that of B. H. Liddell Hart. In a lengthy essay in *Current History*, the famed British military analyst reassessed Pershing and agreed with March's criticism. "What especially impresses one is General March's ability to give logically thought-out reasons for his actions." This in contrast to Pershing's book, which "revealed strange limitations of outlook and of knowledge in a man cast by fate for so big a role." After commenting on the various points of dispute, Liddell Hart wrote:

> The final impression from all this deductive evidence is that of honesty as well as fearlessness in March's testimony. If so, his very honesty may have checked him from disguising his resentment of, and retaliation for, Pershing's attempt to pass the blame to the home authorities for anything that went wrong.[52]

Newton Baker, who had not seen the manuscript, promptly read the copy which March sent him and wrote a detailed critique to his Chief of Staff. In this letter and the others which he exchanged with March in October, 1932, Baker gently corrected the General on several points.[53] Although he wrote that the book was "a very straightforward, strong and helpful contribution to the war story on a side which has until now been inadequately appreciated," he chided March for his criticism of Pershing.[54]

The General of the Armies and his confidants, whom March labelled the "Chaumont crowd," were outraged. Frederick Palmer's book on Baker, which Pershing considered a campaign document to aid the former Secretary's presidential chances in 1932, had caused some consternation among them. Indeed, Pershing asked Fox Conner and George Marshall to read the two volumes with a suspicious eye. "I think," he wrote these two loyal friends, "we must insist on keeping the record straight and not permit an exaggerated impression to be created of the efficiency and foresight of the Administration, the War Department, the War Secretary, or the Chief of Staff." [55] But the blunt criticism in March's book was almost unbearable.

When Pershing's friends considered what action they should take, Harbord at first advised ignoring the book. However, he went along with Pershing's suggestion to help Major General David C. Shanks, who had commanded at Hoboken during the war, publish an excoriation of March.[56] This led to a rebuttal from March, followed by a counter-rebuttal from Shanks.[57] As time passed, the wounds March inflicted did not heal. Although Pershing initially had written Harbord, "There is not one criticism that cannot be conclusively answered, and most of it from my book," he began to consider writing another book in direct refutation of March.[58]

Finally, in the spring of 1934, Pershing accepted Harbord's advice to let the latter write a general history of the American Expeditionary Force which would also refute March.[59] During this period, Baker became involved in a curious manner. In the past few years, he and Harbord had renewed their wartime acquaintance through meetings of the Radio Corporation of America board and correspondence. Although the Secretary deplored the controversy between the two generals, he was pleased that Harbord planned to write a book, but he cautioned him to avoid a sensational approach.[60] After Harbord mailed a draft chapter about March to Baker, the Secretary again urged him not to use such polemical material. He also suggested that he ask the advice of Elihu Root on the matter.[61] When Harbord took the question to the distinguished statesman, then in his late eighties, Root read the two memoirs and Palmer's biography of Bliss as well and concluded that Baker was correct. A full footnote on March's book should suffice, the elderly arbiter advised. Harbord relayed this information to Baker, who promptly volunteered a lengthy footnote on that subject.[62] This footnote was sufficiently critical of March's memoir to satisfy Harbord and Pershing, so Harbord inserted it with minor revision (but without a hint of its author) in his book.[63]

The former Secretary's role in the battle of the memoirs, while minor, is interesting. Since Baker wanted to avoid controversy, he resented March's attitude as represented by his articles and *The Nation at War*. He admired not only March and Pershing but also Scott, Bliss, and many other soldiers with whom he had contact. Yet, he actually had little experience dealing with Pershing in the sense of working day in and day out in an adjoining office as he did with the various Chiefs of Staff. Then, the Secretary, despite his association with the military, retained what he termed "the innocence of my civilian mind."[64] During the war and afterwards he placed Pershing on a pedestal. As he wrote Harbord, "I had always had a feeling about General Pershing that I wanted him to come back to America as our great fighting soldier."[65] When the hero, in his book, skirted affairs, such as the Wood and Edwards cases, which would have provoked controversy or reflected on his own (Pershing's) reputation, Baker was pleased. In turn, March's careful resurrection of controversial matters displeased him. Thus he was willing to join Harbord in criticism of his Chief of Staff. Nevertheless, his admiration for March's contribution to the victory did not wane.[66]

Although *The Nation at War* was March's sole book-length publication, he continued to write after he finished his memoir. As he considered future subjects, his thoughts turned to the Far East. At this time, MacArthur was encouraging him to write about the capture and occupation of the Philippines.[67] While March did not attempt this broad topic, he did write up his reminiscences of the Astor Battery in an article which the *Saturday Evening Post* published after his death.[68] From the Spanish-American War, he shifted his attention to the rising threat of Japan. In an article, "Japanese Strategy in the Far East," which appeared in a 1933 issue of the *Yale Review*, he analyzed the recent moves of this Oriental power.[69]

After these articles, March lost interest in writing, but he did recount his experiences to a limited audience. Annually for several years in the thirties, he delivered a lecture at the Army War College. While he devoted the bulk of these talks to various aspects of his World War I problems, he did range afield occasionally — reminiscing about his days as a military observer, analyzing Japan's military system and the ambitions of the Soviet government, rebutting John M. Palmer, recalling his post-war European tour, and, in his final lecture in 1938, referring to the imminent threat of war.[70] In these talks, March demonstrated the same characteristics which he revealed to the distinguished newsman Mark S. Watson in interviews: "He was a marvellous source of information about men and events, with a fine historical sense, keen perception, excellent perspective, a phenomenal memory and a vigor of expression reflecting his strong opinions." [71]

In addition to his writing, the General was active socially. He and Mrs. March attended the various Embassy receptions and visited the White House several times. On one occasion, President Hoover, who well remembered their wartime contacts, asked March about his progress on the book.[72] Later, during an event at the White House, Secretary of State Cordell Hull recalled for March some of the difficulties of dealing with Congress.[73] At the embassies, March had some interesting encounters. One of his congressional critics, Senator Kenneth D. McKellar, accosted the Marches at a Soviet reception, turned to Mrs. March, and said, "Gen. March was a great Chief of Staff during the war. He was a he-man." [74] The writer Emil Ludwig also found him at a Soviet function and attempted unsuccessfully to elicit an opinion about Franklin D. Roosevelt's service as Assistant Secretary of the Navy.[75] When he met the Soviet ambassador, March discovered that he had served in Manchuria during the Russo-Japanese War; they also discussed the Japanese threat in the Far East.[76] At a party in the garden of the British embassy, he met James W. Wadsworth, who had returned to the Capitol as a Congressman. In their friendly chat, March pleased the former Senator by commenting that the 1920 Defense Act had been beneficial for the army.[77]

After his move to Washington, the General became increasingly interested in politics. While he was in the army, tradition dictated that he be apolitical, but in retirement he began to follow the political scene. In 1928 he told Baker that he would vote for Al Smith.[78] In the next presidential campaign, he was even more enthusiastic about the Democratic candidate. He had known and liked Roosevelt for years. Indeed, in January, 1932, he and Mrs. March received an invitation to Elliot Roosevelt's wedding festivities.[79] In September, F.D.R. wrote the General, "I would appreciate it if you would write me from time to time your reactions on my speeches and on the general progress of the campaign." [80] Throughout that fall, the Marches listened to the addresses over the radio. On October 31, the General congratulated

Roosevelt on the high plane of his speeches and predicted that the election was "in the bag." [81] A few months later, he and Mrs. March saw F.D.R. take the oath of office and heard him deliver his inaugural address. From their reserved seats at the Capitol, they hurried to the State, War, and Navy Building where they watched the parade from the General's office.[82] The Roosevelts later entertained them in the White House. After two years of the New Deal, March wrote to an old army friend, "There is one thing about F.D.R. which he has in common with Helen Wills. He has guts and however much the Democratic leaders may be running around in circles he is apparently the only man in the whole crowd who has kept his head and cheerfulness." [83]

During these years, the General saw a great deal of another exciting personality – the then Chief of Staff. Before he came to Washington, March had written to President Hoover's military aide, Campbell B. Hodges, a recommendation of MacArthur for this coveted assignment.[84] The two generals admired each other very much and enjoyed each other's company. The younger general recalled of his elder, "When I became Chief of Staff, I consulted with him often." [85] In addition to their contact at the War Office, the two exchanged frequent social calls.[86] Theirs was a warm, pleasant relationship.

Despite his active social life, March was able to devote much time to his hobbies. He liked to read and his large library ranged from Rabindranath Tagore and Sinclair Lewis through the war memoirs to a set of *R. E. Lee* which Douglas Southall Freeman presented to him.[87] In the fall of 1932, when he attended a Doubleday party, he was particularly delighted to meet Ellen Glasgow.[88] But the prevailing occupation of his leisure was sports. When possible he attended baseball and football games. He enjoyed the privilege of passes in both major leagues and would sit high up near the press box to watch the game.[89] In football season, he followed the Army team with great interest. Mrs. March remembered that he sat through an Army-Yale game in a pouring rain and his niece, Mrs. Stanley J. Thomas, recalled his taking her and her husband to Army-Navy games.[90] He enjoyed talking about athletics and had many "bull sessions" on this topic with Joe Beacham, the Astor's first Sergeant, who had become a brigadier general.[91]

In 1934, March returned to Easton for the fiftieth reunion of his class. Twenty-three members of '84, including Burr McIntosh, were present for the ceremony. The General wore his uniform, which still fitted him.[92] Since a special act of Congress in 1930 provided all retired officers with the highest rank held during the war, he also wore four stars.[93] That summer he also attended the commencement exercises at Pennsylvania Military College, where the school presented him with an honorary degree.[94] Four years later, he did not attend the fiftieth reunion of his West Point class but merely sent a letter to the seven who did.[95]

During the 1930's, the Marches lived in three different residences in northwest Washington and spent some of the winter months in Florida. In 1939, they moved into a spacious apartment at 1870 Wyoming Avenue with a splendid view of the Capitol. Here they lived for the remainder of the General's life.[96]

As the decade neared its end, March realized that war was imminent. In January, 1938, he told a *Miami Herald* reporter that the Far Eastern situation was "incredibly dangerous." [97] Three months later he confided to an Army War College audience that the next move in Europe "may prove to be the fatal step" and that "it would be the height of folly for us to assume there would be a World War without our being drawn into it." [98]

On the same day that the Germans invaded Poland, a new Chief of Staff took his post. Although George C. Marshall was a close friend of Pershing's, he respected March, whom he considered "a master administrator." [99] His Secretary of the General Staff soon briefed the pertinent parts of *The Nation at War* for his information. This officer, Orlando Ward, later wrote March, "History did repeat itself and your book forewarned the staff." [100]

From beginning to end, March followed the war with great interest. While the European conflict was in its fourth month, he told a reporter that an army of 500,000 would be invaluable to the United States. He added that the draft would be necessary and that the vaunted airplane would not be the decisive weapon in the war.[101] Mark Watson, who interviewed him in this period, noted: "He read everything he could get on the war and expressed himself plainly and without restraint. . . ." [102]

When he celebrated his seventy-ninth birthday in 1943, he told reporters, "You can't whip Germany by whipping somebody in Senegambia. I'm a cross-channel man. . . ." And he warned against premature optimism. "The war hasn't even started. Wait until Germany and Japan begin fighting on their own soil." [103] He also reinforced his remarks on airpower by pointing out the resilience of German industry and the entrenched Japanese on Tarawa. Finally, he advocated, "Tell the people the truth. They've got to know how tough it is. . . ."[104] *Life* magazine devoted a full page to this interview and *Time* ran a column story on the General's comments. This brought him offers to write for magazines, which he declined, and a deluge of mail.[105] A year later, he gave the newsmen some blunt comments on the failure of American intelligence in the Battle of the Bulge and deplored the unconditional surrender doctrine. He also expressed his belief that the Russians would not enter the war against Japan.[106] Meantime, his two sons-in-law, each of whom earned a major general's rank, served with distinction on opposite sides of the world.[107]

March continued in good health, although he celebrated his eighty-first birthday the year World War II ended. An acquaintance who saw him in the Army-Navy Club commented, "Even then he had not faded visibly, but was as sharp as ever in his perceptions and his observations and his hostilities. A marvellous endurance of body and mind and spirit."[108] One of the reporters who had attended his World War I press conferences met him in Farragut Square during a chilling rain. When Bascom Timmons remarked on the General's not wearing a coat, March said that he was in good shape – in fact, that he had walked four miles that day.[109]

When he paid his regular trips to the Army-Navy Club barbershop, he would stop and chat with some of the old-timers, such as Colonel Richard H. McMaster, who had shared a stateroom with him on his 1899 voyage to the Philippines. In his last years, he became acquainted with a retired reserve officer, Colonel George W. Hinman, a witty and urbane gentleman, whose hobby was the club's library. On his visits to the club, March would walk rapidly in long strides down the mezzanine corridor to the library to see Colonel Hinman. Since the General's eyesight was failing, his friend would watch him in fear that he might trip over something.[110]

Although the General was alert and vigorous, he could not escape the sadness of advanced age. He suffered the loss of a son in 1928, and a daughter on Christmas Day of 1932.[111] Then, he was the last survivor of the six March sons after his younger brother, John, died in 1952.[112] It was a distinguished generation, with five of the brothers represented in *Who's Who in America.*[113]

The birthday interview became a regular event following World War II. In 1947, March commented that he was the "despair of the doctors" because of his good health. At that time, he released to the press a letter from his once bitter foe, Fiorello La Guardia, who admitted his error in opposing universal military training in 1919. The former New York mayor added, "I am really writing to say . . . how much and how often I have regretted the ill-advised, unkind, and harsh things I said about you on the floor of the House." [114]

When the United States went to war in Korea, March was in his eighty-seventh year but he still followed the war news. Indeed, he frequently used his knowledge of the Korean terrain to explain the situation to his friends. One day as he and Mrs. March walked across the street to Kalorama Park where they often relaxed in the sun, they met John K. Herr, a former Chief of Cavalry. General Herr, who was naturally a strong enthusiast for his beloved branch, indicted the army: "They have betrayed the horse." He then elaborated on his thesis that with the aid of one regiment of cavalry the United States could win the Korean War. March laughed.[115]

In his first interview after the war began, he refused to comment on the situation. A year later, he did say that it was a "shocking thing" not to bomb the Manchurian bases and that from "a military standpoint, General MacArthur was an ideal man" for the Korean command. Although he would not comment on MacArthur's removal, he did say that the real danger to world peace was in Europe. He added, in a personal vein, that he and his family were relieved that a West Point-trained grandson (Lt. Colonel John Millikin, Jr.) had completed his Korean tour safely.[116]

The high point of March's last years came in July, 1953. Thirty-five years earlier, during that month, he had seen the Atlantic transport reach its peak and had participated in the crucial manpower and Russian intervention decisions. Now, Congress voted on a concurrent resolution tendering him, in the words of Senator Leverett Saltonstall, its "long overdue" Thanks. A lingering hint of old scars remained in that the resolution referred not to his active service but to "his selfless and patriotic interest in the United States Army since his retirement." [117]

On the last day of the month, he went to the White House to receive the engrossed scroll. But the occasion was overshadowed by the concern at the White House over the condition of Senator Robert A. Taft, who was seriously ill, and the ceremony, originally scheduled for mid-afternoon, was moved up to noon. Years before, when March was writing his book in the War Department, he had chatted with the young major who now occupied the presidency. Now, in the presence of Mrs. March, Secretary of the Army Robert Stevens, Senator Saltonstall, Congressman Dewey Short (a family friend), and a few others, President Dwight D. Eisenhower read the resolution and, with the comment that he considered it "a very great privilege," presented it to the General. The aged soldier, who stood erect despite his years, took the document and said, "I think I'll turn it over to Mrs. March."[118] After the President and the General briefly reminisced about the First World War, the ceremony was over.[119] Since the news of Taft's death had just reached the White House, the press secretary prevented photographers from recording the scene.[120]

For the next few months, the General enjoyed a moderate social round. Mrs. March wrote in mid-August that he was "quite well — gay, in fact, since he went to two parties recently!"[121] Sometime before, he had even visited the Pentagon, where he noticed with disdain the amount of time permitted for lunch. In these last years, he took particular pleasure in going for automobile drives with Colonel Hinman. One day they drove out to Mount Vernon and walked about the Washington estate. Shortly after the White House ceremony, they went to Front Royal, Virginia, to visit Beverly Browne. His subordinate of a half-century before was impressed by the General's condition during his four-hour stay; "He was just as keen as he had ever been."[122] Late in the afternoon, when they were having a cocktail, General Browne invited the chauffeur to join them. When the sergeant entered the library, he saw a portrait of the General dating from his years as Chief of Staff. After studying it for a moment, he commented to Browne, "He hasn't changed a bit."[123]

But after this, March began to suffer from the effects of his advanced age. In December, he observed his eighty-ninth birthday in Walter Reed Hospital, where he was recovering from a strained back ligament.[124] He was able to return home, but, on February 3, 1954, he fell and broke a femur.[125] Once again, he went to Walter Reed; this time, he did not return. For the next fourteen months, he occupied the third-floor suite overlooking the formal gardens. At first he was disgruntled because it had been Pershing's quarters, but he soon settled into the hospital routine, occasionally leaving the suite in his wheelchair. On his ninetieth birthday, he enjoyed a cake and presents. In consideration of his failing vision, the hospital orderlies bought him an electric clock with especially large hands.[126] A few months later, at 5 P.M. on April 13, 1955, he died from "the degenerative conditions of old age." [127]

When the nation learned the news, its leaders gave their tributes. President Eisenhower wrote the widow, "To all Americans and to the military personnel in particular, his outstanding accomplishments during World War I have become almost legendary." [128] The then Chief of Staff, Matthew B. Ridgway, called attention to the fact that March's "inspiring leadership . . . contributed to the firm foundation on which our Army stands today" and in General Order # 26 informed the army of the General's death.[129] The Secretaries of Defense and of the Army, as well as George C. Marshall, Bernard M. Baruch, and the French Ambassador added to the praise.[130] One of the editorial eulogies, that of the *Christian Science Monitor*, commented, "Hero no less than officers whose names headlined dispatches from overseas, he deserves his country's reverent tribute." [131]

Some years earlier, March had picked out a burial site among a grove of maple trees on a gentle knoll to the left front of the Lee Mansion in Arlington. On April 19, a cold, gray day, a mile-long cortege, which included a battalion of West Point cadets and representative units from the various services, accompanied the flag-draped caisson, drawn to the cemetery by six white horses. A handsome black horse carrying the traditional saber and reversed boots followed the caisson. Vice President Richard M. Nixon headed the official delegation, which heard a chaplain read the Presbyterian service. After a howitzer boomed the seventeen-gun salute, a rifle squad fired the three sharp volleys. Taps. And the army buried its dead.[132]

Throughout the annals of American history, military leaders have earned distinction on the battlefield. As the evolution of the modern age complicated the structure of war, a new type of leader emerged — the administrator. In order to use the elaborate trappings of twentieth-century war, staff organizations pyramided and men with special skills occupied positions of increasing responsibility. In the United States the beginning of this system dates from the Root reforms of the first decade of this century.

Peyton March spent his early military service in a nineteenth-century army. As a young lieutenant, he served with men who were still lieutenants even though they had seen action in the Civil War. After establishing a reputation for combat gallantry in the wars of empire, he won a place on the first General Staff. Then, the Russo-Japanese War educated him in the intricacies of modern war.

When the First World War came, he went to France, expecting to take part as an artilleryman. Called to Washington, he played a much greater role. As Chief of Staff, by acting vigorously and ruthlessly, he established the power of the General Staff and contributed materially to the victory.

During this period, March was the victim of general misunderstanding. He was a military manager, but most of his contemporaries thought, in rather naive terms, that all military leaders should be in the heroic warrior mold.[133] Thus many considered Pershing, who served as the military manager in France, a hero, while scorning March as a desk officer.

As a modern military manager, March had the significant flaw of failing to recognize the necessity for good relations with Congress. When he thought he was right, he would not attempt a diplomatic, persuasive course. In war he could succeed despite his brusqueness. Without the pressure of war, he encountered opposition from the men in Congress. When March, in a post-war Army War College lecture, compared politicians to soldiers, he commented that the politician must win backing for his plans while the soldier "orders it done."[134] In a democracy, the soldier too must gain support for some major actions. Nevertheless, to fix the blame for the army's post-war problems on him is not justifiable, and is too simple an explanation for a complicated situation. No man – civilian or military – could have turned the tide of reaction.

Fortunately, he outlived the reaction. As the animosities faded, a once bitter AEF division commander admitted, "He could see through things."[135] And a veteran military correspondent added: "He had the great leader's gift of seeing things in the large and also in detail, and assigning the right job to the right lieutenant."[136]

A few years after March's death, Douglas MacArthur reminisced about him and evaluated his old friend. No soldier could ask for a greater tribute: "As a soldier, my opinion of March is of the highest. He was, in my estimation, perhaps the greatest Chief of Staff of all time. . . . He was a man of principle. . . . He would not hesitate to offend the most powerful man on Capitol Hill on a trifle if he thought a principle was involved." The General of the Army continued: "The sights and smells of a battlefield which are repugnant to many were exhilarating to him. He always wanted to go to the front. He was that rare combination — a courageous leader and a skilled administrator. . . . A tremendous officer — a tremendous Chief of Staff." [137]

REFERENCE MATTER

NOTES

Chapter 1. The Beginning of a Soldier's Life

1 James W. Bright, "An Address in Commemoration of Francis Andrew March, 1825–1911," *Publications of the Modern Language Association of America* (1914), XXIX, cxxvi–cxxvii; David B. Skillman, *The Biography of a College: Being the History of the First Century of Lafayette College*, 2 vols. (Easton, Pa., 1932), I, 218; Selden J. Coffin, *Record of the Men of Lafayette: Brief Biographical Sketches of the Alumni of Lafayette College, From its organization to the present time* (Easton, Pa., 1879), 342.

2 Coffin, *Record*, 342; Genealogy prepared by Peyton C. March, Peyton C. March Papers (Library of Congress, Washington, D.C.), Box 6.

3 Memoir draft, March Papers, Box 25; Moncure D. Conway, *Autobiography: Memories and Experiences*, 2 vols. (Boston, 1904), I, 1–9, 11, 46; Mrs. Stanley J. Thomas letter to author, April 7, 1962. Mrs. Thomas, a granddaughter of Professor March and a niece of General March, was most helpful in providing information about the family.

4 Bright, "Address," cxxiii; Skillman, *Biography*, I, 230–34; II, 150. Professor March taught until 1906. Both he and Mrs. March died in 1911.

5 Skillman, *Biography*, I, 233; Clarence L. Barnhart, "Introduction," *March's Thesaurus-Dictionary* by F. A. March and F. A. March, Jr. (Garden City, N.Y., 1958), iii–iv.

6 List of children and dates of birth in 1932 File, March Papers, Box 1; Mrs. Thomas letter; Skillman, *Biography*, I, 119, 213; clipping in 1919 Scrapbook, March Papers.

7 F. A. March to Peyton C. March, Aug. 2, 1870, in possession of Mrs. Thomas.

8 Miss Mildred March interview, February 7, 1959. Mrs. Katherine H. Shaw used questions which I furnished to interview General March's sister. Dr. Benjamin R. Field's account was printed in the Philadelphia *Public Ledger*, March 10, 1918, clipping in 1898 Scrapbook, March Papers.

9 Field, *Ledger* article; Mrs. Thomas letter and interview, April 24, 1962; clipping in 1919 Scrapbook, March Papers; Peyton C. March to Mildred March, April 30, 1932, March Papers, Box 1; Mrs. Peyton C. March interview, Aug. 28, 1961.

10 Peyton C. March questionnaire in his folder in the Alumni Office of Lafayette College; Lafayette College *Catalogue: 1880–1881* (Easton, Pa., 1881), 19.

11 *Melange '82* (Easton, Pa., 1881), 31–35. This was the college yearbook.

12 *Ibid.*, 41, 91–92; *Melange '84* (Easton, Pa., 1883), 3, 80, 112, 125; *Lafayette College Journal*, Vol. 7, # 8 (May, 1882), 100, and Vol 8, # 10 (July, 1883), 289.

13 The quotation is by Dr. J. H. Rohrback in Wilkes-Barre (Pa.) *Leader*, December 14, 1918, clipping in March Folder, Alumni Office, Lafayette College. I found accounts of March's athletic achievements in the yearbooks as well as the *Lafayette College Journals* of his era. Francis A. March, Jr., *Athletics at Lafayette College: Recollections and Opinions* (Easton, Pa., 1926), 36–39, 170, 183, 199, 236, 238.

14 Class statistics in W. A. Cattell Scrapbook, Rare Book Collection, Van Wickle Library, Lafayette College.

15 Class statistics and 1884 Commencement Program in the Cattell Scrapbook. Because of his undergraduate record, March later was granted a Master of Arts degree and admitted to Phi Beta Kappa. Memoir draft, March Papers, Box 25.

16 Typescript of March interview by Joseph E. Bell, September 27, 1932, and March to Newton D. Baker, July 11, 1932, March Papers, Box 1; Skillman, *Biography*, I, 300.

17 Class statistics in Cattell Scrapbook; Memoir draft, March Papers, Box 25; Francis A. March, Jr., account printed in the Philadelphia *Public Ledger*, March 10, 1918, clipping in 1898 Scrapbook, March Papers.

18 F. A. March, Jr., *Ledger* article.

19 *Lafayette College Journal*, Vol. 9, # 9 (June, 1884), 134, 137.

20 Unpublished memoir, Chapter III, John J. Pershing Papers (Library of Congress, Washington, D.C.), Box 377. The last quotation is from Archibald Campbell interview, Aug. 8, 1957. General Campbell was in the class of 1889. (The date of the person's graduating class will be in parentheses when interviews or correspondence are cited.)

21 *Regulations for the U.S. Military Academy at West Point, New York* (Washington, D.C., 1883). *Annual Report of the Board of Visitors for the United States Military Academy* (Washington, D.C., 1887).

22 *Official Register of the Officers and Cadets of the U.S. Military Academy* (West Point, 1884), 21–22. (Hereafter cited as U.S.M.A. *Register* with the appropriate date.) Lewis S. Sorley (1891) gave a particularly graphic description of Beast Barracks training of the period in his interview on August 5, 1957. The course of summer training is detailed in Headquarters, U. S. Corps of Cadets Order Book (U.S.M.A. Archives), Orders # 65 (June 22, 1884) and # 70 (July 6, 1884). (Hereafter cited U.S.C.C.)

23 U.S.M.A. *Register: 1885*, 20; U.S.M.A. *Register: 1888*, 10–11. School History of Candidates (U.S.M.A. Archives). March's tribute to Jervey is in the obituary section of the West Point alumni magazine, *Assembly*, II, # 2 (July, 1943), 4.

24 March's record is in the U.S.M.A. *Registers: 1885*, 17; *1886*, 15, 29; *1887*, 12, 29; *1888*, 10, 29. Archibald Campbell, John P. Hains (Aug. 6, 1957), and W. W. Harts (March 29, 1957)—all of the class of

1889 – in interviews recalled their impressions of March. The first and third quotations are from Spencer Cosby (1891) letter to the author, Feb. 12, 1956. Colonel Cosby supplemented this information in an interview on June 7, 1956. The "Dumbjohn" quotation is from the Sorley interview.

25 William J. Glasgow (1891) letter, March 1, 1956, and the interviews previously cited provided insights of cadet life of this era. U.S.M.A. Library Circulation Records.

26 Charles D. Rhodes (1889), "Intimate Letters of a West Point Cadet," mimeographed copy in U.S.M.A. Archives, May 1 and 22, 1887, March 18, 1888. Sheridan's visits are recorded in Post Headquarters Order Book (U.S.M.A. Archives), Orders # 165 (Sept. 22, 1885), # 91 (June 11, 1886), and # 92 (June 10, 1887).

27 Post Headquarters Order Book (U.S.M.A. Archives), Circular # 25 (Aug. 5, 1885). March praised Merritt in a speech on Jan. 23, 1935, March Papers, Box 3. U.S.M.A. *Register: 1888*, 3. Rhodes, Nov. 6, Dec. 4, 1887. Harts Interview.

28 A pamphlet containing the talks of the One Hundredth Night event is in the Walter N. P. Darrow (1886) Scrapbook (U.S.M.A. Archives). The statistics are from General Committee to Superintendent, Dec. 13, 1918, West Point # 1538, Chief of Staff File, Record Group 165, National Archives. (Hereafter cited C/S File, RG, NA.)

29 Campbell, Harts, and Hains interviews. The quotation is from the Hains interview. U.S.C.C. Order # 67 (June 13, 1885).

30 Charles H. McKinstry (1888) letter, March 5, 1957. Harts interview. The second quotation is from Rhodes, Nov. 27, 1887. The Sorley interview was the source for the bitterness story. In addition to contemporaries already cited, I used these sources to reconstruct March's cadet life: letters to the author from Avery D. Andrews (1886), Sept. 23, 1955; William C. Davis (1890), Feb., 1956; Henry T. Ferguson (1890), Feb. 14, 1956; Melvin W. Rowell (1890), Feb. 6, 1956; interviews with George T. Langhorne (1889), Jan. 30, 1960; Henry D. Todd, Jr. (1890), June 8, 1956; and Hanson E. Ely (1891), June 7, 1956.

31 *New York Times*, June 12, 1888, 5.

32 Organization Return, Third Artillery Regiment, Sept. 1888, RG 94 NA. (Hereafter cited as OR, followed by the unit and date.) Throughout this section, I have depended greatly on interviews with three officers who served in the Third with March at Washington Barracks – Campbell, Hains, and Todd. The quotations are from the Todd interview.

33 OR, Third Artillery, Feb., Aug., Dec., 1889; May, Aug., 1891, RG 94 NA. The description of Chester is from the Hains interview. *Official Army Register: 1889*, 98–101. March's various efficiency reports and service records are in his Appointment, Commission, and Promotion file, # 951 ACP 89, RG 94 NA. (Hereafter cited as ACP.) The comments are by Colonel LaRhett L. Livingston, Feb. 19, 1894, ACP.

34 Campbell, Hains, and Todd interviews. General Todd supplemented this with a letter to the author, March 3, 1956. The quotations are from the Campbell interview. Peyton C. March, *The Nation at War* (Garden City, N.Y., 1932), 83–84.

35 James Totten interview, Nov. 19, 1958. Colonel Totten, who was Mrs. Cunningham's nephew, described his aunt and recalled the courtship. March questionnaire, Feb. 17, 1930, in his file in the U.S.M.A. Association of Graduates Office, West Point. He listed his children and their birthdates there as follows: Mildred, Oct. 4, 1893; Josephine, Nov. 28, 1895; Peyton, Jan. 1, 1897; Vivian, Oct. 29, 1899; and Lewis, May 10, 1904. He did not include Josephine's twin brother, who died ten days after birth. Dec. 7, 1891, Diary, March Papers, Box 7.

36 He was promoted on Oct. 25, 1894. Oath of Office, Dec. 28, 1894, ACP. OR, Fifth Artillery Regiment, Jan. and Feb., 1895, RG 94 NA. Colonel William M. Graham's report, June 30, 1896, ACP.

37 Special Order # 200, Headquarters of the Army, Aug. 25, 1896, ACP. I used the reports of the various faculty department heads which are filed under Artillery School, Fort Monroe, Virginia, Chiefs of Arms Records, RG 177 NA. The class graduated on March 28, 1898. Robert Arthur, *The Coast Artillery School: 1824–1927* (Fort Monroe, 1928), 51. Williams interview, June 5, 1956. During World War I, Hinds became a major general and Chief of Artillery in the AEF.

38 *Official Army Register: 1895*, 333. Peyton C. March, "Mr. Astor Outfits the Army," *Saturday Evening Post*, CCXXXI, No. 3 (July 19, 1958), 25.

Chapter 2. "The Many Acts of Good Soldiership"

1 The title of this chapter is from Arthur MacArthur to The Adjutant General, Feb. 27, 1901, ACP. I have relied greatly on the March, "Mr. Astor Outfits the Army," *Saturday Evening Post*, CCXXXI, No. 3 (July 19, 1958); the quotations are from that source, which was written in 1932.

2 *Philadelphia Press*, May 27, 1898, clipping in 1898 Scrapbook, March Papers.

3 *New York Herald*, June 1, 1898, and undated *San Francisco Chronicle* clippings, 1898 Scrapbook, March Papers.

4 Joseph W. Beacham, in two interviews on March 29, and Aug. 4, 1957, gave me invaluable information and understanding of the Astor Battery, in which he served as a sergeant. The battery's Muster-out roll, Feb. 2, 1899, March Papers, Box 27, supplied the various dates which I have used in reference to March and the unit.

5 The *Chronicle* clipping is in the 1898 Scrapbook, March Papers. T. Bentley Mott, *Twenty Years as Military Attaché* (New York, 1937), 56, 59. Diary, July 25, 1898, Enoch H. Crowder Papers (Western Manuscript Collection, University of Missouri, Columbia, Missouri).

6 Unpublished Memoir, Chapter XVI, 5, Pershing Papers, Box 378.

7 Beacham interviews; Frank D. Millet, *The Expedition to the Philippines* (New York, 1899), 40, 44–45, 57–58.

8 Millet, *Expedition*, 60–63. Clippings of a March interview, Feb. 6, 1899, in "Easton and the Spanish-American War" Scrapbook in the Easton, Pennsylvania Public Library.

9 George Dewey, *Autobiography* (New York, 1913), Chap. XVIII. John F. Bass, "The Fall of Manila," *Harper's Weekly*, XLII (Oct. 15, 1898), 1007.

10 The first quotation is from Bass, "The Fall," 1007. The second is from Oscar K. Davis, *Our Conquests in the Pacific* (New York, 1899), 195.

11 Millet, *Expedition*, 131. Wesley Merritt, Report, Aug. 31, 1898, and March Report, Aug. 16, 1898, in U.S. Congress, House of Representatives, *Annual Report of the War Department, Report of the Major-General Commanding the Army*, 55 Cong., 3 sess., 1898, 41, 120. (Hereafter cited as *Report, 1898*.)

12 *Report, 1898*, 41, 120; Beacham interviews; March, "Astor," 55; Dewey, *Autobiography*, 277; Bass, "The Fall," 1007–08.

13 Arthur MacArthur, Report, Aug. 22, 1898; *Report, 1898*, 79–82. The first quotation is from C. C. Williams to The Adjutant General, Feb. 6, 1899, ACP. The second quotation is from March, "Astor," 55. The final quotations are from the Beacham interviews.

14 Beacham interviews.

15 March lost 3 killed and 4 wounded. Greene's casualties were 1 killed and 6 wounded. Francis V. Greene, Report, Aug. 23, 1898; *Report, 1898*, 71; Beacham interviews.

16 MacArthur, Report, *Report, 1898*, 81. March made these remarks in the Easton interview, Feb. 6, 1899, clipping in Easton Scrapbook. Beacham interview, Aug. 4, 1957.

17 As background for the Astor Battery, I used a scrapbook containing clippings and letters written by a member of the unit to his family. This veteran, Frederick L. Hardenbrook, a Harvard graduate who served as a private in the battery, loaned the scrapbook to me. A microfilm copy of this scrapbook is in the Margaret I. King Library, University of Kentucky, Lexington, Kentucky. Beacham interviews. *New York World*, Jan. 23, 1899, clipping in 1898 Scrapbook, March Papers, Astor Battery Muster-out roll, March Papers, Box 27.

18 March to The Adjutant General, Feb. 24, 1899, and Headquarters of the Army Special Order # 51, March 3, 1899, ACP. *The Lafayette*, XXV, No. 7 (Feb. 10, 1899), 140, 146. Feb. 6, 1899, clipping in "Easton and the Spanish-American War," Scrapbook.

19 "Easton and the . . . War" Scrapbook.

20 MacArthur to March, Dec. 20, 1898, and March to The Adjutant General, March 18, 1899, ACP. Second Division OR, May, 1899, RG 94 NA.

21 March Individual Service Report, Aug. 24, 1899, ACP. List # 3,

"Brevets recommended for service in the Philippine Islands," # 421576, RG 94 NA. (Hereafter cited as List # 3.)

22 Second Division Organization Returns, May through Oct., 1899, RG 94 NA. March lecture at Army War College, April 20, 1933, 13. (These lectures will be cited as AWC lecture and the date.) Douglas MacArthur interview, Dec. 12, 1960. Arthur MacArthur Report, Aug. 15, 1899, ACP.

23 Henry C. Corbin to March, July 12, 1899, ACP.

24 The most valuable source on this regiment is its brief history which Cronin prepared: Marcus D. Cronin to The Adjutant General, April 16, 1899, RG 94 NA. (Hereafter cited as Cronin, "History.") The quotation is by Thomas L. Sherburne, in *Jawbone*, Aug., 1937. The Thirty-third's veterans' newspaper, *Jawbone*, provided much information on March's services with that regiment. Through the generosity of John Boss, Wainwright, Oklahoma; Mrs. Ruth Hamlin, Hannibal, Missouri; and Mrs. Ora Gunn, Wilburton, Oklahoma, I was able to assemble almost a complete file of this paper. *Official Army Register*, 1899, 71, 181.

25 Cronin, "History." Wheaton Report, Nov. 30, 1899, # 308754, RG 94 NA. William T. Sexton, *Soldiers in the Sun: An Adventure in Imperialism* (Harrisburg, Pa., 1939), 73–75.

26 The quotation is from a letter written by M. G. Nixon of Company G, Nov. 9, 1899, printed in *Jawbone*, July, 1956. March Report and Hare Report, both on Nov. 8, 1899, in U.S. Congress, House of Representatives, *Annual Report of the War Department, Report of the Lieutenant-General Commanding the Army*, 56 Cong., 2 sess. (1900), Part 4, 534–36. (Hereafter cited as *Report, 1900.*)

27 *Report, 1900*, 534–36; *Jawbone*, Dec., 1951, and Jan., 1952. List # 3. Hare to Adjutant General, Northwest Luzon, June 6, 1900, # 320748, RG 94 NA.

28 The quotation is from *ibid.* March Report and Hare Report, both on Nov. 12, 1899, *Report, 1900*, 537, 541–43. *Jawbone*, Jan. and March, 1952.

29 Emilio Aguinaldo and Vicente A. Pacis, *A Second Look at America* (New York, 1957), 107. Sexton, *Soldiers*, 204. March Report, Dec. 8, 1899, *Report, 1900*, 330–34.

30 *Report, 1900*, 330–34. Diary, Dec. 2, 1899, March Papers, Box 25. John T. McCutcheon, *Drawn From Memory* (Indianapolis, 1950), Chap. XXIII.

31 March Report, Dec. 8, 1899, *Report, 1900*, 332–33. Diary, Dec. 5 and 25, 1899, March Papers, Box 25. Clipping from Philadelphia *Press*, Feb. 3, 1900, 1898 Scrapbook, March Papers. Jan. 21, 1900, clipping in Easton Scrapbook. For the Tirad Pass fight and the capture of Concepción March received brevet recommendations, List # 3. March Individual Service Reports, Aug. 14, 1900, and Feb. 14, 1902, ACP. *New York Times*, Feb. 10, 1918, Magazine Section, 3. *Jawbone*, May

and Aug., 1937. The quotation is from Kilgore to March, March 23, 1941, March Papers, Box 24.

32 March to The Adjutant General, Jan. 31, 1901, Individual Service Report, Feb. 14, 1902; George W. Davis efficiency report, June 30, 1901; Captain's Oath of Office, May 14, 1901, ACP. Autographed menu of MacArthur farewell dinner, June 26, 1901, March Papers, Box 25.

33 MacArthur to The Adjutant General, Feb. 27, 1901, ACP.

34 Beacham interview, March 29, 1957. C. C. Williams interview, June 5, 1956, and letter to the author, May 21, 1956. Edward Davis, a captain in the Thirty-third, recorded his reminiscences of March in *Jawbone*, Aug., 1958. Gus David, the soldier who offered March the drink, was still disgruntled when he wrote the story for this same issue of *Jawbone*. Another veteran, L. W. Colson, contributed his views in a letter to the author, April 21, 1958.

35 March interview in *New York Times*, Aug. 11, 1918, 2.

Chapter 3. Between Wars

1 *Annual Report of the Secretary of War, 1899*, 58.

2 The two generals were Winfield Scott and William T. Sherman.

3 *Annual Report of the Secretary of War, 1903*, App. C, Regulations for General Staff Corps, Aug. 3, 1903, 483.

4 Henry P. McCain endorsement to March to Adjutant General, Aug. 5, 1901, ACP. OR, Nineteenth Battery, Oct., 1901, RG 94 NA.

5 For information about this period, I am much indebted to Beverly F. Browne. The quotations are respectively from a memo which he prepared in the spring of 1956 and from his Feb. 26, 1959, letter to me. The importance of this maneuver is indicated in J. E. McMahon to the Chief of Staff, Aug. 18, 1913, # 126725, Army War College File, RG 165 NA. OR, Nineteenth Battery, September and October, 1902, RG 94 NA.

6 *Nation*, April 16, 1903, clipping in 1898 Scrapbook, March Papers. March received his orders in May. OR, Nineteenth Battery, May, 1903, RG 94 NA.

7 March to Mrs. John Gibbon, Nov. 3, 1932, March Papers, Box 1. Young to The Adjutant General, Feb. 26, 1901, ACP. March, AWC lecture, April 20, 1933, 14. William H. Carter recalled March's officemates in his *Creation of the American General Staff: Personal Narrative of the General Staff System of the American Army* (Washington, D.C., 1924), 55.

8 March, AWC lecture, Jan. 15, 1930, 2. The duties of the divisions are defined in Otto L. Nelson, *National Security and the General Staff: A Study in Organization and Administration* (Washington, D.C., 1946), 66–68.

9 Nelson, *National Security*, 66, 69.

10 March to The Adjutant General, Oct. 1, 1903, Personal Report File, RG 94 NA. Totten interview.

11 March, AWC lecture, April 6, 1934, 1.

12 The quotation is from the Henry Breckinridge interview, Nov. 12, 1958. The sailing is described in the *San Francisco Chronicle*, March 6, 1904. Crowder gave his reason in his letter to the Secretary of War, March 7, 1906, Crowder Papers.

13 Crowder was also on MacArthur's staff in Manila. David A. Lockmiller, *Enoch H. Crowder: Soldier, Lawyer and Statesman* (Columbia, Mo., 1955), 67, 80. Autographed menu of MacArthur farewell dinner, June 26, 1901, March Papers, Box 25.

14 Lockmiller, *Crowder*, 100–101. Notebook # 1, April 29 – May 15, 1904, March Papers, Box 7.

15 The first quotation is from Frederick Palmer, *With My Own Eyes: A Personal Story of Battle Years* (Indianapolis, 1932), 248. The others are from Palmer interview, June 4, 1956. Notebook # 1, June 15, 1904, March Papers, Box 7.

16 The first quotation is from March, AWC lecture, April 20, 1933, 2. The second is from Max Hoffmann, *The War of Lost Opportunities* (London, 1924), 6. Crowder to his sister, May 23, 1904, Crowder Papers. Palmer interview. Palmer, *With My Own Eyes*, 243.

17 Palmer, *With My Own Eyes*, 247.

18 March, AWC lecture, April 20, 1933, 7.

19 Notebook # 1, July 1, 1904, March Papers, Box 7. Lloyd C. Griscom, *Diplomatically Speaking* (New York, 1940), 243.

20 *Reports of Military Observers attached to the Armies in Manchuria during the Russo-Japanese War*, 5 parts (Washington, D.C., 1906–1907), I, 5, 16, 23. Crowder to his sister, May 23, 1904, Crowder Papers.

21 The first quotation is from Frederick Palmer, *With Kuroki in Manchuria* (New York, 1906), 270. The second is from Palmer letter to the author, March 22, 1956.

22 March's reports are in *Russo-Japanese Reports*, I, 5–56. The quotation is from his AWC lecture in 1905, in which he briefly described and analyzed his observations.

23 Notebook # 2, Oct. 2, 1904, and # 4, Nov. 3–19, 1904, March Papers, Box 7. *Russo-Japanese Reports*, I, 56. Clippings of *Easton Free Press*, April 18, 1905, in 1898 Scrapbook, March Papers.

24 Notebook # 4, Nov. 20 – Dec. 21, 1904, March Papers, Box 7. Mrs. March letter to the author, April 27, 1964.

25 Notebook # 4, Dec. 22, 23, 1904, March Papers, Box 7. March's comments are in the second entry. March, AWC lecture, April 20, 1933, 8.

26 March, AWC lecture, April 20, 1938, 8. The quotation is from the 1905 lecture. Palmer interview; Palmer, *With My Own Eyes*, 255.

27 March, AWC lecture, April 20, 1933, 4–6.

28 March Individual Service Report, Sept. 15, 1906, and March to Military Secretary, Feb. 25, 1905, ACP.

29 Browne letter to the author, Feb. 26, 1959. Bell endorsement to March to Military Secretary, Jan. 26, 1907, ACP. March accounted for his trips in his reports on Oct. 30, 1905, and July 10, and Sept. 1, 1906, Personal Report File, RG 94 NA.

30 Macomb to A. E. Saxton, May 10, 1910, # 5955 filed with # 2094, Fort Leavenworth Service Schools, RG 98 NA. OR, Sixth Artillery, September, 1907, and January, 1908, RG 94 NA.

31 Pennell letter to author, March 10, 1957.

32 Riley letter to author, March 13, 1957.

33 Browne memo, 1956.

34 Blakely interview, May 26, 1959. The Kerr comment is an extract of his report attached to the March Individual Service Report, June 30, 1909, ACP. *Report of Major Peyton C. March, 6th Field Artillery, U.S.A. Chief Umpire Camp of Instruction and Maneuver* (Fort Riley, 1908).

35 The quotation is from the Pennell letter. I also used in preparation of this section the Browne memo; Ben Lear interview, May 16, 1960; and Robert M. Danford letter, April 23, 1959.

36 Riley letter. In his memo General Browne supplemented Colonel Riley's account.

37 MacArthur interview.

38 March Individual Service Report, Dec. 31, 1911, and 1912 and 1913 efficiency reports, ACP.

39 March's promotion was dated February 8, 1912. *Official Army Register: 1913*, 11. *Official Congressional Directory: 63rd Congress, 2nd Session* (Washington, D.C., 1913), 258–59. MacArthur interview.

40 Nelson, *National Security*, 132–66.

41 March to Robert L. Bullard, Aug. 17, 1927, March Papers, Box 22. Peyton C. March, *The Nation at War* (Garden City, N.Y., 1932), 44–45. March to William G. Haan, May 4, 1914, Haan Papers (State Historical Society, Madison, Wis.), Box 2.

42 Moseley interview, Sept. 14, 1960. McCain report, Dec. 31, 1914, ACP. Breckinridge interview; Powell interview, Aug. 6, 1957. Horace M. Albright, who was Lane's assistant, wrote of his encounter with March in his letter to the author of July 1, 1963. I am indebted to Mr. Keith Olson for giving me a lead to Mr. Albright.

43 Nelson, *National Security*, 187–213.

44 March, *Nation at War*, 365. He was promoted on July 1. OR, Eighth Field Artillery, October, 1916, RG 94 NA.

45 My major source for information on this period was the source also of the quotation – Horace L. McBride interview, Aug. 31, 1961. General McBride supplemented this with his letter to the author of March 30, 1961, as did C. W. Neal in his April 6, 1961, letter to the author.

46 Mrs. March letter, April 27, 1964. The cousin was Elise Ficklin.

47 McBride interview, March 28. OR, Eighth Field Artillery, January–

May, 1917, RG 120 NA. The regiment, minus the second battalion, which went to Fort Sill, left Bliss on May 23, 1917.

48 Memoir, March Papers, Box 25.

Chapter 4. A Time of Promise: June, 1917 – February, 1918

1 Frederick Palmer described Baker's wartime service at length in *Newton D. Baker: America at War*, 2 vols. (New York, 1931). C. H. Cramer's *Newton D. Baker: A Biography* (Cleveland, 1961), is a brief biography.

2 MacArthur interview. I also found the interviews with Henry Breckinridge and George Van Horn Moseley helpful in describing both Scott and Bliss. Anne W. Lane and Louise H. Wall, eds., *The Letters of Franklin K. Lane: Personal and Political* (Boston, 1922), 237. Hugh L. Scott, *Some Memories of a Soldier* (New York, 1928).

3 MacArthur, Breckinridge, and Moseley interviews. Frederick Palmer, *Bliss, Peacemaker: The Life and Letters of General Tasker Howard Bliss* (Garden City, N.Y., 1934) is the only biography.

4 March to Baker, Oct. 5, 1932, March Papers, Box 1.

5 *Report of the Chief of Staff, U.S. Army to the Secretary of War, 1919: Annual Reports, War Department*, 18–19. (The page citations are from the single-volume Chief of Staff report. Cited hereafter as *C/S 1919.*) William Hard, "Down the River," *New Republic*, XIII (Dec. 15, 1917), 170–72. Scott to John F. McGee, April 23, 1917, Scott Papers (Library of Congress, Washington, D.C.), Box 28.

6 Bliss memo, March 31, 1917, Bliss Papers (Library of Congress, Washington, D.C.), Letterbook 211.

7 Scott to W. J. Nicholson, April 5, 1917, Scott Papers, Box 28.

8 David A. Lockmiller, *Enoch H. Crowder: Soldier, Lawyer and Statesman* (Columbia, Mo., 1955), Chap. XI. Hugh S. Johnson, *The Blue Eagle from Egg to Earth* (Garden City, N.Y., 1935), 75.

9 Memo of conversation of Joffre, Bliss, and Scott, April 27, 1917, Bliss Papers, Letterbook 212.

10 Memo of conversation of Joffre, Bliss, and Scott; Baker to Wilson, May 2, 1917 (2 letters), Baker Papers (Library of Congress, Washington, D.C.), Box 4.

11 Newton D. Baker, "America in the World War," in Thomas G. Frothingham, *The American Reinforcement in the World War* (Garden City, N.Y., 1927), xx, xxii–xxiii.

12 Scott, *Memories*, 570–71. Scott to William J. Baird, May 14, 1917, Scott Papers, Box 28.

13 Diary, June 15, 1917, Bullard Papers (Library of Congress, Washington, D.C.), Box 2. William M. Black to Baker, July 3, 1917, Baker Papers, Box 1. Bliss to Henry T. Allen, Sept. 28, 1917, Bliss Papers, Letterbook 221. I found the number of General Staff officers in a thorough statistical study of the wartime staff: F. Q. C. Gardner to Chief of Staff, Nov. 16, 1918, # 321 General Staff Corps, The Adjutant General's Office Central File, RG 94 NA. (Hereafter cited as TAGO.)

14 James G. Harbord, *Leaves from a War Diary* (New York, 1925), 92–93. John J. Pershing, *My Experiences in the World War*, 2 vols. (New York, 1931), I, 145–46. Pershing cabled the War Department about unanswered cables on July 11. Cable P # 37, July 11, 1917, RG 120 NA. (The Pershing to War Department cables will be designated by P.)

15 Goethals to his son, George R. Goethals, September 23, 1917, Goethals Papers (Library of Congress, Washington, D.C.), Box 2. L. Ames Brown, "The General Staff," *North American Review*, CCVI (Aug., 1917), 229–40.

16 Baker to Wilson, Sept. 19, 1917, Baker Papers, Box 4.

17 Baker, "America in the World War," xxv.

18 Pershing, *Experiences*, I, 225–26.

19 In this letter of November 13, Pershing wrote: "I have always had a high opinion of March and had often thought of him as timber for Chief of Staff, even before I received your letter." – Pershing, *Experiences*, I, 229. Baker announced Biddle's appointment on October 28. *Army and Navy Journal*, Nov. 3, 1917, 345.

20 Peyton C. March, *The Nation at War* (Garden City, N.Y., 1932), 288–89. Baker to Wilson, May 30, 1917, Baker Papers, Box 4.

21 Harbord, *Leaves*, 100–101.

22 Report of the Chief of Artillery, Major General Ernest Hinds, to the Commander-in-Chief, American Expeditionary Force, May 10, 1919, Inclosure, Part I, "History, Development and Organization of the Office of the Chief of Artillery, A.E.F.," in Report file of the C-in-C, Entry # 1, Folder # 381, RG 120 NA. March, *Nation at War*, 30. The report of the inspection of the French artillery is Nelson E. Margetts, Report, July 29, 1917, # 748, A.E.F. Adjutant General File, RG 120 NA.

23 Walter S. Sturgill, Report on the Training in France of Artillery Brigades of Infantry Divisions of the American E. Forces, December 21, 1918, Part I, # 931, G-3 Reports, A.E.F., G.H.Q., RG 120 NA.

24 Browne letter, March 19, 1958. Floyd Gibbons, *And They Thought We Wouldn't Fight* (New York, 1918), 98. Moseley letter, October 31, 1957. Sturgill and Hinds Reports. General Moseley's diary – War Notes – in Box 1 of his papers is an excellent source for this period.

25 March, AWC lecture, April 16, 1932, 8.

26 March, *Nation at War*, 33–34; Memoir, March Papers, Box 25.

27 Pershing, *Experiences*, I, 173–74; Harbord, *Leaves*, 152.

28 March to Pershing, Nov. 5, 1917, quoted in Sturgill Report, 9–14.

29 *Ibid.*, 14–16. Fox Conner to Harbord, Dec. 10, 1917, # 7616, Malone to Harbord, Dec. 12, 1917, # 5144, A.E.F., A.G. File, RG 120 NA.

30 The quotation is from Heywood Broun, *The A.E.F.: With General Pershing and the American Forces* (New York, 1918), 141. March, *Nation at War*, 220–21.

31 Diary, July 12, Dec. 10–17, 1917, Pershing Papers (Library of Congress, Washington, D.C.), Box 1.

32 Frederick Palmer, *John J. Pershing: General of the Armies: A Biography* (Harrisburg, Pa., 1948), 159. Pershing, *Experiences*, I, 315–16.
33 Robert L. Bullard, *Personalities and Reminiscences of the War* (Garden City, N.Y., 1925), 83, 86. Pershing, *Experiences*, I, 199–200.
34 *Army and Navy Journal*, Dec. 15, 1917, 577.
35 Chamberlain was quoted in the *New York Times*, Jan. 20, 1918, 1. On the next day, the *Times* carried his War Cabinet plan on page 1.
36 *Army and Navy Journal*, Dec. 22, 1917, 629. "The War on the War Department," *Literary Digest*, LVI, No. 3 (Jan. 19, 1918), 16–17. Carbon copies of the minutes of the War Council meetings are located in the Pershing Papers, Box 5, Series 3, RG 316 NA.
37 Lawrence to Wilson, Jan. 28, 1918, copy in the Baker Papers, Box 6. *New York Times*, 1918: Jan. 12, pp. 1, 10; Jan. 27, p. 1; Jan. 29, pp. 1–2; Jan. 30, p. 8. "Secretary Baker's Defense," *Nation*, CVI (Jan. 17, 1918), 54–55.
38 *Army and Navy Journal*, Feb. 16, 1918, 914, 924–25. "Mr. Baker's Vindication," *New Republic*, XIV (Feb. 23, 1918), 97–98.
39 Baker commented on March in "America in the World War," xxvi. Confidential Cable A # 695, Jan. 26, 1918, RG 120 NA. (War Department cables to Pershing will be labelled A.) *New York Times*, Feb. 3, 1918, 1. "Wanted: A Leader," *North American Review*, CCVII, No. 3 (March, 1918), 396.
40 *Chief of Staff Report: War Department Annual Reports*, 1917, I, 133–35.
41 Several publications pointed out that the War Council would limit the Chief of Staff's position that Scott advocated. "Mr. Baker's Vindication," *passim; New York Times*, Feb. 12, 1918, 10; *Army and Navy Journal*, Feb. 16, 1918, 924.
42 The Hinds Report gives the number of artillerymen.
43 The *New York Times* quoted Wadsworth's statement on Feb. 22, 1918, 5; Bullard, *Personalities*, 85.

Chapter 5. Acting Chief of Staff: The First Six Weeks

1 Peyton C. March, *The Nation at War* (Garden City, N.Y., 1932), 35–36; Diary, Feb. 2 and 4, 1918, Pershing Papers, Box 1; Diary, Feb. 4, 5, and 6, 1918, Bliss Papers, Box 65.
2 *New York Evening Sun* interview as quoted in the *Army and Navy Journal*, March 2, 1918, 1001.
3 *Army and Navy Journal*, 1918: Feb. 16, p. 932; March 9, p. 1038; May 11, p. 1398. In the last citation March announced the engagement of his daughter Josephine to his aide, Major Joseph M. Swing. His other daughter, Mildred, had married Captain John Millikin in December, 1917.
4 March, *Nation at War*, 39. Washington *Evening Star*, March 2, 1918, 11. William J. Snow, *Signposts of Experience: World War Memoirs* (Washington, D.C., 1941), 16, 30 (the quotation is on p. 16). Percy P.

Bishop interview, April 29, 1957. F. Q. C. Gardner letter to the author, March 19, 1958. Both of these officers served on the General Staff under both Biddle and March. Crowder to Pershing, Jan. 19, 1918, Pershing Papers, Box 56.

5 March, *Nation at War*, 39–40. Robert L. Eichelberger letter to the author, April 27, 1959.

6 Newton D. Baker, "America in the World War," in Thomas G. Frothingham, *The American Reinforcement in the World War* (Garden City, N.Y., 1927), xv. Bliss to the War Department, Cable # 21, Feb. 3, 1918, RG 120 NA.

7 War Department to Bliss, Cable # 32, March 6, 1918; Confidential Cables A # 918, March 14, 1918; and # 990, March 26, 1918, RG 120 NA.

8 David Lloyd George, *War Memoirs*, 6 vols. (Boston, 1936), V, 410–13.

9 Hoover to E. M. House, Feb. 13, 1917, copy in the Baker Papers, Box 4.

10 Confidential Cable A # 558, Dec. 24, 1917, RG 120 NA. Pershing's agreement with the English appears in *United States Army in the World War: 1917–1919*, 17 vols. (Washington, D.C., 1948), III, 38–39. (Hereafter cited as *USA*.)

11 L. Storr to Tasker H. Bliss, March 3, 1918, Bliss Papers, Letterbook 226. This British staff officer informed Bliss and Pershing of the prime minister's request.

12 Lord Beaverbrook, *Men and Power: 1917–1918* (New York, 1956), 344.

13 John J. Pershing, *My Experiences in the World War*, 2 vols. (New York, 1931), I, 359–67 (the quotation is on p. 365, *n.*).

14 March, *Nation at War*, 79–87 (the quotation is on p. 82). Washington *Evening Star*, March 31, 1918, 12. Confidential Cables A # 1036, April 3, and # 1048, April 6, 1918, RG 120 NA. Edward N. Hurley, *The Bridge to France* (Philadelphia, 1927), 120–24.

15 March to Bliss, March 14, 1918, Bliss Papers, Box 75.

16 *New York Times*, 1918: March 9, pp. 1, 3; March 10, p. 1; March 12, p. 12. Washington *Evening Star*, March 11, 1918, 1.

17 *New York Times*, 1918: April 3, p. 1; April 4, p. 3; April 10, p. 5. Cable WD to Bliss # 48, April 24, 1918. Cable P # 818, March 29, 1918, RG 120 NA.

18 Cable A # 69, July 31, 1917; Confidential Cable A # 390, November 12, 1917; Confidential Cable P # 680, March 4, 1918, RG 120 NA. Pershing to Bliss, Oct. 4, 1917, Pershing Papers, Box 26.

19 March to The Adjutant General, March 12, 1918, Promotions # 210.2, TAGO, Central File 1917–1925, RG 94 NA. (Hereafter TAG.) Snow, *Signposts*, 174. March, *Nation at War*, 264–65.

20 The exchange is in Cable A # 995, March 27, 1918, and Cables P # 834, April 1, and # 954, April 19, 1918, RG 120 NA. Harbord indicated a vulnerable point in Pershing's case when he commented, "If all your recommendations are made you will have some extras." – Harbord to Pershing, April 13, 1918, Pershing Papers, Box 87.

21 Pershing to March, April 23, and March to Pershing, May 10, 1918, Pershing Papers, Box 123, and Pershing to Baker, April 23, 1918, Pershing Papers, Box 19.

22 March to Secretary of War, March 8, 1918; March to TAG, March 12, 1918, General Officers # 538, C/S File, RG 165 NA. Pershing to March, Feb. 24, 1918, Pershing Papers, Box 123. In an undated memo, photostat in the possession of the author, Pershing commented on ten senior officers whom he considered unfit.

23 Palmer to Pershing, Feb. 3, 1918, Pershing Papers, Box 153.

24 Washington *Evening Star*, June 5, 1918, 1. An editorial in the *New York Times*, April 6, 1918, 14, criticized the Illinois mob.

25 *New York Times*, March 24, 1918, Magazine Section, 1.

26 March to Baker, Jan. 22, 1930, Baker Papers, Box 150. An article in the *New York Times*, April 7, 1918, Section 7, 9, provides an intelligent discussion of this matter.

27 Cables A # 915, March 15, and # 956, March 21, 1918, RG 120 NA (the quotation is from the first cable).

28 Harbord to Pershing, March 16, 1918, James G. Harbord Papers (Library of Congress, Washington, D.C.), Volume of Pershing-Harbord Correspondence, 1917–1922.

29 Confidential Cable P # 753, March 19, 1918; Cable P # 793, March 27, 1918; and Cables A # 1227, May 2, and # 1321, May 15, 1918, RG 120 NA (the quotation is from Cable P # 753). Pershing to March, May 5, and March to Pershing, May [June] 6, 1918, Pershing Papers, Box 123. George W. Cocheu interview, August 7, 1957; and F. Q. C. Gardner letter to the author, April 10, 1958.

30 *Army and Navy Journal*, Feb. 16, 1918, 925.

31 *Ibid.*, 924.

32 March to Bliss, March 14, 1918, Bliss Papers, Box 75. For criticism of the War Council, see n. 41 in Chapter 4. March, *Nation at War*, 48–49.

33 Letters to the author of Percy P. Bishop, March 27, 1956; Clifford Jones, Aug. 25, 1958; and F. Q. C. Gardner, March 19, 1958. The quotations are from the Bishop letter.

34 Robert E. Wood interview, Jan. 29, 1960. War Department General Order # 36, April 16, 1918, combined the two divisions.

35 March, *Nation at War*, 187–88. Goethals to George R. Goethals, April 15, 1918, Goethals Papers, Box 2.

36 Goethals to G. R. Goethals, April 15, 1918.

37 Hugh S. Johnson, *The Blue Eagle from Egg to Earth* (New York, 1935), 89–90. Johnson, a bitter enemy of March, described the supply situation and criticized the Chief of Staff in a lengthy letter to Harbord, Jan. 28, 1919. Harbord Papers, World War Military Activities Volume.

38 March, *Nation at War*, 188.

39 *Ibid.*, 369.

40 Cocheu interview. The changes are recorded in: March to TAG, March 5, 1918, Tank Corps # 1420; P. P. Bishop to Director, War Plans Divi-

sion, March 26, 1918, Aviation # 60; March to TAG, March 13, 1918, Construction Division # 313, C/S File, RG 165 NA. War Department General Order # 36, April 16, 1918, created the Coordination Section.

41 Grosvenor B. Clarkson, *Industrial America in the World War: The Strategy Behind the Line 1917–1918* (Boston, 1923), 49–50.

42 March, *Nation at War*, 174.

43 March to Pershing, May 10, 1918, Pershing Papers, Box 123. Baker Memorandum Order, July 8, 1918, General Staff # 538, C/S File, RG 165 NA. March, *Nation at War*, 71.

44 Baruch letter to the author, Feb. 7, 1956, and interview, Nov. 12, 1958.

45 Baruch interview, Nov. 12, 1958.

46 March, *Nation at War*, 72. Hurley, *Bridge*, 120.

47 Hoover letter to the author, Oct. 29, 1957. Mr. Hoover also commented on March in his *The Ordeal of Woodrow Wilson* (New York, 1958), 10.

48 Fosdick letter to the author, March 26, 1957. Mr. Fosdick supplemented this in his *Chronicle of A Generation: An Autobiography* (New York, 1958), 163–65.

49 Frederick P. Keppel, "The General Staff," *Atlantic Monthly*, CXXV (April, 1920), 545. *Army and Navy Journal*, April 20, 1918, 1274; March, *Nation at War*, 52. Keppel's jurisdiction included such matters as the treatment of Negroes and conscientious objectors; thus March never had primary responsibility for these matters.

50 March to Mary W. Herring, Oct. 19, 1920, March Papers, Box 8.

51 March to George O. Squier, March 20, 1918, March Papers, Box 8. Confidential Cable A # 1095, April 13, 1918, RG 120 NA. *Resumé of the Day's Work – General Staff*, April 14, 16, and 24, 1918, in the War Department Historical File, RG 120 NA. (Hereafter cited as *Resumé* and WDHF.)

52 March, AWC Lecture, Jan. 15, 1930, 2. Cable P # 836, April 2, 1918. Confidential Cable A # 1501, June 11, 1918, RG 120 NA. Diary, March 26, 1918, Leonard Wood Papers (Library of Congress, Washington, D.C.), Box 10.

53 Judson to March, March 4, 1918, Russia # 1240, C/S File, RG 165 NA.

54 David F. Trask, *The United States in the Supreme War Council: American War Aims and Inter-Allied Strategy, 1917–1918* (Middletown, Conn., 1961), 104–107. Ruggles' cables are in Russia # 1240, C/S File, RG 165 NA.

55 D. W. Ketcham to March, March 14, 1918, Russia # 1240, C/S File, RG 165 NA. March gave the most explicit statement of his views in his memorandum to Baker on June 24, 1918, Woodrow Wilson Papers (Library of Congress, Washington, D.C.), Box 142, File II. This also appears in his book on pages 116–20.

56 Frederick Palmer, *Newton D. Baker: America at War*, 2 vols. (New York, 1931) II, 157.

57 March, AWC Lecture, Jan. 15, 1930, 2.

58 In March, 84,889 men went to France; the previous high had been

49,515 in December. During April, 118,642 made the trip. Leonard P. Ayres, *The War With Germany: A Statistical Summary* (Washington, D.C., 1919), 37.

59 Baruch interview.

60 Palmer and Cocheu interviews. James G. Harbord, *The American Army in France: 1917–1919* (Boston, 1936), 110; John J. Pershing, *My Experiences in the World War*, 2 vols. (New York, 1931), I, 388.

Chapter 6. The War Department Begins to Hit Its Stride

1 Peyton C. March, *The Nation at War* (Garden City, N.Y., 1932), 366; *New York Times*, April 17, 1918, 13.

2 March, *Nation at War*, 366–67, 369–70.

3 March, AWC Lecture, April 5, 1938, 7.

4 Baker to Bliss, April 29, 1918, Bliss Papers, Box 75.

5 Bliss to March, April 20, 1918, Bliss Papers, Box 75.

6 Baker to Reading and Baker to Wilson, both on April 19, 1918, Baker Papers, Box 8. These letters contain the agreement and its background. Ray S. Baker, *Woodrow Wilson: Life and Letters*, 8 vols. (New York, 1929–1939), VIII, 96–97. Although Pershing did not receive word of the agreement until April 27, March explained its terms in the negotiating stage in Confidential Cable A # 1036, April 3, 1918, RG 120 NA.

7 Confidential Cable P # 961, April 24, 1918, RG 120 NA. John J. Pershing, *My Experiences in the World War*, 2 vols. (New York, 1931), II, 78.

8 Pershing, *Experiences*, II, 7–8; James G. Harbord, *The American Army in France: 1917–1919* (Boston, 1936), 259.

9 Baker to Wilson, April 29, 1918, Baker Papers, Box 8.

10 Wiseman interview, Dec. 14, 1960.

11 Abbeville Notes, Sir William Wiseman Papers (Sterling Memorial Library, Yale University, New Haven, Conn.), Folder 83, Drawer 91.

12 Pershing to March, May 5, 1918, March Papers, Box 22. Pershing discussed this conference in *Experiences*, II, 20–35.

13 Wiseman to E. M. House, May 11, 1918, copy in Wilson Papers, Box 140, File II. Other Allied versions are in, Maurice Hankey, *The Supreme Command: 1914–1918*, 2 vols. (London, 1961), II, 196–97. David Lloyd George, *War Memoirs*, 6 vols. (London and Boston, 1934–1937), V, 441. Georges Clemenceau, *Grandeur and Misery of Victory* (New York, 1930), 71. Also see Thomas N. Lonergan, *It Might Have Been Lost* (New York, 1929), 168–69.

14 *New York Times*, May 9, 1918, 1.

15 Pershing, *Experiences*, II, 74. Diary, June 1, 1918, Pershing Papers, Box 1. B. H. Wells to Bliss, June 3, 1918, Bliss Papers, Letterbook # 227.

16 Weygand letter to the author, Feb. 28, 1958. Diary, June 2, 1918, Pershing Papers, Box 1.

17 Pershing quoted the agreements in his account of this conference, *Experiences*, II, 70–81.

18 Confidential Cable P # 1235, June 4, 1918, RG 120 NA. This appears in Pershing, *Experiences,* II, 82–83, under the date of June 3. Frequently, there is a difference of one day in the dating of cables in the War Department and G.H.Q. cable files.

19 Baker to Wilson, June 5, 1918, Baker Papers, Box 8.

20 Pershing ordered Colonel Moseley to plan the G.H.Q. move. Moseley to C. M. Ragueneau, June 9, 1918, Moseley Papers, Box 3. Pershing, *Experiences,* II, 89–90. Lee Meriwether interview, January 16, 1958. Mr. Meriwether, who was an assistant to the ambassador, explained the precautions at the embassy.

21 *New York Times,* June 6, 1918, 1.

22 Goethals to March, June 15, 1918, and March to Director of Embarkation, June 21, 1918, Troop Movements # 1457; March to Goethals, April 22, 1918, Ships # 1310, C/S File, RG 165 NA. Cable P # 1268, June 8, 1918, RG 120 NA.

23 March to Grosvenor B. Clarkson, Feb. 12, 1921, March Papers, Box 8. Grosvenor B. Clarkson, *Industrial America in the World War* (Boston, 1923), 134–35. Hugh S. Johnson to Harbord, Jan. 28, 1919, Harbord Papers, World War Military Activities Volume. Robert E. Wood letter to the author, Oct. 15, 1962.

24 Baker to Bliss, May 31, 1918, Bliss Papers, Box 75.

25 Confidential Cable A # 1524, June 14, 1918, RG 120 NA. Pershing to March, June 19, 1918, March Papers, Box 22.

26 The main point of the opposition to replacement depots was that they would imply expectation of great losses and thus have a bad psychological effect on the populace. Baker to March, Oct. 3, 1932, March Papers, Box 23. March explained the situation to Senator Gilbert M. Hitchcock in his letter of May 29, 1918, in Thirty-fourth Division # 1434, C/S File, RG 165 NA.

27 Enoch H. Crowder, *The Spirit of the Selective Service* (New York, 1920), 151–57. Pershing to March, June 19, 1918, March Papers, Box 22.

28 Leonard P. Ayres, *The War with Germany: A Statistical Summary* (Washington, D.C., 1919), 37.

29 Pershing, *Experiences,* II, 278; March, *Nation at War,* 256–60.

30 Baker expressed his approval of March in his letter to Bliss, April 29, 1918, Bliss Papers, Box 75. *Army and Navy Journal,* Oct. 6, 1917, 204.

31 Weygand letter to the author; Baker to George Chamberlain, May 14, 1918; and Chamberlain to Baker, May 18, 1918, Secretary of War File, TAGO, RG 94 NA.

32 *Army and Navy Journal,* June 1, 1918, 1520. War Department General Order # 53, May 27, 1918.

33 Foch to March, May 31, 1918, Chief of Staff # 278, C/S File, RG 165 NA.

34 Bliss to March, June 8, 1918, Bliss Papers, Box 75.

35 Pershing to March, June 19, 1918, March Papers, Box 22.

36 *New York Times*, 1918: May 3, pp. 1, 3; May 7, p. 1.

37 Washington *Evening Star*, 1918: June 1, p. 4; July 10, p. 1 (the quotation is from June 1, p. 4).

38 *New York Times*, 1918: April 26, p. 6; May 2, p. 6. Washington *Evening Star*, April 26, 1918, 1. Frederic L. Paxson, *America at War: 1917–1918* (Boston, 1939), 271.

39 Wood interview.

40 Moseley to Wood, June 24, 1918, Moseley Papers, Box 3. Goethals spoke of Johnson's irritating March in his Appointment Book # 2, May 21, 1918, Goethals Papers.

41 Williams interview corroborated by Wood letter to the author, March 19, 1956. Williams' achievements are summarized in Constance M. Green, Harry C. Thomson, and Peter C. Roots, *The Ordnance Department, Planning, Munitions for War* (Washington, D.C., 1955), 25–26, 29, 40.

42 *Resumé*, May 2, 1918, WDHF, RG 120 NA. *Army and Navy Journal*, May 25, 1918, 1478. War Department General Orders # 38, April 18; # 39, April 19; and # 62, June 28, 1918. Leo P. Brophy, "Origins of the Chemical Corps," *Military Affairs*, XX (Winter, 1956), 217–26.

43 *C/S 1919*, 22, March, *Nation at War*, Chap. XV.

44 Baker to Wilson, May 1, 1918; Wilson to Baker, May 4, 1918, Baker Papers, Box 8. March to TAG, June 19, 1918, Italy # 720, C/S File, RG 165 NA.

45 Baker to Wilson, June 19, 1918, Baker Papers, Box 8.

46 William S. Graves, *America's Siberian Adventure: 1918–1920* (New York, 1931), 2.

47 Bishop letter to the author, April 14, 1956.

48 Gardner letter to the author, March 19, 1958.

49 March to Baker, Aug. 30, 1931, March Papers, Box 23.

50 Mark S. Watson letter to the author, April 1, 1958.

51 Carl Hayden letter to the author, March 3, 1958.

52 Tom Connally letter to the author, March 18, 1958.

53 March, AWC Lecture, April 16, 1932, 11.

54 March, *Nation at War*, 223–24.

55 David Lawrence letter to the author, March 6, 1957. Other journalists who recalled these conferences include Bascom N. Timmons in an interview, Nov. 18, 1958; and Jay Hayden, in a letter to the author, April 28, 1958. The account of the first conference is in the *New York Times*, June 16, 1918, 1. March made the arrangements in his memo to Marlen F. Pew, June 14, 1918, Commique # 300, C/S File, RG 165 NA.

56 *New York Times*, April 30, 1918, 13.

57 *Resumé*, May 7, 1918, WDHF, RG 120 NA. *New York Times*, May 27, 1918, 4. Washington *Evening Star*, May 2, 1918, 1.

58 Transcript of Baker-Wood interview, May 27, 1918, Wood Papers, Separate Folio.

59 March, *Nation at War*, 65.

60 Charles E. Kilbourne, who was present, described the Baker-Wood interview in his letter to the author of Feb. 27, 1957. Wood summarized his talk with Wilson in his diary, May 28, 1918, Wood Papers, Box 10.
61 Pershing to March, Feb. 24, 1918, Pershing Papers, Box 123.
62 March, *Nation at War*, Chap. V. The report sympathetic to Wood is in Hermann Hagedorn, *Leonard Wood*, 2 vols. (New York, 1931), II, 301–302. Baker passed Hayden's observations on to Wilson in his letter of June 21, 1918, Baker Papers, Box 8.
63 Pershing, *Experiences*, I, 384.
64 Pershing to Scott, June 28, 1918, Pershing Papers, Box 181.
65 Pershing to March, June 19, 1918, March Papers, Box 22. Pershing eventually received March's letters of May 10 and June 6 (the latter misdated May 6).
66 Cable P # 1196, May 26, 1918, and Cable A # 1499, June 11, 1918, RG 120 NA.
67 *New York Times*, June 21, 1918, 12.
68 Pershing to March, April 23, 1918, and March to Pershing, May 10, 1918, Pershing Papers, Box 123. The fact that March's salutation in this letter was "My dear John J." probably irritated Pershing. In all other letters, both used their last names. Pershing to Baker, June 18, 1918, Pershing Papers, Box 19. Pershing discussed promotoin policy with the Secretary in this letter.
69 Confidential Cable A # 1283, May 10, 1918, RG 120 NA.
70 March, *Nation at War*, 283–84. Two ranking officers on the General Staff testified on this point: Robert E. Wyllie letter to the author, March 31, 1956; and Frank T. Hines interview, Aug. 9, 1957. Confidential Cables A # 942, March 19, 1918, and # 1069, April 9, 1918, RG 120 NA.
71 Cable A # 1317, May 15, 1918, and Cable P # 1172, May 23, 1918, RG 120 NA. James W. McAndrews to Pershing, May 20, 1918, AEF/GHQ Cable File, RG 120 NA. T. Bentley Mott, *Twenty Years as Military Attache* (New York, 1937), 119.
72 Washington *Evening Star*, June 2, picture section, and June 4, 1918, 1.
73 *Army and Navy Journal*, June 1, 1918, 1524.
74 *Ibid.*, June 8, 1918, 1568.
75 *New York Times*, June 15, 1918, 10. Descriptions of the events are in *ibid.*, June 13, 1918, 5, and *Army and Navy Journal*, June 5, 1918, 1610.
76 *New York Times*, June 13, 1918, 5.

Chapter 7. "Men, Men, And Still More Men"

1 The title of this chapter is a quotation from Bliss to March, April 20, 1918, Bliss Papers, Box 75. John J. Pershing, *My Experiences in the World War*, 2 vols. (New York, 1931), II, 118–20.
2 Pershing, *Experiences*, II, 120–24.
3 Pershing to Baker, June 18, 1918, Pershing Papers, Box 19. The quotation is from Pershing to March, June 19, 1918, March Papers, Box 22. See also Confidential Cable P # 1342, June 19, 1918, RG 120 NA. For

a summary of the planning in regard to the AEF's strength, see Edward M. Coffman, "Conflicts in American Planning: An Aspect of World War I Strategy," *Military Review*, XLIII (June, 1963), 78–90.

4 Pershing, *Experiences*, II, 121–24.

5 Confidential Cable P # 1369, June 25, 1918, RG 120 NA. This is the War Department copy.

6 *New York Times*, January 31, 1918, 3.

7 These are round figures. Pershing, *Experiences*, II, 106; James G. Harbord, *American Army in France: 1917–1919* (Boston, 1936), 103–104; Robert L. Bullard, *Personalities and Reminiscences of the War* (Garden City, N.Y., 1925), 75, 165.

8 *New York Times*, June 23, 1918, 1. The ship production record is noted in the *Army and Navy Journal*, July 6, 1918, 1728.

9 March to Bliss, July 8, 1918, Bliss Papers, Box 75.

10 Baker to Bliss, July 8, 1918, Bliss Papers, Box 75.

11 Confidential Cable A # 1640, July 1, 1918, RG 120 NA.

12 War Department to Bliss Cable # 66, July 1, 1918, RG 120 NA.

13 Bliss' estimate was 3,375,000. Bliss to Baker, June 26, 1918, Bliss Papers, Box 74. Clemenceau's estimate was 4,160,000. Bliss to War Department Cable # 139, June 30, 1918, RG 120 NA.

14 Bishop and Cocheu interviews.

15 Goethals, "Report on Military Program 1918–1919 to the Chief of Staff," July 12, 1918, EE [European Expedition] # 570, TAGO, RG 94 NA. An analysis of the tonnage situation is in Frank T. Hines to the Chief of Staff, Feb. 19, 1920, Tonnage # 1440, C/S File, RG 165 NA.

16 Peyton C. March, *The Nation at War* (Garden City, N.Y., 1932), 101–103. James A. Salter, *Allied Shipping Control: An Experiment in International Administration* (Oxford, 1921), 174.

17 Goethals, "Report."

18 Baker to Bliss, March 26, 1920, Bliss Papers, Box 75.

19 See below, Chap. 9.

20 In his interview with the author, Mr. Baruch said that he thought the nation's industries could have supported the larger program; however, in a letter to the Secretary of War, President Wilson drew on facts furnished by Mr. Baruch and emphasized the strain on industry. Ray S. Baker, *Woodrow Wilson: Life and Letters*, 8 vols. (New York, 1929–1939), VIII, 294–95.

21 March, *Nation at War*, 101.

22 Baruch letter to the author, Feb. 7, 1956, and interview.

23 *New York Times*, July 6, 1918, 7.

24 *Ibid.*, July 5, 1918, 1.

25 *Ibid.*, July 7, 1918, 1.

26 March, *Nation at War*, 93–94. In regard to the decision not to use the Canadian ports, General Gardner wrote that March also took into consideration the fact that the British could later use the American-im-

proved ports for commercial purposes in competition with the United States. Gardner letter to the author, March 19, 1958.

27 March to Pershing, July 2 and 5, 1918, Pershing Papers, Box 123. The quotation is from the first letter.

28 Meriwether interview. One aspect of Mr. Meriwether's diplomatic duties was to talk with German prisoners and investigate their situations in captivity.

29 Wilson to Baker, July 24, 1918, War Department # 1503, C/S File, RG 165 NA. This is the letter referred to in n. 20. A study of the impact on industry is in Hugh S. Johnson to March, August 1, 1918, Tonnage # 1440, C/S File, RG 165 NA.

30 March to Bliss, July 8, 1918, Bliss Papers, Box 75.

31 Cables P # 1390, June 29; # 1446, July 11; # 1527, July 28, 1918; Confidential Cable P # 1518, July 26, 1918; and Confidential Cables A # 1686, July 9; and # 1742, July 19, 1918, RG 120 NA. A summary of the entire artillery program is in H. A. DeWeerd, "American Adoption of French Artillery 1917–1918," *The Journal of the American Military Institute*, III (Summer, 1939), 104–16.

32 Cables P # 1419, July 5; and # 1455, July 13, 1918, RG 120 NA. The Liberty motor question is discussed in March to TAG, May 9, 1918, Aircraft # 10; and W. C. Potter to Chief of Staff, Oct. 10, 1918, Liberty Motors # 867, C/S File, RG 165 NA. Confidential Cables P # 904, April 12; # 1308, June 14; # 1394, June 29; # 1623, August 24; and # 1673, September 9, 1918, RG 120 NA. March gave his views on this in *Nation at War*, 204–207.

33 March, *Nation at War*, 100–103. Edward N. Hurley, *The Bridge of Ships* (Philadelphia, 1927), 123–24.

34 According to *C/S 1919*, 10–11, the actual figure was 3,360,000. Jervey in his memo to March, July 15, 1918 (EE # 55.9) used that figure but Goethals in his report used 3,355,000. EE # 570, TAGO, RG 94 NA. Baker to Wilson, July 20, 1918, Wilson Papers, Box 144, File II.

35 Baker to Bliss, July 28, 1918, Bliss Papers, Box 75. March's cable is War Department to Bliss Cable # 74, July 23, 1918, RG 120 NA. The Assistant Secretary of War commented later that crews, bunker coal, and submarines would also be problems. Benedict Crowell, *The Road to France: The Transportation of Troops and Military Supplies 1917–1918* (New Haven, Conn., 1921), 371.

36 Baker used this phrase in his testimony before the Senate Military Affairs Committee. *New York Times*, January 29, 1918, 1.

37 The quotation is from Confidential Cable P # 1608, Aug. 17, 1918, RG 120 NA. Pershing to Baker, Aug. 17, 1918, Pershing Papers, Box 19. Pershing to March, July 19, 1918, March Papers, Box 22. Hurley later flatly declared that if the war had lasted another year the shipping program could not have supplied the AEF. Hurley, *Bridge*, 123–24.

38 Cable P # 1606, Aug. 17, 1918, RG 120 NA.

39 Bliss to Baker, Aug. 7, 1918, Bliss Papers, Box 74.

40 Bliss to Baker, Aug. 27, 1918, Bliss Papers, Box 74. Bliss to War Department Cable # 180, Aug. 14, 1918, RG 120 NA.

41 Diary, Aug. 25, 1918, Box 1, and Notes on Bombon Conference, Aug. 25, 1918, Pershing Papers, Box 50.

42 William J. Wilgus, *Transporting the A.E.F. in Western Europe: 1917–1919* (New York, 1931), 64, 485, 500. *USA*, XII, 173.

43 *New York Times*, Aug. 8, 1918, 1.

44 Erich von Ludendorff, *Ludendorff's Own Story: August 1914 – November, 1918*, 2 vols. (New York, 1919), II, 326–31.

45 *New York Times*, Aug. 16, 1918, 5.

46 H. O. S. Heistand to March, June 14, 1918, and March to Director, War Plans Division, July 18, 1918, Universal Service # 1478, C/S File, RG 165 NA. Baker to Wilson, July 28, 1918, and Wilson to Baker, July 30, 1918, Baker Papers, Box 8.

47 *New York Times*, Sept. 15, 1918, 20. *Army and Navy Journal*, Sept. 7, 1918, 11.

48 Wilson to Baker, Aug. 9, 1918, Baker Papers, Box 8. Pershing informed them of the threat in Confidential Cable P # 1567, Aug. 7, 1918, RG 120 NA. In a later cable (Confidential Cable P # 1603, Aug. 15, 1918), Pershing suggested that the British did this in order to obtain a better bargaining position. March pointed out the problem of ports in Confidential Cable A # 1773, July 25, 1918, RG 120 NA.

49 Confidential Cable P # 1717, Sept. 23, 1918, RG 120 NA. Stettinius to War Department Cable # 541, Sept. 21, 1918, and War Department to Stettinius Cable # 1, Aug. 4, 1918, RG 120 NA.

50 Confidential Cable A # 1935, September 12, 1918, RG 120 NA.

51 Confidential Cable A # 1982, Sept. 25, 1918, RG 120 NA. March explained the situation to Bliss in a letter, on Sept. 26, 1918, in the Bliss Papers, Box 75.

52 Confidential Cable P # 1742, Oct. 2, 1918, RG 120 NA.

53 Frederick Palmer, *Newton D. Baker: America at War*, 2 vols. (New York, 1931), II, 344. Stanley D. Embick Memo, Oct. 5, 1918, Folder # 258, Supreme War Council Records, RG 120 NA.

54 Goethals to George R. Goethals, Oct. 27, 1918, Goethals Papers, Box 2.

55 Palmer, *Baker*, II, 348. March corroborates this, *Nation at War*, 253.

56 Hunter Liggett, the First Army commander, wrote after the war: "General Pershing . . . may have agreed with the urgency of the cable [request for one hundred division], in general, but he knew our own situation too well to be able to indorse it wholly. We had hurried infantry and machine gunners across so rapidly in answer to previous appeals that we had virtually none of any training left at home. Moreover, that priority had held back reenforcements for the Service of Supplies, now badly undermanned. Nor were the French supply services much better off." – *A.E.F.: Ten Years Ago in France* (New York, 1928), 81. Nevertheless, Pershing wrote to Baker on August 17, 1918: "I hope you will pardon me

for referring so persistently to the large program for next year already recommended by Marshal Foch and myself, but I consider it such a vital matter and so important to our success within a reasonable time that I cannot refrain from again impressing it upon you, knowing that you will fully understand my motives." – Pershing Papers, Box 17. Perhaps a study prepared by George C. Marshall in April, 1923, helped shape Pershing's post-war views. The then Chief of Staff asked his aide to analyze the difficulties of the manpower situation during the war. Marshall examined various records, including the War Council Minutes, and submitted his comments which concluded with this paragraph: "When one considers the inevitable confusion incident to coordinating industries in the United States, training, shelter, and shipping, it is surprising that the demands from the A.E.F. were met to the extent they were, and any qualms the Secretary of War may have entertained over further increasing the draft, are not surprising, particularly since he and his Chief of Staff, apparently were the only optimistic members of the War Council." – Marshall to Pershing, April 9, 1923, Pershing Papers, Box 5, Series 3, RG 316 NA.

Chapter 8. The Russian Situation: "Eggs Loaded with Dynamite"

1 The title of this chapter is from William S. Graves, *America's Siberian Adventure: 1918–1920* (New York, 1931), 4. George F. Kennan, *The Decision to Intervene*, Vol. II in *Soviet-American Relations, 1917–1920* (Princeton, N.J., 1958), 56, 59, 345–46.

2 March has two chapters, IX and X, on Russian affairs in *The Nation at War* (Garden City, N.Y., 1932). He has included several of the important cables in his account.

3 Lansing to Wilson, May 11, 1918, Wilson Papers, Box 140, File II. March, *Nation at War*, 133–34.

4 *Ibid.*, 135–36. March actually signed the copy of this Baker to Bliss cable, which is in the National Archives.

5 *Ibid.*, 136–39.

6 *Ibid.*, 146.

7 *Ibid.*, 139.

8 Kennan, *Decision*, 426–27.

9 Diary, Sept. 11, 1918, Breckinridge Long Papers (Library of Congress, Washington, D.C.). Long was an Assistant Secretary of State. March to Stewart Cable, Sept. 14 [19?], 1918, in World War I Organization Records, A.E.F. North Russia, RG 120 NA.

10 Bliss to March, Sept. 3, 1918, Folder # 366, Supreme War Council Records, RG 120 NA.

11 Wilson to March, Sept. 18, 1918, Folder # 366, Supreme War Council Records, RG 120 NA.

12 March to Bliss, Sept. 26, 1918, Bliss Papers, Box 75.

13 Bliss to Baker, June 8, 1918, Bliss Papers, Box 74. In an earlier letter, April 20, 1918, Bliss wrote the Secretary that Japanese intervention

would involve territorial compensation and Japanese domination in Siberia.

14 Baker to March, Sept. 7, 1927, Baker Papers, Box 150. I have corrected typographical errors in the first quotation: "refuse" was spelled with a *v* and used the second time in past tense.

15 House to Wilson and Lansing to Wilson, both on June 13, 1918, Wilson Papers, Box 141, File II.

16 March, *Nation at War*, 116–20. The original is in the Wilson Papers, Box 142, File II. March described his composition of this memo in his AWC Lecture, April 20, 1933, 14. Pershing expressed his opinion in Confidential Cable P # 1253, June 6, 1918. American intelligence agents interviewed Kerensky on June 30 and July 2, in Paris; a report of the conversations is in Confidential Cable P # 1450, July 12, 1918, RG 120 NA. Kerensky thought that the Russians would oppose the Japanese troops.

17 Bliss to March, June 24, 1918, Bliss Papers, Box 75.

18 Foch to Wilson cable, June 27, 1918, copy in Baker Papers, Box 5. David F. Trask discusses the Supreme War Council's part in Russian intervention in Chap. VI of his *The United States in the Supreme War Council: American War Aims and Inter-Allied Strategy, 1917–18* (Middletown, Conn., 1961).

19 Kennan, *Decision*, 394.

20 Memo, July 4, 1918, Robert Lansing Papers (Library of Congress, Washington, D.C.), Box 2. Although journalists knew about the meeting and who was present, they did not know what happened. *New York Times*, July 7, 1918, 1.

21 March, *Nation at War*, 120–23.

22 E. D. Anderson to Chief of Staff, July 6, 1918, photostat in American Forces in Siberia # 21–19.3, WDHF, RG 120 NA. Robert E. Wyllie, who contributed to Anderson's memorandum as Chief of the Equipment Branch of the Operations Division, wrote the author on July 29, 1957: "Regarding the Siberian expedition I do not remember anything whatever about my supply problem, evidently there was little trouble with it. . . ." The Chief of the Embarkation Service, Frank T. Hines, who also contributed to the memo, said in an interview on August 9, 1957: "The Siberian expedition – we hardly knew we had one so far as tonnage went." Robert E. Wood, the Acting Quartermaster General, commented in an interview, January 19, 1960: "There was no problem there since there was so few troops involved." The intervention thus had little impact on the effort in France. Nevertheless, had the United States not limited its forces and had the war in France lasted into 1919 as anticipated, Siberia might have had a greater effect.

23 Memo of White House Conference, July 6, 1918, Lansing Papers, Box 2.

24 Boris A. Bakhmeteff, "Reminiscences," Oral Research Office, Columbia University, 371.

25 March, *Nation at War*, 126.

26 *Ibid.*, 141–46.
27 TAG to Graves, July 17, 1918, World War I Organization Records, AEF Siberia, RG 120 NA.
28 Graves to TAG, July 18, 1918, World War I Organization Records, AEF Siberia, RG 120 NA.
29 March, *Nation at War*, 126, 130. E. F. Glenn to Bliss, July 11, 1918, Bliss Papers, Letterbook 215; James Parker to Baker, Aug. 1, 1917, Bliss Papers, Letterbook 217. Crowder to Pershing, July 22, 1918, Pershing Papers, Box 56. According to his biographer, the old Indian fighter and Civil War general, Nelson A. Miles, also wanted to command this expedition. Virginia W. Johnson, *The Unregimented General: A Biography of Nelson A. Miles* (Boston, 1958), 362.
30 Graves, *Siberian Adventure*, 2–4.
31 *Ibid.*, 4–5.
32 *Ibid.*; Robert Lansing to Wilson, July 8, 1918, and Frank L. Polk to Wilson, July 24, 1918, Wilson Papers, Box 144, File II.
33 Jervey to TAG, Aug. 3, 1918, American Forces in Siberia # 21–19.3, WDHF, RG 120 NA.
34 War Department to Bliss Cable # 88, Sept. 2, 1918, RG 120 NA.
35 General Order # 1, August 16, 1918, World War I Organization Records, AEF Siberia, RG 120 NA. Cables V # 3, August 18; and # 5, August 20, 1918, RG 120 NA. Cables from the Siberian Command to the War Department were labelled "V" while those from the War Department to Siberia were "AV."
36 Cable V # 14, Sept. 3, 1918, RG 120 NA. Graves Report, September 25, 1919, # 4.7–11.4, World War I Organization Records, AEF Siberia, RG 120 NA.
37 Betty M. Unterberger, *America's Siberian Expedition, 1918–1923: A Study of National Policy* (Durham, N. Car., 1956), 99.
38 Cable V # 20, Sept. 11, 1918, RG 120 NA.
39 March to Bliss, Sept. 26, 1918, Bliss Papers, Box 75.
40 Cable AV # 26, Sept. 27, 1918, RG 120 NA.
41 Baker to Wilson, Oct. 17, 1918, Baker Papers, Box 8.
42 March to Bliss, July 8, 1919, Bliss Papers, Box 75.
43 Graves, *Siberian Adventure*, 55.
44 *Ibid.*, 86. Graves to TAG, Oct. 25, 1918, copy in Baker Papers, Box 6.

Chapter 9. March and Pershing: The Friction of War

1 Baker to Wilson, June 8, 1918, Baker Papers, Box 8.
2 Bliss commented on his relationship with Pershing in a letter to Baker, May 11, 1918, Bliss Papers, Box 74: "I do not propose that there shall be the slightest difference of opinion known to exist between him and myself. I discuss things freely and frankly with him in the privacy of his own house or in my office, but when he has once decided upon a course I make it my own also and, so far as anyone else knows, I surrender my judgment to his."

3 James G. Harbord, *Leaves from a War Diary* (New York, 1925), 349. War Notes, July 4, 1918, Moseley Papers, Box 1. Johnson Hagood, who was chief of staff of the S.O.S., differs in judgment of Kernan in his *The Services of Supply: A Memoir of the Great War* (Boston, 1927), 262, 296. A list of the commanding officers and their periods of command is in *Order of Battle of the United States Land Forces in the World War, American Expeditionary Forces: General Headquarters, Armies, Army Corps, Services of Supply, and Separate Forces* (Washington, D.C., 1937), 37.

4 Lloyd George to Reading, May 4, 1918, Wiseman Papers, Drawer 90, Folder 3.

5 Wiseman interview.

6 Notes on interview with Wilson, Jan. 23, 1918, Wiseman Papers, Drawer 90, Folder 43.

7 Wiseman spent an hour with Wilson and discussed this subject on May 29, 1918. Wiseman to Eric Drummond, May 30, 1918, Wiseman Papers, Drawer 91, Folder 129.

8 House to Wilson, May 20, 1918, Edward M. House Papers (Sterling Memorial Library, Yale University, New Haven, Conn.), Drawer 119, Folder 10.

9 House to Wilson, May 12, 1918, Wilson Papers, Box 140, File II.

10 House to Wilson, June 3, 1918, Wilson Papers, Box 141, File II. House's part in this became a controversy in the 1930's when Harbord attempted to disprove March's account of House's role. James G. Harbord, *The American Army in France: 1917–1918* (Boston, 1936), 354–55; Peyton C. March, *The Nation at War* (Garden City, N.Y., 1932), 193–97.

11 Kernan memo, Feb. 2, 1918, Moseley Papers, Box 8.

12 Baker to Wilson, June 8, 1918, Baker Papers, Box 8.

13 Joseph B. and Farnham Bishop, *Goethals – Genius of the Panama Canal: A Biography* (New York, 1930), 31–32, 61, 256–57, 271–72. George R. Goethals letter to the author, Feb. 19, 1957.

14 Goethals to George R. Goethals, June 9, 1918, Goethals Papers, Box 2.

15 Goethals to Pershing, Aug. 3, 1917, and Pershing to Goethals, Sept. 11, 1917, Pershing Papers, Box 83. Goethals to Theodore Roosevelt, Dec. 28, 1917, Goethals Papers, Box 4.

16 Goethals to George R. Goethals, June 9, 1918, Goethals Papers, Box 2.

17 I examined the material under the appropriate dates in Goethals' Appointment Book # 3 and in his letters to his son, George R. Goethals. According to his letter of Aug. 5, he was willing originally to go in a subordinate role to Pershing but Pershing's later cable which opposed the change caused him to believe that he would need full control. The son later wrote March, March 12, 1931, March Papers, Box 23, "I think he always felt that he would go over, if at all, only on a subordinate basis to the Commander of the A.E.F. . . ."

18 Appointment Book # 3, July 6, 1918, Goethals Papers.

19 Goethals to his son, July 14, and Aug. 18, 1918, Goethals Papers, Box 2.

20 March to Pershing, July 5, 1918, Pershing Papers, Box 123.

21 The first letter is in John J. Pershing, *My Experiences in the World War*, 2 vols. (New York, 1931), II, 181–87. The second is in the Pershing Papers, Box 19.

22 Diary, July 26, 1918, Pershing Papers, Box 1.

23 Harbord, *Leaves*, 338–40.

24 Confidential Cable P # 1522, July 27, 1918, RG 120 NA. He supplemented this with a letter, quoted in Pershing, *Experiences*, II, 187–91.

25 Confidential Cable P # 1562, Aug. 6, 1918, RG 120 NA.

26 Baker to Robert Lansing, quoting a cable to be sent to Pershing, July 30, 1918, Baker Papers, Box 6. This message is most revealing as a reflection of the Baker-Pershing-March relationship. The fact that Pershing used State Department cables and that Baker allowed him to do so and responded in the same manner shows Baker's particular regard for Pershing's position. Then, in the text of this message, Baker said, "My whole purpose in this matter is to get all of the data before you and rather to aid you to come to a right conclusion than to impose one of my own."

27 In a letter to Baker on July 28 (another letter of the same date is quoted in Pershing, *Experiences*, II, 187–91), Pershing said that if Baker wanted to, he could send Goethals over with no promise of staying. "Then he could look things over and I could talk with him and get his attitude and possibly reach a conclusion that would be useful." (Hereafter cited as the Letter 2 of Pershing to Baker, July 28, 1918.)

28 Goethals to his son, Aug. 18, 1918, Goethals Papers, Box 2.

29 Pershing, *Experiences*, II, 181–91. Later, Harbord suggested that Pershing commission Stettinius so that, once in uniform, he would be more subject to Pershing's control. Harbord to Pershing, Sept. 23, 1918, Pershing Papers, Box 87.

30 Pershing, *Experiences*, I, 264.

31 March to Pershing, Aug. 12, 1918, Pershing Papers, Box 123. Appointment Book # 3, Aug. 10, 1918, Goethals Papers. Pershing explained his suspicions of March to Baker in his Letter 2 of July 28. He also informed House, through an intermediary, of his attitude. Cables of Arthur Frazier to Lansing and House, Aug. 5, and to House, Aug. 7, 1918, House Papers, Drawer 11, Folder 52.

32 *Army and Navy Journal*, July 6, 1918, 1715–716, 1725.

33 Confidential Cable A # 1283, May 10, 1918, RG 120 NA. Diary, July 11, 1918; Pershing to Baker, June 18, 1918, Pershing Papers, Box 19. Pershing's suavity is shown in this letter: "To make clear my purpose in writing you, permit me to say that in my recommendations of men in active service here it seemed to me that as their abilities to a certain extent have been tested in active service, we should be more likely to obtain efficiency in the new grades than if we should select men without such experience. I do not at all wish to intimate that promotions should be limited to men in France. Such a system would be manifestly im-

practicable and unfair, as well as discouraging to the hopes of good men still in the States. Yet, where you have men with experience available, it would be equally unfair to promote inexperienced men over their heads."

34 Harbord, *Leaves,* 310. Letter 2 of Pershing to Baker, July 28, 1918, Pershing Papers, Box 19.

35 Pershing to Harbord, July 13, 1918, Harbord Papers, Pershing-Harbord Correspondence, 1917–1922.

36 March to Pershing, July 2, 1918, Pershing Papers, Box 123.

37 Pershing to Harbord, July 13, 1918, Harbord Papers, Pershing-Harbord Correspondence, 1917–1922.

38 Harbord to Pershing, July 17, 1918, Pershing Papers, Box 87.

39 Pershing to Baker, July 19, 1918, Pershing Papers, Box 19.

40 Pershing to March, July 25, 1918, March Papers, Box 22. Evidently, Pershing forwarded a draft of this letter to Baker. Pershing to Baker, July 19, 1918, Pershing Papers, Box 19.

41 Letter 2 of Pershing to Baker, July 28, 1918, Pershing Papers, Box 19.

42 March to Pershing, Aug. 12, 1918, Pershing Papers, Box 123.

43 William J. Snow, *Signposts of Experience: World War Memoirs* (Washington, D.C., 1941), 174.

44 Diary, Aug. 22, 1918, Pershing Papers, Box 1. The list appeared in the *New York Times,* Aug. 23, 1918, 5.

45 Confidential Cable P # 1629, Aug. 27, 1918, RG 120 NA.

46 Confidential Cable A # 1885, Aug. 28, 1918, RG 120 NA. March commented that Baker's decisions were, "in questions of policy, along the lines I recommended. So much so, in fact, that General Pershing thought that the Secretary had not been seeing his cables. . . ." – *Nation at War,* 371.

47 *New York Times,* Oct. 4, 1918, 13.

48 Harbord to Pershing, Sept. 23, 1918, Pershing Papers, Box 87. Before the end of the war, Pershing recommended MacArthur for promotion to major general. Confidential Cable P # 1805, Oct. 17, 1918, RG 120 NA.

49 Diary, Oct. 6, 1918, Pershing Papers, Box 1. The distribution of these officers is in R. H. Hearn to March, Oct. 9, 1918, General Officers # 538, C/S File, RG 165 NA.

50 Confidential Cable A # 2176, Nov. 12, 1918, RG 120 NA. There were internal promotion problems in the AEF. Hagood discusses them in his book and blames Pershing's headquarters for these difficulties. Johnson Hagood, *The Services of Supply: A Memoir of the Great War* (Boston, 1927), 241–42, 245, 248–49, 256.

51 Harbord to Pershing, Sept. 23, 1918, Pershing Papers, Box 87.

52 Letter 2 of Pershing to Baker, July 28, 1918, Pershing Papers, Box 19.

53 Pershing to Baker, Aug. 17, 1918, Pershing Papers, Box 19.

54 March, *Nation at War,* 266–67.

55 Since Scott was virtually out of power from the time he left for Russia, I do not include him with Bliss and Biddle. Baker discussed his view of

Pershing's position in "America in the World War," in Thomas G. Frothingham, *The American Reinforcement in the World War* (Garden City, N.Y., 1927), xxii–xxiii. Elihu Root defined the role of the Chief of Staff for Senator James H. Berry in a 1903 letter which is in William H. Carter, *Creation of the American General Staff* (Washington, D.C., 1924), 48: "The purpose of the statute was to enable the President in the discharge of his duties as Commander in Chief, and the Secretary of War in the performance of these specific duties imposed upon him by Congress, to do the practical work of control through the instrumentality of the Chief of Staff."

56 Bliss to Pershing, March 17, 1921, Pershing Papers, Box 26.

57 March, AWC Lecture, April 20, 1933, 6.

58 War Department General Order # 80, August 26, 1918.

59 *Regulations of the Army of the United States: 1913, Corrected to April 15, 1917* (Washington, D.C., 1917), 157.

60 *Ibid.*

61 Otto L. Nelson, Jr., *National Security and the General Staff* (Washington, D.C., 1946), 258.

62 Moseley interview, Sept. 14, 1960.

63 Baker to Harbord, Dec. 14, 1934, Baker Papers, Box 113.

64 Baker to Pershing letter quoted in Pershing, *Experiences*, II, 185. Baker elaborated on this in a letter to Harbord, Feb. 8, 1935, Baker Papers, Box 113.

65 *New York Times*, April 9, 1918, 6.

66 Diary, Sept. 30, 1918, Wood Papers, Box 11.

67 Frederick Palmer, *John J. Pershing; General of the Armies: A Biography* (Harrisburg, Pa., 1948), 253.

68 Goethals to his son, Aug. 25, 1918, Goethals Papers, Box 2.

69 March, *Nation at War*, 261. Hugh S. Johnson wrote that March told him in May that he was going back to France. *The Blue Eagle from Egg to Earth* (New York, 1935), 89, 92. However, both of the Secretaries of the General Staff who worked closely with March in this period stated that he had no ambition to succeed Pershing. Gardner letter to the author, April 10, 1958, and Bishop interview.

70 Frank Owen, *Tempestuous Journey: Lloyd George, His Life and Times* (London, 1954), 476–77.

71 Diary, Oct. 26, 1918, House Papers. Jere C. King, *Generals and Politicians* (Berkeley and Los Angeles, Calif., 1951), 233–38.

Chapter 10. The War Department Strips for Action

1 The quotations are from the MacArthur interview. Crowder was on crutches because of an accident in 1917. David A. Lockmiller, *Enoch H. Crowder: Soldier, Lawyer and Statesman* (Columbia, Mo., 1955), 132, 179–80.

2 Breckinridge interview.

3 MacArthur interview.

4 George Van Horn Moseley to Henry L. Stimson, Nov. 11, 1915, Moseley Papers, Scrapbook of Selected Papers, 1899–1942.

5 Hugh L. Scott, *Some Memories of a Soldier* (New York, 1928), 546.

6 Peyton C. March, *The Nation at War* (Garden City, N.Y., 1932), 46. Crowder's and Baker's opinions are in *War Department Annual Reports: 1916*, I, 70–89. Colonel Cocheu, in his interview, said that newcomers to his section of the General Staff were required to read the two documents.

7 Lockmiller has three chapters – XI, XII, and XIII – on this part of Crowder's career.

8 Bliss to Baker, Aug. 17, and Baker to Bliss, Aug. 18, 1917, Bliss Papers, Letterbook 218.

9 Crowder to Baker, Dec. 8, 1917, Baker Papers, Box 1. Crowder to Pershing, Jan. 19, 1918, Pershing Papers, Box 56.

10 Crowder to Pershing, Jan. 19, 1918.

11 Johnson to Baker, Jan. 31, 1918, Baker Papers, Box 6.

12 According to Colonel House, Brandeis also thought that Baker was exhausted and that his mind was not functioning properly. Diary, Feb. 23, 1918, House Papers.

13 Diary, April 18, 1918, Gordon Auchincloss Papers (Sterling Memorial Library, Yale University, New Haven, Conn.), Drawer 55, Folder 76. Auchincloss was Colonel House's son-in-law.

14 Crowder to March, Sept. 8, 1918, Provost Marshal General # 1157, March to Secretary of the General Staff, Nov. 29, 1918, Conferences and Meetings # 317, C/S File, RG 165 NA.

15 March to Baker, Jan. 7, 1935, March Papers, Box 3.

16 Washington *Evening Star*, 1918: June 29, p. 1; and July 6, p. 8.

17 March endorsement, July 16, on Crowder to March memo, July 16, 1918, Provost Marshal General # 1157, C/S File, RG 165 NA.

18 March to Crowder, July 29, 1918, Provost Marshal General # 1157, C/S File, RG 165 NA. *Resumé*, July 30, 1918, WDHF, RG 120 NA.

19 Crowder to Baker through the Chief of Staff, Aug. 1, 1918, Provost Marshal General # 1157, C/S File, RG 165 NA.

20 March to Baker, Aug. 2, 1918, Provost Marshal General # 1157, C/S File, RG 165 NA.

21 *Ibid.*

22 *New York Times*, 1918: Aug. 7, p. 8; Aug. 8, p. 1; and Aug. 10, p. 1.

23 Baker to March, Aug. 10, 1918. In an accompanying memo, Sept. 5, March wrote Crowder that Baker did not sign the Aug. 10 letter until Aug. 30. Provost Marshal General # 1157, C/S File, RG 165 NA.

24 March to Crowder, Sept. 5, 1918, Provost Marshal General # 1157, C/S File, RG 165 NA.

25 Crowder to March, Sept. 8, 1918, Provost Marshal General # 1157, C/S File, RG 165 NA.

26 Baker to Crowder, Nov. 8, 1918, Provost Marshal General # 1157, C/S File, RG 165 NA. *Resumé*, Nov. 13, 1918, WDHF, RG 120 NA.

27 Crowder to Pershing, Aug. 29, 1918. In another letter to Pershing, on Oct. 15, Crowder expressed his concern about retention of his detail. Both in Pershing Papers, Box 56. Lockmiller, in *Crowder*, 189–90, argues that Crowder was victorious in the dispute.
28 MacArthur interview. General Gardner corroborated this in his letter to the author of April 10, 1958.
29 Clifford Jones (the officer involved) letter to the author, Aug. 25, 1958.
30 McCain to Baker, Jan. 19, and 24, 1920, Baker Papers, Box 12.
31 *New York Times*, Aug. 18, 1918, 8. In this conference March also told the journalists that the Chief of the Militia Bureau, Jesse M. Carter, was leaving that office in order to take command of a division.
32 Appointment Book # 3, Aug. 16, 1918, Goethals Papers.
33 McCain to Baker, Jan. 19, 1920, Baker Papers, Box 12.
34 Cocheu telephone interview, Aug. 25, 1961. March, *Nation at War*, 51.
35 *Official Army Register: December 1, 1918*, 13.
36 March to Judge Advocate General, Aug. 26, 1918, and related correspondence in Staff Corps # 1372, C/S File, RG 165 NA.
37 March to Bliss, July 8, 1918, Bliss Papers, Box 75.
38 This was actually a continuation of the combination which War Department General Order # 36, April 16, 1918, created.
39 Cocheu interview; General Gardner, in his letter to the author of April 10, 1958, and Colonel Jones in his letter also contributed to my description of McIntyre.
40 War Department General Order # 86, Sept. 18, 1918. *C/S 1919*, 50–58.
41 Pierce to March, March 29, 1918, Motor Vehicles # 1019; Lytle Brown to March, July 31, 1918, and related correspondence, Motor Transport Corps #1019, C/S File, RG 165 NA. War Department General Order # 75, August 15, 1918.
42 *C/S 1919*, 62–64.
43 A large portion of the Chief of Staff's 1919 Report is devoted to this division – pp. 108–213.
44 *C/S 1919*, 94–95.
45 *Ibid.*, 215–18.
46 William Bryden interview, Nov. 12, 1960. For biographical background, I also used the *Official Army Register: January, 1925*, 694.
47 Cocheu telephone interview.
48 March to Pershing, May [June] 6, 1918, Pershing Papers, Box 123. Hinds Report, Part I, Enclosure, Report File of the C-in-C, AEF, Entry # 1, Folder 381, RG 120 NA. James G. Harbord, *The American Army in France: 1917–1919* (Boston, 1936), 86–87.
49 *Army and Navy Journal*, Sept. 7, 1918, 21.
50 *New York Times*, Aug. 11, 1918, Magazine Section, 2.
51 *Army and Navy Journal*, Aug. 3, 1918, 1876.
52 Baker to March, Oct. 3, 1932, March Papers, Box 23.
53 War Council Resolution, Jan. 23, 1918, War Council # 1502, C/S File, RG 165 NA.

54 R. I. Rees to March, May 31, 1918, Promotions # 1150, C/S File, RG 165 NA.

55 March to TAG, June 19, 1918, Promotions # 1150, C/S File, RG 165 NA. Cable A # 1793, July 30, 1918, RG 120 NA.

56 March, *Nation at War*, 4–5.

57 *Ibid.*, 5–7. *New York Times*, Aug. 11, 1918, Magazine Section, 1.

58 March to Bliss, Sept. 26, 1918, Bliss Papers, Box 75.

59 Bliss to March, Oct. 9, 1918, Bliss Papers, Box 75.

60 Walter K. Wilson to March, Oct. 19, 1918, Cables # 230, C/S File, RG 165 NA. For a description of the handling of the cable correspondence, see Edward M. Coffman, "The Battle Against Red Tape: Business Methods of the War Department General Staff, 1917–1918," *Military Affairs*, XXVI, No. 1 (Spring, 1962), 5–6.

61 Frank McIntyre to TAG, Oct. 25, 1918, 020.1 TAGO, RG 94 NA.

62 Nolan to James W. McAndrew, Sept. 10, 1918, and Pershing to March, Oct. 24, 1918, both in Pershing Papers, Box 123. Diary, Sept. 5, 1918, Pershing Papers, Box 1.

63 March to TAG, July 27, 1918, Books # 160, C/S File, RG 165 NA.

64 March to TAG, March 22, and Aug. 7, 1918, Aircraft # 10, C/S File, RG 165 NA. March, *Nation at War*, 11, 202.

65 Baker to Bliss, July 8, 1918, Bliss Papers, Box 75. March, *Nation at War*, 208–209. The quotation is from Kenly's study as quoted in I. B. Holley, Jr., *Ideas and Weapons* (New Haven, Conn., 1953), 140. Robert E. Wyllie to March, Oct. 11, 1918, Aircraft # 10, C/S File, RG 165 NA.

66 *Ibid.* The Wyllie memo also paraphrased the Potter message.

67 March, *Nation at War*, Chap. XV. March refers to the changes on p. 207. Holley, *Ideas*, 94.

68 Baker to Wilson, Aug. 24, 1918, Baker Papers, Box 8.

69 *New York Times*, Oct. 20, 1918, 7.

70 *C/S 1919*, 244.

71 *Resumé*, Aug. 10, 12, and 16, 1918, WDHF, RG 120 NA.

72 *Ibid.*, July 30, 1918.

73 March to TAG, Sept. 5, 1918, Infantry School of Arms # 728, C/S File, RG 165 NA.

74 *Resumé*, July 22, 1918, WDHF, RG 120 NA.

75 *Army and Navy Journal*, Oct. 12, 1918, 213.

76 March to Katharine D. Tillman, Oct. 15, 1918, March Papers, Box 8.

Chapter 11. Supplies, Ships, and Victory

1 Moseley letter to the author, April 16, 1956. H. B. Fiske, Pershing's G-5, also supplied information about the operations of the staff in his letter to the author of Feb. 25, 1957.

2 Baruch interview.

3 Goethals recalled the genesis of the reorganization in his post-war testimony before a senate committee. U. S. Senate, Subcommittee of the Committee on Military Affairs, *Hearings, Reorganization of the Army,*

66 Cong., 1 and 2 sess., 1919, 1027. Appointment Book # 3, July 19, 1918, Goethals Papers. Goethals to March, July 18, 1918, General Staff # 538, C/S File, RG 165 NA.

4 Appointment Book # 3, Aug. 10, and 27, 1918, Goethals Papers. March commented on Crowell in a letter to Baker, on Aug. 27, 1926. Baker Papers, Box 149.

5 Appointment Book # 3, Aug. 27, 1918, Goethals Papers.

6 In his endorsement of the supply reorganization, March preserved the General Staff principle by instructing Goethals, "Direct command will not be exercised by the Director of Purchases, Storage and Traffic. The orders which he finds necessary to issue in pursuance to this authority will be, as heretofore, in the name and under the authority of the Secretary of War."—March Memo, Aug. 26, 1918, General Staff # 538, C/S File, RG 165 NA. The evolution of the Quartermaster Corps is described in *C/S 1919*, 195–96.

7 Goethals to his son, Oct. 6, 1918, Goethals Papers, Box 2.

8 Cable P # 1561, Aug. 6, 1918, RG 120 NA. James G. Harbord, *Leaves from a War Diary* (New York, 1925), 349–51; Johnson Hagood, *The Services of Supply: A Memoir of the Great War* (Boston, 1927), 232.

9 War Department to Commanding General, S.O.S. Cable # 1, Aug. 13, 1918. (Cited hereafter as X; the cables of the Commanding General, S.O.S. to the War Department will be cited as S.) Confidential Cable S # 16, Aug. 16, 1918, RG 120 NA.

10 John J. Pershing, *My Experiences in the World War*, 2 vols. (New York, 1931), II, 310, James G. Harbord, *The American Army in France: 1917–1919* (Boston, 1936), 443–44.

11 Cable P # 764, March 22, 1918, RG 120 NA.

12 Confidential Cable P # 1170, Oct. 9, 1918, and Confidential Cable A # 2054, Oct. 15, 1918, RG 120 NA. There had been another cable exchange in July on this subject.

13 Confidential Cable P # 1739, Oct. 12, 1918, RG 120 NA. Pershing, *Experiences*, II, 222, 308.

14 Confidential Cable P # 1686, Sept. 13, 1918, Confidential Cable A # 1949, Sept. 16, 1918, RG 120 NA.

15 Robert E. Wood to March, July 20, 1918, Motor Vehicles # 1019, C/S File, RG 165 NA.

16 Moseley letter to the author, April 16, 1956.

17 Pershing, *Experiences*, I, 263. Hagood, *Services*, 273.

18 Hagood, *Services*, 274.

19 *Ibid.*, 321–29. The first quotation is from a telegram, Harbord to James W. McAndrew, Oct. 21, 1918, as quoted on p. 326. Harbord, *American Army*, 413–14, 508. The last quotation is from Harbord to Moseley, Nov. 2, 1918, copy in Pershing Papers, Box 87.

20 Pershing, *Experiences*, II, 310; Harbord, *American Army*, 443, 495.

21 Stettinius to War Department Cable # 530, Sept. 12, 1918, RG 120 NA.

22 Harbord to Pershing, Sept. 28, 1918, Pershing Papers, Box 87.

23 Stettinius to War Department Cables # 529, Sept. 10, and # 541, Sept. 21, 1918, RG 120 NA.

24 War Department to Stettinius Cable # 23, Sept. 13, 1918, RG 120 NA.

25 H. A. DeWeerd, "American Adoption of French Artillery 1917–1918," *The Journal of the American Military Institute*, III (Summer, 1939), 104–16.

26 Confidential Cable A # 2109, Oct. 27, 1918, RG 120 NA.

27 Confidential Cable P # 1740, Oct. 2, 1918, RG 120 NA. Pershing, *Experiences*, II, 310.

28 Moseley to Dawes, Oct. 3, 1918, Moseley Papers, Scrapbook, 1899–1942.

29 Harbord to Pershing, Oct. 31, 1918, Pershing Papers, Box 87.

30 March to Goethals, Oct. 15, and Goethals to March, Oct. 17, 1918, Cable # 230, C/S File, RG 165 NA. Goethals' methods are demonstrated in his memo to C. C. Williams, Aug. 22, 1918, # 523.93, General Staff, P.S.&T. Division File, RG 165 NA.

31 Bernard Baruch, *Baruch: The Public Years* (New York, 1960), 57–58.

32 War Notes, Oct. 21, 1918, Moseley Papers, Box 1.

33 Hunter Liggett, *A.E.F.: Ten Years Ago in France* (New York, 1928), 249–50.

34 U.S. Senate, Subcommittee of the Committee on Military Affairs, *Hearings, Reorganization of the Army*, 66 Cong., 2 sess., 1919, 1719.

35 Confidential Cable P # 1742, Oct. 2, 1918, RG 120 NA.

36 Confidential Cable A # 1877, Aug. 26, 1918, RG 120 NA. Peyton C. March, *The Nation at War* (Garden City, N.Y., 1932), 276–77.

37 Confidential Cable P # 1861, Nov. 2, 1918, RG 120 NA. March quoted this in his book and commented, "And that was precisely the amount of consideration that was given it." – *Nation at War*, 254–55. A survey from the G.H.Q. standpoint of the replacement problem is in Fox Conner, "Replacements: Life-blood of a Fighting Army," *Infantry Journal*, XL, No. 5 (May, 1941), 2–9.

38 Confidential Cable A # 2134, November 1, 1918, RG 120 NA. William J. Wilgus, *Transporting the A.E.F. in Western Europe: 1917–1918* (New York, 1931), 64, 485, 500. Edward N. Hurley, *The Bridge of Ships* (Philadelphia, 1927), 129, 132.

39 Jervey to March, Oct. 3, 1918, Troop Movements # 1457, C/S File, RG 165 NA. Confidential Cables X # 156 and # 157, both on Oct. 10; and Confidential Cables S # 246, Oct. 8, and # 248, Oct. 9, 1918, RG 120 NA.

40 March, AWC Lecture, Jan. 15, 1930, 7–8. March quotes his own remarks somewhat differently in *Nation at War*, 358–60. Ray Stannard Baker believed that this happened on Oct. 8, and at the White House, but March says that Wilson came over to the War Department. Baker, *Armistice: March 1–November 11, 1918*. Vol. VIII of *Woodrow Wilson: Life and Letters* (New York, 1939), 462–63.

41 *New York Times*, Oct. 1, 1918, 1. Baker, *Armistice*, 446, 457, 462, 494,

505. March to Bliss, Oct. 24, 1918, Bliss Papers, Box 75. March, *Nation At War*, 254.

42 Diary, Oct. 30, 1918, House Papers.

43 *Ibid.*, Nov. 2, 1918.

44 Baker to Pershing, Nov. 5, 1918, and Wilson to Baker, Nov. 7, 1918, Baker Papers, Box 8. Baker took Wilson's advice.

45 March, *Nation at War*, 254–55. Hines interview; Washington *Evening Star*, Oct. 13, 1918, 18.

46 Washington *Evening Star*, 1918: Nov. 8, p. 5; Nov. 11, pp. 1–2. *New York Times*, Nov. 12, 1918, 1–2, 15. Miss Azile Wofford, who as a yeomanette took part in the parade, gave me a vivid account of that day in Washington in an interview on December 18, 1956.

47 *New York Times*, Nov. 12, 1918, 1–2, 15. Diary, Nov. 11, 1918, Frank Polk Papers (Sterling Memorial Library, Yale University, New Haven, Conn.), Drawer 88, Folder 10.

48 Confidential Cable A # 2174, Nov. 11, 1918, RG 120 NA.

49 *New York Times*, Nov. 7, 1918, 13.

50 *Ibid.*, Nov. 12, 1918, 1.

51 Gardner to Directors of General Staff Divisions, Sept. 3, 1918, and March signed copy, dated Nov. 11, 1918, General Staff # 538, C/S File, RG 165 NA.

52 McIntyre to TAG, Nov. 11, 1918, Smithsonian Institute [*sic*] # 1345, C/S File, RG 165 NA.

Chapter 12. "The Right Man in the Right Place"

1 March, AWC Lecture, Jan. 15, 1930, 3. Mrs. Millikin, whose husband was a West Pointer in the AEF, was mentioned as her father's hostess in the Washington *Evening Star*, March 18, 1918, 8.

2 Gardner letter to the author, March 19, 1958. General Bishop in his interview and Colonel Clifford Jones in his letter of Aug. 25, 1958, also commented on the presentation of papers.

3 Bishop interview.

4 See the various papers in the Chief of Staff File, RG 165 NA.

5 Gardner letter, April 10, 1958.

6 Gardner letter, March 19, 1958.

7 *Ibid.*

8 Marshall interview, Nov. 10, 1960.

9 Bishop letter, March 27, 1956.

10 William J. Snow, *Signposts of Experience: World War Memoirs* (Washington, D.C., 1941), 31–32.

11 Bishop letter, March 27, 1956.

12 Browne interview, June 10, 1956. General Gardner corroborated this in his letter to the author, April 10, 1958.

13 Robert L. Bullard to March, Aug. 15, 1927, March Papers, Box 25. The quotation is from an enclosed biographical sketch by Bullard.

14 Baker to March, Aug. 23, 1927, Baker Papers, Box 150.

15 Frederick Palmer, *Newton D. Baker: America at War*, 2 vols. (New York, 1931), II, 204.
16 Snow, *Signposts*, 175.
17 Cocheu interview. Henry T. Ferguson letter to the author, Feb. 14, 1956.
18 Diary, Oct. 18, 1918, Wood Papers, Box 11.
19 March to Robert L. Bullard, Aug. 17, 1927, March Papers, Box 22.
20 Cable A # 1917, Sept. 6, 1917, RG 120 NA.
21 Browne interview, June 10, 1956. March to William I. Westervelt, Dec. 18, 1918, March Papers, Box 8.
22 March, AWC Lecture, April 26, 1937, 6.
23 Raymond B. Fosdick, *Chronicle of a Generation, An Autobiography* (New York, 1958), 160, 164–65.
24 Gardner letter, March 19, 1958.
25 Washington *Evening Star*, Sept. 3, 1918, 15.
26 Peyton C. March, *The Nation at War* (Garden City, N.Y., 1932), 146.
27 *Ibid.*, 370–72. C. H. Cramer, *Newton D. Baker: A Biography* (Cleveland, Ohio, 1961), 124–25.
28 March, AWC Lecture, April 5, 1938, 5.
29 *Ibid.*, 4.
30 Baker to March, Oct. 17, 1932, March Papers, Box 23.
31 Baker to March, March 12, 1936, March Papers, Box 23.
32 Baker to James W. Wadsworth, July 28, 1919, signed copy in March Papers, Box 8.
33 Baker to March, March 5, 1921, March Papers, Box 8.
34 By April 6, 1918, the Army had suffered 2368 casualties, of which 163 were killed in action. *New York Times*, April 7, 1918, Sec. 5, 2.
35 *Ibid.* The number of men in the army at that time was given in the same story. Leonard P. Ayres, *The War with Germany: A Statistical Summary* (Washington, D.C., 1919), 37.
36 Clarence C. Williams, Chief of Ordnance; Robert E. Wood, Acting Quartermaster General; Marlborough Churchill, Director of Intelligence Division; and Frank W. Coe, Chief of Coast Artillery.
37 On October 30, 1918, there were 1073 officers on General Staff duty in Washington. Gardner to March, Nov. 16, 1918, # 321.1 General Staff Corps, TAG Central File, RG 94 NA.
38 Baruch interview.
39 Baker to March, March 12, 1936, March Papers, Box 23.

Chapter 13. Complications of Demobilization

1 *Congressional Record*, 65 Congress, 2 session (1918), Vol. 56, Part 11, 11537.
2 Clifford C. Early letter to author, June 3, 1959. Colonel Early not only worked on problems of mobilization and demobilization in the Opera-

tions Division during this period but also prepared monographs on the subject as well as "considerable parts" of the Chief of Staff's Annual Reports for 1919, 1920, and 1921. His "Lecture on Demobilization of the Men of the Emergency Army," which he delivered before the General Staff College on Jan. 28, 1921, is an invaluable source.

3 Peyton C. March, *The Nation at War* (Garden City, N.Y., 1932), 311–12.

4 Confidential Cable P # 1886, Nov. 11, 1918, RG 120 NA.

5 Ray Stannard Baker, *Armistice: March 1–November 11, 1918*, Vol. VIII of *Woodrow Wilson: Life and Letters* (New York, 1939), 451–53. James R. Mock and Evangeline Thurber, *Report on Demobilization* (Norman, Okla., 1944), 108. Mock and Thurber trace one such proposal back to October, 1917.

6 Hartshorn to Executive Assistant, Oct. 8, 1918; McIntyre to Director of War Plans Division (with March approval), Oct. 14, 1918; and Lytle Brown to March, Nov. 22, 1918, Army # 50, C/S File, RG 165 NA.

7 Frederick Palmer, *Newton D. Baker: America at War*, 2 vols. (New York, 1931), II, 391–92; March, *Nation at War*, 329; Early lecture.

8 March, *Nation at War*, Chap. XIII; Baker to Stettinius Cable # 65, Nov. 11, 1918, RG 120 NA.

9 Early lecture.

10 Peek to W. L. Velie, Nov. 25, 1918, George N. Peek Papers (Western Historical Manuscripts Collection, University of Missouri, Columbia, Mo.), Folder 113 A. He described the plan in a letter to Bernard M. Baruch, Nov. 18, 1918, Folder 111 A.

11 The Frankfurter plan is summarized in Dixon Wecter, *When Johnny Comes Marching Home* (Boston, 1944), 306.

12 Peek to Baruch, Nov. 18, 1918, Peek Papers, Folder 111 A.

13 Crowder to March, Nov. 11, 1918, Crowder Papers.

14 Brown to March, Nov. 22, 1918, Army # 50, C/S File, RG 165 NA.

15 Early lecture.

16 March to James R. Mann, Jan. 23, 1919, Demobilization # 370, C/S File, RG 165 NA.

17 Early lecture. March discussed the demobilization procedure in his article, "Demobilization," *National Service*, V, No. 4 (April, 1919), 201–206.

18 *Ibid.*, 203; *New York Times*, Nov. 17, 1918, 1, 6. E. J. Howenstine, Jr., "Demobilization After the First World War," *Quarterly Journal of Economics*, LVIII (1943–1944), 93–94. Later, the War Department named nineteen more camps as demobilization centers.

19 Peek memo, Nov. 20, 1918, Peek Papers, Folder 111 A.

20 March, "Demobilization," *passim.*

21 Peek memo, Nov. 20, 1918.

22 *C/S, 1919*, 223; Early lecture.

23 Early lecture.

24 March's figures were: British, 355,693 officers and men; American, 740,917. *New York Times*, Jan. 12, 1919, Sec. 1, 9. Winston S. Churchill, *The Aftermath* (New York, 1929), 42–43.

25 The quotation is from Frederic L. Paxson, *The Great Demobilization and Other Essays* (Madison, Wis., 1941), 7.

26 Crowder to W. A. Bethel, Nov. 29, 1918, Crowder Papers.

27 March to Secretary of the General Staff, Nov. 29, 1918, Conferences and Meetings # 317; and March to Jervey, Nov. 14, 1918, War Department # 1503, C/S File, RG 165 NA.

28 Johnson to Harbord, Jan. 28, 1919, Harbord Papers, World War Military Activities.

29 The future New York governor and senator was on the Board of Contract Adjustment. Goethals to March, Dec. 6, 1918, Claims # 280, C/S File, RG 165 NA. In Lehman's biography, there is an amusing story about an encounter which he had with March. Allan Nevins, *Herbert H. Lehman and His Era* (New York, 1963), 58–59.

30 McKellar to March, Dec. 21, 1918, Kenneth D. McKellar Papers (Cossitt Library, Memphis, Tenn.), Box 274. I am indebted to Mr. Joseph Riggs and Miss Jeanne Graham for doing research in these papers for me.

31 *Cong. Rec.*, 65 Cong., 3 sess. (1918–1919), Vol. 57, Part 4, 3287.

32 *Ibid.*, Part 3, 2739–40.

33 March to James R. Mann, Jan. 23, and to Edward J. King, May 21, 1919, Demobilization # 370, C/S File, RG 165 NA.

34 Howenstine, "Demobilization," 102. Wecter, *When Johnny*, 381.

35 U.S. Congress, House of Representatives, Committee on Military Affairs, *Hearings on the Army Appropriations Bill*, 1920, 65 Cong., 3 sess. (1919), 3–4.

36 March to Pershing, Dec. 18, 1918, Pershing Papers, Box 123.

37 Confidential Cables P # 1886, Nov. 11, # 1905, Nov. 18, 1918, RG 120 NA. The quotation is from the last cable. I based my estimate of the strength of the thirty-division force on the customary figure of 40,000 for a division and its support troops.

38 Confidential Cable P # 2021, Dec. 31, 1918, RG 120 NA.

39 Confidential Cable A # 2206, Nov. 16, 1918, RG 120 NA.

40 Confidential Cable A # 2233, Nov. 22, 1918, RG 120 NA.

41 Confidential Cable A # 2805, Feb. 26, 1919, RG 120 NA.

42 Confidential Cable A # 2274, Dec. 1, 1918, RG 120 NA.

43 March to R. Walton Moore, June 23, 1919, EE [European Expedition] # 220.81, TAGO File, RG 94 NA. March, *Nation at War*, 104.

44 *Ibid.*, 104–108. Hines to War Department Cables # 10, Feb. 14, and # 18, Feb. 21, 1919, RG 120 NA.

45 Confidential Cables P # 2164, Feb. 24, # 2596, May 16, and # 2920, Aug. 13, 1919, RG 120 NA. March, *Nation at War*, 106–107.

46 Baker to March, Jan. 23, 1919, and other correspondence in Parades

and Reviews # 1108; Jervey to March, Oct. 4, 1918, Salute # 1250, C/S File, RG 165 NA. *C/S, 1919*, 230.

47 Mock and Thurber, *Report*, 92–94; Wecter, *When Johnny*, 358–59.

48 March, *Nation at War*, 323.

49 *C/S, 1919*, 224.

50 Mimeo. copy of March's statement, June 7, 1919, C/S File, Box 215 RG 165 NA.

51 Mock and Thurber, *Report*, 210.

52 *Army and Navy Journal*, Nov. 30, 1918, 455. Baker to Scott, Nov. 19, 1918, Scott Papers, Box 33.

53 A list of the original thirty-three centers is in *War Department Annual Reports, 1919*, 3 vols. (Washington, D.C., 1920), I, 13. (Cited hereafter as *WDAR, 1919*.)

54 1919 Scrapbook, March Papers.

55 March, *Nation at War*, 327.

56 Mimeo. copy of March's statement, May 10, 1919, C/S File, Box 215, RG 165 NA.

57 *Ibid.*

58 F. Q. C. Gardner to Stanley King, March 10, 1919, War Department # 1503, C/S File, RG 165 NA. Copies of the telegrams are in this folder.

59 1919 Scrapbook, March Papers.

60 Mimeo. copy of March's statement, May 10, 1919.

61 There are correspondence and news clippings on this controversy in the Crowder Papers. See also David A. Lockmiller, *Enoch H. Crowder: Soldier, Lawyer, and Statesman* (Columbia, Mo., 1955), Chap. XIV. Apparently this was a factor in preventing Crowder from getting a post-war promotion to lieutenant general. More important, it led to a reformed version of the Articles of War as a part of the Army Reorganization Act in 1920.

62 Fosdick to Baker, April 17, 1919, Morale # 1010, C/S File, RG 165 NA.

63 *Cong. Rec.*, 65 Cong., 3 sess. (1918–1919), Vol. 57, Part 3, 2248, 2618.

64 *Ibid.*, Part 4, 3395.

65 *Ibid.*, 3301.

66 *Ibid.*, 3475.

67 *Army and Navy Journal*, May 10, 1919, 1266.

68 Fosdick to Baker, April 17, 1919, Morale # 1010, C/S File, RG 165 NA.

69 Buford C. Utley in his interview, May 12, 1960, recalled this incident and the words of the song. Wecter, *When Johnny*, 297.

70 McIntyre to J. S. Frelinghuysen, March 11, 1919, Uniforms # 1470, C/S File, RG 165 NA.

71 Pershing to Baker, July 11, 1919, Pershing Papers, Box 16.

72 Jervey to TAG, July 7, 1921, Sam Browne Belts # 1251, C/S File, RG 165 NA.

73 Harbord to Pershing, April 30, 1919, Pershing Papers, Box 88.

74 *Cong. Rec.*, 65 Cong., 3 sess. (1918–1919), Vol. 57, Part 3, 2736.

75 The officer was George Van Horn Moseley. War Notes, June 29, 1919, Moseley Papers, Box 1. W. M. Wright to Pershing, June 14, 1919, Pershing Papers, Box 217.

76 Pershing to Wilson, Nov. 16, 1918, Commissions # 300, C/S File, RG 165 NA.

77 Confidential Cables A # 2300, Dec. 10, 1918, and # 2397, Jan. 3, 1919, RG 120 NA.

78 Confidential Cable P # 1962, Dec. 7, 1918, RG 120 NA.

79 Confidential Cable A # 2300, Dec. 10, 1918, RG 120 NA.

80 Baker to March, Jan. 25, 1919, Promotions # 1150, C/S File, RG 165 NA.

81 "Commissioned Personnel in the American Expeditionary Forces, 1917–1918," 266. – This is a bound volume prepared at G.H.Q. in May, 1919. Pershing Papers, RG 316 NA. Part IV is devoted to the post-war promotion problem. "Officers – Recommended for Promotion" Folder, Pershing Papers, Box 150.

82 Breckinridge to James W. Wadsworth, Sept. 24, 1942, James W. Wadsworth Papers (Library of Congress, Washington, D.C.), Box 22.

83 William G. Haan to Frank L. Winn, Aug. 8, 1919, and to William Weigel, Oct. 27, 1919, William G. Haan Papers (State Historical Society, Madison, Wis.), Box 5.

84 Correspondence in General Officers # 538, C/S File, RG 165 NA.

85 Charles D. Rhodes, "Diary Notes of a Soldier" (typed MS in the National Archives library), Aug. 14, 1919. Pelham D. Glassford letter to the author, May 4, 1959. Both of these officers had interviews with March. General Bishop, who was Chief of the Personnel Branch, discussed this problem with me in his interview.

86 Rhodes, "Diary," Aug. 23, 1919. This is the same Rhodes who wrote the descriptive letters about West Point during March's cadet days.

87 *Ibid.*, Aug. 25, 1919.

88 Confidential Cables A # 2307, Dec. 12; # 2309, Dec. 15, 1918; # 2806, Feb. 26; # 2837, March 1; # 3082, March 29; and # 3438, May 16, 1919, RG 120 NA.

89 March to Pershing, March 7, 1919, Pershing Papers, Box 123. He made the second comment before a congressional committee. U.S. Congress, House of Representatives, Select Committee on Expenditures in the War Department, *Hearings*, 66 Cong., 1 and 2 sess. (1920), 3277. March wanted McAndrew to be the Director of the War Plans Division but he took Pershing's suggestion and appointed him to the College position.

90 Confidential Cable P # 2480, April 27, 1919; Confidential Cable A # 3438, May 16, 1919, RG 120 NA. Mimeo. March statement, May 10, 1919.

91 *War Department Annual Reports, 1920*, 3 vols. (Washington, D.C., 1921), I, 163. General Pershing's secretary, Ralph A. Curtin, told me

of the general's friendship with Wright in an interview on Nov. 14, 1958.

92 I checked *WDAR, 1919* and *1920,* for the names of bureau chiefs. The Minutes of the Conference of Department Commanders, Jan. 12–19, 1920, C/S File, Box 150, RG 165 NA, gave me a list of the department and division commanders.

93 Cable A # 2280, Dec. 3, 1918, RG 120 NA. March included in his request three officers who later would play important roles in the reorganization struggle – Colonels John M. Palmer and John W. Gulick, and Major Thomas W. Hammond.

94 Confidential Cable A # 2309, Dec. 15, 1918, and Cable P # 1960, Dec. 7, 1918, RG 120 NA.

95 Confidential Cable P # 1995, Dec. 19, 1918, RG 120 NA.

96 Cables A # 3629, June 10, and P # 2761, June 15, 1919, RG 120 NA.

97 Haan to William Weigel, July 10, 1919, Haan Papers, Box 4.

98 Moseley to E. R. Stettinius, June 13, 1919, Moseley Papers, Box 3.

99 Harbord to Pershing, June 14, 1919, Harbord Papers, Personal War Letters. An indication of the attitude of AEF senior officers is in Weigel to Haan, July 2, 1919, Box 4, and Frank L. Winn to Haan, July 29, 1919, Haan Papers, Box 5.

100 Harbord to Pershing, April 30, 1919, Pershing Papers, Box 88.

101 Clipping from *New York World,* June 16, 1919, 1919 Scrapbook, March Papers. Another clipping in this scrapbook carried the story of Baker's denial.

102 Joseph Tumulty to Baker, June 28, 1919, Baker Papers, Box 11.

103 A. D. Tuttle to Moseley, July 12, 1919, Moseley Papers, Box 4. *Army and Navy Journal,* July 19, 1919, 1609.

104 *Cong. Rec.,* 65 Cong., 3 sess. (1918–1919), Vol. 57, Part 1, 444; Part 5, 4534.

105 Fosdick to F. P. Keppel, Jan. 21, 1919, Passports # 1100, C/S File, RG 165 NA.

106 *Ibid.*

107 Wecter, *When Johnny,* 265–71.

108 Curtin interview, Nov. 14, 1958. Pershing to Frederick Palmer, May 8, 1919, Pershing Papers, Box 153.

109 *Cong. Rec.,* 65 Cong., 3 sess. (1918–1919), Vol. 57, Part 4, 3218.

110 Frederick Palmer to Harbord, March 21, 1919, Harbord Papers, Personal War Letters.

111 *New York Times,* 1919: Feb. 19, p. 8; also Jan. 14, p. 6. Hermann Hagedorn, *Leonard Wood,* 2 vols. (New York, 1931), II, 357. Wood referred to political conferences with Allen on Sept. 1, and Nov. 5, 1919; however, there is no mention of the Thirty-fifth Division. Diary, Wood Papers, Box 12.

112 Harbord to Pershing, April 5, 1919, Pershing Papers, Box 88.

113 *Ibid.*

114 Wright to Pershing, June 14, 1919, Pershing Papers, Box 217. Wright

also commented on the Allen charges in this letter. Chap. 2, unpub. memoir, Pershing Papers, Box 377. This indicates that Wright was Pershing's roommate during the fall of 1882 at the Military Academy.

115 Palmer to Pershing, n.d. [Spring, 1919?], Pershing Papers, Box 153.

116 Harbord to Pershing, April 5, 1919, Pershing Papers, Box 88. Baker made a similar suggestion in Confidential Cable A # 2521, Jan. 22, 1919, RG 120 NA.

117 Palmer to Pershing, [Spring, 1919?], Pershing Papers, Box 153.

118 Confidential Cable P # 2942, Aug. 19, 1919, RG 120 NA. *New York Times*, 1919: Sept. 4, p. 3; Sept. 9, pp. 1, 3.

119 *Army and Navy Journal*, Sept. 13, 1919, 54. *New York Times*, 1919: Sept. 10, p. 1; Sept. 11, p. 1.

120 March to Fred Feigl, Sept. 4, 1919, March Papers, Box 8.

121 *New York Times*, Sept. 11, 1919, 1, 2.

122 Washington *Post*, Sept. 13, 1919, 1, 2, 3.

123 *New York Times*, Sept. 18, 1919, 17.

124 This photograph, reproduced in this book, first appeared in *New York Times*, Sept. 14, 1919, Sunday picture section.

125 Confidential Cable P # 1960, Dec. 7, 1918, RG 120 NA.

126 Their last exchange, other than cables and perfunctory notes, was March to Pershing, March 7, 1919, and Pershing to March, April 18, 1919, Pershing Papers, Box 123.

127 Egan to Pershing, Jan. 24, 1919, Pershing Papers, Box 69.

128 March to TAG, Jan. 7, and June 9, 1919, Chief of Staff # 278, C/S File, RG 165 NA. He ended his press conferences in June. *Army and Navy Journal*, June 28, 1919, 1498.

129 Washington *Post*, April 24, 1919, 10.

130 *Army and Navy Journal*, June 21, 1919, 1465.

131 Baker to Hugh M. Dorsey, Nov. 7, 1919, and F. Q. C. Gardner to J. M. Carter, Nov. 4, 1919, National Guard # 1044, C/S File, RG 165 NA. There is a list of incidents in which troops were used in *WDAR, 1920*, I, 70–72. For material on the Washington race riot, see Washington, D.C. # 1503, C/S File, RG 165 NA. Henry C. Frank interview, May 8, 1960.

132 According to *WDAR, 1919*, I, 17, the army discharged 3,280,376 officers and men through August, 1919. *C/S 1919*, 231, gives the figure 952,452 for the period May, 1865, through February 15, 1866.

Chapter 14. Plans for a Post-War Military Policy

1 John M. Dickinson, *The Building of an Army: A Detailed Account of Legislation, Administration and Opinion in the United States, 1915–1920* (New York, 1922), *passim.*

2 *Army and Navy Journal*, April 13, 1918, 1223.

3 Clippings from Kansas City *Times*, June 26, 1918, and the Louisville *Courier-Journal*, June 15, 1918, Crowder Papers.

4 March to Brown, July 18, 1918, Universal Service # 1478, C/S File, RG 165 NA.

5 Brown to March, Aug. 29, 1918, Universal Service # 1478, C/S File, RG 165 NA.

6 Jervey to Brown, Oct. 17, 1918, # 7942–2 War Plans Division File, RG 165 NA.

7 W. F. Clark to J. C. Gilmore, Jr., C. H. Conrad, Jr., John C. Ohnstad, and C. C. Stokeley, Nov. 9, 1918, # 7942, War Plans Division File, RG 165 NA.

8 The Coordination Section wanted to abolish the Inspector General's Department and to change the name of the Purchase, Storage, and Traffic Division to Division of Logistics. In turn, McIntyre advocated weakening the power of the bureau chiefs by selecting them from the generals of the line rather than having them hold rank created specifically for their positions. E. S. Hartshorn to McIntyre, undated memo, and McIntyre to Brown, Nov., n.d., 1918, War Department # 1503, C/S File, RG 165 NA.

9 March, AWC Lecture, April 16, 1932, 16–17. Baker to Charles P. Caldwell, Feb. 1, 1919, Baker Papers, Box 9. Brown received his instructions in a memo from McIntyre, Dec. 2, 1918. Both in Army # 50, C/S File, RG 165 NA.

10 R. D. Black to Chief, War Plans Branch, March 6, 1919, # 7942, WPD File, RG 165 NA. This is a detailed study of reorganization planning up to that point. The plan which Brown submitted to March on Dec. 31, 1918, is in Army # 50, C/S File, RG 165 NA.

11 March to William I. Westervelt, Dec. 18, 1918, March Papers, Box 8.

12 March, AWC Lecture, April 16, 1918, 17.

13 Goethals to his son, Jan. 12, 1919. He expressed a similar view in a letter to his son on Dec. 8, 1918. Both are in the Goethals Papers, Box 2.

14 Jervey to March, Dec. 18, 1918, and McIntyre to March, Dec., n.d., 1918, Army # 50, C/S File, RG 165 NA.

15 Spaulding interview, Nov. 9, 1960. McIntyre gave his version in U.S. Congress, Senate Subcommittee of the Committee on Military Affairs, *Hearings on Army Reorganization*, 66 Cong., 1 and 2 sess. (1919), 1372. March, in *The Nation at War* (Garden City, N.Y., 1932), 331–32, is incorrect in saying that the War Plans Division proposed a universal training scheme at this time. He must have confused this with either the earlier training plan or a later one which was submitted in the spring of 1919.

16 Haan to J. T. Dickman, Oct. 11, 1919, Haan Papers, Box 5.

17 Baker to Charles P. Caldwell, Feb. 1, 1919, Baker Papers, Box 9. March, *Nation at War*, 332.

18 March, *Nation at War*, 332.

19 March, AWC Lecture, April 16, 1932, 17.

20 March, *Nation at War*, 333.

21 U.S. Congress, House of Representatives, Committee on Military Affairs, *Hearings on Army Reorganization*, 65 Cong., 3 sess. (1919), 42, 64. (Cited hereafter as Dent *Hearings.*) *Cong. Rec.*, 65 Cong., 3 sess. (1918–1919), Vol. 57, Part 2, 1578.

22 The bill appears in Dent *Hearings*, 3–12.

23 *Ibid.*, 13, 26, 27; the quotation is on p. 13. Julius Kahn said on the floor of Congress, on February 12, that not a single member of the Committee favored a peacetime army of 500,000 men. *Cong. Rec.*, 65 Cong., 3 sess. (1918–1919), Vol. 57, Part 4, 3207.

24 Dent said that he was not only against the large peacetime army but also against giving the General Staff so much power. *Cong. Rec.*, 65 Cong., 3 sess. (1918–1919), Vol. 57, Part 4, 3204; Dent *Hearings*, 36.

25 Dent *Hearings*, 64.

26 *Ibid.*, 46. After a second request, Pershing agreed to send all of the officers. Confidential Cable P # 1995, Dec. 19, 1918, RG 120 NA.

27 The revisions included increased emphasis on universal training and a modification of the General Staff program. Rather than a permanent staff detail, selected officers on a permanent list would spend at least two in every six years with troops. Fiske memos, Dec. 6 and 23, 1918, File # 1001, Folder # 630, G-3 Reports, AEF/G.H.Q., RG 120 NA. Fiske to James W. McAndrew, Dec. 24, 1918, Pershing Papers, Box 3, Series 3, RG 316 NA.

28 Palmer to Pershing, [Spring, 1919], Pershing Papers, Box 153.

29 Conner to Fiske, Dec. 14, 1918, and Moseley to McAndrew, Dec. 13, 1918, File # 1001, Folder # 630, G-3 Reports, AEF/G.H.Q., RG 120 NA.

30 Pershing to McAndrew, Feb. 7, 1919, File # 1001, Folder # 630, G-3 Reports, AEF/G.H.Q., RG 120 NA.

31 Bowley to March, Dec. 28, 1918, March Papers, Box 22. Fiske memo, Dec. 6, 1918, Army # 50, C/S File, RG 165 NA. This was brought to the War Plans Division by Colonel W. W. Taylor, Jr., one of the staff officers returning from the AEF. Taylor to Le Roy Eltinge, n.d., and Eltinge to Taylor, Dec. 7, 1918, # 20532–C, AEF/AG File, RG 120 NA.

32 March to Pershing, March 7, 1919, Pershing Papers, Box 123.

33 "The Reminiscences of James W. Wadsworth," Oral Research Office, Columbia University, 202.

34 *Cong. Rec.*, 65 Cong., 3 sess., Vol. 57, Part 3, 2419–20.

35 The March quotation is from his press statement, Feb. 1, 1919, C/S File, Box 215, RG 165 NA. Senate, *Reorganization Hearings*, 1178. The three officers were John McAuley Palmer, Tenney Ross, and Allen J. Greer. Cable A # 2280, Dec. 3, 1918, RG 120 NA.

36 Curtin interview, Nov. 10, 1960. Palmer described his earlier plans in his *America in Arms: The Experience of the United States with Military Organization* (New Haven, Conn., 1941), Chaps. XVI, and XVII.

37 The regimental commander, who also was a leader in the Guard during the reorganization period, and, indeed, is one of the outstanding

Guardsmen of the century, Milton A. Reckord, described Palmer in his letter to the author, Feb. 26, 1963.

38 Unsigned memo for McAndrew, Oct. 16, 1918, Folder "Officers-Promotions 1917–1920," Pershing Papers, Box 7, Series 3, RG 316 NA.

39 Palmer to Fiske, Dec. 9, 1918, File # 1001, Folder # 630, G-3 Reports, AEF/G.H.Q., RG 120 NA.

40 Speech before Adjutants General Association, April 21, 1942, John McAuley Palmer Papers (Library of Congress, Washington, D.C.), Box 10.

41 War Notes, Jan. 2, 1919, Moseley Papers, Box 1. Moseley did not think that Palmer's pre-war ideas were good and maintained throughout that his views were not practical. Note on back of Palmer to Moseley, Aug. 20, 1916, Moseley Papers, Scrapbook, 1899–1942. Moseley interview, Sept. 14, 1960.

42 Speech, April 21, 1942, Palmer Papers, Box 10.

43 Palmer to Jervey, March 29, 1919, Microfilm from Palmer Papers, furnished by I. B. Holley, Duke University. The "Outline" is with Brown to March, April 1, 1919, Universal Service # 1478, C/S File, RG 165 NA.

44 Brown to March, April 1, 1919. Accompanying the Brown letter are the various memos. Incidentally, Jervey, in his memo to Palmer on March 21, 1919 (Army # 50), said that he did not agree with the plan.

45 March made this differentiation before the Senate committee. Senate, *Reorganization Hearings*, 27–28. Palmer described the training aspect of his program in *ibid.*, 1180–82, and denied that it was a compulsory service plan.

46 Unpub. memoir, 74, Palmer Papers, Box 22. Palmer established his version of this conflict between the two concepts in his *Washington, Lincoln, Wilson: Three War Statesmen* (Garden City, N.Y., 1930). March commented on this book in his AWC Lecture of April 16, 1932, 17–18.

47 Speech, April 21, 1942, Palmer Papers, Box 10.

48 Brown, "Special Instructions for the Committee on Plans for National Defense, War Plans Branch," April 10, 1919, Universal Service # 1478, C/S File, RG 165 NA. The Devens vote is described in a clipping from the Louisville *Courier-Journal*, March 18, 1919, Crowder Papers.

49 Senate, *Reorganization Hearings*, 39, 43–44.

50 Brown to Committee on Organization, April 15, 1919, Universal Service # 1478, C/S File, RG 165 NA. Speech, April 21, 1942, Palmer Papers, Box 10.

51 Palmer to Wadsworth, July 6, 1942, Wadsworth Papers, Box 31.

52 Speech, April 21, 1942, Palmer Papers, Box 10.

53 Senate, *Reorganization Hearings*, 514, 519. O'Ryan explained his plan on pages 512–29. For a biographical sketch of O'Ryan, see Robert L. Bullard, *Fighting Generals* (Ann Arbor, Mich., 1944), 285–325. A

copy of his plan is in O'Ryan to March, June 6, 1919, Miscellaneous Box 15, C/S File, RG 165 NA.

54 Notes on Gen. O'Ryan's reorganization of the Army, June, n.d., 1919, Miscellaneous Box 15, C/S File, RG 165 NA. Haan to March, June 1, 1919, # 320, TAGO, RG 94 NA.

55 Senate, *Reorganization Hearings*, 1835–51, 1942, 1957. O'Ryan told Pershing, on Oct. 30, 1919, that it would be hopeless to try to get the support of the Adjutants General. O'Ryan interview, Pershing Papers, Folder "Army Reorganization Interviews," Box 6, Series 3, RG 316 NA.

56 March quotation is in a clipping from *National Guardsman* in the 1919 Scrapbook in the March Papers. March explained his views on the National Guard before the House Committee also. U.S. Congress, House of Representatives, Committee on Military Affairs, *Hearings on Army Reorganization*, 66 Cong., 1 and 2 sess. (1919–1920), 44–45, 163–173. An interesting analysis of the National Guard question appears in Dickinson, *Building of an Army*, 351–62. The most thorough discussion of the issue from the Guard point of view is in Jim Dan Hill, *The Minute Man in Peace and War: A History of the National Guard* (Harrisburg, Pa., 1964), Chap. XIII.

57 *Army and Navy Journal*, Nov. 8, 1919, 305. *New York Times*, 1919: Nov. 25, p. 10, and Dec. 5, p. 3.

58 *Resumé*, May 26, 1919, WDHF, RG 120 NA. In June, 1919, the War Plans Division made its long awaited move from the War College to the State, War, and Navy Building. E. S. Hartshorn to WPD, May 27, 1919, War Plans Division # 1508. By the end of March, 1920, there were only 351 General Staff officers on duty in Washington. The P.S.&T. Division was in the Munitions Building; M.I.D. was located in three different places in the city and the rest of the staff were in the State, War, and Navy Building. March to Clifford Ireland, March 29, 1920, General Staff Corps (Organization) # 538, C/S File, RG 165 NA.

59 March to TAG, Dec. 19, 1919, G.S.C. (Detail) # 538, C/S File, RG 165 NA. For the description of Wright, I drew on the Curtin interview, Nov. 14, 1958, and the Gardner letter of April 10, 1958.

60 Senate, *Reorganization Hearings*, 215–16.

61 March to Director, P.S.&T., May 12, 1919, and Hartshorn to McIntyre, Dec. 11, 1919, G.S.C. # 538, C/S File, RG 165 NA.

62 Senate, *Reorganization Hearings*, 230–31, 543–44. Rogers took this office in February, 1919. He was a friend of Daniel R. Anthony of the House Military Affairs Committee. Harbord to Pershing, June 26, 1921, Pershing Papers, Box 88. Goethals wrote his son on March 4, 1919 (Goethals Papers, Box 2), ". . . Rogers isn't going to submit to control by Burr. . . ."

63 William J. Snow to March, Dec. 5, 1918 (with March approval), Field Artillery material # 481. The report of this board, which was chaired by March's former adjutant, William I. Westervelt, is in Miscellaneous Box 215, C/S File, RG 165 NA.

64 E. D. Anderson to TAG, Nov. 17, 1919, Boards of Officers # 168, C/S File, RG 165 NA.

65 The quotation is from Edwin B. Winans to Haan, Nov. 17, 1919, Haan Papers, Box 5. Winans detailed several of his complaints in this letter. During one day of the Senate Hearings, pay and low morale were discussed at length. Senate, *Reorganization Hearings*, 1459–553. *Cong. Rec.*, 66 Cong., 1 sess. (1919), Vol. 58, Part 5, 5776. The situation is also discussed in E. D. Anderson to March, Dec. 18, 1919, and Baker to Franklin D'Olier, Jan. 28, 1920, Recruits # 1180, C/S File, RG 165 NA.

66 Haan to March, Dec. 23, 1919 (with March approval), Conferences and Meetings # 317, C/S File, RG 165 NA.

67 Minutes of the conference are in Box 150 of the C/S File, RG 165 NA. Among those who attended the January 12–19, 1920, conference were Hunter Liggett, Robert L. Bullard, John L. Hines, Charles P. Summerall, Leonard Wood, and Harbord. The decentralization order was War Department General Order # 132, Dec. 19, 1919. Evidently it resulted from Haan to March, Sept., n.d., 1919, Army # 50, C/S File, RG 165 NA.

68 Harbord to Dawes, Jan. 25, 1920, Charles G. Dawes Papers, (Northwestern University Library, Evanston, Ill.), Harbord Box 1920–1937. According to the minutes, March was present to hear Baruch lecture but he did not attend any of the other sessions after his opening talk.

69 March memo, Jan. 23, 1920, Uniforms # 1470, C/S File, RG 165 NA.

70 March, *Nation At War*, 259.

71 A description of conditions at the Academy is in William A. Ganoe, *MacArthur Close-Up: More Then and Some Now* (New York, 1962), 13–20. For a former Harvard president's (Charles W. Eliot) criticism of the Academy, see *New York Times*, May 9, 1920, 19.

72 *Army and Navy Journal*, Sept. 6, 1919, 7.

73 March gave his views in a memo to Baker, May 12, 1919. Jervey to TAG, Nov. 16, 1918, The General Committee to the Superintendent, Dec. 13, 1918, West Point # 1538, C/S File, RG 165 NA.

74 *Army and Navy Journal*, Dec. 21, 1918, 569. Brown to March, Dec. 24, 1918, and March 7, 1919, West Point # 1538, C/S File, RG 165 NA. Pershing's views are in *Cong. Rec.*, 66 Cong., 2 sess. (1919–1920), Vol. 59, Part 3, 3034.

75 March to Baker, May 12, 1919, West Point # 1538, and March Press Statement, May 10, 1919, C/S File, Box 215, RG 165 NA.

76 MacArthur interview.

77 March to C. B. Hodges, March 18, 1930, March Papers, Box 22. *Cong. Rec.*, 66 Cong., 2 sess. (1919–1920), Vol. 59, Part 3, 2921–22, 3033–34; Part 4, 4674–75, 5061. General Danford wrote in his letter to the author, April 23, 1959, that both he and General MacArthur wanted to return to the four-year system. The correspondence in West Point # 1538, C/S File, and Ganoe's *MacArthur* illustrate the changes made at the Academy at that time.

Chapter 15. Congress Forges a Military Policy

1 Swope interview, June 16, 1960. Dixon Wecter, *When Johnny Comes Marching Home* (Boston, 1944), 371.
2 *Cong. Rec.*, 66 Cong., 1 sess. (1919), Vol. 58, Part 5, 4476.
3 Charles P. Caldwell to Baker, Feb. 1, 1919, Baker Papers, Box 9.
4 March, AWC Lecture, April 26, 1937, 9.
5 March, AWC Lecture, April 16, 1932, 11.
6 McKellar to March, Jan. 25, 1919, McKellar Papers, (Cossitt Library, Memphis, Tenn.), Box 274.
7 F. Q. C. Gardner to Operations and others, Jan. 12, 1919, Correspondence # 320. See the letters for May 2–7, 1919, in Discharges # 390, C/S File, RG 165 NA.
8 March, AWC Lecture, April 26, 1937, 7.
9 *Cong. Rec.*, 65 Cong., 3 sess. (1918–1919), Vol. 57, Part 2, 1408–10; Part 3, 2530; the quotation is from the last page.
10 *Ibid.*, 2735–42. The quotation is on page 2736. Senator Wadsworth described Frelinghuysen in his "Reminiscences," Oral Research Office, Columbia University, p. 202.
11 The first three quotations are from a clipping of the Boston *Evening Transcript*, Feb. 7, 1919; the last quotation is from a clipping of the *Washington Post*, March 25, 1919. Both are in Scrapbook, Vol. 11, Pershing Papers, Box 391.
12 March to Marlborough Churchill, Feb. 18, 1919, March Papers, Box 22.
13 Moseley to O'Ryan, March 1, 1919, Moseley Papers, Box 3.
14 Crowder to Pershing, Feb. 10, 1919, Pershing Papers, Box 56.
15 See debate on February 11–15 in *Cong. Rec.*, 65 Cong., 3 sess. (1918–1919), Vol. 57, Parts 3 and 4.
16 *Ibid.*, Part 4, 3388.
17 *Ibid.*, Part 5, 4889, 4892–93.
18 Peyton C. March, *The Nation at War* (Garden City, N.Y., 1932), 347.
19 The first quotation is from Wadsworth, "Reminiscences," 198; the second from the Spaulding interview.
20 Spaulding interview.
21 Wadsworth described his background in his "Reminiscences," 30–34. See also Henry F. Holthusen, *James W. Wadsworth, Jr.: A Biographical Sketch* (New York, 1926), *passim.*
22 *Cong. Rec.*, 66 Cong., 1 sess. (1919), Vol. 58, Part 1, 776, 861, 867. The Adjutant General reported (*War Department Annual Report, 1919*, Vol. I, 496) that the strength of the Army on June 30, 1919, was 936,578 officers and men. This figure included Philippine Scouts.
23 *Cong. Rec.*, 66 Cong., 1 sess. (1919), Vol. 58, Part 1, 977–1006, 1051–52.
24 *Ibid.*, Part 2, 1069–83. T. W. Hammond to McIntyre, June 27, 1919, Army # 150, C/S File, RG 165 NA.
25 *Cong. Rec.*, 66 Cong., 1 sess., Vol 58, Part 1, 876.
26 *Ibid.*, Part 2, 1083.
27 *Ibid.*, 1492, 1557–1604, 1636–78, 1730–50; Part 3, 2196.

28 *Ibid.*, Part 3, 2196; Part 5, 4481.

29 *Ibid.*, Part 3, 2187.

30 Harold and Margaret Sprout, *Toward a New Order of Sea Power: American Naval Policy and the World Scene, 1918–1922* (Princeton, N.J., 1943), 107.

31 Hammond to March, May 22, 1919, Secretary of War # 1299, C/S File, RG 165 NA. Under Army # 50, there are two Hammond to McIntyre letters, June 10 and 27, 1919, which March noted. Hammond was one of the officers March requested from Pershing in Dec., 1918. Cable A # 2280, December 3, 1918, RG 120 NA.

32 *Cong. Rec.*, 65 Cong., 3 sess. (1918–1919), Vol. 57, Part 1, 926.

33 *Ibid.*, Part 4, 3198, 3378, 3736; Part 5, 4892.

34 March Press Statement, March 29, 1919, C/S File, Box 215, RG 165 NA.

35 U.S. Congress, Senate, Subcommittee of the Committee on Military Affairs, *Hearings, Army Appropriations Bill,* 66 Cong., 1 sess. (1919), 97.

36 *Cong. Rec.*, 65 Cong., 3 sess. (1918–1919), Vol. 57, Part 1, 841, 979. The officers in order of rank given by Baker were Generals March, Pershing, and Bliss, and Lieutenant Generals Liggett and Bullard.

37 *Cong. Rec.*, 66 Cong., 1 sess. (1919), Vol. 58, Part 3, 2852.

38 Brown to Harbord, July 19, 1919. Harbord forwarded this letter to Pershing with the comment that it was "very interesting," on Aug. 4. Pershing Papers, Box 88. The *New York Times* (July 19, 1919, 5) generally corroborates Brown's description of the scene.

39 *Ibid.*, July 21, 1919, 10.

40 Clipping of *New York Sun*, July 19, 1919, March Papers, Scrapbook 1919.

41 The Committee vote was as follows: 3 Republicans joined 5 Democrats in the majority while 6 Republicans and 1 Democrat were in the minority. *New York Times*, July 31, 1919, 16.

42 Clipping from Washington *Evening Star*, Aug. 22, 1919, March Papers, Scrapbook 1919. The others who filed protests were Daniel R. Anthony, Rollin B. Sanford, Alvan T. Fuller, Charles C. Kearns, and the Democrat, Charles P. Caldwell. *Army and Navy Journal*, Aug. 23, 1919, 1769.

43 Baker to Wadsworth, July 28, 1919, signed copy, March Papers, Box 8. March, *Nation at War*, 349–50.

44 Diary, Oct. 6, 1919, Josephus Daniel Papers (Library of Congress, Washington, D.C.), Box 3. I am indebted to E. David Cronon for calling my attention to this.

45 *Cong. Rec.*, 66 Cong., 1 sess. (1919), Vol. 58, Part 5, 4465, 4467. The Clark quotation is on the first page. Guy E. Campbell's comments are on the second page.

46 *Ibid.*, 4973–74. The "discordant note" quotation is from an editorial in the *Washington Post*, Sept. 8, 1919, 6.

47 *Cong. Rec.*, 66 Cong., 1 sess. (1919), Vol. 58, Part 5, 4975–76; a description of Schall is in Part 6, 6062. Those who voted with Schall

were Tom Connally, Marvin Jones, and Robert Y. Thomas — all Democrats. *Ibid.*, Part 5, 4468.

48 *Ibid.*, Part 6, 5560–62. The quotations are on pages 5560–61. The description of Pershing is from *New York Times*, Sept. 20, 1919, 16.

49 In preparing this section on the hearings, I used both the Senate and House *Hearings*, but I relied primarily on U.S. Congress, Senate, Subcommittee of the Committee on Military Affairs, *Hearings on Army Reorganization*, 66 Cong., 1 and 2 sess. (1919), which I read in entirety. The House *Hearings* are U.S. Congress, House of Representatives, Committee on Military Affairs, *Hearings on Army Reorganization*, 66 Cong., 1 and 2 sess. (1919–1920), 2 vols.

50 Baker to Wadsworth, Aug. 3, 1919, Army # 50, C/S File, RG 165 NA.

51 Senate, *Reorganization Hearings*, 55. Although there seems to be a discrepancy between the figure of 509,000 mentioned in January and the 576,000 which Johnson used, there actually is not. March explained that Congress would only have to appropriate for the smaller number of enlisted men since the larger number included officers and unassigned recruits — a safety valve for recruiting. House of Representatives, *Reorganization Hearings*, 131.

52 The Baker quotations are from Senate, *Reorganization Hearings*, 211, and House of Representatives, *Reorganization Hearings*, 1774–75. March's explanations are in House of Representatives, *Reorganization Hearings*, 76–77, 131.

53 Ray S. Baker and William E. Dodd (Editors), *The Public Papers of Woodrow Wilson: War and Peace*, 2 vols. (New York, 1927), II, 412. For the navy, see H. and M. Sprout, *Toward A New Order of Sea Power*, 73–75. Baker was also tentative about a permanent peacetime army strength in his "A Permanent Military Policy for the United States," *Saturday Evening Post*, CXCI, No. 48 (May 31, 1919), 29–30, 165.

54 Haan to John P. Smith, Nov. 2, 1919, Haan Papers, Box 5. The March quotation is from Senate, *Reorganization Hearings*, 60. Ten years later, Baker wrote Beecher Stowe and enclosed a copy of his letter to March (Sept. 20, 1929, March Papers, Box 22). In this letter the former Secretary said that the choice was between world co-operation and armaments. He added, ". . . so far as the military policy of 1919–1920 is concerned, including the so-called Baker-March bill, I am personally responsible for that. President Wilson's mind was far too much occupied with other things to expect him to give that any attention." Since he had just read Palmer's interpretation of the bill, he wrote that he did not think Palmer was correct in applying the Washington *vs.* Upton thesis to the situation and that Palmer's views of a proper military policy were suitable for a very different country in a very different world situation. Colonel Cocheu first called my attention to the influences on March in his August 7, 1957, interview.

55 Senate, *Reorganization Hearings*, 63, 150–57; House of Representatives, *Reorganization Hearings*, 32–33, 1781.

56 Haan to March, Aug. 15, 1919, Army Transport Service # 59, C/S File, RG 165 NA.
57 George W. Haan to Haan, Aug. 22, 1919, Haan Papers, Box 5.
58 Both Baker and March said that officers were free to express their opinions, and the testimony before both committees certainly indicates that this was the case. Baker to Wadsworth, Oct. 27, 1919, Universal Service # 1478, and March to Johnson Hagood, Sept. 15, 1919, Legislation # 840, C/S File, RG 165 NA. Wadsworth, "Reminiscences," 307. Although March later wrote, "At no time in the consideration of this reorganization did the War Department imagine that Congress would appropriate the money for 500,000 men" (*Nation at War*, 341), he gave no indication of this attitude in 1919.
59 John M. Palmer, *America in Arms: The Experience of the United States with Military Organization* (New Haven, Conn., 1941), 167–68.
60 Spaulding interview.
61 Wadsworth, "Reminiscences," 307.
62 *Ibid.*, 308.
63 Senate, *Reorganization Hearings*, 1177.
64 *Ibid.*, 832.
65 The first quotation is from Wadsworth's introduction to John M. Palmer, *Statesmanship or War* (Garden City, N.Y., 1927), xv. The second is from Wadsworth, "Reminiscences," 308.
66 The first two quotations are from Wadsworth, "Reminiscences," 306. The last is from Wadsworth, introduction to Palmer, *Statesmanship*, xv. Baker to Wadsworth, Oct. 18 and 27, 1919, and Chapter File, Box 17, Vol. 13 in Holley microfilm of Palmer Papers.
67 Wadsworth, introduction to Palmer, *Statesmanship*, xiv.
68 Virginia Conner, *What Father Forbade* (Philadelphia, Pa., 1951), 88–89.
69 These twenty interview transcripts are in Folder "Army Reorganization – Interviews," Pershing Papers, Box 6, Series 3, RG 316 NA.
70 Fox Conner to Robert C. Davis, Oct. 20, 1919, Folder "Army Reorganization," Pershing Papers, Box 3, Series 3, RG 316 NA.
71 John M. Palmer to James W. Wadsworth, March 11, 1940, Wadsworth Papers, Box 21.
72 March-Pershing interview, Oct. 30, 1919, Folder "Army Reorganization – Interviews," Pershing Papers, Box 6, Series 3, RG 316 NA.
73 Curtin interview, Nov. 10, 1960; Colonel Curtin was the stenographer.
74 March-Pershing interview, Oct. 30, 1919.
75 March to Pershing, March 7, 1919, Pershing Papers, Box 123.
76 Haan to John P. Smith, Nov. 2, 1919, Haan Papers, Box 5. Pershing appeared on three days, Oct. 31, Nov. 1 and 5. At his side were George C. Marshall and Fox Conner. George C. Marshall, "Some Lessons of History," *Maryland Historical Magazine*, XL, No. 3 (Sept., 1945), 177. Senate, *Reorganization Hearings*, 1610.
77 Senate, *Reorganization Hearings*, 1605.

78 *Ibid.*, 1572.

79 *Ibid.*, 1578, 1649, 1651. A comment on the citizen army that Pershing made to the Quartermaster General, Harry L. Rogers, during one of the interview sessions probably reflected the General of the Armies' private attitude on this subject: "It is high time we are all working for the good of the service; otherwise we will have a big citizen army and we will all be thrown out." Rogers interview in Folder "Army Reorganization – Interviews," Pershing Papers, Box 6, Series 3, RG 316 NA.

80 Clipping from the *Stars and Stripes*, Nov. 8, 1919, in Scrapbook, Vol. 14, Pershing Papers, Box 394.

81 Chamberlain's statement, a Senate Committee Print, is bound with the Senate, *Reorganization Hearings*; the quotation is from p. 8.

82 Senate, *Reorganization Hearings*, 1575, 1618, 1623–25. On the first page, he did say that some of the War Department General Staff actions were the result of the lack of trained personnel.

83 *Ibid.*

84 *Ibid.*, 544–46, 604, 686–97, 1149–50.

85 *Ibid.*, 395–408.

86 *Ibid.*, 337.

87 House of Representatives, *Reorganization Hearings*, 108–10, Chamberlain called attention to this in his statement on the Baker-March bill. Senate Committee Print, Senate, *Reorganization Hearings*, 5–8.

88 U.S. Congress, Senate, Subcommittee of the Committee on Military Affairs, *Hearings, Army Appropriations Bill*, 66 Cong., 1 sess. (1919), 95.

89 Senate, *Reorganization Hearings*, 1256–57.

90 March, *Nation at War*, 209.

91 *Cong. Rec.*, 66 Cong., 1 sess. (1919), Vol. 58, Part 1, 877; MacArthur interview.

92 Mitchell to Arnold, July 25, 1919, William Mitchell Papers (Library of Congress, Washington, D.C.), Box 7.

93 Baker cover letter with the Crowell Report, Aug. 11, 1919, Baker Papers, Box 11. Baker wrote Crowell, who was in Paris, on June 2, 1919, "I do not wish a study of separate Air Service for the United States to be made in France." Aviation # 60, C/S File, RG 165 NA. Baker expressed his indignation to Daniels. Diary, July 23, 1919, Daniels Papers, Box 3.

94 Senate, *Reorganization Hearings*, 105, 185, 278–81.

95 *Ibid.*, 743.

96 Menoher to March, July 28, 1919, Aviation # 60, C/S File, RG 165 NA.

97 U.S. Congress, House of Representatives, Subcommittee of the Military Affairs Committee, *Hearings on United Air Service*, 66 Cong., 2 sess. (1919), 125.

98 Foulois interview, Nov. 7, 1960.

99 U.S. Congress, House of Representatives, Subcommittee of the Military

Affairs Committee, *Hearings, Army Appropriations Bill,* 66 Cong., 1 sess. (1919), 96.

100 Senate, *Reorganization Hearings,* 278.

101 *Ibid.,* 266.

102 *C/S, 1919,* 244.

103 Menoher to Pershing, Dec. 16, 1919, and Pershing to Menoher, Jan. 12, 1920, Aviation # 60, C/S File, RG 165 NA.

104 Senate, *Reorganization Hearings,* 33–35, 93–96, 163, 178, 1763.

105 *Cong. Rec.,* 66 Cong., 2 sess. (1919–1920), Vol. 59, Part 4, 4296; Part 5, 4560. Spaulding interview.

106 Spaulding interview. *Cong. Rec.,* 66 Cong., 2 sess., Vol. 59, Part 6, 5898.

107 Pershing to Julius Kahn, Nov. 24, 1919, Pershing Papers, Box 109.

108 March to TAG, Jan. 30, 1920, and Baker to Wadsworth, June 12, 1920, GSC (Details) # 538, C/S File, RG 165 NA.

109 *New York Times,* 1920: Jan. 22, p. 21; Jan. 23, pp. 4, 12. The *Times* supported Baker on this point in an editorial on the last page cited.

110 *Cong. Rec.,* 66 Cong., 2 sess. (1919–1920), Vol. 59, Part 2, 1501–07.

111 *Ibid.,* Part 5, 5241. In October, 1919, Wadsworth introduced a bill which authorized three lieutenant generals, with the understanding that March, Liggett, and Bullard would be appointed. After a brief debate on Jan. 17, 1921, the Senate dropped the measure without a vote. *Cong. Rec.,* 66 Cong., 3 sess., Vol. 60, Part 2, 1492–93.

112 *Cong. Rec.,* 66 Cong., 2 sess. (1919–1920), Vol. 59, Part 4, 4310.

113 Thomas W. Harrison of Virginia protested: "Now, I know nothing so irresponsible as a young negro boy rigged out in brass buttons and with a gun. In communities where the negro largely predominates he would be a positive menace to the safety of the community." Percy Quin of Mississippi was more intemperate in his remarks. *Cong. Rec.,* 66 Cong., 2 sess. (1919–1920), Vol. 59, Part 4, 4033, 4043; the quotation is from p. 4033. John Dickinson, *The Building of an Army: A Detailed Account of Legislation, Administration and Opinion in the United States, 1915–1920* (New York, 1922), 367–72. The President's request is Wilson to Baker, Feb. 7, 1920 (which the Secretary forwarded to the congressmen), Baker Papers, Box 11.

114 Spaulding interview; Colonel Spaulding was Kahn's companion.

115 Wadsworth, "Reminiscences," 313.

116 *Ibid.*; Palmer, *America in Arms,* 179–81.

117 In addition to these provisions, Palmer's proposal for a General Staff committee consisting of regulars and civilian component personnel remained. Frelinghuysen made the motion on April 8, 1920. *Cong. Rec.,* 66 Cong., 2 sess. (1919–1920), Vol. 59, Part 5, 5323–33; Part 6, 5402.

118 Wadsworth to Baker, Feb. 26, 1920, Baker Papers, Box 13.

119 *Cong. Rec.,* 66 Cong., 2 sess. (1919–1920), Vol. 59, Part 5, 5240. Warren won a Medal of Honor in the battle of Port Hudson. *Congressional Directory,* 66 Cong., 1 sess. (1919), 127.

120 *Ibid.,* 86–87. *Cong. Rec.,* 66 Cong., 2 sess., Vol. 59, Part 4, 4186.

121 *Ibid.*, Part 6, 5548. McKellar to C. H. Totten, May 31, and to E. C. Felts, June 1, 1920, McKellar Papers, Box 281.

122 In the House, the vote was 245 to 92, with 89 not voting. In the Senate, 46 voted for it with 10 against it and 40 absent. *Cong. Rec.*, 66 Cong., 2 sess., Vol. 59, Part 5, 4560; Part 6, 5898.

123 Kahn to Pershing, March 12, 1920, Pershing Papers, Box 109.

124 The conferees were Senators Wadsworth, Howard Sutherland, Harry S. New, Charles S. Thomas, and George E. Chamberlain; and Representatives Kahn, Daniel R. Anthony, Jr., John C. McKenzie, William J. Fields, and S. Hubert Dent. *Cong. Rec.*, 66 Cong., 2 sess., Vol. 59, Part 6, 5898, 5990. Palmer in his Notes on WPD Plan of April 1, 1919, prepared July 17, 1942 (Palmer Papers, Box 10), indicated the differences. Senator Wadsworth also commented on the conference problems in *Cong. Rec.*, 66 Cong., 2 sess., Part 7, 7331–32.

125 *Ibid.*, 7263–67, 7298–319, 7331–34; Part 8, 7813–44, 7893; Reckord letter.

126 Palmer, *America in Arms*, 182–83.

127 *Ibid.*, 173. In his letter, General Reckord praised the Section 5 Committee: "This plan has worked spendidly since it was initiated in 1920, and it is definitely General Palmer's brain child." While Section 47d provided for volunteer training camps, Palmer also wanted a four-month program for National Guard and Organized Reserve enrollees. Notes on WPD Plan of April 1, 1919, prepared July 17, 1942.

128 Wilson to Baker, undated pencilled note, Baker Papers, Box 13.

129 Baker to Wilson, June 3, 1920, Baker Papers, Box 13. In this same location is another Baker to Wilson letter, June 4, 1920, in which Baker pointed out the potential ill effects of a veto.

130 *Cong. Rec.*, 66 Cong., 2 sess. (1919–1920), Vol. 59, Part 8, 8662.

131 The Act is printed along with the conference report in *ibid.*, 7813–33. Baker analyzed and criticized the Act in a letter to Clifford Ireland, Aug. 16, 1920, Army # 50, C/S File, RG 165 NA. In his interview, General Foulois remarked that the Act did nothing for the Air Service. The annual report of the Judge Advocate General gives a summary of the revisions of the Articles of War. *WDAR*, *1920*, I, 346–47.

132 Burr to Acting Chief of Staff, June 2, 1920, Organization # 1080, C/S File, RG 165 NA.

133 Gilmore to Haan, June 2, 1920, Organization # 1080, C/S File, RG 165 NA. See also in this folder the other General Staff memos about the bill, in particular the undated one signed by Wright, Haan, and Jervey.

134 *Cong. Rec.*, 66 Cong., 2 sess. (1919–1920), Vol. 59, Part 6, 5664; Part 8, 8178–82, 8418–24, 8453. See the editorial in the *New York Times*, May 29, 1920, 14. Wadsworth gave his analysis of the Act in "Reminiscences," 311–13. Palmer summarized his views on the period in his *Washington, Lincoln, Wilson: Three War Statesmen* (Garden City, N.Y., 1930), 361–68.

135 *Army and Navy Journal*, May 22, 1920, 1177.

136 *WDAR, 1920,* I, 162. In my study of this period, I used, in addition to works already cited, Edward B. Lee, Jr., *Politics of Our Military National Defense* (76 Cong., 3 sess., Senate Document # 274, Washington, 1940); Ben. G. Franklin, "The Military Policy of the United States, 1918–1933; A Study of the Influence of World War I on Army Organization and Control" (Unpub. Ph.D. thesis, Univ. of Calif., 1943); Russell F. Weigley, *Towards an American Army: Military Thought from Washington to Marshall* (New York, 1962); and Forrest C. Pogue, *George C. Marshall: Education of a General* (New York, 1963).

Chapter 16. The Trials of Peace

1 Browne interview, June 10, 1956.
2 Whitlock to Baker, June 23, 1920, Baker Papers, Box 13. Clippings in Scrapbook 1919–1928, March Papers. Browne interview, June 10, 1956. In World War II, Somervell headed the army's supply program.
3 Henry T. Allen, *My Rhineland Journal* (Boston, 1923), 117. For Pershing's political awareness, see his letter to Charles G. Dawes, May 26, 1920, Dawes Papers.
4 *War Department, Annual Reports, 1920,* 3 vols. (Washington, D.C., 1921), I, 239–41. "Preparation for the Advance of the First Division East of the Rhine," n.d., # 201–32.8, First Division Historical File, World War I Organization Records, RG 120 NA.
5 Robert L. Bullard, *Fighting Generals: Illustrated Biographies of Seven Major Generals in World War I* (Ann Arbor, Mich, 1944), 87–95; the quotation is on p. 93.
6 Clipping from the *Amaroc News,* June 11, 1920, in Scrapbook 1919–1928, March Papers.
7 Allen to Pershing, June 25, 1920, Henry T. Allen Papers (Library of Congress, Washington, D.C.), Box 13.
8 Allen to W. W. Harts, June 14, 1920, Allen Papers, Box 13.
9 *Army and Navy Journal,* July 10, 1920, 1397. Clippings in Scrapbook 1919–1928, March Papers. For the Davis mission and the German problem, see Allen, *Journal,* 119, and March to Baker Cable, June 17, 1920, Germany # 530, C/S File, RG 165 NA.
10 March to Allen, June 23, 1920, Allen Papers, Box 13. The critique – March to Allen, June 17, 1920 – is in the same location.
11 Baker to Allen, July 12, 1920, Allen Papers, Box 13.
12 Browne interview, June 10, 1956, and letter to the author, Feb. 4, 1959. *New York Times,* June 21, 1920, 17.
13 *WDAR, 1920,* I, 237–39.
14 Bliss to War Department Cable # 358, Dec. 9, 1919, RG 120 NA.
15 Baker to Secretary of State, Aug. 12, and Nov. 16, 1920, Military Missions # 987, C/S File, RG 165 NA.
16 March to Sir Herbert J. Creedy, Aug. 10, 1920, Chief of Staff # 278, C/S File, RG 165 NA. Browne interview, June 10, 1956.
17 *New York Times,* June 29, 1920, 17.

18 *Ibid.*, July 8, 1920, 10; and July 11, 1920, 4. March's rank is reflected by his serial number – 06. The officers who ranked him and who held serial numbers 01 through 05 were, in order, Pershing, Leonard Wood, Hunter Liggett, John F. Morrison, and Charles G. Morton, *Official Army Register: July 1, 1921* (Washington, D.C., 1922), *Official Army Register: January 1, 1925* (Washington, D.C., 1925).

19 *Army and Navy Journal*, July 17, 1920, 1416.

20 Peyton C. March, *The Nation at War* (Garden City, N.Y., 1932), 147.

21 John Cudahy [A Chronicler], *Archangel: The American War with Russia* (Chicago, 1924), 2. On one occasion in north Russia, there was a case of near mutiny in an American unit. March, *Nation at War*, 150–53.

22 Diary, Dec. 14, 1918, Polk Papers, Drawer 88, Folder 12.

23 Wilds P. Richardson, Monograph on the North Russian Expedition, # 319.1, TAGO, RG 94 NA; the information about the withdrawal is on p. 65.

24 *Ibid.* The quotation is from an article by John Cudahy in the *Milwaukee Journal*, May 9, 1926, Feature Magazine, 3.

25 Betty Miller Unterberger, *America's Siberian Expedition, 1918–1920: A Study of National Policy* (Durham, N.C., 1956), 105.

26 *Ibid.*, 119–23.

27 Baker to Wilson, Nov. 27, 1918, Baker Papers, Box 8. The first letter was dated Nov. 6.

28 Diary, Dec. 14, 1918, Polk Papers, Drawer 88, Folder 12.

29 Unterberger, *America's Siberian Expedition*, 151.

30 *Cong. Rec.*, 66 Cong., 1 sess., Vol. 58, Part 5, 4899.

31 Wilson to Baker, Aug. 21, 1919, Baker Papers, Box 11.

32 The first quotation is from Robert L. Eichelberger letter to the author, April 27, 1959; the second is from an interview with the general's son, Sidney C. Graves (Aug. 29, 1961), who also served on the general's staff in Siberia.

33 William S. Graves, *America's Siberian Adventure: 1918–1920* (New York, 1931), 54, 118–19, 219–24.

34 March to Graves, May 13, 1919, March Papers, Box 22.

35 Graves, *Siberian Adventure*, 160.

36 Diary, Oct. 8 and 10, 1919, Daniels Papers, Box 3.

37 Diary, Nov. 30, 1919, Lansing Papers, Box 2.

38 Cable AV # 502, Dec. 29, 1919, RG 120 NA.

39 Unterberger, *America's Siberian Expedition*, 176–80.

40 Dewitt C. Poole, "Reminiscences," Oral Research Office, Columbia University, 486.

41 Cables V # 661, Jan. 20, and # 797, April 1, 1920, RG 120 NA. Graves, *Siberian Adventure*, 328.

42 Graves, *Siberian Adventure*, 326–28. Eichelberger letter.

43 Unterberger, *America's Siberian Expedition*, 203.

44 March, *Nation at War*, 131.
45 Wright to March, June 11, 1920, Board of Officers # 168, C/S File, RG 165 NA.
46 Wright listed the officers on the various boards in a memo to TAG, June 7, 1920, Board of Officers # 168, C/S File, RG 165 NA. Spaulding interview.
47 Special Committee Report, July 8 ,1919, mimeo. copy, Pershing Papers, Box 4, Series 3, RG 316 NA.
48 Baker to state governors, June 11, 1920; Hartley A. Moon to TAG, July 20, 1920, # 320, TAGO, RG 94 NA. *Report of the Chief of Staff, United States Army, to the Secretary of War: 1921* (Washington, D.C., 1921), 68. [Cited hereafter as *C/S 1921*.] The quotation is from the Reckord letter. John M. Palmer, *Washington, Lincoln, Wilson: Three War Statesmen* (New York, 1930), 365.
49 March note on E. D. Anderson to March, Sept. 18, 1920, Business Methods # 227, C/S File, RG 165 NA.
50 *C/S, 1921*, 11.
51 *Ibid.*, 65–68.
52 Wadsworth to Palmer, June 26, 1920, Palmer Papers, Holley microfilm. *C/S, 1921*, 12–13.
53 Report of A.E.F. Superior Board on Organization and Tactics, June 16, 1920, with Pershing to Baker, July 9, 1920, Pershing Papers, Box 4, Series 3, RG 316 NA.
54 James H. McRae to Pershing, July 17, 1922, # 210.2, TAGO, RG 94 NA. Under this file number also see James W. Wadsworth to Secretary of War, Sept. 28, 1921, and TAGO memo on promotion list problems, Oct. 14, 1921.
55 Harbord to Henry T. Allen, Jan. 12, 1921, Allen Papers, Box 16.
56 Baker to Pershing, Sept. 9, 1920, Pershing Papers, Box 6, Series 3, RG 316 NA.
57 *Cong. Rec.*, 66 Cong., 3 sess. (1920–1921), Vol. 60, Part 3, 2384. The Congressman was Daniel R. Anthony, Jr.
58 *Cong. Rec.*, 67 Cong., 1 sess. (1921), Vol. 61, Part 3, 2150.
59 Harold and Margaret Sprout, *Toward a New Order of Sea Power: American Naval Policy and the World Scene, 1918–22* (Princeton, N.J., 1943), 126, 143. *Cong. Rec.*, 66 Cong., 3 sess. (1920–1921), Vol. 60, Part 4, 4316–17. Senator Wadsworth compared the army requests with the actual appropriations.

	Requests	*Appropriations*
1919	$1,300,000,000	$900,000,000
1920	1,000,000,000	392,000,000
1921	690,000,000	346,000,000

The 1921 appropriation did not go into effect because of a presidential veto. *Cong. Rec.*, 67 Cong., 1 sess., Vol. 61, Part 2, 2142.

60 U.S. Congress, House of Representatives, Committee on Armed Services, *Hearings, The National Defense Program – Unification and Strategy,* 81 Cong., 1 sess. (1949), 604.

61 *C/S, 1921,* 19. *Cong. Rec.,* 66 Cong., 3 sess. (1920–1921), Vol. 60, Part 1, 1019; Part 2, 1533–37, 1856.

62 *Cong. Rec.,* 66 Cong., 3 sess. (1920–1921), Vol. 60, Part 3, 2684, 2719.

63 *C/S, 1921,* 25.

64 *Cong. Rec.,* 67 Cong., 1 sess. (1921), Part 3, 2150, 2184.

65 *Ibid.,* 2147.

66 *Ibid.,* 2185, 2728. Senator William H. King recalled the Victorian standard, while Percy Quin suggested the low figure.

67 *Ibid.,* 2251–53.

68 *Ibid.,* 2256.

69 *Ibid.,* 2732. Greene's remark on the "sitting down" army is from *Cong. Rec.,* 66 Cong., 3 sess. (1920–1921), Part 4, 4473.

70 Harbord to Pershing, June 26, 1921, Pershing Papers, Box 88.

71 Bascom N. Timmons interview, Nov. 18, 1958.

72 James H. Durbin letter to the author, July 24, 1964.

73 Harbord to Pershing, June 26, 1921, Pershing Papers, Box 88.

74 Hammond to March, Sept. 15, 1920, Legislation # 840, C/S File, RG 165 NA.

75 Gardner letter, March 19, 1958.

76 *C/S, 1921,* 20–21, 30–32, 67–68, 75–76.

77 March memo, Aug. 20, 1920, GSC (Details) # 538, C/S File, RG 165 NA. In connection with Nolan's appointment, it is interesting to note that Paul B. Malone, another AEF officer critical of March, also served on the War Department General Staff in this period. *Army List and Directory: April, 1920,* 151.

78 *Ibid.,* Aug., 1920, 65.

79 March to TAG, Sept. 5, 1920, Board of Officers # 168, C/S File, RG 165 NA.

80 March to Attorney General, Aug. 15, 1919, Claims # 280, C/S File, RG 165 NA. March signed this letter as Acting Secretary of War.

81 The quotation is from Baker to Vance C. McCormick, March 19, 1921, Baker Papers, Box 14. March gave his opinion in a letter to Baker, Aug. 27, 1926, Box 149. In addition to his support of an independent air service and his drive for more power, Crowell angered Baker by endorsing Harding in the 1920 campaign.

82 R. H. Hearn to Secretary of the General Staff and others, Oct. 18, 1920, Supply Division # 1403, C/S File, RG 165 NA.

83 Dewitt to Director of Supply Division, Nov. 4, 1920, Supply Division, # 1403; Wright memo with Baker approval, Dec. 1, 1920, Service of Supply # 1298, C/S File, RG 165 NA.

84 March memo, Aug. 20, 1920, GSC (Details) # 538, C/S File, RG 165 NA.

85 A. S. Fleming memo, Dec. 4, 1920, Supply Division # 1403, C/S File, RG 165 NA.

86 Mitchell to Arnold, Jan. 11, 1921, Mitchell Papers, Box 9.

87 Mitchell to March, Feb. 1, 1921; March buckslip, Feb. 10, 1921, Navy # 1040, C/S File, RG 165 NA.

88 Cost of project for bombing, March 28, 1921; Haan to March, March 23, 1921; Wright to March, June 22, 1921, Navy # 1040, C/S File, RG 165 NA.

89 March, *Nation at War*, 210.

90 *Ibid.*, 363–64. March to Joseph M. Swing, March 15, 1921, March Papers, Box 8.

91 March to Beverly Browne, March 15, 1921, March Papers, Box 8.

92 Baker to March, March 5, 1921, March Papers, Box 8.

93 March to Swing, March 15, 1921, March Papers, Box 8.

94 Baker to Hugh L. Scott, March 8, 1921, Baker Papers, Box 13.

95 James W. Wadsworth, "Reminiscences," Oral Research Office, Columbia University, 202. Weeks' career is sketched in Charles G. Washburn, *The Life of John W. Weeks* (Boston, 1928).

96 Baker to Scott, March 8, 1921, Baker Papers, Box 13.

97 March to Browne, March 15, 1921, March Papers, Box 8.

98 On March 12, 1921, the *Army and Navy Journal* (781) mentioned Harbord, Haan, and Charles P. Summerall as possible successors. The next month, the *Journal* (April 23, 1921, 933) added the names of Wright, David C. Shanks, and Clarence R. Edwards to the list of possibilities. Pershing wrote Harbord on Feb. 1, 1921, ". . . your name has been mentioned more frequently in this connection than any other." Pershing Papers, Box 88.

99 Clipping from *New York Times*, June 8, 1920, in Scrapbook, Vol 17, Pershing Papers, Box 397.

100 *New York Times*, 1920: Jan. 22, p. 21; and Jan. 23, pp. 4, 12. For Pershing's recognition of the possibility of becoming commanding general, see n. 103 below.

101 Otto L. Nelson, Jr., *National Security and the General Staff* (Washington, D.C., 1946), 284–85.

102 Pershing's recommendations are in the Folder "Officers – Recommendations 1917–1920," Pershing Papers, Box 7, Series 3, RG 316 NA.

103 Pershing closed his headquarters on Aug. 31, 1920. Pershing to Baker, Aug. 2, 1920, # 323.31, TAGO, RG 94 NA. In a letter to Harbord on March 12, 1921, the General of the Armies discussed his future and recognized the possibility of returning to the pre-Root commanding general system: "As for myself, there is considerable talk, first of my being Chief of Staff, second, commanding general in fact, then, third, possibly Ambassador to France or England." Pershing Papers, Box 88.

104 Bliss to Pershing, March 17; Pershing to Bliss, March 22; Conner memo, March 22, 1920, Pershing Papers, Box 26. Conner expanded on his

views in his AWC Lecture on Nov. 4, 1920, and in his memo to Pershing, April 9, 1921, Pershing Papers, Box 52.

105 Pershing to Bliss, March 22, 1920, Box 26; and to Harbord, March 12, 1921, Pershing Papers, Box 88. In the letter to Bliss, Pershing agreed on the concept of a G.H.Q. but he added, "Just what powers should be given such a headquarters is a difficult question."

106 *Army and Navy Journal*, April 30, 1921, 957. For Weeks' announcement, see *ibid.*, April 23, 1921, 932–33. The *New York Times* also commented on the problem on April 23, 1921, 10.

107 Harbord to Pershing, March 20, 1921, Pershing Papers, Box 88.

108 Weeks made the announcement on May 13, to go into effect on July 1. *Army and Navy Journal*, May 14, 1921, 997.

109 Gardner to March, Jan. 11; Gardner to Haan, May 7, 1921, GSC (Details) # 538, C/S File, RG 165 NA.

110 March, AWC Lecture, April 20, 1933, 1. General Moseley wrote: "Harbord dealt with Pershing as the Commanding General of the Army, and with Mr. Baker [Weeks] as Secretary of War, but Harbord was really Chief of Staff." Memoir, II, 48, Moseley Papers, Box 1a.

111 L. D. Gasser memo, June 30, 1921, Correspondence, # 320, C/S File, RG 165 NA.

112 *Cong. Rec.*, 67 Cong., 1 sess. (1921), Vol. 61, Part 3, 2716, 2732–34, 2895, 2897; Part 4, 3238.

113 Wright to Pershing, June 23, 1921, Pershing Papers, Box 217. In this five-page letter, Wright made a comprehensive analysis of the situation for his friend.

114 Harbord to Pershing, May 24, 1921, Pershing Papers, Box 88. *New York Times*, May 15, 1921, II, 1. *Army and Navy Journal*, July 9, 1921, 1206. For a brief discussion of the future development of the G.H.Q., see Ray S. Cline, *Washington Command Post: The Operations Division* in *The War Department: United States Army in World War II* (Washington, D.C., 1951), 20–21, 31–34.

115 *Army and Navy Journal*, May 14, 1921, 997.

116 Weeks to March, June 16, 1921, March Papers, Box 8.

117 *New York Times*, Feb. 13, 1921, VII, 2.

118 *Ibid.*, June 20, 1921, 12.

119 *Army and Navy Journal*, June 18, 1921, 1133.

Chapter 17. Years of Retirement

1 March, AWC Lecture, April 6, 1934, 2.

2 *Ibid.*, 4. Weeks to Secretary of State, June 21, 1920, Chief of Staff # 278, C/S File, RG 165 NA.

3 *New York Times*, 1921: July 2, p. 4; July 20, p. 4. Henry T. Allen, *My Rhineland Journal* (Boston, 1923), 230.

4 Davis letters in *Jawbone*, August, 1958, and to the author, Aug. 23, 1958.

5 March, AWC Lecture, April 26, 1937, 10.

6 *Ibid.*, March to W. D. Puleston, Nov. 5, 1934, March Papers, Box 3.
7 March, AWC Lectures, April 16, 1932, 8–9, and April 20, 1933, 3. The last quotation is from the second lecture.
8 AWC Lectures, April 20, 1933, 3 and April 6, 1934, 7.
9 Davis letter, Aug. 23, 1958.
10 March, AWC Lectures, April 16, 1932, 9; April 20, 1933, 3; and April 6, 1934, 7. "A Visit to Hindenburg," March Papers, Box 23.
11 March to Weeks, Aug. 2, 1921, in March, AWC Lecture, April 6, 1934, 8.
12 AWC Lectures, April 6, 1934, 8, and April 20, 1933, 2–3.
13 The first and last quotations are from March, AWC Lecture, April 6, 1934, 6. The second and third quotations are from March, AWC Lecture, April 20, 1933, 4.
14 March apparently referred to this when he mentioned a "special mission" in a letter to Baker, July 16, 1932, March Papers, Box 1. Mrs. March, in her May 12, 1961, interview with the author, said that he was offered the post.
15 March, AWC Lecture, April 5, 1938, 3.
16 *New York Times*, 1921: Sept. 22, p. 19, and Oct. 15, p. 5. The quotation is from the last source. On Nov. 1, March retired from active service. *New York Times*, Nov. 1, 1921, 19.
17 *New York Times*, Dec. 9, 1926, 16. March, AWC Lecture, April 6, 1934, 5. Speech at Doubleday, Doran party, Oct. 11, 1932, March Papers, Box 1.
18 Peyton C. March, *The Nation At War* (Garden City, N.Y., 1932), 108–11. March to Weeks, June 1, and Aug. 26, 1922, March Papers, Box 1. Allen, *Rhineland Journal*, 536–42.
19 Harbord to Pershing, July 5, 1922, Pershing Papers, Box 88.
20 Speech at Doubleday, Doran party.
21 *New York Times*, Dec. 9, 1926, 16. Mrs. March interviews, May 12, and Aug. 28, 1961. Clipping from *Army and Navy Journal*, Sept. 1, 1923, in March folder, Association of Graduates, USMA.
22 *New York Times*, Dec. 9, 1926, 16.
23 Clippings in Scrapbook 1919–1928, March Papers. Mrs. March interview, Aug. 28, 1961.
24 John N. Wheeler, "They Never Tell All," *American Magazine*, CXII, No. 6 (Dec., 1931), 38.
25 March to Baker, Aug. 17, 1927, March Papers, Box 22.
26 Baker to March, June 21, and March to Baker, June 22, 1921, March Papers, Box 8.
27 Baker to March, March 20, 1926, March Papers, Box 22.
28 Baker to March, Sept. 7, 1927, March Papers, Box 22.
29 *New York Times*, Oct. 21, 1927, 9.
30 *Ibid.*, July 1, 1928, V, 1–2.
31 The draft memoir is in the March Papers, Box 25.
32 March to Baker, July 17, 1928, Baker Papers, Box 150.

33 The Wood article was syndicated and appeared on Dec. 14, 1930, in the *New York World*, among others.
34 Wheeler, "They Never Tell All," 37–38.
35 Unpublished memoir, Epilogue, 3, Pershing Papers, Box 379. Frederick Palmer, *Newton D. Baker: America at War*, 2 vols. (New York, 1931), I, v–vii.
36 March to Baker, Jan. 22 and 30, 1930, Baker Papers, Box 150.
37 March to Baker, Nov. 2, 1931, March Papers, Box 1.
38 Baker to March, March 1, 1931, March Papers, Box 23.
39 March to Baker, March 4, 1931, March Papers, Box 23.
40 *Ibid.*
41 March to Russell Doubleday, Dec. 3, and to Baker, Oct. 23, 1931, March Papers, Box 1.
42 March to John N. Wheeler, Dec. 10, 1931, March Papers, Box 1.
43 March to Baker, Oct. 23, 1931.
44 Gordon Dorrance to March, July 7, 1927, and George Shively to March, Feb. 3, 1929; Cass Canfield to March, Nov. 28, 1931; Russell Doubleday to March, March 24, 1933, March Papers, Boxes 22, 23, and 2.
45 George R. Goethals to March, Feb. 25, March 5, and March 12, 1931; March to Hugh S. Johnson, Oct. 22, 1931, March Papers, Boxes 23 and 1. March, *Nation at War*, 259–60.
46 March to Russell Doubleday, Sept. 9, 1932, and Doubleday to March, April 28, 1932, March Papers, Box 1.
47 March to Baker, June 13, 1932, March Papers, Box 1.
48 Clippings in Scrapbook, 1932, March Papers. March to Mark S. Watson, Sept. 22, 1932, March Papers, Box 1.
49 March to Watson, Sept. 22, 1932; Mrs. March interview, May 12, 1961.
50 Advertising flyer, March Papers, Scrapbook, 1932. This announced September 21 as the publication date and $3 as the price.
51 S. T. Williamson in the *New York Times*, Sept. 25, 1932, V, 3, 25.
52 B. H. Liddell Hart, "Pershing and His Critics," *Current History* (Nov., 1932), 135–40.
53 Baker to March, Oct. 3, 7, 12, 17, 22, and 26, 1932, March Papers, Box 23.
54 Baker to March, Oct. 3, 1932.
55 March's reference to the "Chaumont crowd" is in his letter to Baker, April 10, 1933, March Papers, Box 2. The quotation is identical in both Pershing to Conner and to Marshall, Nov. 30, 1931, Pershing Papers, Boxes 52 and 124.
56 Harbord to Pershing, Sept. 7, and Pershing to Harbord, Sept. 24, 1932, Pershing Papers, Box 88. Harbord to Newton D. Baker, May 11, 1934, Baker Papers, Box 113.
57 *New York Times*, 1932: Oct. 9, VIII, 4–5; Oct. 23, II, 6; Dec. 11, IV, 2.
58 Pershing to Harbord, Dec. 5, 1932, Pershing Papers, Box 88. Baker to Harbord, May 14, 1934, Baker Papers, Box 113.
59 Harbord to Baker, May 11, 1934, Baker Papers, Box 113.

60 Baker to Harbord, May 14, 1934, Baker Papers, Box 113.
61 Baker to Harbord, Sept. 27, and Oct. 4, 1934, Baker Papers, Box 113.
62 Root to Harbord, Dec. 3, 1934 (photostat); Harbord to Baker, Dec. 10, 1934; Baker to Harbord, Dec. 14, 1934, Baker Papers, Box 113.
63 Harbord to Baker, Dec. 31, 1934, Baker Papers, Box 113. The footnote appears on pages 110–11 in James G. Harbord, *The American Army in France: 1917–1919* (Boston, 1936). The only revisions of the text Baker sent Harbord are "Major General Henry W. Halleck" for "General Halleck," and "principle" for "plan" in the last sentence.
64 Baker to Harbord, Feb. 8, 1935, Baker Papers, Box 113.
65 *Ibid.*
66 Baker to March, Oct. 17, 1932; April 4, 1933; and March 12, 1936, March Papers, Box 23. Baker to Pershing, Dec. 22, 1930, Pershing Papers, Box 16. C. H. Cramer, *Newton D. Baker: A Biography* (Cleveland, Ohio, 1961), 165–66.
67 March to Julian M. Cabell, Aug. 11, 1932, March Papers, Box 1.
68 March, "Mr. Astor Outfits the Army," *Saturday Evening Post*, CCXXXI, No. 3 (July 19, 1958), 24–25, 53, 55.
69 *Yale Review*, XXIII (Sept., 1933), 78–87.
70 The lectures are cited in the bibliography.
71 Watson letter to the author, April 1, 1958.
72 March to Alden March, Dec. 11, 1931, March Papers, Box 1. In 1932, March denied and objected strongly to some material about his social life that he considered offensive, in Robert S. Allen and Drew Pearson, *More Merry-Go-Round* (New York, 1932). The publisher promptly agreed to delete the passage. March to Baker, Sept. 23, 1932, and T. R. Smith to March, Oct. 7, 1932, March Papers, Box 23.
73 March, AWC Lecture, April 26, 1937, 9.
74 *Ibid.*
75 *Ibid.*, April 5, 1938, 2–3.
76 *Ibid.*, April 6, 1934, 16–17.
77 Wadsworth to John M. Palmer, March 8, 1940, Palmer Papers, Holley Microfilm.
78 March to Baker, July 17, 1928, Baker Papers, Box 150.
79 March to Florence Stratton, April 10, 1934; and to Alden March, Jan. 14, 1932, March Papers, Boxes 3 and 1. Mrs. Roosevelt in a letter to the author, Feb. 28, 1957, said that her husband admired General March.
80 Roosevelt to March, Sept. 23, 1932, March Papers, Box 23.
81 March to Roosevelt, Oct. 31, 1932, March Papers, Box 1.
82 March to John Millikin, March 23, 1933, March Papers, Box 2.
83 March to Julian M. Cabell, June 14, 1935; March to Alden March, May 17, 1933, March Papers, Box 2.
84 March to Hodges, March 18, 1930, March Papers, Box 22.
85 MacArthur interview. See also MacArthur to March, Nov. 22, 1930, March Papers, Box 22.

86 Mrs. March interview, May 12, 1961. *New York Times*, Dec. 28, 1934, 17.

87 I base my comments on his library on an examination of the books while they were temporarily located in the Manuscripts Division of the Library of Congress. They are now in the library of Lafayette College. Freeman to March, Nov. 27, 1935, located in the set.

88 March to Baker, Oct. 14, 1932, March Papers, Box 1.

89 March to John A. Heydler, March 19; to William Harridge, April 6, 1932, March Papers, Box 1. Mrs. March interview, March 15, 1957.

90 Mrs. March interview, March 15, 1917; Mrs. Thomas interview.

91 Beacham interview, March 29, 1957.

92 *Lafayette*, LX, No. 55 (June 8, 1934). *New York Times*, June 9, 1934, 8.

93 *New York Times*, June 27, 1930, 20, 23.

94 March to Eli A. Helmick, July 3, 1934, March Papers, Box 3.

95 "The Association of the Graduates of the United States Military Academy, Sixty-ninth Annual Report," June 13, 1938, 46–48.

96 Mrs. March interview, Aug. 28, 1961. At first they lived on Seventeenth Street, Northwest, March to Russell Doubleday, Dec. 3, 1931; then they rented a house on California Avenue from John Gulick, who had worked with John M. Palmer in the reorganization struggle, Gulick to March, June 21, 1934, March Papers, Boxes 1 and 2. For the Florida sojourn, see *New York Times*, Dec. 27, 1939, 14.

97 Clipping from *Miami Herald*, Jan. 12, 1938, March Papers, Scrapbook 1932–1938.

98 March, AWC Lecture, April 5, 1938, 3.

99 Marshall interview, Dec. 7, 1956, by Forrest C. Pogue. General Marshall added that March's great weakness was that he antagonized people. I am indebted to Dr. Pogue and the G. C. Marshall Research Foundation for this information.

100 Ward to March, June 22, 1949, March Papers, Box 24.

101 Clipping of *Washington Times-Herald*, Dec. 6, 1939, March Papers, Scrapbook 1939–1948. Earlier in the decade, March expressed his approval of the Baker Board's decision against a greater autonomy for the Air Corps. March to Mrs. March, July 24, 1934, March Papers, Box 3.

102 Watson letter.

103 *Life*, XVI, No. 2 (Jan. 10, 1944), 32.

104 *Time*, XLIII, No. 2 (Jan. 10, 1944), 19.

105 Clipping of Washington *Evening Star*, Jan. 11, 1944, March Papers, Scrapbook 1939–1948.

106 Clippings in Scrapbook 1939–1948, March Papers. *New York Times*, Dec. 28, 1944, 3.

107 Major General John Millikin served in Europe while Major General Joseph M. Swing served in the Pacific. Swing later became a lieutenant general.

108 Watson letter.

109 Timmons interview. The General's hearty appetite is another indication

of his condition in his advanced years. According to Mrs. March, he regularly ate a large breakfast – two three-minute eggs, fruit, one piece of toast with marmalade, one cup of coffee, and eight pieces of bacon. At lunch, he would have only a glass of milk. For dinner, he would eat meat and two vegetables. Sometimes, he would walk a couple of blocks to a bar to enjoy a martini. Mrs. March interviews, May 12, and Aug. 28, 1961.

110 Hinman interview, March 29, 1957. McMaster interview, Nov. 7, 1958.

111 His youngest child, Lewis, died within a week of his twenty-fourth birthday. March Questionnaire, Feb. 17, 1930, Association of Graduates, USMA. His daughter, Vivian, died at thirty-three. March to Baker, Jan. 20, 1933, March Papers, Box 2.

112 *New York Times,* Dec. 4, 1952, 35. John March was Professor Emeritus of Psychology at Union College, Schenectady, New York.

113 D. A. Hatch (editor), *Biographical Register of the Men of Lafayette: 1832–1948* (Easton, Pa., 1948), 70, 101, 105, 113, 117.

114 *New York Times,* Dec. 28, 1947, I, 14. La Guardia to March, Dec. 30, 1946, March Papers, Box 24.

115 Mrs. March interviews, March 15, 1957, and May 12, 1961. Hinman interview, March 20, 1957.

116 *New York Times,* Dec. 28, 1951, 23. The *Times* magazine carried a feature article on the General on Jan. 13, 1952, VI, 14.

117 Senator Saltonstall and Congressman Dewey Short backed the measure (Senate Concurrent Resolution # 43 and House Concurrent Resolution # 170). *Cong. Rec.,* 83 Cong., 1 sess. (1953), Vol. 99, Part 7, 9309, 9621. The Saltonstall quotation is from the last page. *Ibid.,* 9852; Part 8, 10422–23. The last quotation is from the resolution as it appeared in the *New York Times,* July 22, 1953, 9.

118 *New York Times,* Aug. 1, 1953, 13. White House Memo, undated, March Papers, Box 24. March referred to Major Eisenhower in a letter to Baker, Oct. 19, 1932, March Papers, Box 1.

119 Eisenhower letter to the author, May 28, 1963.

120 Mrs. March interview, March 15, 1957. *New York Times,* Aug. 1, 1953, 13.

121 Mrs. March to Charles N. Branham, Aug. 19, 1953, Association of Graduates, USMA.

122 Browne interview, June 10, 1956. Hinman interview, March 20, 1957. Mrs. March told me about the Pentagon visit in the interview on Aug. 28, 1961.

123 Browne interview, June 10, 1956.

124 *New York Times,* Dec. 27, 1953, 14.

125 *Ibid.,* Feb. 6, 1954, 3.

126 Mrs. March interviews, March 15, 1957, and May 12, 1961. Pfc. Wilbur M. Hargreaves, one of the orderlies, gave a brief description of the General's last days and a warm tribute in a letter to Mrs. March, *Cong. Rec.,* 84 Cong., 1 sess. (1955), Vol. 101, Part 10 D, A 3205.

127 Washington *Post*, April 14, 1955, 22.

128 Eisenhower to Mrs. March, April 14, 1955, *Cong. Rec.*, 1 sess. (1955), Vol. 101, Part 10 F, A 6230.

129 *Ibid.*, Part 10 C, A 2613. DAGO # 26, April 14, 1955.

130 *Cong. Rec.*, 84 Cong., 1 sess. (1955), Vol. 101, Part 10 C, A 2613; Part 10 D, A 3205. Baruch to Joseph M. Swing, June 11, 1955 (photostat), in March Papers (a copy was in Mrs. March's possession).

131 *Christian Science Monitor*, April 15, 1955, 18.

132 Mrs. March interview, March 15, 1957. *New York Times*, April 19, 1955, 31.

133 The terms "military manager" and "heroic leader" are from Morris Janowitz, *The Professional Soldier: A Social and Political Portrait* (Glencoe, Ill., 1960).

134 March, AWC Lecture, April 26, 1937, 9.

135 Hanson E. Ely interview, June 7, 1956.

136 Watson letter.

137 MacArthur interview.

BIBLIOGRAPHY

Manuscript Collections

Library of Congress, Washington, D.C.
- Henry T. Allen Papers.
- Newton D. Baker Papers.
- Tasker H. Bliss Papers.
- Henry Breckinridge Papers.
- Robert L. Bullard Papers.
- Josephus Daniels Papers.
- George W. Goethals Papers.
- James G. Harbord Papers.
- Robert Lansing Papers.
- Breckinridge Long Papers.
- Peyton C. March Papers.
- William Mitchell Papers.
- George Van Horn Moseley Papers.
- John M. Palmer Papers (Including some microfilm furnished by Professor I. B. Holley).
- John J. Pershing Papers.
- Hugh L. Scott Papers.
- James W. Wadsworth Papers.
- Woodrow Wilson Papers.
- Leonard Wood Papers.

Oral History Research Office, Columbia University, New York
- Boris A. Bakhmeteff Reminiscences.
- DeWitt Clinton Poole Reminiscences.
- Gerard Swope Reminiscences.
- James W. Wadsworth Reminiscences.

United States Military Academy Library and Archives, West Point, New York
- U.S.M.A. Post Order Books: 1884–1888.
- U.S. Corps of Cadets Order Books: 1884–1888.
- Peyton C. March Record Card.
- School History of Candidates.
- Library Circulation Records: 1884–1888.
- W. N. P. Darrow Scrapbook.
- Charles D. Rhodes, "Intimate Letters of a West Point Cadet" (Mimeographed).

Association of Graduates Office, U.S.M.A., West Point, New York
- Peyton C. March File.

Van Wickle Library, Lafayette College, Easton, Pennsylvania
- W. A. Cattell Scrapbook in the Rare Book Collection.

Alumni Office, Lafayette College, Easton, Pennsylvania
Peyton C. March File.
Public Library, Easton, Pennsylvania
"Easton and the Spanish-American War" Scrapbook.
Sterling Memorial Library, Yale University, New Haven, Connecticut
Gordon Auchincloss Papers.
Edward M. House Papers.
Frank Polk Papers.
Sir William Wiseman Papers.
Newberry Library, Chicago, Illinois
William V. Judson Papers.
John T. McCutcheon Papers.
Western Historical Manuscripts Collection, University of Missouri, Columbia, Missouri
Enoch H. Crowder Papers.
George Peek Papers.
Cossitt Library, Memphis, Tennessee
Kenneth D. McKellar Papers.
Northwestern University Library, Evanston, Illinois
Charles G. Dawes Papers.
National Archives Library, Washington, D.C.
Charles D. Rhodes, "Diary Notes of a Soldier."
State Historical Society of Wisconsin Library, Madison, Wisconsin
William G. Haan Papers.
Margaret I. King Library, University of Kentucky, Lexington, Kentucky
Frederick L. Hardenbrook Scrapbook (Microfilm).

Records in the National Archives

Record Group 94
Peyton C. March Appointment, Commission, and Promotion File.
Personal Reports, Peyton C. March File.
United States Military Academy Register, 1884–1885.
Organization Returns.
Nineteenth Battery, Field Artillery.
Third Artillery Regiment.
Fifth Artillery Regiment.
Sixth Field Artillery Regiment.
Eighth Field Artillery Regiment.
Second Division, Department of Pacific and Eighth Army Corps.
Cablegrams: Work Copies of A cables.
Secretary of War Correspondence File.
Office of The Adjutant General – Central File. (This is the great official record file of the army. The large bulk of documents are filed merely by number; however, I shall list three sub-groups which I used in addition to many other documents in the numerical file.)
European Expedition File.

Philippine Insurrection File.
Brigadier General Wilds P. Richardson monograph on the North Russia Expedition.
Record Group 98
Records of United States Army Commands.
Fort Leavenworth Army Service Schools.
Record Group 120
American Expeditionary Force Adjutant General's File.
Report File of the Commander-in-Chief.
American Expeditionary Force, General Headquarters.
G-3 Report File.
Special Orders.
Supreme War Council File.
War Department Cable Section File.
War Department to American Expeditionary Forces (A).
American Expeditionary Force to War Department (P).
War Department to Commanding General, Services of Supply (X).
Commanding General, Services of Supply to War Department (S).
War Department to General Tasker H. Bliss.
General Tasker H. Bliss to War Department.
War Department to Edward R. Stettinius.
Edward R. Stettinius to War Department.
War Department to American Expeditionary Force in Siberia (AV).
American Expeditionary Force in Siberia to War Department (V).
War Department to Colonel G. W. Winterburn.
Colonel G. W. Winterburn to War Department.
War Department to Brigadier General Frank T. Hines.
Brigadier General Frank T. Hines to War Department.
War Department to Military Attaché in London.
Military Attaché in London to War Department.
War Department Historical File.
American Forces in Siberia 21–19–3.
General Staff History.
History of the Bureau of Military Aeronautics 7–62.1.
Papers Relating to the Formation of the Tank Corps 7–61.13.
Resumé of the Day's Work – General Staff.
World War I Organization Records.
American Expeditionary Force.
First Field Artillery Brigade, First Division Historical File.
First Division Document File.
First Division Historical File.
First Army Artillery Correspondence File.
American Expeditionary Force in Siberia.
Cables of San Francisco Quartermaster Depot to American Expeditionary Force in Siberia.

Cables of American Expeditionary Force in Siberia to San Francisco Quartermaster Depot.
General and Special Orders.
Historical File 4.7–11.4.
Telegrams of War Department to Major General William S. Graves.
Telegrams of Major General William S. Graves to War Department.
American Expeditionary Force in North Russia.
History of the American Forces in Germany: July 3, 1919, to December 31, 1921, prepared by the G-2, American Forces in Germany.
Record Group 165
Army War College File.
Chief of Staff Correspondence File.
General Staff: Purchase, Storage, and Traffic Division.
Brigadier General Hugh S. Johnson File.
War Plans Division File.
Record Group 168
National Guard Bureau File.
Fort Riley Maneuvers.
Record Group 177
Records of Chief of Arms.
Artillery School, Fort Monroe, Virginia.
Record Group 316
John J. Pershing Personal Papers.

Interviews

Baruch, Bernard M. New York, November 12, 1958.
Beacham, Brigadier General Joseph W. Washington, D.C., March 29, and August 4, 1957.
Bishop, Major General Percy P. Washington, D.C., April 29, 1957.
Blakely, Brigadier General Charles S. Louisville, Kentucky, May 26, 1959.
Breckinridge, Colonel Henry. New York, November 12, 1958.
Browne, Brigadier General Beverly F. Front Royal, Virginia, June 10, 1956; Washington, D.C., October 29, 1958.
Bryden, Major General William. Washington, D.C., November 12, 1960.
Campbell, Brigadier General Archibald. Alexandria, Virginia, August 8, 1957.
Cocheu, Colonel George W. Washington, D.C., August 7, 1957; August 25, 1961 (telephone).
Cosby, Colonel Spencer. Washington, D.C., June 7, 1956.
Curtin, Colonel Ralph A. Washington, D.C., November 14, 1958; November 10, 1960.
Early, Colonel Clifford C. Atlanta, Georgia, November 13, 1959.
Ely, Major General Hanson E. Washington, D.C., June 7, 1956.
Foulois, Major General Benjamin D. Andrews Air Force Base, Maryland, November 7, 1960.
Frank, Henry C. Memphis, Tennessee, May 8, 1960.
Grant, Major General U. S., III. Washington, D.C., November 20, 1958.

Graves, Sidney C. Washington, D.C., August 10 (telephone), and August 29, 1961.
Hains, Colonel John P. Washington, D.C., August 6, 1957.
Harts, Brigadier General William W. Washington, D.C., March 29, 1957.
Hines, Brigadier General Frank T. Washington, D.C., August 9, 1957.
Hinman, Colonel George W. Washington, D.C., March 20 and 29, 1957; August 28, 1961.
Langhorne, Colonel George T. Chicago, Illinois, January 30, 1960.
Lear, General Ben. Memphis, Tennessee, May 16, 1958.
MacArthur, General of the Army Douglas. New York, December 12, 1960.
McBride, Lieutenant General Horace L. Washington, D.C., August 31, 1961.
McMaster, Colonel Richard H. Washington, D.C., November 7, 1958.
March, Miss Mildred. Schenectady, New York, February 7, 1959 (interviewed by Mrs. Katherine Harelson Shaw).
March, Mrs. Peyton C. Washington, D.C., March 15, 1957; May 12, July 27, and August 28, 1961.
Marshall, Brigadier General Richard C. Washington, D.C., November 10, 1960.
Meriwether, Lee. Memphis, Tennessee, January 16, 1958.
Moseley, Major General George Van Horn. Atlanta, Georgia, November 12 and 13, 1959; Washington, D.C., September 14, 1960.
Palmer, Colonel Frederick. Charlottesville, Virginia, June 4, 1956.
Powell, Jesse. Washington, D.C., August 6, 1957.
Sorley, Colonel Lewis S. Washington, D.C., August 5, 1957.
Spaulding, Colonel Thomas M. Washington, D.C., November 9, 1960.
Swope, Honorable King. Lexington, Kentucky, June 16, 1960.
Thomas, Mrs. Stanley J. Bethlehem, Pennsylvania, April 24, 1962.
Timmons, Bascom N. Washington, D.C., November 18, 1958.
Todd, Major General Henry D. Washington, D.C., August 8, 1956.
Totten, Colonel James. Washington, D.C., November 19, 1958.
Utley, Buford C. Memphis, Tennessee, May 12, 1960.
Williams, Major General Clarence C. Woodstock, Virginia, June 5, 1956.
Wiseman, Sir William. New York, December 14, 1960.
Wofford, Miss Azile. Lexington, December 18, 1958.
Wood, Brigadier General Robert E. Chicago, Illinois, January 29, 1960.

Correspondence

Albright, Horace M. July 1, 1963.
Andrews, Brigadier General Avery D. September 23, and October 24, 1955.
Baruch, Bernard M. February 7, 1956; December 3, 1958.
Bishop, Major General Percy P. March 27, and April 14, 1956.
Breckinridge, Colonel Henry. May 3, 1959.
Browne, Brigadier General Beverly F. April 8, May 3, and undated memo, 1956; April 15, July 26, 1957; March 19, 1958; February 4, February 26, and March 4, 1959.
Byrnes, Honorable James F. April 16, 1959.

Colson, L. W. April 21, 1958.
Connally, Honorable Tom. March 18, 1958.
Cosby, Colonel Spencer. February 12, 1956.
Danford, Major General Robert M. April 23, 1959.
Davis, Colonel Edward. August 23, and undated memo, 1958.
Davis, Major General William C. February, 1956.
Durbin, James H. March 18, 1957, and July 24, 1964.
Early, Colonel Clifford C. June 3, 1959.
Eichelberger, General Robert L. April 27, 1959.
Eisenhower, General of the Army Dwight D. May 28, 1963.
Ely, Major General Hanson E. December 9, 1955.
Ferguson, Colonel Henry T. February 14, 1956.
Fiske, Major General Harold B. February 25, 1957.
Fosdick, Raymond B. March 26, 1957.
Gardner, Major General Fulton Q. C. March 19, and April 10, 1958; June 14, 1961.
Glasgow, Brigadier General William J. March 1, 1956.
Glassford, Brigadier General Pelham D. May 4, 1959.
Goethals, Colonel George R. February 19, 1957.
Grant, Major General U. S., III. March 19, 1956; January 5, 1959.
Harts, Brigadier General William W. February 4, 1956.
Hayden, Senator Carl. March 3, 1958.
Hayden, Jay G. April 28, 1958.
Hines, Brigadier General Frank T. June 9, 1958.
Hoover, Honorable Herbert. October 29, 1957; November 29, 1960.
Hoyle, Major General R. E. D. April 9, 1957; June 15, 1959.
Jervey, Mrs. Henry. July 12, 1962.
Jones, Colonel Clifford. August 25, 1958.
Kilbourne, Lieutenant General Charles E. February 11, 1957.
Lawrence, David. March 6, 1957.
Lee, Lieutenant General John C. H. February 22, 1957.
MacArthur, General of the Army Douglas. November 28, 1960.
McBride, Lieutenant General Horace L. March 30, 1961.
McKinstry, Brigadier General Charles H. March 5, 1957.
McMaster, Colonel Richard H. December 6, 1958.
March, Brigadier General Francis A, III. March 23, 1962.
Moseley, Major General George Van Horn. April 16, and 30, 1956; October 31, 1957; October 3, 1958; July 8, 1960.
Neal, Colonel Carroll W. April 6, 1961.
Palmer, Colonel Frederick. March 22, 1956.
Parker, Major General Cortlandt. April 12, 1957.
Pennell, Major General Ralph McT. March 10, 1957.
Reckord, Lieutenant General Milton A. February 26, 1963.
Riley, Colonel James W. March 13, 1957.
Roosevelt, Mrs. Eleanor. February 28, 1957.
Rowell, Colonel Melvin W. February 6, 1956.

Schoeffel, Lieutenant Colonel Francis H. February, 1956.
Shotwell, James T. May 13, 1959.
Sorley, Colonel Lewis S. February 9, 1956.
Thomas, Mrs. Stanley J. April 7, 1962.
Swope, Herbert Bayard. May 13, 1958.
Timmons, Bascom N. December 1, 1958.
Todd, Major General Henry D. March 3, 1956.
Watson, Mark S. April 1, 1958.
Weygand, General Maxime. February 28, 1958.
Williams, Major General Clarence C. May 21, 1956.
Wood, Brigadier General Robert E. March 19, 1956; October 15, 1962.
Wyllie, Brigadier General Robert E. February 23, March 31, 1956; July 29, 1957.

Miscellaneous Unpublished Material

George B. Duncan, "Reminiscences of the World War." (Typed MS in possession of Henry T. Duncan, Lexington, Kentucky).
Franklin, Benjamin G. "The Military Policy of the United States, 1918–33: A Study of the Influence of World War I on Army Organization and Control." (Unpublished Ph.D. dissertation, University of California, 1943).
Peyton C. March, Army War College Lectures, 1905; January 15, 1930; April 16, 1932; April 20, 1933; April 6, 1934; April 26, 1937; and April 5, 1938. (Typed and Mimeographed MSS in the author's possession).

Public Documents

Annual Reports of the Boards of Visitors to the United States Military Academy: 1885, 1886, 1887, 1888.
Annual Reports of the Chief of Staff: 1918, 1919, 1920, 1921.
Annual Reports of the Secretary of War: 1899, 1900, 1901, 1902, 1903, 1905.
Annual Reports of the War Department: 1898, 1899, 1900, 1901, 1913, 1916, 1918, 1919, 1920, 1921.
Army List and Directory: April, 1920.
Biographical Directory of the American Congress: 1774–1949, 1950.
Carter, William H. *Creation of the American General Staff: Personal Narrative of the General Staff System of the American Army.* (68 Congress, 1 session, Senate Document # 119, 1924).
Congressional Directories, 63 Congress, 2 session (1913); 66 Congress, 1 session (1919).
Congressional Records, 65 Congress, 2 (1918) and 3 sessions (1918–1919); 66 Congress, 1 (1919), 2 (1919–1920), and 3 sessions (1920–1921); 67 Congress, 1 session (1921); 71 Congress, 2 session (1929–1930); 83 Congress, 1 session (1953); and 84 Congress, 1 session (1955).
Epitome of the Russo-Japanese War (prepared by the Second Division, General Staff), 1907.
General Orders and Bulletins: War Department, 1918.

Hearings: U. S. Congress.

Senate, Committee on the Philippines, *Hearings on Affairs in the Philippine Islands*, 57 Congress, 1 session (1902).

House of Representatives, Committee on Military Affairs, *Hearings on Army Reorganization*, 65 Congress, 3 session (1919).

Senate, Subcommittee of the Committee on Military Affairs, *Hearings on Army Appropriation Bill*, 66 Congress, 1 session (1919).

House of Representatives, Committee on Military Affairs, *Hearings on the Army Appropriation Bill*, 66 Congress, 1 session (1919).

Senate, Subcommittee of the Committee on Military Affairs, *Hearings on Reorganization of the Army*, 66 Congress, 1 and 2 sessions (1919).

House of Representatives, Committee on Military Affairs, *Hearings on Army Reorganization*, 66 Congress, 1 and 2 sessions (1919–1920).

House of Representatives, Select Committee on Expenditures in the War Department, *Hearings*, 66 Congress, 1 and 2 sessions (1920).

House of Representatives, Subcommittee of the Committee on Military Affairs, *Hearings on a United Air Service*, 66 Congress, 2 session (1919).

House of Representatives, Committee on Armed Services, *Hearings, The National Defense Program – Unification and Strategy*, 81 Congress, 1 session (1949).

Lee, Edward B., Jr. *Politics of Our Military National Defense.* (76 Congress, 3 session, Senate Document # 274, Washington, 1940).

Official Army Registers: 1889, 1895, 1899, 1904, 1905, 1913, 1918, 1921, 1924, 1925.

Official Register of the Officers and Cadets of the U. S. Military Academy, West Point, New York: 1885, 1886, 1887, 1888.

Order of Battle of the United States Land Forces in the World War: American Expeditionary Forces, Divisions. 1931.

Order of Battle of the United States Land Forces in the World War: American Expeditionary Forces, General Headquarters, Armies, Army Corps, Services of Supply, and Separate Forces. 1937.

Regulations for the Army of the United States: 1913. Corrected to April 15, 1917.

Regulations for the U. S. Military Academy at West Point, New York: 1883.

Report of the Commission appointed by the President to investigate the Conduct of the War Department in the War with Spain, 1900.

Reports of Military Observers Attached to the Armies in Manchuria During the Russo-Japanese War. 5 parts, 1906–1907.

Report of Major Peyton C. March, 6th Field Artillery, U.S.A., Chief Umpire Camp of Instruction and Maneuver, Fort Riley, 1908.

Second Report of the Provost Marshal General to the Secretary of War on the Operations of the Selective Service System to December 20, 1918.

State Department, Papers Relating to Foreign Relations of the United States, 1919: The Paris Peace Conference, Volumes III, XI, and XII, 1942.

———, Papers Relating to the Foreign Relations of the United States. Russia: 1919, 1937.

United States Army in the World War: 1917–1919 (prepared by the Historical Division, Department of the Army). 17 Vols., 1948.

Newspapers

Army and Navy Journal: Gazette of the Regular and Volunteer Forces.
Christian Science Monitor, April 15, 1955.
Easton Daily Express, June 6, 1884; September 9 and 12, 1911.
The Evening Star (Washington, D.C.).
Jawbone (monthly newspaper of the veterans of the Thirty-third Volunteer Infantry).
Lafayette College Journal.
The Lafayette.
New York Times.
Washington (D.C.) *Post.*

Books

Addresses Delivered At a Celebration in Honor of Professor Francis A. March, LLD, LHD at Lafayette College October 24, 1895. Easton, Pa., 1895.
Addresses to the Graduating Classes U.S.M.A. Volume 1 (1827–1897). Bound volume of pamphlets.
Aguinaldo, Emilio and Vincente A. Pacis. *A Second Look At America.* New York, 1957.
Alger, Russell A. *The Spanish American War.* New York, 1901.
Allen, Henry T. *My Rhineland Journal.* Boston, 1923.
Andrews, Avery D. *My Friend and Classmate John J. Pershing: With Notes From My War Diary.* Harrisburg, Pa., 1939.
Arnold, Henry H. *Global Mission.* New York, 1949.
Arthur, Robert. *Coast Artillery School: 1824–1927.* Fort Monroe, Va., 1928.
Association of the Graduates of the United States Military Academy. Sixty-Ninth Annual Report. Newburgh, New York, 1938.
Association of the Graduates of the United States Military Academy Annual Report. West Point, New York, 1940.
Ayres, Leonard P. *The War With Germany: A Statistical Summary.* Washington, D.C., 1919.
Baclagon, Uldarico S. *Philippine Campaigns.* Manila, 1952.
Bailey, Thomas A. *Wilson and the Peacemakers.* New York, 1947.
Baker, Ray Stannard. *Armistice: March 1–November 11, 1918.* Vol. VIII of *Woodrow Wilson: Life and Letters.* New York, 1939.
———, and William E. Dodd, editors. *Public Letters of Woodrow Wilson: War and Peace.* 2 Vols., New York, 1927.
Baruch, Bernard. *Baruch: The Public Years.* New York, 1960.
Beaverbrook, Lord. *Men and Power, 1917–18.* New York, 1956.
Bernardo, C. Joseph and Eugene H. Bacon. *American Military Policy: Its Development Since 1775.* Harrisburg, Pa., 1955.
Bishop, Joseph B. and Farnham Bishop. *Goethals — Genius of the Panama Canal: A Biography.* New York, 1930.

Blount, James H. *The American Occupation of the Philippines: 1898–1912.* New York, 1912.

Broun, Heywood. *The A.E.F.: With General Pershing and the American Forces.* New York, 1918.

Bullard, Robert L. *Fighting Generals: Illustrated Biographical Sketches of Seven Major Generals in World War I.* Ann Arbor, Mich., 1944.

———. *Personalities and Reminiscences of the War.* Garden City, N.Y., 1925.

Burtis, Mary E. *Moncure Conway: 1832–1907.* New Brunswick, N.J., 1952.

Cameron, W. J. *Washington in War Times.* Detroit, 1918.

Churchill, Winston S. *The Aftermath.* New York, 1929.

Clarkson, Grosvenor B. *Industrial America in the World War: The Strategy Behind the Line, 1917–1918.* Boston, 1923.

Clemenceau, Georges. *Grandeur and Misery of Victory.* New York, 1930.

Clendenen, Clarence C. *The United States and Pancho Villa: A Study in Unconventional Diplomacy.* Ithaca, N.Y., 1961.

Cline, Ray S. *Washington Command Post: The Operations Division in The War Department: United States Army in World War II.* General Editor, Kent R. Greenfield. Washington, D.C., 1951.

Coffin, Selden J. *Record of the Men of Lafayette: Brief Biographical Sketches of The Alumni of Lafayette College From its organization to the present time.* Easton, Pa., 1879.

Coit, Margaret L. *Mr. Baruch.* Boston, 1957.

Conner, Virginia. *What Father Forbade.* Philadelphia, 1951.

Conway, Moncure D. *Autobiography: Memoirs And Experiences.* 2 Vols., Boston, 1904.

Cramer, C. H. *Newton D. Baker: A Biography.* Cleveland, Ohio, 1961.

Creel, George. *The War, The World and Wilson.* New York, 1920.

Crowder, Enoch H. *The Spirit of Selective Service.* New York, 1920.

Crowell, Benedict and R. F. Wilson. *How America Went to War.* 6 Vols., New Haven, 1921.

Crozier, Emmet. *American Reporters on the Western Front, 1914–1918.* New York, 1959.

Crozier, William. *Ordnance and the World War: A Contribution to the History of American Preparedness.* New York, 1920.

Cudahy, John [A Chronicler]. *Archangel: The American War With Russia.* Chicago, 1924.

Cullum, George W. *Biographical Register of the Officers and Graduates of the U.S. Military Academy at West Point, New York since its establishment in 1802.* Vol. VI, Edited by Wirt Robinson. Saginaw, Mich., 1920.

Davis, Oscar King. *Our Conquests in the Pacific.* New York, 1898.

Dawes, Charles G. *A Journal of the Great War.* 2 Vols., Boston, 1921.

Dewey, George. *Autobiography.* New York, 1913.

Dickinson, John. *The Building of An Army. A Detailed Account of Legislation Administration and Opinion In the United States, 1915–1920.* New York, 1922.

Dupuy, Ernest R. *Where They Have Trod: The West Point Tradition in American Life*. New York, 1940.

Ekirch, Arthur A. *The Civilian and the Military*. New York, 1956.

Foch, Ferdinand. *The Memoirs of Ferdinand Foch*. Translated by T. Bentley Mott. Garden City, N.Y., 1931.

Forman, Sidney. *West Point: A History of United States Military Academy*. New York, 1950.

Fosdick, Raymond B. *Chronicle of a Generation, An Autobiography*. New York, 1958.

Fuess, Claude M. *Stanley King of Amherst*. New York, 1955.

Ganoe, William A. *MacArthur Close-Up: Much Then and Some Now*. New York, 1962.

———. *The History of the United States Army*. New York, 1943.

Gibbons, Floyd. *And They Thought We Wouldn't Fight*. New York, 1918.

Gleaves, Albert. *A History of the Transport Service: Adventures and Experiences of United States Transports and Cruisers in the World War*. New York, 1921.

Graves, William S. *America's Siberian Adventure: 1918–1920*. New York, 1931.

Green, Constance McLaughlin, Harry C. Thomson, and Peter C. Roots. *The Ordnance Department: Planning Munitions for War in The Technical Services: United States Army in World War II*. General Editor, Kent R. Greenfield. Washington, D.C., 1955.

Griscom, Lloyd C. *Diplomatically Speaking*. New York, 1940.

Hagedorn, Hermann. *Leonard Wood*. 2 Vols., New York, 1931.

Hagood, Johnson. *The Services of Supply: A Memoir of the Great War*. Boston, 1927.

Hallgren, Mauritz A. *The Tragic Fallacy: A Study of America's War Policies*. New York, 1937.

Hamilton, Sir Ian. *A Staff Officers Scrapbook During the Russo Japanese War*. London, 1906.

Hammond, Paul Y. *Organizing for Defense: The American Military Establishment in the Twentieth Century*. Princeton, N.J., 1961.

Hankey, Maurice. *The Supreme Command, 1914–18*. 2 Vols., London, 1961.

Harbord, James G. *Leaves from a War Diary*. New York, 1925.

———. *The American Army in France: 1917–1919*. Boston, 1936.

———. *The American Expeditionary Forces: Its Organization and Accomplishments*. Evanston, Ill., 1929.

Hatch, D. A., Editor. *Biographical Record of the Men of Lafayette, 1832–1948*. Easton, Pa., 1948.

Hayes, Ralph A. *Secretary Baker at the Front*. New York, 1918.

Hill, Jim Dan. *The Minute Man in Peace and War: A History of the National Guard*. Harrisburg, Pa., 1964.

History of the First Division during the World War: 1917–1918. Philadelphia, 1922.

Hittle, J. D. *The Military Staff: Its History and Development.* Harrisburg, Pa., 1949.

Hoffmann, Max. *The War of Lost Opportunities.* London, 1924.

Holley, I. B., Jr. *Ideas and Weapons.* New Haven, Conn., 1953.

Holliday, E. M. *The Ignorant Armies.* New York, 1960.

Holthusen, Henry F. *James W. Wadsworth, Jr.: A Biographical Sketch.* New York, 1926.

Hoover, Herbert. *The Ordeal of Woodrow Wilson.* New York, 1958.

Hunt, Frazier. *The Untold Story of Douglas MacArthur.* New York, 1954.

Huntington, Samuel P. *The Soldier and the State: The Theory and Politics of Civil-Military Relations.* Cambridge, Mass., 1957.

Hurley, Edward N. *The Bridge of Ships.* Philadelphia, 1927.

Janowitz, Morris. *The Professional Soldier: A Social and Political Portrait.* Glencoe, Ill., 1960.

Johnson, Hugh S. *The Blue Eagle from Egg to Earth.* New York, 1935.

Johnson, Thomas M. *Without Censor: New Light on Our Greatest World War Battles.* Indianapolis, 1928.

Johnson, Virginia M. *The Unregimented General: A Biography of Nelson A. Miles.* Boston, 1962.

Kennan, George F. *The Decision to Intervene.* Vol. II, in *Soviet-American Relations 1917–1920.* Princeton, N.J., 1958.

King, Jere C. *Generals and Politicians.* Berkeley and Los Angeles, Calif., 1951.

Kriedberg, Marvin A., and Merton G. Henry. *History of Military Mobilization in the United States Army, 1775–1945.* Washington, D.C., 1955.

Lafayette College Catalogue, 1880–81. Easton, Pa., 1881.

Lane, Anne W. and Louise H. Wall. Editors. *The Letters of Franklin K. Lane: Personal and Political.* Boston, 1922.

Levine, Issac. *Mitchell: Pioneer of Air Power.* New York, 1943.

Liddell Hart, B. H. *Through the Fog of War.* New York, 1938.

Liggett, Hunter. *A.E.F.: Ten Years Ago in France.* New York, 1928.

———. *Commanding an American Army: Recollections of the World War.* Boston, 1925.

Lloyd George, David. *War Memoirs.* Vols. III, IV, London, 1934; Vol. V, Boston, 1936; Vol. VI, Boston, 1937.

Lockmiller, David A. *Enoch H. Crowder: Soldier, Lawyer and Statesman.* Columbia, Mo., 1955.

Lonergan, Thomas C. *It Might Have Been Lost: A Chronicle from Alien Sources of the Struggle to Preserve the National Identity of the A.E.F.* New York, 1929.

Ludendorff, Erich von. *Ludendorff's Own Story: August 1914–November 1918.* 2 Vols., New York, 1919.

MacArthur, Charles G. *A Bug's-Eye View of the War.* Oak Park, Ill., 1919.

McClendon, R. Earl. "The Question of Autonomy For the United States Air Arm: 1907–45." Maxwell Air Force Base, Ala., 1950. (Mimeographed Air University Documentary Research Study.)

McClure, Nathaniel F. *Class of 1887, United States Military Academy: A Biographical Volume.* Washington, D.C., 1938.

McCutcheon, John T. *Drawn From Memory*. Indianapolis, Ind., 1950.
March, F. A., Jr. *Athletics At Lafayette College: Recollections and Opinions*. Easton, Pa., 1926.
March, Peyton C. *The Nation at War*. Garden City, N.Y., 1932.
Melange, 1882, 1883, 1884, 1885. Easton, Pa., 1881, 1882, 1883, 1884.
Millis, Walter. *Arms and Men: A Study in American Military History*. New York, 1956.
Millett, Frank D. *The Expedition to the Philippines*. New York, 1899.
Mock, James R., and Evangeline Thurber. *Report on Demobilization*. Norman, Okla., 1944.
Morison, E. E. *Turmoil and Tradition, A Study of the Life and Times of Henry Stimson*. Boston, 1960.
Mott, T. Bentley. *Twenty Years as Military Attaché*. New York, 1937.
Murray, Robert K. *Red Scare: A Study in National Hysteria*. Minneapolis, Minn., 1955.
Nelson, Otto L. Jr. *National Security and the General Staff*. Washington, D.C., 1946.
Nevins, Allan. *Herbert H. Lehman and His Era*. New York, 1963.
Owen, Frank. *Tempestuous Journey: Lloyd George: His Life and Times*. London, 1954.
Owen, W. B. *Historical Sketches of Lafayette College*. Easton, Pa., 1876.
Palmer, Frederick. *Bliss, Peacemaker: The Life and Letters of General Tasker Howard Bliss*. New York, 1934.
———. *John J. Pershing; General of the Armies: A Biography*. Harrisburg, Pa., 1948.
———. *Newton D. Baker: America at War*. 2 Vols., New York, 1931.
———. *With Kuroki in Manchuria*. New York, 1906.
———. *With My Own Eyes: A Personal Story of Battle Years*. Indianapolis, Ind., 1932.
Palmer, John M. *America in Arms: The Experience of the United States With Military Organization*. New Haven, Conn., 1941.
———. *Statesmanship or War*. Garden City, N.Y., 1927.
———. *Washington, Lincoln, Wilson: Three War Statesmen*. Garden City, N.Y., 1930.
Parker, James. *The Old Army: Memories 1872–1918*. Philadelphia, 1929.
Paxson, Frederic L. *America at War: 1917–1918*. Vol. II in *American Democracy and the World War*. Boston, 1939.
———. *Pre-War Years: 1913–1918*. Vol. I in *American Democracy and the World War*. Boston, 1936.
———. *The Great Demobilization and Other Essays*. Madison, Wis., 1941.
Pershing, John J. *My Experiences in the World War*. 2 Vols., New York, 1931.
Pogue, Forrest C. *George C. Marshall: Education of A General*. New York, 1963.
Register of Graduates and Former Cadets: United States Military Academy. New York, 1953.
Repington, C. à Court. *The First World War 1914–1918: Personal Experiences*. Vol. II, Boston, 1931.

Riker, William H. *Soldier of State: The Role of the National Guard in American Democracy.* Washington, D.C., 1957.

Robertson, Sir William. *Soldiers and Statesmen: 1914–1918.* 2 Vols., New York, 1926.

Salter, James A. *Allied Shipping Control: An Experiment in International Administration in Economic and Social History of the World War* (British Series). Edited by James T. Shotwell. Oxford, 1921.

Scott, Hugh L. *Some Memories of a Soldier.* New York, 1928.

Sexton, William T. *Soldiers In the Sun: An Adventure in Imperialism.* Harrisburg, Pa., 1939.

Sims, William S. and Burton J. Hendrick. *The Victory at Sea.* Garden City, N.Y., 1920.

Skillman, David B. *The Biography of A College: Being the History of the First Century of the Life of Lafayette College.* 2 Vols., Easton, Pa., 1932.

Smith, Louis. *American Democracy and Military Power: A Study in Civil Control of the Military Power in the United States.* Chicago, 1951.

Snow, William J. *Signposts of Experience: World War Memoirs.* Washington, D.C., 1941.

Sonnichsen, Albert. *Ten Months a Captive Among Filipinos.* New York, 1901.

Sparks, George F., editor. *A Many Colored Toga: The Diary of Henry Fountain Ashurst.* Tucson, Ariz., 1962.

Sprout, Harold and Margaret. *Toward a New Order of Sea Power: American Naval Policy and the World Scene, 1918–22.* Princeton, N.J., 1943.

Stimson, Henry L. and McGeorge Bundy. *On Active Service in Peace and War.* New York, 1947.

Storey, Moorfield and Marcial P. Lichauco. *The Conquest of the Philippines By the United States, 1898–1925.* New York, 1926.

Strakhovsky, L. I. *Intervention at Archangel: The Story of Allied Intervention and Russian Counter-Revolution in North Russia, 1918–1920.* Princeton, N.J., 1944.

———. *Origins of American Intervention in North Russia: 1918.* Princeton, N.J., 1937.

Sweetser, Arthur. *The American Air Service.* New York, 1919.

Syrett, Harold. Editor. *The Gentleman and the Tiger: The Autobiography of George B. McClellan, Jr.* Philadelphia, 1956.

The Russo-Japanese War: The Battle of Liao-Yan and The Battle of Scha-ho. Prepared in Historical Section of the German General Staff. London, 1909–1910.

Thomas, Sewall. *Silhouettes of Charles S. Thomas: Colorado Governor and United States Senator.* Caldwell, Idaho, 1959.

Tobin, Harold J., and Percy Bidwell. *Mobilizing Civilian America.* New York, 1940.

Trask, David F. *The United States in the Supreme War Council: American War Aims and Inter-Allied Strategy, 1917–18.* Middletown, Conn., 1961.

Unterberger, Betty Miller. *America's Siberian Expedition, 1918–1920: A Study of National Policy.* Durham, N.C., 1956.

Walworth, Arthur. *World Prophet.* Vol. II in *Woodrow Wilson.* New York, 1958.

Wardlaw, Chester. *The Transportation Corps: Responsibilities, Organization, and Operations in The Technical Services: United States Army in World War II.* General Editor, Kent R. Greenfield. Washington, D.C., 1951.

Washburn, Charles G. *Life of John W. Weeks.* Boston, 1928.

Watson, Mark S. *Chief of Staff: Prewar Plans and Preparations in The War Department: United States Army in World War II.* General Editor, Kent R. Greenfield. Washington, D.C., 1950.

Wecter, Dixon. *When Johnny Comes Marching Home.* Boston, 1944.

Weigley, Russell F. *Towards An American Army: Military Thought From Washington to Marshall.* New York, 1962.

White, Howard. *Executive Influence in Determining Military Policy in the United States.* Urbana, Ill., 1925.

Wilgus, William J. *Transporting the A.E.F. in Western Europe: 1917–1918.* New York, 1931.

Williams, William A. *American-Russian Relations: 1781–1947.* New York, 1952.

Wolff, Leon. *Little Brown Brothers: How The United States Purchased and Pacified The Philippine Islands At the Century's Turn.* Garden City, N.Y., 1961.

Zaide, Gregorio F. *The Philippine Revolution.* Manila, 1934.

Articles

Allen, Henry. "Wanted – Army Re-organization," *North American Review,* CCX (July, 1919), 39–47.

Baker, Newton D. "America in the World War," Introduction to Thomas G. Frothingham, *The American Reinforcement in the World War.* Garden City, N.Y., 1927, v–xxxv.

———. "A Permanent Policy For the United States," *Saturday Evening Post,* CXCI, No. 48 (May 31, 1919), 20–30, 165.

———. "Making Ready the Army," *The Independent,* XC (April 14, 1917), 109.

Barnhardt, Clarence L. "Introduction," *March Thesaurus-Dictionary.* Garden City, N.Y., 1958, iii–v.

Bass, John F. "The Fall of Manila," *Harper's Weekly,* XLII (October 15, 1898), 1007–08.

Bright, James W. "An Address in Commemoration of Francis Andrew March, 1825–1911," *Publications of the Modern Language Association of America,* XXIX (1914), cxvii–cxxxvii.

Brooks, William E. "Peyton March – A Study in Development," *The Outlook,* CXIX (August 7, 1918), 549.

Brophy, Leo P. "Origins of the Chemical Corps," *Military Affairs,* XX (Winter, 1956), 217–26.

Brown, L. Ames. "The General Staff," *The North American Review,* CCVI (August, 1917), 229–40.

"Bureaucracy and the Army," *The Forum,* LVI (November, 1916), 619–27.

Carter, William H. "A General Staff for the Army," *The North American Review,* CLXXV (October, 1902), 558–65.

———. "After the War," *The North American Review,* CCVIII (December, 1918), 854–57.

———. "Army Reformers," *The North American Review,* CCVIII (October, 1918), 548–57.

———. "The American General Staff," *Scribner's Magazine,* LXIV (September, 1918), 352–56.

Coffman, Edward M. "Conflicts in American Planning: An Aspect of World War I Strategy," *Military Review,* XLIII, No. 6 (June, 1963), 78–90.

———. "The Battle Against Red Tape: Business Methods of the War Department General Staff, 1917–18," *Military Affairs,* XXVI (Spring, 1962), 1–10.

Conner, Fox. "Replacements: Life-blood of a Fighting Army," *Infantry Journal,* XLVIII (May, 1941), 2–9.

Davis, Oscar King. "The Astor Battery Arrives Out," *Harper's Weekly,* XLII (September 17, 1898), 919.

Derthick, Martha. "Militia Lobby in the Missile Age: The Politics of the National Guard," in Samuel P. Huntington, editor, *Changing Patterns of Military Politics,* Glencoe, Ill., 1962, 190–234.

DeWeerd, H. A. "American Adoption of French Artillery," *The Journal of the American Military Institute,* III (Summer, 1939), 104–16.

———. "American Industrial Mobilization for War, 1917–1918," *The Ohio State Archaeological and Historical Quarterly,* XLIX (1940), 249–61.

Eliot, George F. "Unified Command: Lessons from the Past," *Foreign Affairs,* XXII (October, 1942), 11–20.

"Experiments in Reorganization: Building over the War Department Machinery," *The Outlook,* CXVIII (January 16, 1918), 91.

Fosdick, Raymond B. "America at War," *Foreign Affairs,* X (January, 1932), 316–23.

Foulois, Benjamin D. "Why Write a Book?" *The Air Power Historian,* II, No. 2 (April, 1955), 17–35.

"From an old Soldier," *Time,* XLIII, No. 2 (January 10, 1944), 19.

"General March," *Life,* XVI, No. 2 (January 10, 1944), 32.

Greene, Francis V. "The Capture of Manila," *The Century Magazine,* Vol. LVII, No. 5 (March, 1899), 785–91; No. 6 (April, 1899), 915–37.

Hanson, Joseph M. "The Historical Section, Army War College," *The Journal of the American Military History Foundation,* I (Summer, 1937), 70–74.

Hard, William. "Down the River," *The New Republic,* XIII (December 15, 1917), 170–72.

———. "Pursuing Mr. Baker," *The New Republic,* XIII (January 26, 1918), 366–68.

Howenstine, E. J., Jr. "Demobilization After First World War," *Quarterly Journal of Economics,* LVIII (1943), 91–105.

Irvine, Dallas D. "The Origin of Capital Staffs," *The Journal of Modern History,* X (June, 1938), 161–79.

Keppel, Frederick P. "Newton D. Baker," *Foreign Affairs*, XVI (April, 1938), 503–14.

———. "The General Staff," *The Atlantic Monthly*, LXXV (April, 1920), 539–49.

Kester, Randall B. "The War Industries Board, 1917–1918: A Study in Industrial Mobilization," *The American Political Science Review*, XXXIV (August, 1940), 655–84.

Liddell Hart, B. H. "Pershing and His Critics," *Current History* (November, 1932), 135–40.

Lowry, Edward G. "The Emerging Mr. Baker: A Pacifist who is in this war business 'to see it through'," *Collier's Weekly*, LX (October 6, 1917), 6–7, 35–36.

Luberoff, George. "Early Pioneering in France," *Quartermaster Review*, VIII, No. 6 (May–June, 1929), 42–49.

McLean, Ross H. "Troop Movements on the American Railroads during the Great War," *The American Historical Review*, XXVI (April, 1921), 464–88.

March, Peyton C. "Demobilization," *National Service*, V, No. 4 (April, 1919), 201–06.

———. "Henry Jervey Obituary," *Assembly*, II, No. 2 (July, 1943), 4.

———. "Japanese Strategy in the Far East," *Yale Review*, XXIII (September, 1933), 78–87.

———. "Mr. Astor Outfits The Army," *Saturday Evening Post*, CCXXXI, No 3 (July 19, 1958), 24–25, 53, 55.

Marion, John H. "Organization for Internal Control and Co-ordination in the United States Army," *The American Political Science Review*, XXXII (October, 1938), 877–97.

Marshall, George C. "Some Lessons in History," *Maryland Historical Magazine*, XL (September, 1945), 175–84.

Merrill, James M. "Submarine Scare, 1918," *Military Affairs*, XVIII (Winter, 1953), 181–90.

Millett, F. D. "In Front of Manila," *Harper's Weekly*, XIII (September 24, 1898), 934.

———. "With General Merritt," *Harper's Weekly*, XLII (August 13, 1898), 799–800.

Mott, T. Bentley. "The Fall of Manila," *Scribner's Magazine*, XXIV (December, 1898), 683–87.

"Mr. Baker and the War Department," *The World's Work*, XXX (February, 1918), 354–55.

"Mr. Baker's Vindication," *The New Republic*, XIV (February 23, 1918), 97–98.

Paxson, Frederic L. "The American War Government, 1917–1918," *The American Historical Review*, XXVI (October, 1920), 54–76.

Riepma, Siert F. "Portrait of an Adjutant General: The Career of Major General Fred C. Ainsworth," *The Journal of the American Military History Foundation*, II (Spring, 1938), 26–35.

Rogers, Lindsay. "Civilian Control of Military Policy," *Foreign Affairs*, XVIII (January, 1940), 280–91.

"Secretary Baker and the General Staff," *The Outlook*, CXIV (November 29, 1916), 713.

"Secretary Baker's Defense," *The Nation*, CVI (January 17, 1918), 54–55.

Selden, Charles A. "The Chief of the General Staff," *The World's Work*, XXXIV (May, 1918), 39–41.

Soule, George. "The Brain of the Army," *The New Republic*, XIII (December 22, 1917), 203–5.

Swisher, Carl B. "The Control of War Preparations in the United States," *The American Political Science Review*, XXXIV (December, 1940), 1085–1103.

"The Call for a War Lord," *The Literary Digest*, LVI (January 26, 1918), 10–11.

"The General Staff (1903–16)," *The Military Historian and Economist*, I (October, 1916), 385–93.

"The Investigation of the War Department," *The Nation*, CV (December 20, 1917), 680–81.

"The Responsibility of Congress for Military Delay," *The New Republic*, XIII (December 29, 1917), 236–37.

"The War on the War Department," *The Literary Digest*, LVI (January 19, 1918), 16–17.

"Wanted: A Leader," *The North American Review*, CCVII (March, 1918), 321–44.

Wheeler, John N. "They Never Tell All," *American Magazine*, CXII, No. 6 (December, 1931), 36–38, 80.

Wilhelm, Donald. "How Big is Baker?" *The Independent*, XCIII (February 9, 1918), 229–30, 244.

INDEX